INTRODUCING
PHILOSOPHY

INTRODUCING
PHILOSOPHY

KNOWLEDGE

and

REALITY

JACK S. CRUMLEY II

broadview press

BROADVIEW PRESS— www.broadviewpress.com
Peterborough, Ontario, Canada

Founded in 1985, Broadview Press remains a wholly independent publishing house. Broadview's focus is on academic publishing; our titles are accessible to university and college students as well as scholars and general readers. With over 600 titles in print, Broadview has become a leading international publisher in the humanities, with world-wide distribution. Broadview is committed to environmentally responsible publishing and fair business practices.

Library and Archives Canada Cataloguing in Publication

Crumley, Jack S., author
    Introducing philosophy : knowledge and reality / Jack
S. Crumley II.

Includes bibliographical references and index.
ISBN 978-1-55481-129-8 (paperback)

    1. Philosophy—Introductions. 2. Knowledge, Theory of.
3. Metaphysics. I. Title.

BD21.C78 2016   100   C2016-903541-7

Broadview Press handles its own distribution in North America
PO Box 1243, Peterborough, Ontario K9J 7H5, Canada
555 Riverwalk Parkway, Tonawanda, NY 14150, USA
Tel: (705) 743-8990; Fax: (705) 743-8353
email: customerservice@broadviewpress.com

Distribution is handled by Eurospan Group in the UK, Europe, Central Asia, Middle East, Africa, India, Southeast Asia, Central America, South America, and the Caribbean. Distribution is handled by Footprint Books in Australia and New Zealand.

Broadview Press acknowledges the financial support of the Government of Canada through the Canada Book Fund for our publishing activities.

Canada

Edited by Robert M. Martin
Book design by Michel Vrana
Illustrations by Gillian Wilson

PRINTED IN CANADA

For Andie
and
the angels in my life

CONTENTS

PREFACE

M y guiding thought for this text was someone reading about topics in philosophy for the first time, most likely students, but also someone who was just curious. I wanted students to be able to read the text and then have questions that pursued the topics further. Whether students read the text because of an assignment or out of curiosity, I very much want that the text allows them to learn about the issues simply from their reading. And part of that is that they will see the issues in context—both contemporary and historical. I hope students are able to see—as a result of the text—not only the "why" of the issues, but how they arose in the history of philosophy. Of course, they will learn more from further conversation or discussions in class. But my hope is that they will already know something before those conversations or the discussions.

I intend the text to offer professors the ability to adapt it to their own classes. To that end, like the philosophy of mind and epistemology texts, I wanted to keep my own views in the background, as much as possible, and to let the philosophers and issues and arguments speak for themselves. Thus, while providing the framework for discussion and evaluation of positions and arguments, I intend that different professors will be able to pursue more detailed analysis and evaluation in the direction they choose. And I tried to strike a balance between presenting the arguments and overwhelming the reader.

I hope I also achieved a balance between historical material and contemporary questions and approaches. (In my mind, "contemporary" runs roughly from the second half of the twentieth century onward; although "Two Dogmas" and the *Investigations* are now closing in on their 75th anniversaries.) In presenting the views of philosophers from our history, I have relied on both my own and others' interpretations. My preferred interpretations I also tried to keep in the background; inevitably, however, some of my predilections will be apparent (e.g., Daniel Sherman on Plato's forms or A.A. Luce on Berkeley's view of the external world). And perhaps I have misinterpreted some of those commentators.

Somewhere I think Nietzsche said "We Mandarins with Chinese brushes ...," indicating that what appeared on the page was not the text as it originally came to him. Space limitations require choices; yet I included some indications of further directions in which some of these issues might be pursued: sections on Whitehead and Heidegger, text boxes on Emerson, Sartre, Hinduism, Mayahana Buddhism, or the love affair between Abelard and Heloise. Doubtless these "indications" reflect considerably some of the interests I have.

The organization and topics too reflect a choice. The individual chapters are largely self-contained, as much as possible to allow professors to sequence the topics as they see fit or to select only some. The choice of chapter topics reflects two considerations. First, I relied on the input that I had from others and what I discovered on my own about preferred topics. Second, I chose topics that I thought might represent a sort of meeting point between professors and students on their interests. There are other topics of course that I would have very much liked to include. And here once again, I plead space. Perhaps there will be some later opportunity to present those topics.

I never thought I would write textbooks. Much less did I think I would write an "Introducing Philosophy" textbook. And here I "blame" Don LePan of Broadview Press. Don first approached me some years ago about my interest in writing about metaphysics. I demurred. As I did when Stephen Latta, my editor at Broadview, later inquired about my interest in writing about metaphysics. But in my decade-plus as chair of University of San Diego's philosophy department, I pressed myself into service as the instructor for our upper-division metaphysics class for a few semesters in a row. (Subsequent chairs followed suit.) In the months preceding my sabbatical semester and my immediately following reassigned time semester, Don approached me with another idea—this text. Somehow he made it seem a less daunting task than it actually was. After reflecting on it on my own and talking to my then Executive Assistant, Leeanna Cummings—who knows very well my weaknesses in time management—I decided to try. I must thank Broadview and especially Stephen Latta for their patience; I especially thank Stephen for his guidance, his understanding, and his commitment to the project ... and to my completing the project. Given the many stresses of bringing a book to print, for publishers and authors, Broadview is exceptional in making the process a genuinely friendly collaboration.

I am especially grateful to Broadview for selecting as gifted an artist as Gillian Wilson to provide the illustrations for the text. I am flattered that she consented to take on the project and am thrilled with the results. For more information on Gillian's art, visit www.gillianwilson.ca.

The text has greatly benefited from the detailed comments of both Laura Buzzard, senior editor at Broadview, and a Broadview copy editor, Bob Martin, philosophy professor emeritus, Dalhousie University. The evident care, attention to detail, and concern for making the text better was reflected in their comments and suggestions. I continue to be amazed that they can read a section, and a page or two later, see that some paragraph or paragraphs ought to be moved back or forward. Occasionally—very, very occasionally—I chose not to follow a suggestion. I sometimes think there should be a little "reader warning" at various places in the text along the lines of "Jack chose not to heed Laura or Bob's good suggestions for making this paragraph or section better." More seriously, I can't thank them enough.

This is the second text of mine for which Bob has served as copy editor. Although I was already impressed with his own work and certainly impressed with how he helped me on the second edition of the epistemology text, I am truly grateful to have such a gifted philosopher and clear thinker as my copy editor.

As I worked on the text, so often I thought of my Momma's patience as books and papers piled round in her otherwise immaculate home. Mostly, I thank her for insisting that I get my undergraduate degree ... for her love and support ... and Saturday morning hotcakes. I still miss her.

And Andie. Seventeen pounds of joy. He naps for a couple of hours. Wakes up, stretches, comes over underneath the table, puts his little paws up in my lap and stretches as if to observe, a little love makes philosophy much better, don't you think?

INTRODUCTION

Metaphysics and Epistemology

Aristotle said that philosophy begins in wonder. The lore of Western philosophy has it that Thales—its first philosopher—fell into a well while he was walking and "wondering."

Aristotle—we'll meet him later—also said that "All men by nature desire to know." This is the first sentence of his treatise called *Metaphysics*. Epistemology asks about this "knowing," addressing as one of its principal topics the nature of knowledge. Conveniently, but not entirely coincidentally, we find metaphysics and epistemology in close proximity.

Philosophy comprises several areas; metaphysics and epistemology are two of its most basic areas. So, one of our first "wonderings" is this: what are these—these areas *metaphysics* and *epistemology*?

Epistemology addresses topics in the theory of knowledge. We claim to know lots of things and lots of different kinds of things—that the Milky

Way is at least 100,000 light years in diameter, that moose are mammals, that a given book is red, that books as well as moose as well as you and I are made up of atoms. Epistemology theorists try to explain what it takes for a person to know. Not just *claim* to know—but when some claim or belief is a genuine instance of knowledge. And a theory of knowledge attempts to explain what all these genuine instances have in common. From the physicist to the meteorologist on Channel 9 to the history professor to you in the art museum, a theory of knowledge says "here are the requirements for some claim to be a bit of knowledge." Of course, these requirements will be very general, if they are the requirements from areas as diverse as science or art. But that is what it means to ask about the *nature* of knowledge: what is common to all these instances of knowledge? Or as a philosopher might ask: In virtue of what are all these examples or instances of knowledge in fact knowledge?

A quick survey of the contents of this book shows that epistemology ranges into other areas as well, including the sources of knowledge, whether or not we can have knowledge at all, and when is some claim or belief of ours not just arbitrary, but based on good reasons or evidence. Epistemologists think of this latter as *justification*, and the nature of justification is a main concern of much contemporary epistemological theory.

Another bit of philosophical lore serves to introduce metaphysics. Aristotle's treatise was titled *Metaphysics* because in one of the first libraries of Aristotle's work, this particular treatise came *after*—in Greek "meta"—a treatise entitled *Physics* (which should not be confused with the physics texts of today).

Aristotle observes he is engaged in the study of being *qua* being. "Qua" is a Latin word, which means "in its character as" or a bit roughly, "as this kind of thing." Looking at students *qua* students thus is considering them *just as* students, leaving aside issues of their biological makeup or family backgrounds or the movies they like. And to say that we want to study *being qua being* is to say that we want to look at all the things there are just insofar as they are. Metaphysics is sometimes identified with an important subdiscipline: ontology. Ontology may be understood as the study of the *kinds* of being(s) that exist. In another of Aristotle's works, the relatively brief *Categories*, he identifies different categories, such as "being a quality or characteristic of something else." And all that *exists* falls into one or another category. This "all-encompassing" character perhaps leads to a second characterization of metaphysics. Metaphysics is a more general study than our other specific disciplines, whether art, religion, science—that is, metaphysics attempts to describe and explain general features of reality. But what are these "general" features? Isn't psychology a pretty general study of human beings? Isn't biology pretty general in its study of the animal kingdom? Or chemistry and physics pretty general in studying just about everything that there is? Metaphysics, however, looks at all these different disciplines—as well as others—and notices still further general questions. Questions about free will and whether human beings have it, about the conditions under which an object remains the same object (or the same person!), or whether there are more kinds of things than those that science studies (is everything physical, or are there some non-physical things?)—all of these are metaphysical questions. Metaphysics then, in its most general form, asks about what kinds of things there are in the world, about their nature, and about the structure or relationship between these things.

It is not always easy to draw the line between science and philosophy, or religion and philosophy, or art and philosophy, or logic and philosophy. The psychologist or neuroscientist who claims we have no free will, or the scientist who claims that there is nothing beyond the natural world, or the theologian who insists on the existence of a nonphysical soul, or the poet who claims there is something more to love than chemical or psychological states, has most likely begun raising metaphysical questions, and hence philosophical questions. And this perhaps invites the question of how to characterize philosophy.

Unsurprisingly, the English language inherits the term "philosophy" from ancient Greek, "philosophia." And it was Aristotle's teacher Plato who shaped the meaning of the term. Before Plato's writings, a group of people we now call *Sophists* were often known as philosophers. Traveling teachers in Greece, they offered to teach rhetoric—the art of speaking—to those willing to pay the tuition. Although Greek writing had been around for a few hundred years at the time, it was still very much an oral culture. Speaking ability and the ability to persuade were honored and celebrated. And in the course of teaching the ability to speak persuasively, some of the sophists took positions on the nature of knowledge and reality, and on how to behave or act, what we now call ethics or morals.

We see in Plato's writings, however, a different notion of philosophy. In one of his works, he characterizes the philosopher as someone who loves the truth and the whole of truth. In another—still one of the most famous works on the *nature* of love—Plato represents the philosopher as the lover of beauty. Not the lover of beautiful bodies or beautiful minds, though love may begin there, but of beauty itself. It's not difficult to draw the conclusion that for

Plato the love of beauty and truth, as well as of "good," finds its expression in the love of wisdom. The literal rendering of the Greek word "philosophia" is "love of wisdom." Everyone by nature may desire to know, but the philosopher loves knowing, loves wisdom, and not just some of it, but all of it.

Philosophy includes many areas or disciplines. We've seen two, metaphysics and epistemology. Two other main areas are ethics and logic. But there are many others, including political philosophy, philosophy of mind, philosophy of language, philosophy of science, of mathematics, of religion, of art, of history, of technology. Indeed, name an area of human endeavor or inquiry, and there is likely to be a series of *philosophical* questions worth asking: What's the difference between science and pseudo-science? Is faith rational? What makes something a work of art? Rightly or wrongly, philosophers think there are *basic* or *foundational* issues or questions that go beyond the boundaries of science or art or religion or linguistics, and that these questions are the province of philosophy. Mathematicians may tell us that there are two different ways to represent numbers in set theory. But to ask whether numbers are just handy tools made up by people, or whether they exist "on their own," or why the physical world seems to have mathematical properties—well, those are philosophical questions.

Some Important Concepts

Like any discipline, philosophy has a set of concepts or terms it employs. Some you have undoubtedly come across, but perhaps with a slightly different sense given to them. Other concepts are more likely unfamiliar. The first concept we'll discuss is that of *concept*.

Concepts refer to or pick out certain properties or objects. For example, my concept of a university refers to some things and not to others. The place where I teach is a university; the restaurant where I occasionally dine is not. We sometimes want to explain or analyze concepts by saying when the concept applies. Analyzing "university" should explain the basis for identification of things that are and those things that aren't universities.

The idea that an analysis of a concept gives us the conditions that pick out all and only things of a certain kind is sometimes characterized as providing necessary and sufficient conditions for the application of a concept. Necessary conditions are like minimum requirements. A necessary condition of being President of the United States is being at least thirty-five years of age. Somewhat more technically, A is a necessary condition of B if and only if B cannot occur without the occurrence of A. But sufficient conditions are enough to bring about a particular event or property. That is, it is a sufficient condition of being president-elect of the United States that one gets a majority of the votes cast by the Electoral College. More technically, A is a sufficient condition of B if and only if whenever A occurs, B also occurs.

At various times and in various eras, philosophers attempted to provide the necessary and sufficient conditions of central concepts in epistemology and metaphysics. For example, attempts at providing the necessary and sufficient conditions for considering something to be a *substance* or considering a given belief to be *knowledge*. Of course, such attempts involve trying to explain why a certain analysis of a concept is the best analysis. A somewhat related term might be introduced here: "logically possible." Put simply, a sentence (or a proposition—what's expressed by a sentence) is logically possible if it is not self-contradictory. "Polar bears are white" is logically possible, and so is "Polar bears are green." Neither is self-contradictory, though one is in fact true, and the other false. Alternatively, we might say that a proposition is necessary if its denial or contradictory is not logically possible. A sentence is not logically possible when it is self-contradictory. For example, "A triangle has four sides" is self-contradictory and therefore not logically possible. Thus, "A triangle has three sides" is necessary. Logical possibility is different from physical possibility, which only asserts that something doesn't contradict physical law. For example, it is not physically possible that my car goes faster than the speed of light, or that I can fly by flapping my arms. Both are, however, logically possible.

These notions of necessary and logically possible propositions turn out to be important for many of the claims philosophers give, as well as many of the arguments they offer.

As we will use the concept, a belief is a mental state that has a particular content; this content represents some object as having some property or characteristic. Beliefs, then, are representational states by virtue of their having certain contents. Typically, the contents of a belief—what the belief is about—is described by means of propositions. Thus, for example, my belief that the coffee is cold represents that the coffee is cold. By virtue of their propositional content, beliefs can be either true or false. That is, they can represent things either correctly or incorrectly. If Andy believes that the ball is in the backyard, then his belief is either true or false, depending on whether the proposition which is the content of the belief—that the ball is in the backyard—is true or false; that is, on whether the ball is actually in the backyard. If Sally believes that Santa knows if she's been bad or good, her belief is false, but not because Santa actually knows this; rather because (too bad!) there isn't any such person; she's just representing the world the way it isn't.

When philosophers talk about "beliefs," that word doesn't have the common everyday meaning, in which something is called a "belief" when it's implied that it's "just a belief"—that is, an opinion without backing—an unfounded guess or a matter of faith. Some of what philosophers call beliefs are certainly like that. Sara's belief that her ticket for tomorrow's California Super Lottery has the winning numbers for the grand prize is a belief supported by virtually no evidence. But all of us also have beliefs for which we have a great deal of backing. In fact, the notion of belief we are using also leaves open the possibility that some beliefs are instances of knowledge.

There are venerable traditions in philosophy, in both epistemology and metaphysics. Two principally epistemological traditions are rationalism and empiricism. Each of these traditions has a general view of the nature of knowledge, including its extent and how we acquire it. Empiricism is the view that our beliefs about the world can be instances of knowledge or justified belief only if those beliefs derive from information gained in sense experience. Empiricists hold that our five senses—vision, hearing, smell, taste, and touch—are the door to *empirical* knowledge, or knowledge about the world. It is ultimately by means of the operations of the senses that we come to know that the coffee is cold or that the leaves have turned brown or that quarks are flavored. Some empiricists allow that, in addition, we have knowledge of certain semantic or conceptual truths, based on our understanding of the words or concepts. (For example, that if you have an uncle, that person is the brother of one of your parents.) Such truths, however, convey no empirical knowledge. Empiricism then holds that all of our knowledge of the world must arise from sense experience.

Rationalism is the view that the epistemic legitimacy or acceptability of some of our beliefs depends not on sense experience, but on the operation of reason. Rationalists often hold that some of our knowledge is *innate*—inborn—that is, that everyone, regardless of their particular experiences, already has such knowledge. They divide knowledge into two types: *a posteriori* and *a priori*. A posteriori knowledge is knowledge that depends on our sense experience. I could not know that the radio is on unless I had a certain sense experience—say, hearing the music or seeing an indicator light. A priori knowledge is knowledge that I could have independently of the senses. An uncontroversial example of *a priori* knowledge is that all bachelors are unmarried. A more contentious example is that all events have causes. Rationalists frequently claim that we have *a priori* knowledge, while empiricists frequently doubt the existence of at least certain kinds of *a priori* knowledge.

Many epistemological questions and answers can be traced back to Socrates, Plato, and Aristotle, in the fifth and fourth centuries BCE, and the same is true for metaphysics. One metaphysical tradition with ancient roots is Realism: the idea that some particular kinds of thing exist independently of our beliefs—and are thus *mind-independent*. A person might be a realist, for example, about numbers and arithmetic, holding that even if there were no people who thought about it or ever performed division or addition, 2+2 would still equal 4. One can also be a realist about colors, thinking that even if there were no sentient beings to perceive them, objects would still have color.

A more general—and more obvious—realism is about the external world, the world of common sense. A realist about the external world holds that, independently of whatever we believe, independently of our thoughts about it, stars and starfish, planets and people, rocks and rutabagas, apples and animals exist. The second notion is a realism *about truth*. For a significant range of propositions or statements, the truth (or falsity) of those statements is an objective fact independent of what we think. Anti-realism about truth, by contrast, holds that (at least in some areas) "true" statements are just those that we individually, or as a culture, approve of.

This brings us to another venerable "fault line" in philosophy, a line that is significant for both metaphysics and epistemology. Some have suggested that the natural or the physical world is all that exists. Such a view is known as naturalism or physicalism. Since, in the physicalist view, there is only one kind of thing—physical things—this view is a type of monism. ("Monism" comes from the Greek word "monos," meaning "one"; in this context, it refers to the belief that everything that exists is the same type of thing.) Holding to physicalism is one way of being a monist. Some have thought that, in addition to the physical world, there are also nonphysical objects or kinds or properties. Among the objects typically offered as nonphysical are souls or minds, as well as mental "contents" like ideas or experiences. As hinted above, many take numbers or geometrical objects to be nonphysical. Properties or attributes similarly might be nonphysical. Dualism is the view that in addition to our normal physical objects and properties, there also exist nonphysical or immaterial objects, namely, minds and their properties. In this view then, for example, the belief that *tin is a major export of Peru* is a mental state, a property of a mind, and both mind and its "state" are nonphysical. One type of dualism thus claims, for example, that we not only have brains and neurons firing, but also nonphysical minds and their nonphysical properties.

But there is also a view that holds that there are no physical things, only nonphysical things, such as minds and their properties: idealism.[1]

Argument, Counterexample, and Explanation

A story is told about a "contest" in the emperor's court in ancient China, during the Warring States period (about 470 to 220 BCE): debates between "orthodox" philosophers and the *Logicians* or the *School of Names* (ming chià). The impetus for the contest seems to have been that the Logicians frequently offered brief, apparently paradoxical claims to summarize their views about the relation between names and reality, such as "An egg has feathers" and "A white horse is not a horse."[2] The denouement of the story is that one of the orthodox philosophers' representatives concluded the contest by asking the emperor which he'd rather believe: the difficult and the false (the ming chià's view) or the "simple and the true." This *argument* apparently had the desired effect; little remains of the School of Logicians work.

This historical vignette points to something important about philosophy. Philosophers present their views in different ways, sometimes in long treatises, sometimes "axiomatically," sometimes in paradox or aphorism. Now some philosophers are happy with the notion of a "philosophical method," while others are more suspicious. Still, philosophers with very different philosophical temperaments and intuitions rely on what we might call basic *forms* of presenting their views, forms that can be found in philosophers' work from China to Greece, from Heraclitus to Heidegger, from Augustine to Wittgenstein. And one standard form is argument.

Deductive arguments are those intended to be "truth preserving." That is, the truth of the premises (the reasons) is intended to guarantee the truth of the conclusion. In *valid* deductive arguments—deductive arguments that are "structured" properly—the premises in fact guarantee the truth of the conclusion. In other words, valid deductive arguments always satisfy this condition: If the premises are true, then the conclusion *must* be true, e.g.,

---

1   This philosophical term does not carry the meaning it has in ordinary language: the pursuit of ideals, possibly neglecting practicality.

2   Fung 1962.

Philosophy professors are snappy dressers.

Sam is a philosophy professor.

So, Sam is a snappy dresser.

If these two premises are true, because of the form or pattern of the argument, the conclusion is guaranteed to be true. And if it turns out that the premises are indeed true, then the argument is not only valid, but *sound*. Find yourself a sound argument, and you have found—many would claim— an indisputable conclusion! This little argument above is valid, but almost everyone would dispute its *soundness*. Most introductory logic books present students with ways of identifying valid and invalid arguments. The soundness of an argument is harder to judge, and often requires looking outside of logic (or philosophy), to other areas, such as history or science, to assess the truth of the premises.

Philosophers—and introductory logic textbooks—are often interested in *bad* arguments, too. Not that they recommend your using them. Rather they worry that some *other* philosophical position relies on a bad argument, in particular what is called an *informal fallacy*: a common pattern of bad reasoning that looks persuasive at first glance, but is actually flawed. Introductory logic textbooks typically list, explain, and give examples of at least a couple dozen informal fallacies. Here we note one in particular, that of *begging the question*.[3] Arguments that beg the question are *circular arguments*. They use as a premise or a reason what they are supposed to prove. It should be noted that it is sometimes controversial whether or not a given argument begs the question. Indeed some famous arguments in philosophy have critics who maintain that they beg the question. This sort of disagreement about the evaluation of an argument is part of the give and take of philosophical analysis.

One way to help understand a philosopher's position—and especially to understand the "strength" of the philosopher's claims—is to identify the premises and conclusion of the argument being made. Yet it is not always an easy task to identify the premises or structure of an argument. As a means of identifying an argument's structure, it is sometimes helpful to see the argument as part of a larger context or in connection with a philosopher's other arguments. This "getting clear" about the structure of an argument is one form of philosophical analysis, or more generally, understanding a text.

---

3   The mistake of taking "begging the question" to mean *raising the question* has become common. Correcting your friends when they use the term this way may make them respect you more. Or not.

In Book I of Plato's *Republic*, Socrates responds to his host's definition of justice, which Socrates characterized as in part "paying what is owed." Socrates argues against this definition of justice as "paying one's debts" by means of a *counterexample*. Socrates points out that if a neighbor left weapons with you, and later returned for them, while clearly intoxicated, you should not return the weapons. By means of the counterexample, Socrates thus implies that "paying one's debts" can't be the right definition of justice, because sometimes *not* paying one's debts is the right thing to do.

Arguing by counterexample is a frequent tool of philosophers. Counterexamples highlight *inconsistent* beliefs or statements—two or more statements that cannot all be true at the same time. Socrates suggests that it's *inconsistent* to believe both that justice is paying one's debts and that there are times one should not return what is owed. More generally, if a philosopher's position leads to some claim or statement that is inconsistent with an obviously or apparently true statement, then that is reason to wonder about the philosopher's position.

Philosophers also frequently rely on *explanation* as a means of articulating and defending a view. They take a concept or a set of concepts and explain how those concepts are useful for understanding some set of phenomena or some aspect of our lives. For example, the concept of consciousness has figured prominently in the views of philosophers of very different philosophical persuasions. We find philosophers putting forward these different views by providing an explanation of different "types" of consciousness or how they are related to one another.

In a sense this is explaining by a kind of "conceptual configuring" or bringing together a "constellation" of concepts. The relations between (or the "configuration" of) these concepts shows us how to think about a certain area or topic. Sartre, for example, relies on the notions of consciousness and negation (among others) to explain the nature of human freedom. Wittgenstein relies on the concepts of game, of "form of life," and use to explain the nature of linguistic meaning.

This type of explanation is perhaps different from the type of explanation that interests scientists. Some have thought that scientists explain an event or some phenomenon by citing a hypothesis (or law) and then deducing (providing a deductive argument) for the cause of that event or phenomenon. Whether or not this is the correct understanding of scientific explanation, philosophical explanation should not be restricted to this pattern.

"Philosophical method" is not exhausted by the above. Contemporary interpreters of Plato, for example, have argued that properly understanding Plato requires understanding the dramatic setting of Plato's dialogues.[4] The aphoristic style of a Nietzsche or the numbered propositions with subsequent "explanation" of a Paul Weiss in his *Modes of Being*[5] are other examples of the diverse ways in which philosophers sometimes present their positions, and their arguments. Consequently, philosophers—and philosophy professors, especially—often suggest that the best way to see how philosophers proceed or to see what the philosophical positions are is to ... well ... go take a look.

Key Concepts

- epistemology
- metaphysics
- concepts
- necessary and sufficient conditions
- proposition
- logically possible
- necessary
- belief
- content
- representational states
- empiricism
- rationalism
- *a posteriori* knowledge
- *a priori* knowledge
- realism
- physicalism
- monism
- dualism
- idealism

---

4   E.g., Strauss 1964; Rosen 2008; Griswold 1988.
5   Weiss 1958.

CHAPTER ONE

SKEPTICISM

In Charles Schulz's classic comic strip, *Peanuts*, Linus tells Charlie Brown's younger sister, Sally, that "life is peculiar." He asks rhetorically about wishing to live one's life over "if you knew what you know now." After a moment's pause, Sally asks (philosophically?) "What do I know now?" According to some philosophers, the answer (for all of us) is "Not much ... not much at all." Following the adventures of Snoopy and the gang may seem a roundabout way to raise intimations of skepticism. Yet skeptical worries, again according to some, are never far away.

The fact that responding to the skeptic is a central question of epistemology is sometimes greeted with puzzlement. Why should so many philosophers have worried about what seems so obvious? Of course we know many things! And if we individually fall short, if we haven't quite achieved knowledge in some areas, there are more than enough people who have succeeded. At the very least, many of our beliefs are rational or justified. What could be more obvious?

Skepticism and Epistemic Standards

Skepticism is the view that we do not have knowledge or justified beliefs in some area. Global skepticism about knowledge holds that *none* of our beliefs are instances of knowledge; despite our having reasons for those beliefs—being justified—those reasons simply are not enough to yield knowledge. While global skepticism about justification is very rare, some skeptics think we fail to have justified beliefs in certain areas. In claiming this either partial or global failure, the skeptic claims that our beliefs don't "measure up." Our beliefs don't satisfy the requisite epistemic standards.

Three famous arguments for skepticism dominated modern philosophy, two of them offered by René Descartes and the third by David Hume. These arguments have had a lasting influence on epistemology. We first try to get a little clearer about the notion of epistemic standards.

Epistemic Standards

Academic and Pyhrronian Skepticism

In the third and second centuries BCE, two schools of skepticism arose in Greece. *Academic skepticism* held that we know but one thing: that we have no knowledge. *Pyhrronian skepticism* thought that position too dogmatic, but instead recommended suspension of belief unless some proposition was completely evident. Sextus Empiricus (160–210), the foremost exponent of Pyhrronian skepticism, held that we must content ourselves with appearances only. After all, it is always possible to give equally compelling arguments for and against any belief. Interestingly, Sextus thought we would be happier if we learned to suspend judgment. The rise of modern skepticism, which culminated in Descartes, came about with the rediscovery of Greek skepticism.

We evaluate our beliefs differently, according different beliefs different *epistemic status*. We count some of our beliefs as mere opinion, unsupported by evidence, while others we count as more "grounded," as more trustworthy. And why do we trust some beliefs and not others? Trustworthy beliefs, we hold, are supported by some evidence or principle or both. For example, Andrew tells Andrea that she left her epistemology book in the car. When asked to defend that claim—that is, when challenged to explain *why* he thinks or believes that—he replies that he thinks he recalls seeing it there. In some circumstances, we demand more to defend a belief than this weak evidence: a scientist or a doctor ought to be able to provide us with rather convincing evidence before we count some claim as an instance of knowledge. Often we might reject a claim because it has not been *proved*. Thus, we have different types of epistemic status—different degrees of trustworthiness—from the very low, an unsupported belief, to the highest, knowledge.

To have a certain epistemic status, a belief must satisfy some *epistemic standard*. We are familiar with grading standards, e.g., a grade of "D" is poor, while a grade of "A" is excellent. Many other things can be "graded," for example, potatoes in the US are graded US No. 1, US Commercial, or US No. 2 depending on their size, regularity of shape, freedom from defects, etc.

An epistemic standard is a way of grading beliefs, a way of assessing their epistemic status. Typically we think that the standard for knowledge is more demanding that the standard for, say, reasonable belief.

It might seem a bit odd to talk about beliefs in this way—identifying some beliefs as mere opinion or simply as a matter of faith without evidence, identifying other beliefs as justified to some small or great degree, or some as instances of knowledge. But belief is a *representation* of some aspect or feature of the world. So, Andrew believes that the book is still in the car. He represents the world as being a particular way. Standards are there, then, because meeting them is supposed to make it more likely that the way we represent the world is the way it really is. Of course, identifying the relevant epistemic standards is no small task; but even if we do, the skeptic will ask: what makes you think that a belief that gets an A on your standard-test is therefore more likely to represent the world the way it really is?

Our commonsense epistemic practices—the way we normally "grade" beliefs—are the central concerns of the skeptic. The skeptic claims, for example, that our normal practice requires that we are "sure," or that we should always be able to provide some positive reason for a belief to be justified. The skeptic of course wants to insist on various conclusions, such as, "None of our beliefs are instances of knowledge" or "You can't trust the (five) senses to give you knowledge" or "Relying on this inference method is never rational." Much more important, the skeptic claims to have arrived at such conclusions by *relying on those standards that we normally accept!* This will be explained.

Of Dreams and Demons: Descartes's Skeptical Arguments

Rainbows: Descartes, the Scientist

We know Descartes's "armchair philosophy" and his work in algebraic geometry. His empirical side is often overlooked, including his work on optics and meteorology, first published in 1637. In his work on meteorology, Descartes offered the explanation of the various colors in the rainbow as resulting from a double diffraction within the raindrop and then through the cloud (or collection of raindrops in the air).

Interestingly Descartes devised and executed an *experiment* to *test* his hypothesis. This included filling a large round flask with water to simulate a raindrop! And, like a student lab report, the Eighth Discourse of *Meteorology* contains several tables of detailed measurements and calculations.

Descartes was the first to give a complete explanation of the rainbow. Some three centuries earlier a German monk, Theodoric, had also developed aspects of the diffraction theory, and later in the seventeenth century, Newton explained the general effects of a prism. But the next time someone mentions Descartes's "I think, therefore I am," ask them if they know that it was Descartes who first told us how nature produces rainbows.

René Descartes (1596–1650) was not a skeptic. He thought that—if we followed the right method—we were in a position to know many things, including some very surprising things, for example, about the difference between mind and body, and about the existence of God.

Why would philosophers who believe we have knowledge nonetheless give not just any skeptical arguments, but the most powerful skeptical arguments they could muster? Descartes had two reasons.

First, he thought the best way to defeat skepticism was to defeat its best argument. Descartes wanted the best the skeptic could offer. Thus, at the very beginning of the *Meditations*, he discounts weak skeptical arguments, such as the argument based on the fact that our senses sometimes mislead us: Occasional failure of the senses does not show that our senses never yield knowledge. The two principal arguments in the first Meditation are, in Descartes's view, the strongest skeptical arguments. Indeed, versions of each of these arguments continues to reappear at various times in the history of philosophy.

The second reason may have been more important for Descartes. Despite his confidence in a particular method of gaining knowledge, he nevertheless wanted to show that what is often supposed to be the best method for acquiring knowledge about the world was in fact not the best. Descartes thought that many previous thinkers—both philosophers and scientists—had settled on a basic means for acquiring knowledge about the world, a means or a method that was in their view fundamental. Perhaps you can surmise this means or method, since it still animates our commonsense view about knowledge: You open your eyes ... and look! You reach out ... and touch! Listen or smell or taste. The way we learn about the *ultimate nature* of the world, the way we acquire knowledge about the things in the world and their properties, is through our senses. Unfortunately, Descartes thought, we had been misled. Our senses do not *really* show us what is *really out there in the world*. Our experience—our senses—do not tell us about the ultimate nature of that world. If genuine knowledge is to be ours, we must go about acquiring it in a different way.

Another World: What Our "Dreams" Don't Tell Us

How could anyone think our senses mislead us, not just on occasion, but even under the best of circumstances? I look across the table, and only a Michael Jordan's arm-length away are two red candles. I can lean over, pick them up, smell the fragrance; I can tap them against the table, or, I suppose, if I were so inclined, take a waxy bite. Look at what our senses tell us. There's a world out there of objects, many of them solid. They "resist" us and one another. When I tap the candle against the table, they don't merge into each other. The table is solid, as are the candles. And they have *sensory properties*, such as color and scent and feel and sound and taste. The reds and greens and magentas and indigos are really out there, part of those objects; the scent of pine or rose are part of the tree or the flower.

Yet for a long time now, you have probably been aware of "another world." The table is made of wood, yes; but the wood is made of molecules. These molecules comprise atoms, which—well, you know the story—are protons, neutrons, electrons. And these are composed of still smaller things. It turns out that these little *insensible* particles are not colored. They don't have a fragrance or a taste. Our everyday objects are composed of these tiny particles surrounded by a great deal of empty space. The table isn't nearly as solid as our senses tell us!

Descartes was not alone in thinking that the new physics of the sixteenth and seventeenth centuries was about to reveal "another world," wholly unlike our sensory world. And Descartes thought that in order to have *knowledge* about this world, we would need a new route to that knowledge. As he says on the first page of the first Meditation:

> It is now some years since I detected how many were the false beliefs that
> I had from my earliest youth admitted as true, and how doubtful was
> everything I had since constructed on this basis; and from that time I was
> convinced that I must once for all seriously undertake to rid myself of all
> the opinions which I had formerly accepted, and commence to build anew
> from the foundation, if I wanted to establish any *firm and permanent structure*
> *in the sciences....*[1]

But what kind of argument could ever persuade us that our senses should not be trusted?

A "Dream-Like" World: The Dream Argument

Indubitable and Infallible

In Descartes's view, indubitability is not merely a subjective matter of whether an agent thinks there are reasons to doubt. Rather, indubitable beliefs involve the absence of *objective* reasons for doubting the truth of the belief. That is, there are no good reasons, independently of what the person believes or thinks, that could provide grounds for doubting. Thus, if the belief is indubitable, there is no *possible* doubt about the belief. We can compare the notion of indubitability with two other notions, infallibility and incorrigibility. Infallible beliefs are beliefs that cannot be mistaken or that cannot turn out to be false. Incorrigible beliefs are beliefs about which it is impossible to show that the person is mistaken.

These three notions—indubitability, infallibility, and incorrigibility—are independent of one another. For example, we might be unable to produce evidence showing that a person's belief is mistaken—thus we might agree that it is incorrigible—but this does not imply that the belief *cannot* be mistaken—that it is infallible. Whether Descartes actually thought that there was

---

1   Descartes 1968b, Meditation 1; emphasis added.

a connection between indubitability, infallibility, and incorrigibility is not our immediate concern. Contemporary responses to skepticism often consider infallibility to be the critical target.[2] In what follows, we will take Descartes to hold that a requirement for knowledge is infallibility. If the goal is infallibility, then we must find infallible methods, methods that yield infallible beliefs.

The Dream Argument, as it is known, accomplishes two things for Descartes. It provides a skeptical argument about the senses, but it also helps to clear the way for Descartes to make his case that *our senses do not tell us about the ultimate nature—the real make-up—of the world.*

The Dream Argument has been interpreted in many different ways, some of them quite illustrative and insightful,[3] others less so. Perhaps you've heard a "summary" version: how do I know whether I'm dreaming or awake? Admittedly, Descartes occasionally makes comments that invite such summaries—but a closer look at his argument might reveal something interesting.

Descartes, like the skeptic, accepted an extremely rigorous epistemic standard for knowledge. The criterion for knowledge, according to Descartes, is infallibility. A belief of ours is an instance of knowledge only if that belief is infallible, that is, it is *not possible* for that belief to be mistaken. In other words, a proposition is knowledge only if it is not possible that it's false. Notice that the fact that a particular belief is true is not sufficient to make it knowledge. It's rather that there is no possible way that this belief could have turned out to be false.

With this as the standard for knowledge, Descartes's task in undermining our confidence that we achieve knowledge by means of the senses is clear. He needs to find some reason to think that our senses *possibly* might be giving us false or misleading representations about the nature of the world. That is, he must show that there is at least some reason to suspect our "sensory beliefs." And Descartes thinks he has found that possible reason: dream "experiences" and sensory experience have various features in common. Yet dream experiences can't be trusted. Might that lead to doubt about our senses? What would that mean for our knowledge of the world?

Margaret Wilson, in her book on Descartes's *Meditations*, offers an elegant statement of the Dream Argument.

---

2   Lehrer 1990, Chap. 9, and Audi 1988, Chap. 9.
3   E.g., Wilson 1978.

1. I believe in the past I have dreamed that I was perceiving various physical objects at close range when it was false that I was really perceiving any such objects (when my experience was thoroughly delusory).
2. If I see no certain marks to distinguish waking experience of physical objects from dream experience when, I believe, I was deceived, I have reason to believe my waking experience, too, may be deceptive.
3. I see no such certain marks to distinguish waking experience from dreams.
4. Therefore, I have reason to suppose that waking experience, too, may be deceptive (thoroughly delusory).
5. But if I have reason to suppose my waking experience may be deceptive (thoroughly delusory), I have reason to doubt the existence of physical objects (for at present we are supposing this experience to be the best foundation for our belief in physical objects).[4]

Note the conclusion of the argument: the existence of physical objects is open to doubt. And our understanding of physical objects—what we take them to be and what we think they are like—derives from our senses, according to both common sense and the expert. But why think that what happens in a dream in any way undermines our *certainty* about what our senses tell us?

We can see why we don't trust our "dream experiences." They seem to tell us about the same kinds of objects that sensory experiences convey information about—everyday, ordinary objects, with their everyday properties. Yet we come to discount dream experiences precisely because the *object as experienced in the dream does not match the real cause of the experience.* Ordinary objects aren't causing those dream experiences. Imagine that Andrew dreams that he is tossing a light green tennis ball in the air. Now notice: the cause of that dream experience isn't a ball, much less anything light green. The cause of that dream experience is something *internal* to Andrew that *is nothing like a light green tennis ball.*

Descartes's challenge to defenders of the senses as giving us knowledge about objects now comes into focus: What if our sensory experiences are like the dream experiences? Our sensory experiences tell us that the world is made up of solid, colored, scented (etc.) objects. Not only do we think the *external* objects are the cause of our sensory experiences, we take our sensory experiences to represent those objects *the way they really are.* But our "dream

---

4   Wilson 1978, pp. 22–23.

beliefs" suggest another possibility: What if our sensory experiences are more about *what's going on inside of us than what's going on out there in the world*? What if our senses are more a reflection of us than of the real nature of those external objects?

My senses tell me the table is uniformly solid, but another sort of investigation suggests that the real nature of the table is quite different from what our senses reveal.

That sort of possibility, for Descartes, is enough to rule out "sense knowledge" about the objects presented to us in sense experience. Knowledge, once again, requires infallibility. The possibility that our senses misrepresent the real nature of the world and the nature of those objects—that our sensory experiences might be "dream-like"—is enough, in Descartes's view, to eliminate most of our sensory experiences as a source of knowledge.

Yet perhaps an important *dissimilarity* between dream and sensory experience has been overlooked: Andrew wakes up to find out that he is not playing with a light green tennis ball. We don't trust our dreams because we find out that they are wrong, by means of ... the senses! Indeed our senses keep reconfirming the very nature of the objects we encounter: they're colored and textured ... and occasionally tasty.

This, however, is not a line of argument open to the defender of the senses. We cannot use the senses to verify our senses. If I think I see a blue book on the table, I cannot verify this belief by appealing to other sense-based beliefs, because it is the senses that are in question. An analogy: you can't check that your calculator is working right by doing the same sum on it again. You could use pencil-and-paper to check the sum. You could call your high school math teacher for a quick check. But are we able to "get outside" our senses to check them? Of course not. We do not have an independent check of our senses. All that is available to us is the character or nature of our own experiences, and it's the correctness or accuracy of those experiences that's in question. And this is why Descartes thinks that the representational character of my sense experiences cannot guarantee that the world really is the way those experiences represent it.

Because there is no guarantee of the accuracy of our sensory representations, it is possible that our senses are *not* telling us the truth about the world. And that possibility—the possibility that we are mistaken—is enough to rule out our having the knowledge we think we have based on our senses.

Demons

Descartes is not quite finished. We might not be able to trust the accuracy of our sensory representation of the color of the geranium bloom or the scent of the rose. Still—green is a color; $2 + 2 = 4$; a triangle has three sides. I can't be mistaken about these beliefs. I can't even imagine what it would be like for these beliefs to be false. *That just doesn't seem possible.*

Descartes recognizes that the truth of beliefs such as these—*rational truths*, we might call them—is rationally compelling, and is not based on our senses, which the dream argument has shown are doubtable. Nonetheless, he suggests that even they could be false. He has in mind another *alternative scenario*, which we cannot rule out, in which it is possible for us to have the same beliefs, yet they turn out false.

In the 1999 movie *The Matrix*, we see a world in which everything a person believes is "conjured" by some very powerful force, and thus false. Descartes imagines an even more powerful being than that imagined in *The Matrix*. For all we know, some extremely powerful being, or demon, might cause us to believe seemingly obvious propositions—that green is a color or that a triangle has three sides—even though such propositions were in fact false. The belief that a triangle has three sides might be only *apparently* true, and thus we cannot rule out a *possible* alternative scenario undermining our knowledge. Our inability to rule out this alternative scenario means that we must admit the possibility that such beliefs come from a deviant source. The mere possibility that these beliefs might come not from the way the world really is, but from a demon intent on deceiving us, is sufficient to show that these beliefs are fallible. We could be mistaken about the truth of these beliefs. And because we could be mistaken, we do not *know* that $2 + 2 = 4$, or that everything that has color has a shape. Spelled out, the Demon Argument might run as follows:

1. I have some beliefs that are compelling.
2. It is possible that an evil demon, intent on deceiving me, could be the causal source of these beliefs.
3. If the origin of the beliefs is sufficiently deviant, then the beliefs are false.
4. I cannot rule out the evil demon scenario.
5. Hence, it is possible that the origin of the beliefs is sufficiently deviant.
6. Hence, it is possible that the beliefs are false.
7. Hence, I do not know.[5]

---

5   Crumley 2009, p. 28.

It is hard to imagine a more globally skeptical argument. Not only can we not trust our apparent sensory knowledge of the world around us, but we cannot claim to know some very basic truths!

Descartes wants exactly this. He wants to take on the strongest skeptical argument, the argument widest in scope and most difficult to refute. If he can show that the strongest skeptical argument can be defeated, then he will have succeeded in showing that, yes, indeed we have knowledge. At the beginning of the second Meditation, Descartes believes he does just that in perhaps one of the most famous arguments ever given:

> I was persuaded that there was nothing in all the world, that there was no heaven, no earth, that there were no minds nor any bodies; was I not then likewise persuaded that I did not exist? Not at all; of a surety I myself did exist since I persuaded myself of something. But there is some deceiver or other, very powerful and very cunning, who ever employs his ingenuity in deceiving me. Then without doubt I exist also if he deceives me, and let him deceive me as much as he will, he can never cause me to be nothing so long as I think that I am something ... we must come to this definite conclusion: *I am, I exist, is necessarily true each time that I pronounce it, or mentally conceive it.*[6]

Descartes claims that he has arrived at a proposition that he cannot be mistaken about, and hence, he knows. He knows at least this much: "I am, I exist, is necessarily true each time that I pronounce it, or mentally conceive [think] it." Hence, whenever I think, I *know*—at least while I'm thinking—I am. Or: I think; therefore, I am—in Descartes's famous Latin version, "*cogito ergo sum.*"

The Dream and Demon Arguments presented a radical challenge to those who held that, of course, we have knowledge of things in the world and about rational truths. Knowing requires being able to rule out any possible alternative scenario. And Descartes thinks he has done just that for at least one belief: "Let him deceive me as much as he will," no possible alternative scenario—not even the demon scenario—could arise that could make this belief false: "I am, I exist, is necessarily true each time that I pronounce it, or mentally conceive it." Descartes has found a truth about a real thing (the "I" of *cogito ergo sum*). And there is no way he could be mistaken. Hence, he claims he knows.

---

6   Descartes 1968b, p. 150.

Is Infallibility Necessary for Knowledge?

The Reformation and Infallibility

Descartes did not "dream up" the infallibility requirement for knowledge. The history of skepticism is populated with similar ideas.

It is interesting to note how the Reformation contributed to worries about knowledge and infallibility. The German monk, Martin Luther, nailed 95 theses to the door of the Wittenburg church in 1517, an act many consider to have begun the Reformation. Part of Luther's challenge centered on the Church's claim to infallibility in matters of doctrine and interpretation of the Bible. Luther, citing various inconsistencies and errors, rejected that notion, turning instead to one's own conscience, or one's own conscientious reading of the Bible. Of course, the Church's response was (in part) that appealing to conscience allowed too many interpretations.

Once the idea of infallibility is abandoned, how are we supposed to tell when we have attained religious truth? Indeed infallibility might seem essential to being able to tell that we have attained any truth. Richard Popkin 1979, Chap. 1 explores these matters in more detail.

There is much that Descartes still hasn't shown that he knows. He hopes the rest of the *Meditations* will suffice to show *what* this "I" or this "thinking thing" is, that God exists, that the mind is distinct from the body and that we can know some very general features of the physical world. Some are willing to grant that Descartes knows that he exists, without also being willing to grant that Descartes succeeds in showing that we know these other propositions, e.g., that God exists.[7] Others question whether or not Descartes is right to insist that infallibility is a necessary criterion for knowledge.

The Cartesian skeptic is no doubt right in claiming that infallibility is sufficient—enough—for knowledge. But this skeptic has not shown us that it is necessary—required—for knowledge. We realize that the skeptic wants to avoid the possibility of mistake. But it isn't clear why we should be so cautious in our epistemic pursuits. After all, it is not just good fortune that has led us to many of the things we have claimed to know. Relying on evidence, applying certain methods, and correcting methods that have misled us in the past—all of these, while admittedly fallible, have led us to genuine instances of knowledge. Thus, Cartesian skeptics have yet to show that we must accept their preferred epistemic standard.

---

7   Curley 1978.

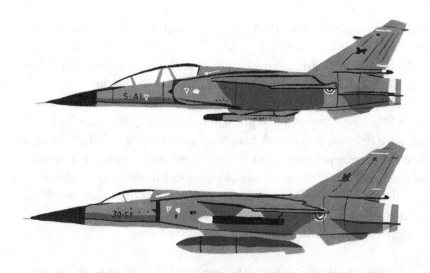

Similarly, the skeptics' view that knowledge requires ruling out *every* alternative scenario is uncompelling. A fallibilist—one who thinks we have knowledge despite the possibility of mistake—could argue that our ordinary epistemic standards require only ruling out *relevant* alternative scenarios, not every *possible* alternative scenario. Consider a case of the sort presented by Thompson Clarke, about plane spotters who must distinguish very similar aircraft.[8] The spotters' manual tells them that the friendly planes have characteristic F and the hostile planes have characteristic H. The manual is not at fault: the planes in that area with F are American or British—friendly—and those with H are hostile—Iraqi. But the twist in the story is this: French planes are also participating in this war, on the same side as the British and Americans. Their planes, however, have characteristic H. The manual doesn't mention this, because the French planes are operating in a totally different area. A spotter sees a plane with H, and correctly identifies it as hostile. Does the spotter know it's hostile? If, contrary to fact, a French plane had lost its way and wandered into the spotter's sector, then that plane would have been misidentified as hostile by the spotter using the manual's test. It's fortunate that this unlikely event did not happen; but what this shows is that the manual's test is not an infallible one—it could have resulted in a false belief under certain circumstances.

So what should we say about this example? Sometimes it is argued that this belief wasn't genuine knowledge—it was based on correct use of the manual, and thus had a very high probability of truth, but it was nevertheless

---

8   Clarke 1972.

not real *knowledge*—rather, a lucky guess, because the method used didn't rule out every possible scenario for mistake. On the other hand, it seems more reasonable to say that the spotter is justified in coming to the belief he did, in the circumstances, and that he knew that the plane was hostile.

This second reaction, which reflects perhaps a more commonsense view of knowledge, suggests that the skeptic is mistaken in requiring a test for knowledge that rules out *every possible* competing scenario. Which alternatives must be ruled out may vary from case to case. This makes the skeptical requirement of a more stringent standard for knowledge—infallibility—questionable.

The fallibilist view of knowledge can point to many cases where we arrived at true beliefs on the basis of good reasons, using reasonable methods. Richard Feldman succinctly characterizes this fallibilist position:

> Our experiences provide us with very good evidence, but not absolutely conclusive evidence, for propositions such as the proposition that we really do see a book (and thus are not dreaming ...). This evidence is good enough to justify our ordinary beliefs and thus to satisfy the justification conditions [a standard or requirement] for knowledge. All the arguments for skepticism rely on the mistaken assumption that justification, and thus, knowledge, require conclusive evidence.[9]

We might quibble with Feldman about what is "conclusive." What this means is *decisive* or *convincing*—enough to *conclude* wondering and draw *conclusions*. This is what ordinary (but not infallible) justification provides.

Questions still remain, of course, about the nature of perception and perceptual knowledge. (See Chapter 5: Perception, for a discussion of some of these.) And some have suggested that the Demon Argument raises questions about the connection between proof and truth—a connection we normally take for granted, that *proving* a hypothesis is enough to show it true.[10] Others doubt whether we can coherently raise "demon questions."[11] Those further questions remain interesting and worth pursuing.

Here is an interesting argument against skepticism.[12] Skeptics suggest that they have as much evidence for rival hypotheses, e.g., evil demons or dreams, as we do for our commonsense view of the world. Yet there is perhaps a *best*

---

9   Feldman 2003, p. 128.
10   Hacking 1973 in Honderich 1984, especially pp. 216–17.
11   E.g., Bouwsma 1949.
12   A version of this argument can be found in Feldman 2003, Chap. 7.

explanation of our experience, which is better supported by the evidence we have. Suppose, for a moment, that a skeptic suggests that our world is really like the world of the movie *The Matrix*. Notice that a "Matrix world" would apparently be consistent with our evidence and would seemingly count against the justified status of our beliefs about the world. Philosophers have raised questions about what is the best explanation and why. But it is sometimes suggested that the best explanation of our evidence is that the world is just the world of commonsense (of course, as "corrected" by our best science). What does need some attention here, however, is the assumption that when there are two explanations that fit all our observations, the one that's "better" in terms of our criteria for explanation is therefore more likely to be true.

Hume and Our Reasons for Induction

You are doubtless familiar with a common instruction on various tests: *Show your work*. Merely providing an answer is insufficient; you have to show how you arrived at the answer. You are instructed to provide your reasons. Indeed, the right answer based on bad reasons may not be worth more than a wrong answer. The rationale for the instruction is fairly simple, if not always stated: You are not "entitled" to that answer if you do not know the right way to get there. Indeed for many years, wrong answers on the SAT test were penalized—something was subtracted from one's score—but when no answer was given, that merely failed to add to the score. This was an attempt to prevent guessing, and to counteract the grading credit that would have been provided by a lucky guess. Guessing did not entitle a person to the answer.

David Hume's (1711–76) skeptical worry ran in a somewhat different direction from Descartes. He was interested in our beliefs about the world, of course. And Hume was willing to grant that we often get things right; many of our beliefs about the world are no doubt true, or at the very least are likely to be true.[13] But Hume thought that if we claim that some of our beliefs are rational because of our reliance on some method, then we must have some good reason to rely on that method. He argued, however, that one important method cannot be shown to be rational.

Hume has in mind a particular view of what makes our beliefs rational or justified. We should not be satisfied with some belief simply because we have some reason or other for it. Wagering on a football game because of a

---

13   Hume 1975, pp. 54–55; Hume 1978, pp. 173–78.

preference for the mascot or on a horse race because a horse has the same name as a favorite relative may provide one's reasons for the bets. Win or lose, however, these are not good reasons. Instead Hume thinks we have to have *good reasons* or *positive reasons* for our beliefs, and that includes having good reasons for the methods that lead us to those beliefs. Being able to provide good reasons for our beliefs is necessary for our beliefs to count as rational. When asked to show our work, to give our *good* reasons for certain types of belief, Hume argues we can't. And unlike the compassionate teacher, Hume won't give partial credit.

Hume's Assumptions

Types of Induction

Inductive inferences purport to show that their conclusions are probable. Hume focuses on a particular type of **induction**, generally known as *enumerative induction*. Enumerative inductions proceed by noting that certain members of a group have a certain property. It is then concluded that any other member of the group likely will have that property.

Another type of frequently used induction is inference to the best explanation. With this type of inductive inference, the claim is that a certain conclusion is probable because it is the best explanation of a certain fact or event. For example, one might claim that it is probable that there is a green cup in front of me, because that is the best explanation of my having the sense experience of a green cup. This type of inference is sometimes called *abduction*. We will see this sort of argument in this and a later chapter.

Hume thinks we are *naturally* inclined to a lot of our beliefs about the world. For example, when I leave the room and return a few minutes later to my computer, I *naturally* believe that it is the same computer I just left. I believe that the computer continues to exist independently of my being there to observe it. My belief in this constancy and continued existence is not anything that I *rationally infer*, according to Hume. Hume claimed:

> It seems evident, that men are carried, by a natural instinct or preposses-
> sion, to repose faith in their senses; and that, without any reasoning, or even
> almost before the use of reason, we always suppose an external universe, which
> depends not on our perception, but would exist, though we and every sensible

creature were absent or annihilated. Even the animal creations are governed by a like opinion, and preserve this belief of external objects, in all their thoughts, designs, and actions.[14]

While Hume did not doubt that many of our beliefs are natural, he doubted that we are *rationally entitled* to at least some of those beliefs. Hume held that we cannot explain how we could have rationally or justifiably arrived at our beliefs about the persistence of objects, or about the reality of cause-and-effect relationships, or at beliefs arrived at by means of inductive inferences. Induction, a type of non-deductive reasoning, takes summaries or records of past experience and extend them to new cases.

Now, Hume was willing to allow us this much: beliefs about present experience are justified, as well as memory beliefs about past experience. For example, I am justified in believing that in the past, my turning the knob on the stove was followed by the boiling of the water. But how do we use these beliefs to predict the future?

The Rationality of Our Inductive Inferences

In the 1960s television series "The Beverly Hillbillies," the character Jethro never quite mastered the concept of doorbell. He eventually came to believe, however, the conclusion of a particular inductive inference. Jethro noticed that a rather elegant-sounding chime wafting through the Clampett mansion was invariably accompanied by visitors at the front door. Upon hearing the sound, he would find someone standing there. Jethro's experience was of a *constant conjunction* between these two events, the ethereal sound of the chime and the subsequent discovery of someone standing at the front door. Jethro consequently and, according to Hume, naturally came to believe that upon hearing the chime, he would find someone at the door.

We can represent Jethro's inference in the following manner:

1. In the past, whenever I have heard the sound of the chime, I have subsequently experienced someone at the front door.
2. I am currently hearing the sound of the chime.
3. Thus, I will find someone at the front door.

---

14   Hume 1975, Bk. 1, Sect. XII, Pt. 1.

(My dog has apparently "reasoned" to a similar conclusion. Whenever he hears the doorbell, he flies madly to the front door and remains there, barking insistently, until the front door is opened to reveal whoever is standing there.)

Hume's special interest is the general pattern of inference, which we can represent:

> (1) All observed A's have been followed by B's.
> (2) An A is currently being observed.
> (3) Thus, a B will follow.

Hume asked a difficult question: why does believing (1) and (2) entitle us to believe (3)?

His point is perhaps subtle but can be drawn out this way. Imagine an instance of the inference pattern you learned to call "modus ponens": *If P, then Q; P; therefore, Q*:

> (P1) If it rains in April, then Sacramento will have a good almond crop.
> (P2) It rains in April.
> (Con) Therefore, Sacramento will have a good almond crop.

When we ask why (P1) and (P2) support the conclusion, the ready answer is *modus ponens*, a pattern of deductive inference that *legitimizes* or *licenses* the conclusion, given the logical form of those premises. More than that, we can give some pretty good reasons why we trust that rule of inference, *modus ponens*. *Modus ponens* gives us a "license" or an okay to trust the argument about Sacramento's almond crop. It can easily be shown to be *truth-preserving*: if the premises are true, and *modus ponens* gets you the conclusion, then this conclusion has to be true. But is there a similar "license" for induction? Is there some rule of inference or principle that supports the conclusion of the inductive inference? What rule tells us that connections between A's and B's in the past *entitle* us to believe that a similar connection will now occur? What principle or rule tells us that it is legitimate to move from the two premises in the induction pattern to the conclusion?

This leads to one of Hume's central claims. When we use induction, he claimed, we are tacitly relying on an *unstated* principle, which supports our inductive inferences. That is, the "inductive rule of inference" allowing us to move from (1) and (2) to (3) is something like the following:

That instances, of which we have had no experience, must resemble those, of which we have had experience, and that the course of nature continues always uniformly the same.[15]

Accepted practice identifies this principle as the Uniformity Principle (UP). Notice how this principle—this "inductive rule of inference"—is supposed to work. Jethro once again hears the doorbell. And he *tacitly relies on UP* in drawing the connection between past events and the current sound of the doorbell. Of course, Jethro isn't consciously thinking "Hey; UP says I'm entitled to conclude...." Far from it, and Hume was not suggesting anything like that. Rather Hume argued that explaining how Jethro's inference might be rational requires tacit reliance on something like UP.

One point requires clarification. Hume was trying to explain why we think inductive conclusions are acceptable. He claimed that our reliance on induction makes sense only if we are tacitly relying on UP. He was not arguing for adoption of the principle.

And here is the core of Hume's skeptical critique of induction. The fact that we rely on UP is not enough to show that our inductions are rational. Hume challenged us to explain why we should trust UP. Why do we count on UP? Hume argued that we cannot give good reasons for trusting UP.

Is UP Rational?

We've seen that some claims can be justified by argument; but others can be justified all by themselves. According to Hume, there are only two ways to justify any claim. Any proposition—no matter its content—is, in Hume's view, either a claim about the world (e.g., "ducks are quackers" or "Jupiter is larger than Mars" or "protons are made up of quarks"), or a claim about definitions or the connection between concepts (e.g., "a triangle has three sides" or "vixens are female foxes"). And we have only two means or ways for justifying propositions. We draw on experience—more precisely, sensory experience—to justify claims about the world. And we draw on reason to justify a claim involving conceptual connections. We can reason out its truth—we know independently of experience that it is true—because we can see that it is true by definition,

---

15   Hume 1978, Bk. 1, Pt. 3, Sect. VI.

or that its denial is a self-contradiction. That's it. Reason or experience. Those are the only two avenues available for justifying the Uniformity Principle.

How might UP be justified by reason? We can justify UP this way only if we can show that it's a "truth of reason"—a conceptual or logical truth. The way to show that some proposition is a truth of reason or a logical or definitional truth is to show that denying it is self-contradictory. Thus, "all bachelors are unmarried" is a truth of reason because denying it leads to contradiction. The definition of the word "bachelor" includes being unmarried. The concept of being a bachelor must include the concept of being unmarried. Thus claiming that some bachelors are married tacitly asserts the self-contradictory claim that "some *unmarried men* are married."

But is the proposition "the future will *not* resemble the past" self-contradictory? If it were true, that would mean that the world is very confusing—and dangerous! Yet there's nothing self-contradictory about this proposition, which denies UP.

You might protest that people change their minds, but not nature. Notice, however, there is nothing self-contradictory about nature "changing course." It is not self-contradictory to hold that although the sun has risen every day of human history thus far, it may not do so tomorrow. Our long overdue galactic supernova might occur just before sunrise. Thus, the Uniformity Principle cannot be established by reason.

Casual readers sometimes surmise that we can stop here: Hume has shown that we can't justify UP. But that would be to walk out of the movie before the climactic scene. Hume now set himself the task of showing that experience cannot justify UP, and there are two options here. First, note that UP contains a reference to unobserved, not yet actual events. And our experience does not include those future events. We haven't observed the not-yet-occurred.

But how, then, might a justification based on experience proceed? Perhaps something like the following will do:

(1) Reliance on UP in the past has led to true beliefs.
(2) I am relying on UP now.
(3) Hence, this use of UP will lead to a true belief.

This pattern of inference ought to seem familiar—it is merely an instance of the inference pattern we set out to establish as legitimate in the first place! We begin with a summary of our past experience, that reliance on UP has worked in the past. We further note that we are currently relying on UP.

Consequently, we infer that this reliance on UP will have the desired result: acquiring a true belief.

This justification of UP presumes precisely what is at issue—that the future will be relevantly like the past. Hume rightly noted that we should reject this move. It is a circular argument, which cannot provide the *good reason* we are seeking. If it is our confidence in UP that is in question, we cannot use UP to justify that confidence. So, attempts to justify UP based on experience are either irrelevant or circular.

The main outline of Hume's argument is then clear. Inductive inferences are legitimate only if something like the Uniformity Principle licenses or permits the inference. The task of justifying inductive inference thus becomes the task of justifying our reliance on the Uniformity Principle. Yet there is a problem in doing so. First, UP is not evidently established by reason alone: its denial is not a self-contradiction. Second, we can't simply appeal to past experience, because UP refers to the future. Nor, more importantly, is it justified by the appeal to the fact that past inductions, which relied on UP, worked in the past. This latter appeal is, for Hume, fatally circular. But then we have exhausted our possible ways of justifying UP. Reason and experience have failed. Thus, Hume claims, we are not entitled to claim that our inductive beliefs are based on some sort of rational deliberation. We cannot claim that we have good reasons for our inductive beliefs. According to Hume, such beliefs reflect nothing more than a habit or custom. We do it ... we just do it. Like Jethro, we make inferences, but we don't know what justifies them.

Hume's argument, again, doesn't deny that we have a lot of true beliefs. Hume objected rather to our trying to take credit for what nature has done! Before we pride ourselves on our *rational* reliance on inductive inference, Hume asks us whether we really can give good reasons for so relying. And Hume thinks his arguments show that if there are good arguments for the rationality of induction, we have yet to provide them.

Responding to Hume

Responding to Hume presents a different and perhaps more daunting challenge than responding to Descartes. We generally agree with Hume that being rational means being able to give reasons. And we can see his point: if inductive inferences are rational, there must be some way of explaining *why* they are.

One approach is to suggest that Hume misunderstands the standard for rationality in these types of context. The British philosopher Peter Strawson

(1919–2006) argues that accepting the conclusions of inductive arguments is precisely what we mean by "rational." We are justified in accepting inductive conclusions only and precisely to the extent that they are supported by the evidence:

> It is an analytic proposition [a proposition that is true by definition, whose denial is an implicit self-contradiction] that it is reasonable to have a degree of belief in a statement which is proportional to the strength of the evidence in its favour; and it is an analytic proposition ... that, other things being equal, the evidence for a generalization is strong in proportion as the number of favourable instances, and the variety of circumstances in which they have been found is great. So to ask whether it is reasonable to place reliance on inductive procedures is like asking whether it is reasonable to proportion the degree of one's convictions to the strength of the evidence. Doing this is what "being reasonable" *means* in such a context.[16]

Strawson appeals to our concept of "being reasonable": *all other things being equal*, this is what it means to be reasonable—trust induction.

Strawson is here claiming what Hume denied: that UP can be established by reason alone. He is claiming that "UP is reasonable" is a truth by definition. Many are tempted by this type of response, but should they be? In Strawson's view, a conceptual connection exists between rationality and reliance on induction. Using induction is part of what we mean by "rational." And, says Strawson, if Hume is asking for more than pointing out this connection, then Hume has not quite understood what is meant by "justification" or "rationality." Consider a simple analogy. Suppose that Sam is about to climb a ladder, and Sara tells him to be careful. After Sam gives the ladder a shake, checks on the dog, and starts climbing, Sam insists that he's done everything he needs to do to be careful. But we can reply, on behalf of Hume, that if that's what these words mean, then his question could be rephrased: what makes us think that a "justified" belief, arrived at through "rationality," is likely to be true?

In a later work, Strawson takes a somewhat different tack, suggesting that the way to respond to the skeptic is not by means of a counterargument. Rather, we should be content to show that certain beliefs or claims are fundamental to human thought: "Our inescapable natural commitment is to a general frame

---

16   Strawson 1952, pp. 256–57.

of belief and to a general style (the inductive) of belief-formation."[17] Our best response, according to Strawson, is to illustrate the way in which induction plays a role in our belief system and our methods of acquiring and revising belief. Induction is thus part of our fundamental practice, our fundamental engagement with the world.

17   Strawson 1983, p. 14.

Oddly enough, Hume and Strawson agree here: that no argument against the skeptic justifying induction is possible, and that induction is a natural fundamental practice. So Strawson is not really providing what Hume denied can be provided: a justification for this practice.

Hume insists that we should not be taking credit for what nature has done. Nature has instilled in us and the rest of animal creation a certain style of belief formation, namely, induction. This style seems to work. But the fact that it works, Hume claims, is nature's doing, not ours. Because no *argument* of ours underlies the efficacy of induction, he says, our rational abilities do not guarantee the effectiveness of induction. At best, we can hope that nature provides the guarantee—a hope, Hume notes, we have no epistemic right to count on. Strawson and Hume thus disagree at a very basic level.

Another approach suggests that Hume has misdescribed our inductive practice. Hume supposes that we "enumerate" our experiences. We see that some object has a certain feature on one occasion, notice that it does so on a second, a third, and, after enough observations summarize that experience in "All A's are B's." The generalized summary is, in a way, "naked," unconnected to other beliefs. Hume supposes this bit of summary of our experience proceeds independently of our other beliefs. It is no surprise then that when we go to apply it to a new case, we can give no reason *why*.

Some have suggested, however, that the generalization is never as naked or unconnected as Hume supposes and that induction always takes place against a background of other beliefs, a background that licenses some inductive inferences but prohibits others.[18]

Suppose, to vary an example from the pyschologist and computer scientist John Holland, that a friend points to a certain bird and says that it is an American goldfinch. On the basis of this one case, you might infer that American goldfinches have bright yellow neck and breast plumage. Suppose also that a few moments later, the same friend points to a nattily attired man walking by and says, "That's my philosophy teacher." You are unlikely to conclude on the basis of this one case that all philosophy teachers are smartly dressed. The difference in the two cases—that you draw the conclusion in the former case but not the latter—is due to the operation of certain background beliefs. Your background beliefs are likely to tell you that there is some connection between being a particular species of bird, and having a certain plumage—in other words, that it's likely that the plumage of birds inside a single

18   Holland 1986; Bogdan 1976, pp. 217–36.

species is uniform. It's no mere coincidence, or an accidental regularity that can't be counted on to continue. Other background beliefs, however, tell you it would be quite remarkable if there were some connection between being a philosophy teacher and being nattily attired.

In this view, inductive arguments are always relative to certain contexts. If we want to understand why an inductive argument is legitimate (or illegitimate), we need to look to the context, to the relevant background beliefs. *Justifiably* concluding that all American goldfinches have bright yellow plumage requires that there are relevant background beliefs.[19] But to the extent that this contextualized view is a more accurate account of our inductive practice, then Hume has *misdescribed* our actual cognitive situation. *If* Hume's skepticism depends on such misdescription, then we have some reason for thinking that Hume has not provided us with a compelling argument.

The skeptic's view of induction assumes that particular inferences are "isolated." We begin with particular beliefs about our observations in particular cases. Generalizing on these particular cases, we apply that generalized belief to a new case. The only evidential support for this *inductive application*, according to the Humean, is the generalized summary of past observations. And none of our other beliefs seem relevant, in the skeptic's view.

Does the Humean skeptic provide us with any compelling reason to think that induction is like this? It might be suggested that we understand how particular observations support inductive conclusions *by virtue of* our having certain general beliefs about the context in which the induction occurs.[20] The skeptic seemingly disregards this other view of induction.

Clearly, Hume will want to know what entitles us to these general beliefs that are part of the background of particular inductive inferences. We acquire such beliefs as we acquire the concepts that we use in making particular observations. The process of acquiring the concept also involves the acquisition of associated general beliefs about when certain kinds of inference are legitimate. We acquire or master concepts in "groups," as it were. For example, in learning to identify *kinds* of birds, I learn, if only tacitly, that the kind is characterized by certain natural features or properties, such as being able to fly or having distinctive plumage. We may later discover that there are exceptions (penguins don't fly) or further related concepts (plumage is determined by genetic code).

---

19   Bogdan 1976.
20   Cf. Everitt and Fisher 1995, pp. 174–78.

It is then as legitimate to accept the general beliefs as it is to accept the particular observation beliefs that make use of the relevant concepts.

The Humean skeptic may wish to reject this view of concept acquisition. Nonetheless, the view illustrates the sense in which the Humean view of induction depends on a certain view of how we acquire the concepts we use in making particular judgments about what we observe ... and *inferences based on those observations*. If Hume is wrong about concept acquisition, then he may well be wrong about the legitimacy of our inductively based beliefs. In any case, the Humean has yet to provide us with a compelling case for accepting the empirical and conceptual claims that underlie such skepticism.

But perhaps Hume's skepticism could be reformulated to accommodate what might be this more realistic view of how we get general beliefs. If any particular induction depends on our already believing other general truths, we can then ask how experience gives us these *other* truths. The central problem here is how experience justifies beliefs about the unexperienced. If this justification is done "holistically," fitting it into a "framework," the question still arises why we think that the structured collection of general beliefs we have about future experiences is justified by past experiences.

Key Concepts

- skepticism
- Dream Argument
- infallibility
- Demon Argument
- induction
- Uniformity Principle

Reading/Discussion Questions

1. Explain the connection between epistemic standards and knowledge. How would you describe the epistemic standard invoked by the Cartesian skeptic—that is, what is the criterion of knowledge for that skeptic?

2. As clearly as you can, explain the Dream Argument. Begin by stating the aim of the argument. What do you see as the most questionable premise or assumption in the argument? Why?

3. Philosophers sometimes refer to versions of the Evil Demon Argument as a "brain in a vat" argument for skepticism. We are to imagine that we

are but "disembodied brains," kept functioning in some manner, and "fed" experiences by evil scientists. The movie *Matrix*, of course, presents a sort of "body in a cocoon" version of this argument. Do you think that if we were deceived by a demon, or were brains in vats, or bodies in cocoons, that we could discover that? Why or why not?

4. Hume's argument concerning the rationality of induction is sometimes summarized as "it's logically possible that the past might not be repeated." Explain what's right *and* what's wrong about this summary.

5. Which skeptical argument—Dream, Demon, or Induction—do you see as the most threatening; that is, which do you see as the most challenging and difficult to refute? Explain.

6. What do you think is the best response to the Dream Argument? to the Demon Argument? Do you think there is an adequate response to Hume? Explain.

For Further Reading

Several excellent introductions to epistemology consider the skeptical arguments, including, Keith Lehrer 1990, Richard Feldman 2003, and Robert Audi 2005; Lehrer's classic 1974, more advanced than the introductions, considers the skeptical position. Crumley 2009 is similar to the approach in this text.

Richard H. Popkin 1979 provides an excellent account of the cultural context and the work of earlier skeptical thinkers that led to Descartes. There are many studies of Descartes; Margaret Wilson's 1978 is an excellent and very accessible account of the arguments of the *Meditations*. In the same series, Barry Stroud 1975 is similarly an excellent and very accessible examination of Hume's positions and arguments.

In the past few decades, contextualism as a response to skepticism has drawn more attention, largely due to the work of Keith DeRose. DeRose and Warfield 1999 contains essays representing the many different types of response to skepticism. Perhaps the twentieth century's simultaneously most famous and, for many, most exasperating response to skepticism are G.E. Moore 1966 and 1957. Moore's essays are difficult, with disputed interpretations and analyses; see DeRose and Warfield 1999 and Jones and Fogelin 1997, Chap. 3. (The section on Moore's essay is written by Fogelin.)

Descartes 1968a is his *Discourses*; a nice explanation of his work on rainbows can be found at http://farside.ph.utexas.edu/teaching/302l/lectures/node131.html.

CHAPTER TWO

KNOWLEDGE

Various philosophers have offered accounts or analyses of the nature and extent of our knowledge. These accounts, however, may be classified as one of two broad types. Setting aside details, an account might be seen as belonging to the empiricist tradition or the rationalist tradition. Seeing these two traditions in more detail begins the chapter. The latter half of the chapter surveys a few recent analyses of knowledge.

Two Traditions

Empiricism and rationalism are the dominant approaches to understanding the nature and sources of knowledge. They have been so since Plato (c. 425 BCE–?) and Aristotle (384–322 BCE). Both Plato and Aristotle held that real knowledge was of universal truths, for example that *all* humans are mortal or that *all* rectangles are four-sided plane figures. Aristotle, however, held that all our knowledge begins with the information—presumably about particular things—we get through the five senses. Plato thought that genuine knowledge was attained only by the exercise of mind or intellect. Earlier thinkers, such as Parmenides (510 BCE–?), had also claimed that genuine knowledge comes only from reason's exercise. Plato's view was truly revolutionary, however, in scope and depth. He held that genuine knowledge consists in our intellectual apprehension of a special, nonphysical object, which he called *Forms* (today, more often thought of as *universals*).[1]

Plato's influence traces through Neoplatonism, a school of thought that arose in the third century CE, led mainly by Plotinus (204–270), and is especially evidenced in the epistemological theory of Christian philosophers St. Augustine (384–430) and later St. Bonaventure (1271–74). Augustine's view, in keeping with the Neoplatonic tradition, held that we could not have knowledge of sensible things:

> Whatever is attained by sense, what we call the sensible, never for an instant ceases to change. Always it is in a state of uninterrupted becoming. And the perpetually changing cannot be comprehended. No genuine truth and hence no knowledge can be had by the senses.

It was a commonplace, in this epistemological view, to hold that we could only have knowledge of necessary and unchanging truths. This view is not now widely held, but a simple example perhaps illustrates the motivation. If 2 + 3 constantly and arbitrarily took on different values—one moment 5, the next 7, or 131—we would hesitate to say we *know* that 2 + 3 = 5. Julia claims to know that the coffee is hot ... but no, wait—now it's merely warm ... or is it now cold? Characteristics that change are superficial—they are not part of the real nature of something, which must be constant as long as that thing exists. Real knowledge cannot be of the superficial, but must be of the essential. What then can we know? Well, the unchanging. And the objects that had this characteristic of immutability—unchanging objects—are Platonic Forms or universals. Universals, like numbers and geometric objects, are *ideal* objects: nonphysical, hence unchanging, non-sensible objects that exist in an ideal world. (Views like Plato's or Augustine's are sometimes known as *idealism*[2] because the objects of knowledge are nonphysical, ideal objects.) Numbers

---

1   E.g., compare White 1976 and Sherman 2013.

2   As mentioned in the Introduction, this philosophical term does not carry the meaning it has in ordinary language: the pursuit of ideals, possibly neglecting practicality.

don't change, any more than arithmetic or algebraic formulas change; similarly universals don't change.

More than immutability, this Platonist view of knowledge offered *certainty*. Once you understand what *two* and *three*, *addition* and *equals* and *five* are, not only do you know, you're certain: $2 + 3 = 5$. These objects, whether mathematical objects or universals, are of course not known by the senses; they are, after all, *in*-sensible. They are in fact apprehended or "cognized" by the mind. Different thinkers may call this mental ability to apprehend universals "reason" or "intellect" or "understanding." But a fundamental claim remained for earlier rationalists, such as Augustine: genuine knowledge occurs when the mind apprehends the universal. Augustine described this power of the mind as a *divine illumination* view. A "light of the mind," he claimed, furnished by God enables the mind to see or grasp or apprehend the universal. Later thinkers characterized this power as the *natural light of reason*. The seventeenth-century philosopher, G.W. Leibniz (1646–1716), calls this reflective capacity the *natural light*.[3] Leibniz also claims that this natural light is a power within each of us.[4] And this reflective capacity is an innate capacity.

The more controversial feature of rationalism is its assertion that reason alone can yield truths about the nature of the world. Sensory experience might trigger or give us the requisite concepts. Yet reason alone allows us to apprehend or recognize the truth of such claims as "all shapes are colored." Not only does reason provide knowledge of conceptual truths, but it can also yield knowledge about features of the world. Leibniz, for example, thought we could know by reason alone that this is the best of all possible worlds or that the soul is simple and indivisible.

Like rationalism, empiricism too traces its history to antiquity—in this case to Aristotle. Like Plato, Aristotle held that we had certain knowledge, and that scientific knowledge was always of the universal. But in the Aristotelian view, all knowledge begins with our senses. Later empiricism, which flourished beginning in the seventeenth century, gave the senses a more pervasive role in knowledge; but what we have here is the heart of empiricism: no sensory information, no knowledge. The medieval philosopher St. Thomas Aquinas accepts the Aristotelian dictum that all knowledge begins with the senses: "The philosopher [Aristotle] proves that the principle of our knowledge is in

---

3   Leibniz 1979, pp. 550–51.
4   Copleston 1974, pp. 33–34; also Crumley 2009, Chap. 9.

the senses."[5] As finite human beings with limited cognitive powers, we are unable to form or acquire any concept without first having had some sensation or sense impression.[6]

This brief exploration of the family trees of empiricism and rationalism of course leaves out much; it simply reminds us of their Greek parentage—Plato and Aristotle. It also suggests this question: Can reason alone give us at least some knowledge?

Why A Priori?

Absolute Knowledge and Non-Dual Vedānta

Of interest here is the Hindu professor Adi Śaṅkara's (788–820), distinction between absolute and relative knowledge. The latter includes processes for acquiring knowledge such as perception, inference, and testimony.

Far more important is absolute knowledge. This type of knowledge is immediate and intuitive and self-validating. As self-validating, it is perhaps like a priori knowledge: having the knowledge requires no further checks. As intuitive, however, absolute knowledge probably differs. Note that a priori knowledge requires first grasping the concepts. But as intuitive, absolute knowledge is perhaps seen as "non-conceptual"; it is not bound by our understanding of certain concepts.

How might you learn—come to know—the color of the shirt Sam is wearing? Obviously: you go look. You rely on one of your senses. Or how might you learn—come to know—whether there is enough oregano in the sauce? Again obviously: you taste it. Senses again. And how might you learn whether the universe comprises only physical things or both physical and nonphysical things? Or whether the universe is one single thing or a collection of a lot of individual things? Or whether a person *is* an immaterial soul? Could you just look? Sniff? Take a bite out of a few things? Reach out and touch someone?

Consideration of the nature of *a priori knowledge*—of knowledge that is "prior to," independent of, sense experience—affords a way of drawing more sharply the contrast between rationalism and empiricism. Remember that

---

5   Aquinas 2008, Pt. I, Q. 84, Art. 6.
6   Gilson 1940, p. 249.

empiricism insists that our knowledge of the world around us, from the most mundane observation to the deepest scientific fact, depends fundamentally on our senses. Rationalism, however, believes that *reason alone* is at least on some occasions the source of important truths *about the world*. Thus, rationalists typically hold that at least some of our knowledge about the world is *a priori*. Empiricism, however, insists that if knowledge is about the world, its source is ultimately one or more of our senses. This is but a rough characterization, but it is a place to start.

Although the divide between empiricism and rationalism can be found at almost any point in the history of philosophy, the seventeenth and eighteenth centuries saw extended argument between the two views. And one of the principal foci of the dispute was over *a priori* knowledge. The twentieth century sees the issue emerge again, with some quite striking results.

Rationalism and the Traditional View of A Priori Knowledge

While the rationalist view of *a priori* comes to the forefront during the seventeenth and eighteenth centuries, it has had defenders throughout various eras, including the twentieth century. Differences exist between particular thinkers, but some common aspects emerge. Roderick Chisholm provided a succinct summary of the view:

> Once we have acquired some concepts (once we know, with respect to certain attributes, just *what* it is for something to have those attributes), we will also be in a position to know just *what* it is for a proposition or state of affairs to be necessary—to be necessarily such that it is true or necessarily such that it obtains. Then, by contemplating or reflecting upon certain propositions or states of affairs, we will be able to see that *they* are necessary.[7]

Two important features are apparent. First, the rationalist view claims that simply "contemplating" or "reflecting" enables us to see or grasp certain truths. All we need do is understand the concepts. This is the source of our *a priori* knowledge. Second, these truths known *a priori* are necessary—that is, they must be true—they will be true under any circumstances. Laurence

---

7   Chisholm 1977, p. 40. "Truths of Reason," the relevant chapter of this book, is
      reprinted in Moser 1987.

BonJour, a contemporary advocate of a rationalist view of the *a priori*, remarks that we are "able simply to see or grasp or apprehend that the proposition is *necessary*."[8] Of course "seeing" is at best a metaphor—but one often used by rationalists in an attempt to capture the immediacy of the thought process that recognizes certain truths as necessary.

Why does the rationalist think that these truths are necessary? Their answer is along the following line. If reason alone is sufficient for such knowledge, then the course of events—what happens out in the world, what events occur or the character of objects and their properties—makes no difference to the truth of these propositions. No matter how our experience might go, no matter what kinds of sensations or experiences we have, *a priori* truths remain true. These propositions are then true in any *possible world*—given any actual or merely possible sequence of events. Hence, they are necessarily true. Chisholm and BonJour thus suggest the view that Chisholm called the traditional view of *a priori* knowledge: Once we have acquired the relevant concepts, we can see or grasp by reason alone that a proposition must be true.

Some of these necessary propositions may seem straightforward, indeed trivial, but, importantly, some reflect something deeper. "All vixens are female foxes" or "A square has four sides" are obvious and frequently cited examples of *a priori* knowledge. These truths, however, seem fairly trivial—perhaps merely matters of definition, or of conceptual inclusion. (This sort of case was the only one that Hume would allow as *a priori*.) Many rationalists have thought that reason enables us to grasp the necessary truth of more important truths. "All events have a cause" or "The self is a substance" or "There are two distinct created substances, mind and body" convey something more than a definition or semantic connection. Such *metaphysical truths* tell us how the world is put together; they tell us about the ultimate nature and structure of the world. The rationalist epistemological view thus holds that metaphysical truths like these can be the objects of *a priori* knowledge.

While rationalists may have doubted the reliability of the senses in various circumstances, we perhaps detect a more important motive for holding that there is *a priori* knowledge. This motive is the underlying belief that our senses were simply not suited to detect the *real* things of the world. Plato is frequently understood as claiming that the senses could not give us knowledge because of the changeability and instability of the objects of sense. The mutability,

---

8   BonJour 1998, p. 106.

the "changing-ness," of the physical precludes our sensory knowledge of the physical. Only reason could grasp the ideal nature of reality. Indeed some hold that Plato thought only the Forms were truly real.[9]

Similarly Descartes thought that our senses are not good "detectors" of what is *really* out there in the world. Descartes acknowledged the reality of physical objects, but he was suspicious of the senses ability to detect the real nature of those physical objects. Our senses seemed to tell us about an object's qualities—e.g., color or scent—but those qualities were suspect. What if the qualities were simply a reflection of us, and not of the actual character of the world? (Think about our basic scientific picture: the candle is red, but the molecules that make it up aren't red at all.)

This distrust of our senses doesn't quite explain why then we should trust *reason* to give us knowledge about metaphysical features of the world. Again, perhaps tracing back to Parmenides and Plato, we see an underlying assumption that the real world is fundamentally a rational world—not the world our senses reveal. The human capacity of reason is naturally and best-suited to learning of these metaphysical truths.

Thus we come to know these metaphysical truths, in the rationalist view, only if we accept that we come to know them *a priori*. This view, however, proves to be very controversial.

Empiricism and A Priori *Knowledge*

In general empiricism rejects the idea that reason alone can give us knowledge of the world, but it accepts that we know some truths *a priori*. David Hume, as we have seen, held that we have *a priori* knowledge, or as he called it, knowledge of *relations between ideas*. Such knowledge is always about necessary connections between concepts.[10] The concept *bachelor* is necessarily tied to the concept *unmarried male*. Yet this sentence—"All bachelors are unmarried males"—contains no *empirical* information about, for example, who are the bachelors or how many there are or what they look like. Tell your psychology instructor that your semester project is surveying the bachelors on campus to find out how many are unmarried, and it's *very* unlikely that your instructor

---

9   But see Penner 2006; Welton 2002; Sherman 2013 *passim*.
10   Hume 1978, Bk. III, I, Sect. I.

will be impressed. In short and roughly, in Hume's view, to know *a priori* some truth is merely to know the relations of the concepts involved.

The real source, then, of the disagreement between rationalists and empiricists is over the extent of our *a priori* knowledge. The disagreement is nicely expressed by A.J. Ayer, a twentieth-century proponent of what is known as the linguistic view of the *a priori*: we know that certain propositions are true independently of experience because we know the meanings of the words. A little more precisely, the necessity and *a priori* character of certain truths is due to the meanings of the words—"vixen" *means* "female fox." *A priori* knowledge is linguistic knowledge.

More importantly, this linguistic view undermines the motivation for the rationalist view, Ayer claims:

> For the fundamental tenet of rationalism is that thought is an independent source of knowledge ... And the ground for this view is simply that the only necessary truths about the world which are known to us are known through thought and not through experience. So that if we can show either that the truths in question are not necessary or that they are not "truths about the world," we shall be taking away the support on which rationalism rests.[11]

Ayer, along with other empiricists, held that the linguistic view was sufficient to explain how we could know *a priori* mathematical, logical, and conceptual truths. However, since empirical truths—*facts* about the world—went beyond understanding the meanings of words, our knowledge of those facts depended on our senses. We can know *a priori* that all bachelors are male or that the cube root of 27 is 3. We know this by virtue of our linguistic competence. We know this, Ayer says, because we know the "rules of language." That grapefruit trees fare best in soil with a pH of 6–7 or that Thailand is home to a population of elephants are truths that cannot be discerned simply by knowing the meaning of "grapefruit" or "elephant." We need to *look and see*; we depend on the senses for such truths.

If Hume and Ayer are right, reason alone cannot give us knowledge about the world. Although much more can be said about this dispute, there are three interesting responses to the traditional historical picture of the *a priori*, each one pivotal in its own right.

---

11   Ayer 1952, p. 73.

Kant and the Synthetic A Priori

Immanuel Kant (1724–1804) argued for a second Copernican Revolution: the mind imposes structures or organization on our sensory information. Kant agrees with Hume that we know *a priori* sentences that assert connections between concepts, which Kant called *analytic* propositions. Synthetic propositions, however, tell us something new. In synthetic propositions, we learn something new about the subject—what the sentence is about. This new information is given by the predicate, that part of the proposition that tells us what the subject is doing or about some features of the subject. Sam learns something new when he learns that the shirt (subject) is turquoise (predicate). Normally our knowledge of synthetic propositions is *a posteriori*, achieved by means of the senses. But Kant held that in virtue of the mind's "organizing structures," we have knowledge of synthetic *a priori* propositions. Such propositions are necessarily true, and so are known *a priori* rather than through the senses. These are propositions that tell us something about the world. Kant offered a unique and dramatic rationale for the existence of synthetic *a priori* knowledge.

Kant argued for the existence of categories, innate concepts that organize or structure incoming sensory information. (Kant called these "pure concepts of the understanding.") What does it mean to say that the categories *structure* sensory information? In part, it means the categories organize that information. As I look out the bay window, I don't merely sense patches of different greens, of yellow, of brown, of purple, of arbitrary bobbing up and down. On the contrary, I see a finch lighting on the branch of the giant leaf philodendron, and that leaf bobbing up and down, and the subsequent movement of the flowers. Both finch and philodendron are *substances*. Similarly, to use an example of Kant's, when we say, "The sun warms the rock," we are asserting that there is a causal connection between the sun and the rock. The existence of causal connections, however, is not something we learn by means of sense experience. Rather we organize our experiences *causally* because of the innate structure of the mind. Because of the structure of the human mind, we see every event—whether it's the warming of the rock or the warming of the hearth or the "warming" of the heart—as caused. Thus, for Kant, "every event has a cause" is a synthetic proposition, and it's known *a priori*. Similarly that the self is an enduring subject is a proposition known *a priori*. Neither Julia nor Jack learn from experience that Julia is the same self that was here a moment ago. Indeed, according to Kant, we could not make sense of our experience except for our awareness that it is *this self* that experiences. The categories are the necessary conditions for us to have coherent experience. Indeed all *experience* is *category-structured* experience. And we can come to know about categories and their impact on our experience, according to Kant. (The *Critique of Pure Reason*—one of the more challenging works in philosophy—is Kant's critical examination of these aspects of the mind and our knowledge of the world around us.[12])

No sensations, however, justify *a priori* knowledge. How could they? Instead the innate categories of *causality* and *substance* organize experience this way—pre-determine how we experience reality, as consisting of enduring things with causal relations. They impose a *conceptual structure* on the world. We have a framework for understanding and interpreting our interaction with the objects of the world. And our reflection on the mind and the nature of our experience leads us to see the necessary truth of a range of synthetic *a priori* propositions. Reflection leads us to see that the nature of our experience is structured by the categories, and this is reflected in these synthetic *a priori* propositions.

Kant explains why he takes this to be the "Copernican revolution" in philosophy:

> Up to now it has been assumed that all our cognition must conform to the objects; but all attempts to find out something about them *a priori* through concepts that would extend our cognition have, on this presupposition, come to nothing. Hence let us once try whether we do not get farther with the problems of metaphysics by assuming that the objects must conform to our cognition, which would agree better with the requested possibility of an *a priori* cognition of them, which is to establish something about objects before they are given to us. This would be just like the first thoughts of Copernicus, who, when he did not make good progress in the explanation of the celestial motions if he assumed that the entire celestial host revolves around the observer, tried to see if he might not have greater success if he made the observer revolve and left the stars at rest. Now in metaphysics we can try in a similar way regarding the intuition of objects.[13]

12   Kant 1965.
13   Kant 1965, B xvi–xviii.

The Kantian view has an important *metaphysical* consequence, too. If we only experience objects through or by means of our categories, then we never experience or come in contact with the object as it was independently of us. We never know the "thing-in-itself" (Kant's term). We know that things-in-themselves exist. But that's it. We can't know any more about some thing-in-itself; it is always apprehended by us as *categorized*. We can never take off our "category-tinted" glasses and view objects as they actually are.

The Kantian view is pivotal, both for epistemology and metaphysics. Some see it as shaping the dominant philosophical outlooks in the nineteenth and twentieth centuries.

Quine and Two Dogmas of Empiricism

On the surface it might not seem that Ayer's and other empiricists' linguistic view of the distinction between analytic and synthetic statements was importantly different from Kant's way of drawing the distinction: that in an analytic statement, the predicate concept was *contained* in the subject concept; for example, the concept *unmarried male* is contained in the concept *bachelor*. So, how might it matter if instead we drew the distinction, as Ayer and other empiricists did, in terms of words and their definitions?

For the empiricists, the linguistic view allows us to "separate" two sorts of contributions to our knowledge: from the world, and from our language. Since analytic statements are true *in virtue of the meaning of the words*, they can be known *a priori*. For the empiricists, but of course, not for Kant, analytic statements provide the only *a priori* knowledge there is. (As we've seen, Kant postulates also synthetic *a priori*.) Thinking that the only way *a priori* knowledge is possible is because the sentences known are analytic, the empiricists held that *a priori* knowledge is not knowledge about what occurs in the world; our empirical knowledge is reflected solely in synthetic propositions.

The empiricists' view, based on separating the factual from the linguistic component in our knowledge, opened the door to two possibilities: 1) undercutting the rationalist claim that we can have *a priori* knowledge of the world, and 2) *reconstructing* the acquisition of our empirical knowledge, that is, seeing how we start with very basic "unconceptualized" sensory information about the world, and showing how from that we arrived at our sophisticated scientific theories. This approach traces back at least to Hume, but it became reinvigorated in the twentieth century.

Reinvigorated, that is, until the publication of what some have thought was the most influential philosophy essay of the twentieth century, "Two Dogmas of Empiricism," by Willard Van Orman Quine.[14] The "first dogma" of empiricism Quine wished to refute is that we can in principle distinguish between analytic and synthetic statements. (While most of the essay concerns the first dogma, the second, related dogma is that experience might justify synthetic truths one by one; this will be discussed in Chapter 3: Theories of Justification.)

Empiricists, Quine held, uncritically—dogmatically—accepted the distinction between analytic and synthetic, thinking that "true solely in virtue of the meaning of the terms" was, as a definition of "analytic," sufficient to enable us to tell the difference between analytic and synthetic statements. Quine had other ideas.

Quine's argument is quite detailed, and tied to many views held at the time, but the intended general outline of the argument is clear. The argument's aim is to show that the linguistic view of "analytic" is circular. If Quine is right, then we don't have a way of explaining what it is to be an analytic sentence. He traces the circularity through this series of concepts: analytic, synonymy, necessarily true, and then back to analytic. Again, the significance of this "circle" is that we have to rely on the concept of analytic ... to explain that concept!

So start with the idea that analytic propositions are those that have subject and predicate terms *that mean the same thing*. "Bachelor" and "unmarried male" have the same meaning. "Square" and "polygon having four equal sides and four equal angles" have the same meaning. Terms that mean the same thing are *synonymous*. So, "analytic" leads to "synonymy."

We have made the first move now in the circle: to understand "analytic sentence," we need to understand "synonymy" or "sentences containing synonymous expressions." Which sentences are those? Quine says, "The necessarily true sentences." That all bachelors are unmarried males *has to be true*; it's necessarily true, according to the linguistic view of the *a priori*. Compare the assertion that bachelors make up 70% of the male population in the US aged 20–34. That is true, but it doesn't have to be true—it might have turned out differently. So "being an unmarried male" is definitionally connected with "bachelor," but "being, as a group, 70% ..." is not. Similarly "all squares are polygons with four equal sides and four equal angles" must be true. So,

---

14   Quine 1951.

now we will understand "analytic" if we understand "necessary truths." Notice where we are now in the circle: from analytic to synonymy to necessary truth.

And now, to show that the explanation of "analytic" is ultimately circular, ask this question: which sentences are the necessarily true sentences? Quine says the obvious answer is—the analytic sentences.

Ooops. Circle completed. We started out wanting to understand "analytic sentence." And our dogma of empiricism tells us that the analytic sentences are those containing synonymous terms. Those sentences in turn are the sentences that have their truth values necessarily. Which sentences were the necessarily true sentences? The analytic sentences.

There is an old joke: How do you get a million dollars? First, get a million dollars. The *circular explanation* that Quine reveals is not much more explanatory: analytic leads to synonymous leads to necessary ... and back to analytic. Right where we started. We seem unable to break out of the circle.

Quine believes that if we have no non-circular account of "analytic," then we really don't understand "synthetic." Hence, we have no real understanding of the analytic-synthetic distinction, a fundamental dogma of empiricism.

Now Quine drew some interesting consequences for epistemological theory and ontology. The empiricists thought that basic synthetic knowledge was directly tied to the senses—was confirmed or overthrown by observation; in contrast, analytic truths were immune from any observation. But Quine claims that no matter how undeniable a sentence appears—whether because it's so obviously tied to the senses or so obviously tied to meaning—we can always deny it, if we are willing to make "compensatory" conceptual changes. This claim is controversial on its own. Yet he challenged a distinction that had been at work in philosophy spanning three different centuries. And many still consider the undermining of analytic-synthetic distinction to have closed out various options for empiricism.

Quine's view was then and continues to be controversial. Peter F. Strawson and Paul Grice argued that distinctions could still be useful, despite the absence of a clear dividing line. And the analytic-synthetic distinction was one of these. The boundary between the two types of sentence might not be sharp, but that alone does not suffice to show that we should abandon the distinction.[15] Others, such as Michael Dummett and Richard Rorty, have argued that Quine's argument is not only successful, but has significant consequences for our understanding of the nature of truth and meaning, knowledge, and what

---

15   Strawson and Grice 1956.

we must say about the structure of reality.[16] The arguments of "Two Dogmas" were thus instrumental in changing (at least some) empiricists' view of their own project.

Kripke and the Necessary A Posteriori

Empiricists and rationalists alike assumed that any sentence knowable *a priori* is also necessarily true. Indeed Kant thought that a mark of the *a priori* is its necessity. Yet in a series of three lectures, entitled "Naming and Necessity," given in 1970 at Princeton University, Saul Kripke argued *inter alia* that some truths known *a posteriori* are nonetheless necessarily true.[17]

A little more simply: some facts about the world are very special kinds of facts. These are facts about identities. You are quite familiar with some of them. For example, water is H_2O or gold is the substance with atomic number of 79. And as identities, they are necessary: this clump of stuff simply *cannot* be gold unless it has 79 protons in its nucleus. Or, find some water and you have also found H_2O, and necessarily so. So, it's *necessarily true* that water is H_2O and that gold has 79 protons. If an element only has atoms with 78 protons, then it is not gold: it's platinum.

How do we find out about these identities? By *experience*. We depend on our senses. We don't learn that water is H_2O by the natural light of reason or by understanding the meaning of the terms. Socrates knew very well what water was. And although he apparently didn't own any, he knew very well what gold was too. He knew the meaning of the Greek words for gold and water. No natural light of reason told Socrates that water is H_2O; reason alone did not lead him to that truth. Instead, it would be almost 2000 years before this identity would be discovered. And it would be discovered by experiment, experience, and inference; but at bottom discovering that truth depended on the senses.

We have then a number of *a posteriori* necessary truths (and more are being discovered all the time). These truths are known *a posteriori*; knowledge of them depends on the senses. And yet, they are necessary, since identity statements are always necessary.

Like Quine, Kripke draws attention to an assumption about the nature of an aspect of our knowledge. The connection between *a priori* and necessity

---

16   Richard Rorty 1972; Richard Rorty 1976, Pt. II, but especially Chaps. 4 and 6; Richard Rorty 1982; Dummett 1978, Chap. 22.

17   Kripke 1972, especially pp. 314–23.

had been presumed for centuries. Kripke's arguments, however, undermine that presumed connection by leading to the conclusion that we have necessary *a posteriori* knowledge. Also like Quine, Kripke's arguments are controversial. But his conclusion about the necessary *a posteriori* is widely held.

A priori knowledge is of course but one aspect of knowledge in general. And during the latter half of the twentieth century, there was special interest in whether we could say what knowledge in general is. Ok—there's *a priori* and *a posteriori* knowledge. Scientific knowledge. Perhaps religious knowledge. But can we say what knowledge in general is? Can we give an analysis of the concept of knowledge?

Analysis of Knowledge

In Plato's dialogue *Meno*, a conversation about virtue turns to questions about knowledge. Socrates (Plato's teacher [?–399 BCE]) notes that true belief is just as useful as knowledge: if you have a *true belief* about which road leads to Megara, that true belief will get you to Megara, no differently than if you had *known* the road to Megara. Of course, Meno then wonders: if true belief will get you to the same result as knowledge, why would knowledge be more prized than true belief?

Socrates then appeals to a classic myth, likening true beliefs to lifelike statues which ran away if not "tied down":

> True opinions [beliefs] are a fine thing and do all sorts of good so long as they stay in their place, but they will not stay long. They run away from a man's mind, so they are not worth much until you tether them by working out the reason.[18]

This true belief "running away" is perhaps a familiar experience. Sara has the right answer to a particular logic homework problem, but she can't quite explain why; she has a feeling, but it's not backed up with good reasons. As a matter of fact, her answer is right, but Sam insists it isn't: he remembers a different answer from his logic class last year. Persuaded by Sam, she forsakes her true belief; that true belief "runs away."

We are, however, a little ahead of ourselves. So let us step back for a moment. Sara didn't *know*. Likewise, upon arriving at school your roommate

---

18   Plato 1961b, p. 380.

confidently asserts that she *knew* she had enough gas to get to school; that belief was right, because the car made it. But it was just a hunch—the gas gauge in the car doesn't work. Like Sara, your roommate had a true belief. But neither knew. What was missing? What would have made either of these instances an instance of knowledge?

An *analysis of the concept of knowledge* tells us what conditions must be satisfied—what requirements must be met—in order for someone to have knowledge. Now, we aren't talking about the items or facts one must have in order to know or know how to solve a problem; we aren't talking about, e.g., "You need to know this formula to calculate the density of that liquid." We are instead interested in a more general formula, an "epistemological formula," that says, "Any instance of knowledge satisfies these conditions...." where we now have to fill in the blank. And what goes in the blank are the necessary and sufficient conditions of knowledge. Fairly explicit in Socrates story about the moving statues is that true belief is *not sufficient for knowledge*. If true belief is not enough for knowledge, then what are those requirements? What are those conditions of knowledge?

Consider first the idea that knowledge is a special kind of *belief*. Socrates and Meno seemed very much at ease with the idea. Why *belief*? Belief is, to make matters simple, a kind of mental state. It's a representation or a "mental description" of some aspect of the world. Sam *believes* that he left his keys on the kitchen counter. That's what he *thinks*. Now, to say that some belief is also an instance of knowledge is to say this is the very best we can do with this belief. If Sam not only believes, but *knows* that his keys are on the counter, then he's achieved the best he can do. Not only is this representation or this mental description correct, but also something makes it the best Sam could have done *cognitively* regarding the whereabouts of his keys.

Ordinary conversation often uses other terms for the notion of belief: "thinks," "has the idea that," "is of the opinion," and so on. For our purposes, we can treat each as capturing the sense "This is how I think (or someone thinks) the world is...." Apart from being little maps of the world—maps by which we steer, as the British mathematician and philosopher, Frank Ramsey, once suggested—beliefs have two other features that are especially important for us now.

Beliefs can be either true or false. Sam either has a true belief or a false belief about the location of his keys. Julia's belief that Macy's opens at 10 on Sundays, not, as Jack believes, at 9, is either true or false. And we typically take it that whether a belief is true or false depends on the world, not on us.

This is a *realist* view: it holds that there are objective facts, that the way the world is does not depend on us. Not everyone shares this view, but it will serve well enough here.

Typically we have a belief for some reason; it is "supported" in some way. Our support, our *evidence*, for a belief varies. Andy's belief that he left the tennis ball outside may be supported by a vivid memory, whereas his belief that he's having steak for dinner may be supported by not much more than a hunch or wishful thinking, or by his seeing a wrapped-up package in the fridge earlier that rather looks like it might contain steak. Sara's belief that her logic proof is correct might be supported by very strong evidence—the hours of study she has spent, or the many similar proofs she has completed correctly. It seems that there's a connection between *truth* and *evidence*: the better our evidence, the more likely it is a belief is true. A theory of *justification* explains what it is for a belief to be justified. (See Chapter 3: Theories of Justification.) And appropriately supported beliefs are *justified beliefs*.

John Dewey: Knowing and Doing

John Dewey (1859–1952) was the most recent of the three great American pragmatists; the others are C.S. Peirce (1839–1914) and William James (1842–1910). Dewey had an unusual perspective on the nature of knowledge. For Dewey, knowing *is* doing.

Dewey objected to what he saw as the traditional epistemological view of emphasizing *theory* over *practice*. This distinction is the same as the knowing vs. doing distinction. In Dewey's view, "doing" is the method we use, or should use. And that method is the *experimental method*.

Dewey saw the theory-approach to knowledge—the spectator view—as stemming for a concern with the "greatest attainable security of values."[19] If we could locate value in a "higher" world, a world of pure thought or theory, our values could be secured. And it was knowledge of that higher world—a theoretical knowledge—that could secure our values.

But Dewey thought the best way to secure the values of greatest concern to us was to rely on the experimental procedure, which "is one that installs doing at the heart of knowing."

---

19 This quotation is from Dewey 1929, p. 35. Those following are from the same work, pp. 36, 259, and 255.

The value of knowledge over mere true belief is thus explicit: it secures our values, or those things that matter most to us. And the experimental procedure is a reliable, if not perfect, guide to realizing those values.

And what, in Dewey's view, is "value"? Value is the enjoyment which comes about as the result of intelligent action—that is, action guided by the experimental method. And "action" is the means by which we resolve a problematic situation—one which conflicts with our beliefs or makes intended action more difficult.

The experimental method of course reminds us of the "scientific method," and Dewey is explicit about the role of the scientific revolution (which he traces to the early modern philosopher Francis Bacon) in philosophy. The experimental procedure opens a new path for philosophy, a pragmatic path. In this he was very much in agreement with Peirce and James. Dewey saw the integrating of our beliefs about the world with our values and purposes as the "deepest problem" of modern life. Indeed, Dewey thought the experimental procedure could be extended to all areas of human endeavor—including education, politics, morality, and art.

(By the way, you might be wondering whether this is the same Dewey responsible for the Dewey decimal system, still used in some libraries. Although Dewey was very interested in education, the decimal system was developed by *Melvil* Dewey, a late-nineteenth- and early-twentieth-century American librarian.)

These three elements—belief, truth, and justification—are the elements of a traditional "epistemological formula" for knowledge, what has been called the *traditional analysis of knowledge*. A person knows some proposition or statement if and only if the person has a justified, true belief (where the content of the belief is the proposition or statement that is believed). The force of the "if and only if" is that justified, true, and belief are the necessary and sufficient conditions for knowledge—to have knowledge, you must meet all three conditions, and you don't need to have anything else. Kiersten *knows* that this painting is a Chagall if and only if (1) she *believes* that this painting is a Chagall; (2) it's *true* that this painting is a Chagall; (3) Kiersten is *justified in believing* that this painting is a Chagall—e.g., she is in Lincoln Center, and she remembers reading that Chagall painted these murals for the Lincoln. This type of knowledge is called propositional or factual knowledge; it is not intended to be an analysis of "knowing how," as in "Kiersten knows how to use Photoshop." This traditional analysis provides us something like a general definition of propositional knowledge. Whether it's a mathematical or chemical formula, whether it's some recondite historical fact or a fact about what Kiersten wore to her interview, *knowing that*—according to the traditional analysis—is having a justified true belief.

The traditional analysis of knowledge has something of an interesting history. Some have interpreted the *Meno* as providing this sort of analysis because of Socrates' suggestion that, in addition to the true belief, a "tying down" or a "working out the reason" of the belief must be added to yield knowledge. Justification is this "tying down" or giving of an "account." A.J. Ayer, in the mid-twentieth century, offered a slightly different version in which the criteria are that the belief is true, that the holder of the belief is sure, and that the holder of the belief has the right to be sure.[20] There are reasons to prefer the justified true belief analysis to Ayer's so we will continue working with it.[21] One intriguing aspect of this traditional analysis is that it came to a rather sudden and abrupt end in 1963, as we see now.

Gettier and the Traditional Analysis

Can a person be right, have good reasons, and still not know? More specifically, might someone have the right belief, have good reasons for the belief, but not have the *right reasons*, and hence, not know? In 1963, a very short essay, authored by Edmund L. Gettier, appeared. It was entitled "Is Justified True Belief Knowledge?"[22] The traditional view, of course, answers "yes." But Gettier offered examples of situations in which justified true belief did *not* seem to be *sufficient* for knowledge. Virtually overnight philosophers, in essay after essay, set about trying to fix this problem, offering new analyses of knowledge, only to be rebuffed by newer and ever more ingenious Gettier-type counterexamples, thus producing a new round of analyses and beginning the cycle again.

Two counterexamples nicely illustrate Gettier's point about the inadequacy of the traditional analysis, the first offered by Keith Lehrer.[23]

Imagine a case in which a person we'll call S has a coworker, Ms. Nogot. Suppose now that S has good reason to believe that Ms. Nogot owns a Ford. Imagine, for example, that S has seen Nogot driving a Ford, S has been told

20   Ayer 1956, pp. 31–35.
21   Crumley 2009, Chap. 2.
22   Gettier 1963.
23   Lehrer 1965.

by persons who have in the past been reliable that, yes, Nogot owns a Ford, and so on. Hence, S has justification for her belief that Nogot owns a Ford. From this she infers—by a completely acceptable logical inference—a further belief that *someone in the office owns a Ford.* Call this belief content "P." Lehrer now asks us to suppose that Ms. Nogot does not own a Ford. Nevertheless, S's belief that someone in the office owns a Ford is true, because *in fact* Ms. Havit owns a Ford.

Now S has a justified true belief. The belief that *someone in the office owns a Ford* is indeed true. Moreover, S had good evidence for arriving at this belief, so it seems apparent that S is justified in believing that P. Yet is it obvious that S's justified true belief is also an instance of knowledge?

We might be tempted to say "no." S was just lucky. Whatever else knowledge is, you shouldn't be able to achieve it because you were lucky. It just so happened that someone owned a Ford, but not the person S thought owned the Ford. Thus, we might conclude that S has reasons, even good reasons. But those reasons aren't connected in the right way to the truth of her belief.

A second well-known counterexample from the literature was invented by Alvin Goldman.[24] Imagine a film crew has put up a number of barn façades

---

24   Goldman 1976.

in a rural area, which from the road are indistinguishable from the real barns that are in the area. Imagine a father taking his son through the country for the first time, pointing out and identifying silos, tractors, combine harvesters, and barns. The father just happens to point to a real barn, instead of the façade across the road, and correctly announces, "That's a barn."

As in the Ford-Nogot case, the father has a justified true belief. He sees the barn, can recognize barns, and so on. But is this justified true belief also knowledge? We might reasonably hesitate to claim that it is. After all, he *just as easily* could have pointed to a barn façade and thus have had a justified, yet *false* belief. (Remember: there can be good justification for a false belief. In this case, because the barn façades look, from the front, just like real barns, the father would have exactly the same good degree of justification for the belief that there's a barn there, from seeing a real barn, and from seeing a façade from the front.)

Cases like Havit and Nogot, or even the barn case, might seem out of the ordinary, and thus not the best rationale for overturning the traditional analysis. How often are we the victims of an "unwitting conspiracy of ignorance," as in the Ford case? Yet it is not too difficult to imagine more ordinary cases that might suggest that we sometimes have a true and justified belief, yet not know. Imagine that Kiersten has the justified true belief that the cab in front of her apartment building is the cab that will take her to the airport. As she has often done before, she called the taxi company, which in fact dispatched a cab. Her appointed driver, however, is stuck in traffic, and she has merely fortuitously found a driver that pulled over to make a phone call, but is happy to take her to the airport.

Or again, suppose that Kiersten is running for Congress and that she has put the false statement on her website that she once served in the Coast Guard. On this basis she believes that there is a false statement on her website. Unbeknownst to Kiersten, however, hackers have replaced that statement with the equally false statement that she was once arrested for defacing a government building. Now, she has a justified true belief. But the explanation of why she is justified differs from the explanation of why her belief is true. Hence, we are strongly inclined to say that Kiersten doesn't know.

Sometimes such cases might occur in science, such as reported by a 1997 issue of *Science News*. Scientists had thought that yo-yo dieting might increase the risk of cancer. The studies suggested they were right, *but for the wrong reasons*. Of course, they didn't get those reasons by consulting a fortune teller. They had evidence, but the evidence did not point to the real cause of the increased risk. We might think then that they had a justified true belief, but the justification somehow didn't "get it right."[25]

Still, why don't we notice such cases more frequently? Often we may not notice that we are in a Gettier-ized environment. Our true belief is good enough, and we might not encounter any information that something is wrong with our justification. Think of the father pointing to a real barn in an area full of façades, or Kiersten getting into the cab without confirming it is the one she called. Since our belief is true, and absent any indication that something is amiss—or came very close to being amiss—we aren't practically or "epistemically disappointed."

All of these cases suggest a general lesson. Of course they are intended to show that justified true belief is not sufficient for knowledge. Indeed they are *counterexamples* to the traditional analysis for just this reason. But this doesn't tell us the "why": they don't tell us the underlying cause of the problem. It is not difficult to see why, however. The traditional analysis leaves open the possibility that a person's reasons or justification might not be appropriately connected to what it is that makes the belief true. In other words, a person's evidence or reasons for a belief may not adequately reflect the circumstances that underlie the truth of the belief. Notice that, in the Nogot-Ford case, S has all kinds of reasons for believing that someone owns a Ford, but these do not indicate why her belief is indeed true. In a sense then, S, of the Nogot case, has evidence—so she is justified—but it is the wrong evidence for the belief that she has. Gettier's challenge suggests that the traditional analysis is too *weak*—it counts cases that should not be counted as instances of knowledge. And one way of understanding this "weakness" is seeing that the explanation of why a belief is justified points in a different direction than the explanation of why the belief is true.

If Gettier cases tell us what's wrong with the traditional analysis, they also give us some hint of what we should expect from a satisfactory analysis of the concept of knowledge. Gettier-cases suggest that, in cases where a belief might be justified and true, had things been just a little different, we might have had a false belief. Thus, it was merely good fortune or a happy accident that we arrived at a true belief. Now, knowledge, as we've already noted, is not

---

25   The earlier evidence was the well-known facts that yo-yo dieting is a causal factor for obesity, and that obesity is a causal factor for certain cancers. The *Science News* story (Raloff 1997), reported that yo-yo dieting indeed increased the risk of cancer, but for a different reason (the burning of body fat increased the circulation in the body of cancer-causing substances).

something we think should be achieved by luck. Note that many standardized multiple-choice tests attempt to rule out "lucky guesses." Again, Gettier cases then suggest an "anti-luck" account of knowledge, and several theorists have suggested versions of such a view.[26]

On the other hand, remember the plane-spotter example from the previous chapter? This was a case in which the suggestion was that the spotter *did* have knowledge, despite the fact that, had things been a little different, he would have had a false belief. In a sense the spotter made a lucky guess! But we were tempted to ascribe his true belief the status of knowledge. Things are not simple here.

While other responses may place less emphasis on the "anti-luck" factor, any adequate response to Gettier cases will, it seems, find some way to "close the gap" between being justified and having a true belief. An initially attractive way is to suggest that the justification itself must meet certain conditions; this thought gives rise to the first two approaches below. The second type of approach, as we will see, asks us to view the nature of knowledge and justification in a manner quite different from the traditional view.

Knowledge and Indefeasibility

What Do You Know? Look at the Artifacts

In a very different understanding of the nature of knowledge, Barry Allen identifies knowledge as "superlative artifactual performance." As the title of his book *Knowledge and Civilization* suggests, Allen ties knowledge to civilization and evolution.

The existence of knowledge, Allen argues, depends on its best examples. And we find those best examples—not in simple examples of propositional knowledge, such as $1 + 1 = 2$—but in a cultivated capacity. Knowledge is a cultivated capacity—the capacity for eliciting, creating, and amplifying superlative performance in *artifacts*. Thus, for example, the iPhone is a superlative performance. It gives us a novel way of seeing, organizing, managing, and thinking about our world or some aspect of our lives.

---

26   For example, Heller 1999; Zagzebski 1994; Pritchard 2004; Pritchard 2009, especially Chaps. 2 and 4.

Our normal way of thinking of artifacts is that they are things we make. All of reality is artifactual, however, in Allen's view. He notes that the elliptical orbit of, say, Mars, is no less artifact than Kepler's theory.

Yet Allen is principally interested in the things we make. Allen views the paper clip or the iPhone or Post-its or the original Lascaux cave paintings or the first jewelry made some 10,000 years ago as the expressions or manifestations that constitute our knowledge. Importantly, it is the original making or creating that matters. Once the artifactual breakthrough occurs, mere copies or mass production do not manifest "superlative artifactual performance."

Unsurprisingly Allen rejects the idea that we can give necessary and sufficient conditions for knowledge, since there are too many different ways for artifactual performance to occur.

Indeed Allen argues that "the 'justified true belief' formula should be set aside ... because knowledge is not belief-*plus*. Knowledge is deeper than language, different from belief, more valuable than truth. It is exemplified in exemplary performances with artifacts of all kinds."[27]

Gettier cases might be thought to identify *defective* justifications. In such cases, the justifying beliefs are not *good enough*. And they aren't good enough because of some fact or bit of information. Let the person become aware of a proposition describing that fact, and the person's beliefs would change. Then the proposition that describes the "Gettier fact" *defeats* a person's justification. Again, a proposition *defeats* a justification if it undermines the justification; the *defeater* provides some reason for thinking that one or more of the justifying beliefs or assumptions is mistaken.

This leads to a type of view known as the indefeasibility view: a belief is an instance of knowledge if and only if it is true *and indefeasibly justified*. A person's belief is indefeasibly justified only if there are in fact no defeaters, no actually true propositions that would undermine the person's justification. One theorist defines knowledge as having a justified belief when that justification is factually undefeated.[28] The "factual" reference is important. Merely *possibly* true claims, such as those envisioned by the skeptic (see Chap. 1), are not the worry here. Rather, the concern is with the facts, with the way things really are—there really are barn façades nearby.

---

27   Allen 2004, p. 59.
28   Steup 1996.

Indeed we can see why, in the barn case, the father's justification is defective and has a relevant defeater: "There are a number of barn façades in this area." This proposition defeats—undermines—the father's justification. Give the father this bit of information, make him aware of this proposition—faux barn alert!—and he would no longer think he was justified *enough* to claim "That's a barn." We are thus able to explain why the father's justification is defective, that is, why it's *defeasible*. The father's justification is not good enough for knowledge because there's a defeater that his justification can't handle.

Similarly, the Ford-Nogot case has an easily seen defeater: Nogot doesn't own a Ford. Make S aware of this fact—and assuming no other changes in her justification—and she would no longer be justified in her belief that someone owns a Ford.

(And similarly: the fact that friendly French planes in Iraq have characteristic H, the one the spotter uses to identify hostiles, undermines the spotter's justification for his true belief.)

A sound intuition seems to lie behind indefeasibility theory. If you know something—if you *really* know it—your reasons should be good enough or strong enough to withstand new information. In a sense, knowledge ought to be *extendible*. New information shouldn't weaken your justification. Your reasons should be good enough to "take on all comers," (where "all comers," of course, are propositions expressing new information).

The challenge for indefeasibility theorists has been to find a principled way to identify genuine defeaters. Marshall Swain suggests that there can be *misleading defeaters*.[29] A misleading defeater undermines a justification because only a part of the story is known. A recent case serves to illustrate the issue.

There is plenty of good evidence that the common vaccine against measles, mumps, and rubella is safe and effective. But a 1998 paper in a distinguished medical journal claimed that the vaccine caused autism; this certainly would defeat this evidence (and a considerable number of people refused the vaccine as a result). By 2010 the journal had fully retracted the paper, when it was discovered that the author's research claims were fraudulent and his conclusions utterly false. But in 1999, there was clearly a defeater to the general belief; nevertheless, we want to say, people who hadn't heard about the paper then, and consequently still believed the vaccine was safe, knew it was safe.[30]

---

29   Swain 1974.
30   See Atwell 2010 and McCarthy 2013.

Pockets of evidence or circumstances, without the "full story," might mislead. Beliefs based on induction or sampling might give us such misleading pockets. The important point here is that we *have knowledge* only if our justification is strong enough to withstand such pockets of evidence.

Assuming, however, that we have a way of distinguishing misleading from genuine defeaters, and assuming a way of saying when a justification is strong enough to withstand misleading information, indefeasibility seems a viable theory of knowledge: to know is to have an indefeasibly justified true belief.

No False Premise

Achieving knowledge, we suspect, is in part getting there the right way, or by the right kind of reasoning. But relying on *false beliefs* for justification is not one of the right ways.

Some have thought Gettier cases depend on the agent having some false belief. S relies on an obviously false belief: "Nogot owns a Ford." Similarly, the father relies, at least tacitly, on a false belief: "If it looks like a barn, it is a barn." So, perhaps we can address Gettier cases by amending the justified true belief analysis: add a condition that says "no false beliefs allowed in the justification."[31] Thus, a belief is an instance of knowledge if and only if it is true, it is justified, and no false belief is an essential part of the justification. This is the no false premise view.

Richard Feldman suggested that some Gettier cases might not depend on a false belief. Imagine a clever reasoner who skips the "false belief step." A *clever* person might not explicitly consider and come to believe the false proposition. In the Ford-Nogot case, our ever-present S might never explicitly think "Nogot owns a Ford." She just "skips ahead," straight from her evidence to the belief that *someone* owns a Ford.

If, however, we understand "beliefs essential to the justification" as including *tacit beliefs*, then this objection might well be avoided.[32] Indeed, more recently Feldman suggests that the no false premise view allows for such tacit beliefs.[33] Of course, the no false premise theorist needs to provide some sense of how to identify the relevant tacit or background beliefs. But if this can be done, this view also seems a promising strategy as a post-Gettier account of knowledge.

---

31   Meyers 1988; Harman 1986.
32   Crumley 2009, Chap. 2.
33   Feldman 2003, pp. 36–37.

Both the indefeasibility strategy and the no false premise view respond to the challenge raised by Gettier by looking at what goes wrong in a person's justification. A dramatically different alternative, however, is posed by a view known as *reliabilism*.

Reliabilism

"The Rocking Horse Winner," a somewhat dark short story by D.H. Lawrence published in 1927, tells of Paul, a boy determined to help his family. Paul has happened on the "method" of riding his toy rocking horse, for as long as it takes, until he discerns clearly, in something resembling a clairvoyant state, the winner of a horse race. The "rocking horse method" proves perfectly reliable, winning significant sums on the racing bets. The young Paul dies on the night of his greatest prediction. The account is of course fictional. But the idea of a *generally reliable* method of producing our beliefs is part of the story of recent epistemology.

Reliabilism is an account of knowledge and justification that came to prominence beginning in the 1970s. Almost immediately it drew significant criticism. Nonetheless it remains very influential in epistemology, while exchanges between critics and defenders still continue. Alvin Goldman, perhaps the most widely known proponent, has articulated and defended reliabilism against significant objections in books and essays. Others have also proposed and defended versions of reliabilism.[34] Despite different versions, there is a broad and motivating tenet of the view: reliabilism sees the connection to truth as the primary element in justification and hence knowledge. Thus, very roughly, reliabilism holds that a belief is justified or an instance of knowledge only if there is a reliable connection between the belief and truth. Some views, like Goldman's, tend to focus on the *reliable* cognitive or psychological processes, such as perception or memory, that produce belief. David Armstrong, whose contributions have been significant in philosophy of mind, metaphysics, and epistemology, emphasizes the connection between belief and environment. Not only do our beliefs arise as a result of our interactions with the environment, our beliefs are *reliable indicators* of what is happening in that environment. Common to these views is the thought that a belief—in order for it to be *epistemically* acceptable as an instance of knowledge or justified belief—must be brought about in such a way that it tends to be or is likely to be true.

---

34 Schmitt 1992; Armstrong 1973.

Goldman argues that beliefs resulting from *reliable belief-forming processes* are, in general, justified beliefs, and hence candidates for instances of knowledge. Reliable belief-forming processes are just those that tend to produce true beliefs. So, roughly, a "reliable belief" is likely to be true *because* it results from a generally reliable cognitive, or belief-forming, process. Beliefs arising from wishful thinking, guessing, or what a palm reader tells us are notorious for *not* being closely connected to truth. Beliefs, if brought about by perception, memory, or appropriate deductive reasoning, however, tend to be true. Generally, if Kiersten spies a red book on the couch, there is a red book there. Andy *remembers* his keys lying on the counter ... so that memory belief is *likely to be true*. And roughly, for Goldman, beliefs brought about by reliable cognitive processes are justified.

This account is designed to answer questions raised by Gettier examples. Reliabilism promises to close the "gap" between justification and truth that is the basis of Gettier cases, precisely because a belief is justified because it is produced by a reliable process, and thus *is likely to be true* (again, waiving some qualifications that must be included; see below).

In a reliabilist account of perceptual knowledge, three conditions must be satisfied. (The account here is somewhat less formal than Goldman's.) First, the belief must be the result of a reliable process. Second, given the person's relevant alternatives, there must be no perceptual equivalents that could lead the agent to have a false belief. And of course, third, the actual belief must be true.

The notion of relevant alternatives points to the recognition that *abnormal* environments can undermine our ability to acquire knowledge. The father's belief in the barn case, for example, relies on visual perception, a reliable belief-forming process. But there is something unusual about his immediate vicinity that is relevant to his knowing. Moreover, the father is unable to distinguish between façades and real barns. Notice: a faux barn is a *relevant alternative* for the father, and he can't tell the difference between the two (façade and real). Thus, although this true belief is reliably formed, it might as easily have been a false belief.[35]

Notice that the definition of knowledge above makes no mention of justification as a condition, which is a departure from the traditional analysis. In an influential essay, Goldman presents a reliabilist analysis of justification

---

35   Goldman 1976.

that identifies a belief brought about by a reliable process *as justified*.[36] This identification of "being reliably produced" with "justified" is a much disputed point between reliabilist and critic. Goldman refined the definition of reliabilist justification in response to objections. Indeed criticisms of the reliabilist view of knowledge still focus on the reliabilist concept of justification, despite Goldman's refinements.[37]

Yet, intuitively, the reliabilist account has a certain appeal. We think that processes such as perception, not only usually produce true beliefs, but also *normally* yield knowledge. When I see that there is coffee in the cup, we don't hesitate to say I *know* that there is coffee in the cup. Sometimes things can go a bit awry—Hollywood filmmakers, epistemologists, and practical jokers (imagine two identical salt shakers, one containing sugar and the other salt) can sometimes place "perceptual equivalents" in our way. Such abnormal environments can trick our normally reliable belief-forming mechanisms. When our environment cooperates, when things are as they normally are, then we might, like Goldman, be inclined to think that it is the reliability of the processes involved that leads to our having beliefs that are instances of knowledge.

Externalism and Internalism

In the last quarter of the twentieth century, *externalism* became a widely held and very controversial view regarding knowledge and justification. The contrary view, also frequently held to be the more traditional view, is *internalism*. Internalist views hold that the factors or conditions relevant to knowledge and justification are internal to a person's beliefs. In principle, reflection can lead to the person holding the belief becoming aware of whether those conditions are satisfied.

Externalism, as represented in Goldman's reliabilist view, for example, holds that whether a person knows or has a justified belief is judged from a third person or "God's eye" perspective. It's a *fact*, and one not necessarily determinable by the believer, whether some process is a reliable cognitive process.

The relative merits of internalism and externalism are still debated, and the matter remains controversial.

---

36   Goldman 1979.
37   See Crumley 2009, Chap. 3.

From among the various objections that have been raised to the reliabilist theory of knowledge, we consider one classic criticism: Laurence BonJour's case of Norman, the reliable clairvoyant, which challenges the sufficiency of reliabilism.[38] BonJour argues that reliabilism fails because it counts cases of *irrational belief* as justified and hence as knowledge. Irrational beliefs should not count as knowledge, BonJour protests. This sort of situation can arise, according to BonJour, because reliabilism does not require that a person have reasons for the belief or reasons about the reliability of the relevant process. Reliabilism only requires that the belief is reliably produced. And this invites a simple counterexample, BonJour claims.

Norman is a reliable clairvoyant. That means he can "see" the future, and his predictions turn out amazingly often to be true. But he has no evidence or reason to believe that he is a clairvoyant, much less a reliable clairvoyant. One day—without any other evidence or information—as a result of his clairvoyant power, Norman comes to have the *true* belief that the President is in New York City. According to the reliabilist view, Norman *knows* that the President is in New York City, since it is both true and reliably produced. Yet Norman has no reasons for his belief. BonJour then asks:

> Why is not the mere fact that there is no way, as far as he knows or believes, for him to have obtained this information a sufficient reason for classifying this belief as an unfounded hunch and ceasing to accept it? And if Norman does not do this, is he not thereby being epistemically irrational and irresponsible?[39]

The answer BonJour expects we'll give to these rhetorical questions is: Norman will, and should, reject these beliefs. BonJour begins with what seems an uncontroversial assumption: knowledge can't be irrational. That is, knowledge can't be arbitrary or seemingly come from nowhere; knowledge requires having reasons for one's belief. So any view that allows "irrational knowledge"— knowledge without reasons—is an inadequate account of knowledge. And BonJour claims that reliabilism, as the Norman case illustrates, allows just this—"irrational knowledge." So, reliabilism is inadequate as an explanation of knowledge.

---

38   BonJour 1980; also BonJour 1985, Chap. 3.
39   BonJour 1980, pp. 62–63.

BonJour identifies a fundamental difference between reliabilism and its critics. Traditionally, justification, and hence knowledge, require that a person is able to provide reasons for a belief. Reliabilism, however, seems to suspend this requirement. Goldman's view differs:

> [Reliabilism] requires only, in effect, that beliefs in the external world be suitably caused.... If one wishes, one can so employ the term 'justification' that belief causation of *this* kind counts as justification. In this sense, of course, my theory does require justification. But this is entirely different from the sort of justification demanded by Cartesianism.[40]

And BonJour's criticism trades on the idea of justification comprising having reasons for one's belief. Consequently, he finds the reliabilist view of justification and knowledge wanting.

Goldman accepts BonJour's suggestion that this is not knowledge; but he suggests that reliabilism can explain that sort of case. He claims that Norman did not make the best use of his "cognitive processes." Norman failed to reason in an appropriate way; he failed to make use of other reliable processes that would have "alerted" him to the epistemic inadequacy of his belief about the President's whereabouts. Norman should realize (and we do, or should, as well) that hunches that appear out of the blue are in general unreliable. They are, in general, reliably unreliable. More generally then, reliabilism says that a reliable belief—a reliably produced belief—is justified *unless* some other reliable process would undermine that belief. In Norman's case, his hunch, despite previous reliability, is undermined by the general fact that hunches aren't a good guide to truth.

Reliabilism remains a widely held and influential view. The exchanges between reliabilism's advocates and the critics have led, in some cases, to modifications of the view.[41] We should not lose sight, however, of a motivating intuition: both knowledge and justification seem intrinsically aimed at truth. And when we ask what accounts for our ability to acquire true beliefs, we are led to consider the connection between ourselves and our environment—and the cognitive processes that allow us to acquire reliable information about that environment.

---

40   Dancy 1988, pp. 63–64.
41   See Crumley 2009, Chap. 3.

Key Concepts

· traditional view of *a priori* knowledge
· linguistic view of the *a priori*
· synthetic *a priori* propositions
· categories
· analytic-synthetic distinction
· *a posteriori* necessary truths
· Gettier cases
· indefeasibility view
· no false premise view
· reliabilism

Reading/Discussion Questions

1. Think of various literary works—novels, poems, plays, short stories. Do we or can we acquire knowledge from such art works? More specifically, can we acquire, e.g., knowledge of human nature, or of emotions, or of the human condition? Try to explain your view, relying on one of the views of knowledge in the text.

2. Try to explain *a priori* knowledge. Explain how this notion can be used to illustrate some of the differences between rationalism and empiricism. What are the differences between the traditional, the linguistic, and the Kantian views of the *a priori*?

3. Why are Gettier cases important for the traditional analysis of knowledge? Can you identify a "real life" example of a Gettier case? Try to construct your own Gettier case; explain why your example allows for a justified true belief that is not an instance of knowledge.

4. In indefeasibility theory, what are (genuine) defeaters? Why are they important? How do they differ from misleading defeaters?

5. If you had to argue that the no false premise view is the best analysis of knowledge, what would you say is its strongest point? Why?

6. What is BonJour's objection to reliabilism, recounted in this chapter? Do you agree with him? Explain.

For Further Reading

While there are many histories of philosophy, some pay a little more attention to the epistemological themes in that history, drawing together related
themes such as rationalism and empiricism, *a priori* knowledge, and the nature
of knowledge. W.T. Jones's five-volume *A History of Western Philosophy* 1969
does so in a manner very accessible to someone just starting out. All the vol-
umes contain considerable quotations from the various philosophers. A recent
secondary source provides survey essays by a number of contemporary scholars
on the key philosophers in the history of epistemology: *Epistemology: The
Key Thinkers*, Hetherington 2012.

Three collections of essays contain many of the most important recent
articles on *a priori* knowledge: Harris and Severens 1970; Moser 1987;
Boghossian and Peacocke 2000.

A comprehensive history of twentieth-century responses to Gettier is
Shope 1980. The work contains over 100 Gettier-type counterexamples, along
with analysis of and commentary on the various proposals, in light of the counterexamples, for the analysis of knowledge. Richard Foley 2012 is a more recent
work, which addresses Gettier-inspired worries, including various related issues,
such as the value of knowledge. Kvanvig 2003 is a book-length treatment of
the value of knowledge and arrives at a somewhat more modest view of the
value of knowledge. John Dewey's epistemological writings are found primarily in Dewey 1929, 1920, 1938 (especially the first six chapters); his 1954,
which he gave as the first William James Lecturer in 1932 at Harvard, is also
interesting, not only for his views on aesthetics, but his view of the nature of
experience. Pritchard 2009 is an accessible and careful work that explains an
alternative view of knowledge, which he calls "anti-luck virtue epistemology."

Armstrong 1973, Goldman 1986, and Schmitt 1992 are each elegant
elaborations and defenses of reliabilism. As noted, reliabilism is a controversial view. In addition to BonJour 1980 and 1985, Feldman 1985 and 2003
contain important criticisms of reliabilism as a theory of justification. See also
Crumley 2009, Chap. 3 for a survey of some of the issues.

Discussions of externalism and internalism can be found in most of the
epistemology surveys noted above. Discussion of both internalism and externalism can be found in Steup 2001 and Steup and Sosa 2005.

A nice summary of Śaṅkara's view of knowledge may be found in Carl
Olson 2007, Chap. 5.

CHAPTER THREE

THEORIES OF JUSTIFICATION

Deirdre believes that Steller's jays mate for life. She can *tell you why* she believes this—she remembers reading it in her book on the birds of North America. Providing reasons or evidence for our beliefs—the *why* of a belief—occurs in any number of settings. Some of those settings are technical or require precision, as when a doctor makes a diagnosis. Some are more ordinary, as in Deirdre's case above. Some are more outlandish, such as in the story told by Daniel Dennett of an ornithologist who received a phone call and being asked to settle a bar bet: are rabbits birds? On being told "no," the dejected bar patron said, "Damn," and hung up.[1] What could his reason have been for initially thinking rabbits are birds? Anyway, he now had a reason to think they are not. Sometimes the evidence is simply noting something about one's own mental state, as when Kiersten refers to her subjective perceptual experience: "Well, that paint sure looks magenta to me!" Justified beliefs are

---

1   Dennett 1998, p. 14.

of course beliefs that are somehow appropriately supported by reasons or evidence. And a *theory of justification* or a *theory of justified belief* explains what it is for a belief to be appropriately supported. That is, such a theory proposes necessary and sufficient conditions for justified belief.

Two motivations might be suggested for our interest in a theory of justification. The first might be thought of as "initial credibility"—we want to know the source of the epistemic credibility of our beliefs. How do they become epistemically credible in the first place?

To ask about the credibility of some belief is to ask about the reasons supporting the belief. For example, Andy announces that he believes bees are in the attic. Andrea of course will want to know *why* he thinks this. Has he heard buzzing? Has he seen bees flying into one of the vents?

How do any of our beliefs *initially* come to have any "epistemic credibility"? If beliefs are supported by other beliefs, is there some first, unsupported, belief that starts this justification project, and that needs no justification itself? Descartes argued for this in his *Meditations*. Or do we start with a group of beliefs that are somehow initially epistemically credible? Plato has been interpreted as holding that justification—and hence knowledge—gets started based on a large group of beliefs, a picture of the whole of reality.[2] On the other hand, some theorists suggest that a small subset of beliefs is necessary for initial epistemic credibility. And some of these beliefs may be innate, some may be acquired.

A second motivation for our interest in such a theory is the *aim* of justified beliefs. Why does having a *justified* belief matter more than just having the belief? We think justification gets us closer to knowing, which requires "justified truth." And justification is intrinsically connected to truth. That is, our understanding of justification is that it provides the reason(s) why the belief is likely to be true. After all, this is what justification is: evidence in support of the likely truth of some claim. In leading to truth, then, justification can also lead to knowledge.

Beliefs as Reasons for Other Beliefs: Justification

We often give reasons for some belief of ours, some claim that we make. The reasons provide our evidence; in fact, we often use the notions of reason

---

2   White 1976 argues that Plato holds that we acquire knowledge only when we have a grasp of the whole.

and evidence interchangeably. Imagine that Andy believes that there will be chicken for dinner. And suppose you could ask Andy, "Why do you believe that?" He might offer you a couple of different types of *beliefs*. The first might be a perceptual belief—that he saw the chicken thawing on the counter. He might further offer a "background" belief—that chicken is usually thawed out on the day it will be used. We might then conclude that Andy has adequate reasons for his belief about this evening's dinner fare; Andy's belief is *justified*.

We thus provide reasons for our belief by citing other beliefs. The other beliefs *justify* the belief in question. Justifying beliefs may be of different kinds. Sometimes they are perceptual beliefs. Sometimes they are background beliefs, that is, beliefs that a person has acquired over time about various subjects (e.g., Andy's belief about when chicken is thawed or your belief that water flows downhill). Very often and importantly the justifying beliefs are beliefs based on the testimony of others. Andrea believes, for example, that Einstein thought our ordinary views of past, present, and future are misguided. She believes this *because* her physics teacher told her so. It seems that a lot of our beliefs are like that: we acquire beliefs by reading the newspaper, or a magazine, or by reading a textbook or a history book. Andy believes that the Reformation began in 1517 because he read it in a history book; he relies on the testimony of the author. Of course, not all testimony is reliable—witness much of what you find on the Internet!—and often our "epistemic task" is to figure out which sources provide genuine evidence, which sources provide beliefs that are true, and really do justify other beliefs.

Two rival views of justification have been prominent, especially during the twentieth century. These are foundationalism and coherentism. Foundationalism is the view that at least some of our beliefs do not depend on other beliefs for their justification, but are nonetheless justified. Such beliefs are the foundation for the justification of our other beliefs. Coherence theory or coherentism holds that the justification of any given belief derives from the coherence—that is, the mutual support—of an agent's beliefs.

Each view has different versions, and the history of each is complex, as is their rivalry. No doubt foundationalism has generally been the more widely held view. Indeed many characterize the history of epistemology, at least since Descartes, as primarily foundational in nature.[3] Coherentism's fortunes have varied with time and place, it seems. Various idealist views of nineteenth-century Europe can be seen as coherentist; and the publication of Willard

---

3   Quine 1969; Richard Rorty 1976, especially Chap. III.

Van Orman Quine's "Two Dogmas of Empiricism" in 1951 led to a wider acceptance of coherentism in Anglo-American philosophy. By the mid-1980s, however, foundationalism seemed again the more dominant view.

Foundationalism

Although others have been identified with the view, Descartes is perhaps the most recognized exemplar of the foundationalist approach to knowledge and justification. The opening paragraph of his first Meditation tells us:

> It is now some years since I detected how many were the false beliefs that I had from my earliest youth admitted as true, and how doubtful was everything I had since constructed on this basis; and from that time I was convinced that I must once for all seriously undertake to rid myself of all the opinions which I had formerly accepted, and commence *to build anew from the foundation*, if I wanted to establish any firm and permanent structure in the sciences....[4]

Descartes of course was interested in the nature of knowledge, but his view also assumes a foundationalist view of justification.

There are two principal versions of foundationalism. Both versions are held to have their principal motivation in the *regress argument*.

A Motivation for Foundationalism: The Regress Argument

How do we justify our beliefs? By citing other beliefs, of course. This appears to be the case even when Andrea's belief that Andy was at the concert is justified by her belief that she saw him there from the other side of the audience. But that depends on the reliability of her identification. Her reason for thinking that was Andy was the unusual hat she could see him wearing. But what makes her so sure that it was unlikely that anyone else would be wearing that hat? And so on. Each newly cited justification itself needs justification. Well, we cite still newer beliefs ... wait: how long can this process go on? How long are we supposed to keep citing beliefs to justify other beliefs?

The recognition that there might be some problem with a seemingly unending justification process is the core of the **regress argument**, which is the principal motivation for foundationalism. The regress argument notes

---

4   Descartes 1968b; emphasis added.

that every belief offered as supporting or justifying some other belief must itself be justified. But this seems to set us on an unending process, a *regress*.

According to the regress argument, there are four options for stopping the regress. The first two—that the regress never ends or that it ends somewhere just arbitrarily with an "unjustified" belief—are considered obviously unsatisfactory. The first option apparently unacceptably requires an infinite number of beliefs. But the second one fares no better, because the first belief, being itself unjustified, would not provide the epistemic credibility for the series that it is supposed to justify. The flaw in these two options points us back to the idea of "initial credibility." How could a process that never ends explain why any of our beliefs are epistemically credible in the first place? Similarly, it seems extremely puzzling how a belief that lacks epistemic credibility itself could ever render any other belief credible.

There is a third option—a "circular option"—that leads from one belief to another to another, until we arrive back at the original belief. (This is something like the picture given by coherence theory, which will be discussed later.) But it seems that credibility is a concern again here. If we want to know why some belief has any initial epistemic worth, surely it won't do to, in the end, say that it vouches for itself.

And that leaves us with the fourth—the foundationalist—option: the regress terminates. But it terminates not just arbitrarily, but with a very special kind of belief. We find a belief that is itself justified, but doesn't depend on other beliefs for its justification. Such "regress-terminating beliefs" are known as *basic beliefs*.

Common Features

The first and most important aspect of foundationalism is the commitment to foundational or *basic beliefs*.[5] Basic beliefs are *epistemically independent*, which means that they are themselves justified but do not depend on other beliefs for their justification. A simple example illustrates the idea.

Suppose Julia tells Andrea that Jack has returned from his Christmas shopping. Andrea asks why she thinks that, why she *believes* that. Julia replies that there is box of Godiva truffles under the Christmas tree. Asked now why she believes this, Julia replies that she *sees* the box under the tree. Julia thus has a perceptual belief—a belief based on her senses—that there is a distinctive box of candy under the tree. This simple "reasoning chain" is easy

5   Audi 2005, especially Chap. 9; Audi 1993, Pt. I; see also Crumley 2009, Chap. 4.

to trace. Julia believes that Jack has returned home because she believes that there is a box of truffles beneath the tree; and she believes this because she believes she can *see* the box. The "epistemic buck" stops here, as it were, with the perceptual belief of *seeing that the box is there*. Some foundationalists do not accept perceptual belief as basic; but all foundationalists agree in this tenet: Find where the epistemic buck stops, and you've found a basic belief.

Justification *begins* with basic beliefs, and hence they are the *source* of justification. Basic beliefs are themselves justified, but not by virtue of their connection to other beliefs. Basic beliefs are the source of epistemic credibility, but are epistemically independent.

No doubt you've guessed one of the main questions for foundationalism. Why are basic beliefs justified? If it isn't other beliefs that justify them, what does? So we need the foundationalist to explain why basic beliefs are justified.

Different versions of foundationalism identify different types of belief as basic. Some count perception or memory or *a priori* reasoning as yielding basic beliefs. Other views suggest that beliefs about one's own mental states or sensations—we might call them *introspective beliefs*—are basic. No matter these differences, foundationalists agree on the fundamental idea that any justification of *nonbasic* beliefs ultimately derives from or can be traced back to one or more basic beliefs. This "structure" of the connection between beliefs is sometimes characterized as a pyramid. Paraphrasing Descartes a bit, we build justification from the foundation, and basic beliefs make up this foundation.

Descartes is sometimes described as holding one basic belief: the "I think therefore I am" belief, from which his other beliefs about the existence of God, about the natural world, and about the distinctness of mind from body are derived (see Chapter 1 for a discussion of this). Most foundationalists, however, recognize many basic beliefs. Indeed, if contemporary foundationalists are right, we are acquiring a large but undetermined number of basic beliefs, all during our waking hours—open your eyes and look! Eat a peach! Remember what you had for breakfast!—and you will acquire basic beliefs ... likely lots of them.

Our "reasoning chain" regarding Jack's Christmas shopping highlights the second common feature that both approaches to foundationalism share. Both views assert that between basic and nonbasic beliefs there is an inferential, justifying connection. A belief is justified if and only if that belief is either a basic belief or a belief that can be traced back to some one or more basic beliefs. Perhaps more to the point, such a belief fails to be justified if it cannot be traced to basic beliefs. Versions of foundationalism disagree about the nature of this inferential connection. Some, like Descartes, insist on deductive connections between basic and nonbasic beliefs. (Recall from the Introduction that valid deductive arguments are truth-preserving: if the premises are true, then the conclusion must be true.) Most contemporary foundationalists hold that inductive inferential connections suffice to transmit justification from basic to nonbasic beliefs. (The conclusion of an inductive argument goes beyond or "amplifies" the information contained in the premises; the stronger the argument, the more likely the conclusion.) But this common feature remains: nonbasic beliefs "inherit" their epistemic credibility or justification *by means of* their inferential connections to basic beliefs.

Distinguishing deductive from inductive inferential connections leads to the two main versions of foundationalism, which we will call strong and modest foundationalism. The principal difference between these two is that the latter but not the former adopts **fallibilism**. Theories of justification that are fallibilist hold that further evidence—in other words, the acquisition of further beliefs—can override a previously accepted and otherwise acceptable justification. Hence, the currently but fallibly justified belief will cease to be justified. Sara, for example, might believe that friends are taking Sam to lunch to celebrate his new job. She believes this because one of those friends, Deirdre, told her that was the plan, which is a perfectly acceptable justification. Later Sara discovers that Sam preferred an afternoon at the local bowling alley to sitting in a noisy chain restaurant. Hence, Sara's "loses" her original justification. Thus, fallible justification is justification that can be overridden by new evidence—but is still justification, nonetheless.

Strong Foundationalism

Strong foundationalism, sometimes called Cartesian or infallible foundationalism, holds that basic beliefs cannot be mistaken and that justification is inherited or transmitted only through deductive inferential connections. Since the basic beliefs cannot be mistaken, they are infallible. Because the conclusion of a successful deductive argument is certain, deductive connections to such basic beliefs guarantee that nonbasic beliefs are similarly infallible. Descartes's "I think" belief was, in his view, just such an infallible belief. He couldn't be mistaken. And he argued that, given that belief, he could prove certain other beliefs, e.g., the existence of God.

Some of the more recent strong foundationalists see basic beliefs as *introspective beliefs*, beliefs about our own mental states. Such beliefs cannot be mistaken. And if they can't be mistaken, surely they are justified. But one doesn't need to rely on other beliefs to "introspect." It is, after all, direct ... and easy. One just "looks inside" to access one's own mental states. Andrea is immediately aware, for example, and hence cannot be wrong that *it seems to her* or *looks to her* like Sara is walking up the driveway. Andrea need rely on no other belief to introspect—infallibly—that *it looks to her* as if Sara is wearing a white dress. No matter that it's at night, and in fact it's Deirdre, not Sara, wearing a yellow dress. Andrea wasn't wrong—and could not be wrong—about how it *seemed* to her, no matter what the reality was.

This idea of *how it seems* or *how it appears* to me has proved important in much epistemology, surfacing, for example, in various accounts of perception and perceptual knowledge.[6] The underlying thought is that a person might be mistaken about what's out there in the world, about the color of a dress or the cause of some sound. But a person simply cannot be mistaken about *how it seems*. Imagine Julia telling Jack that he's wrong that the shirt appears to him to be indigo. Julia and Jack might disagree about the color, but clearly Jack is the best authority on *how it seems to him*. Clearly then, the strong foundationalist claims, introspective beliefs are justified but don't depend on other beliefs for their justification. They are justified because they cannot be wrong. Some have identified these as "self-evident" or "self-presenting" beliefs.

---

6   E.g., Chisholm 1957.

The infallibility of introspective beliefs is a vexed, intricate, and ongoing issue, and not only in epistemology. Philosophers and psychologists have raised questions about the infallibility of introspective beliefs. Various findings suggest that we are often wrong about the source of or the temporal order of such beliefs. Lehrer provides a case suggesting an introspective belief may be the result of an unconscious inference, rather than the immediate, noninferential belief.[7] And if such criticisms are correct, that would undermine the strong foundationalist position. Many contemporary foundationalists take a different approach, however—the modest foundationalist approach.

Modest Foundationalism

Virtue Epistemology

Virtue ethics, which emphasizes character traits as basic to moral evaluation, is usually traced back to Aristotle, but it achieved something of a comeback in the later decades of the twentieth century. And some theorists began to look at virtue ethics as a model for thinking about epistemological issues; thus, *virtue epistemology*. This approach suggests that whether a person is justified or knows depends on certain intellectual traits and whether those traits were exercised appropriately in a particular circumstance.

Some versions of the view are more externalist in nature, while others tend to be more internalist. Perhaps the more important point is that knowledge is achieved when a person's "habits of mind" are well-developed and are appropriately directed toward some important epistemic goal, such as truth or explanatory adequacy.

How does this work in practice? We might find some hint from the Greek word for "virtue": it suggests the idea of excellence in performance of a function. Suppose then, for example, that our "epistemic function" is acquiring beliefs directed toward explanatory adequacy. An epistemically virtuous character is one which contributes to excellence in performing that function. E.g., such a character will avoid wishful thinking, will seek out more evidence, and will rely on valid inferences.

And like the virtuous moral character, the virtuous epistemic character can be molded or shaped. In some virtue epistemology views, we are therefore *responsible* for the beliefs we hold.

---

7   Lehrer 1990, pp. 49–50; Lyons 1986, Chap. 3.

According to modest foundationalism, a basic belief can still be considered justified even if subsequent evidence might override the justification of the basic belief. So for modest foundationalism, basic beliefs need only be fallibly justified. Modest foundationalists also hold that justification can be transmitted *inductively* while acknowledging that in some instances deductive connections also transmit justification. If Sam believes that he hears the garage door going up, he might infer that the family has come home from shopping. This inference is not deductive, only inductive. Nonetheless the belief about the garage door raising justifies the belief about who is home.

Modest foundationalism, with its fallibilistic view, thus sees many types of basic beliefs. Sam's belief about his hearing the garage door going up is a perceptual belief. Of course, it is fallible, according to modest foundationalism. Yet this belief can count as basic. Thus, perceptual beliefs—beliefs that we have as a result of our senses—about what's going on in the world are basic beliefs. Similarly, memory beliefs, or apparent memory beliefs, beliefs reached by *a priori* reasoning, in the modest foundationalist view, can be basic beliefs.

Robert Audi, who has for some time articulated and defended a version of modest foundationalism, identifies a number of principles that tell us when a belief is basic.[8] For example, suppose Sara has a "memorial impression," a seeming to remember, of setting the keys next to a sculpture of cardinals and bluebirds. Now suppose that Sara reflects on this impression and on that basis she comes to believe "The keys are by the sculpture." This latter belief, in Audi's view, is a basic belief, justified by the memorial impression. Some *non-belief* impression serves a person's basis for a subsequent basic belief. The person comes to have the basic belief on the basis of the relevant impression.

Why, we might wonder, should such beliefs count as justified? The answer to this question illustrates one of the more interesting features of modest foundationalism. Modest foundationalists such as Audi typically think of basic beliefs as supported by an experience or a sensory impression or sensation; yet the experience or impression or sensation is not itself a belief. Basic beliefs are thus epistemically dependent on "nonbelief"—*nondoxastic* is the technical term—sensations. Such beliefs are thus justified but are basic because they don't depend on other beliefs for their justification.

A simple example may serve to illustrate the modest foundationalist thought here. Julia looks in the direction of the Christmas tree and has a

---

8   Audi 1988; Audi 1998.

sensation, that of a gold box. *Because of this nondoxastic sensation*, she comes to have the perceptual belief that there's a gold box under the tree. It might turn out of course that's she's wrong; there might be no box (an ornament may have fallen on the floor) or that it's not gold (perhaps it is the reflection of colored light). But usually, generally, when she has this sort of sensation, she comes to have the perceptual belief. And it's generally true! The sensation is a *generally reliable* intermediary between the "out there" and the subsequent "in here" belief. The having of a sensation *is good evidence for* or a *good indication of* the truth of the corresponding perceptual belief.

Now notice: a sensation is not a belief, or at least, this is the claim of the modest foundationalists. It *supports* the perceptual belief, however. So, the perceptual belief is justified; it has good evidence (the sensation). But it doesn't depend on other beliefs for its justification, only on the non-belief—the *nondoxastic*—sensation. Hence, we have a basic belief: a fallibly justified belief that does not depend on other beliefs for its justification.

Can Experiences Justify Belief?

Perhaps you sense a criticism that's lurking. Foundationalists offer experiences or impressions or sensations as the justifying factor for basic beliefs. Yet it's claimed that since these sensations or experiences aren't beliefs, they don't need justification themselves. But how can this be, critics want to know. If sensations play an *epistemic* role, don't they too need their epistemic status validated? Sensations can only lend their epistemic credibility to perceptual beliefs *if the sensations already have epistemic credibility*—that is, if they are reliable sources of information. Critics then ask, where did these sensations get *their* initial epistemic credibility? If they are justified or epistemically credible, doesn't our search for the source of their justification or epistemic credibility start the regress again? But if they are not credible, sensations wouldn't seem to be able to serve as the justification for basic beliefs.[9]

This disagreement between foundationalists and critics has not yet been resolved. Foundationalists respond that this is part of the nature of coming to have certain sorts of beliefs. Our sensory interactions lead to our having sensations. It's because this sensation is caused by those interactions that our basic beliefs are likely to be true. Our normal interactions with the environment

---

9   BonJour 1985.

produce sensations, sensations which eventually give rise to beliefs. And the foundationalist thinks this sensory experience makes it more likely that the belief is true. This is a complicated issue, one that undoubtedly requires much more investigation into the nature of sensation, belief, and justification.[10]

This disagreement also points to a different approach to justification, one that eschews basic beliefs, and instead sees justification as a feature of the connections or relations between beliefs.

Hanging Together: The Coherence View of Justification

At the signing of the Declaration of Independence, Benjamin Franklin observed to his fellow rebels, "We must indeed all hang together, or most assuredly, we shall all hang separately." Ben of course was not making an epistemological observation. But *coherence*, as an epistemological concept, is animated by the thought that beliefs must hang together, if they are to "survive" epistemically.

Three philosophers in the latter half of the twentieth century have been especially associated with coherence views of the nature of knowledge and justification: Willard Van Orman Quine, Keith Lehrer, and Donald Davidson.[11] Other coherence theorists include Jonathan Kvanvig and Laurence BonJour (who eventually rejected it for foundationalism).[12] Quine's views are more typically termed "holism," and his "Two Dogmas of Empiricism" paper is one of the most influential essays of the twentieth century. His notion of a "web of belief" is frequently invoked to characterize coherence views.[13] While there are differences among different coherentists' views, the broad outlines of the coherentist idea of justification are relatively clear.

Coherence theory makes both a positive and a negative claim. The positive claim is hinted at in the "hanging together." In the coherentist view, justification derives from the coherence of a person's beliefs. That is, a person's beliefs *mutually support* each other. Explaining the concepts of mutual support or coherence is thus crucial for coherence theorists; different interpretations lead to different versions of coherentism.

The negative claim of coherentism is quite specific: there are no epistemically independent beliefs. Every belief depends on other beliefs for its justification. Hence, there are no basic beliefs. Perceptual beliefs, memory

---

10   For more on sensation and justification, see Smith 2002, especially Pt. I.
11   Quine 1951; Lehrer 1974, 1990, and 2002; Davidson 1986a and 1986b.
12   Kvanvig and Riggs 1992; BonJour 1985.
13   Quine and Ullian 1978.

beliefs, even beliefs about sensation may nonetheless play an important role in a person's "belief systems." The justification for these beliefs, however, arises from the connection to, or the support of, the person's other beliefs. Imagine, for example, that Julia is trying to determine whether any of the cantaloupes are sufficiently ripe. And now imagine, after picking up a particular cantaloupe and sniffing, that she comes to have a belief that the "cantaloupe scent" is still faint, and hence believes that the fruit is not yet ripe. This "olfactory belief" about the scent of the cantaloupe is, according to the coherence theorist, justified because of its connection to other beliefs, for example, her belief about how ripe cantaloupes smell, her memory belief that she has been successful in identifying ripe cantaloupes before, and her belief that there's nothing amiss with her senses. There is an epistemic connection between the olfactory belief and Julia's other beliefs. And it is this epistemic connection—this *coherence*—among beliefs that constitutes justification. There is no basic belief to be found here.

Mutual Support

Coherence as Constraint Satisfaction

In his 2000 book, *Coherence in Thought and Action*, Paul Thagard characterizes coherence as *maximal constraint satisfaction*. He notes also that this is a fitting together, or, in the absence of coherence, it is a resistance to fitting together.

Thagard may be best known outside the philosophy discipline for his *The Brain and the Meaning of Life*, and his work in cognitive science overlaps thematically with his work in philosophy. He has for many years researched topics in connectionist networks, neural network modeling, and various topics in metaphysics and epistemology.

Thagard applies the notion of coherence, not just to epistemic justification, but to other areas such as our ideas about the general nature of reality and emotions.

The details of Thagard's constraint satisfaction are a little technical, but a few points are worth noting. First, he applies coherence to not only beliefs but several types of representations, e.g., images, concepts, goals. Second, the idea of multiple constraint satisfaction includes notions such as probability, explanation—one belief explaining another—and deductive consistency or inconsistency. Very, very roughly, the idea is to align as many of the positives and negatives, and then to choose which is the more likely or the best fit. For example, deliberative coherence involves choosing an action that is more likely to facilitate or help bring about some goal. That action then coheres with an overall set of "elements," and is thus justified.

Like Lehrer, who has applied coherence to different areas, Thagard's view is wide-ranging, taking into account a wide range of empirical findings from various disciplines, especially psychology and cognitive psychology.

When a belief of ours fits with, or "hangs with," other beliefs, we are no doubt inclined to give greater epistemic weight or credibility to that belief. It is not very difficult to see why. Recall this feature of beliefs: They provide a picture of or a representation of the world. That's just what it means to talk about the *content* of a belief—it's a little bit of information (about the world). Indeed, that's why theorists are inclined to talk about beliefs as *representational*. Of course, for various reasons we might have doubts about whether to trust any particular bit of information. We are understandably encouraged to "trust" some particular belief if we find that its particular information *fits* with other pieces of information—other beliefs—in our possession. The more the belief fits, the greater our trust. A single belief is a bit like a piece of jigsaw puzzle. By itself, a single piece of the puzzle does not make a lot of sense. Yet once we see how the piece fits together with other pieces, once we see the way it interlocks with other pieces, we understand where the piece fits in and why we need it. The pieces "hang together." Similarly, as some particular belief content fits with more and more other contents—other beliefs—the more inclined we are to trust that first belief. That is, if some bit of "belief information" can be seen as a piece of a larger picture presented by our other beliefs, then we are more inclined to see that belief as epistemically trustworthy.

Now some beliefs might seem to make sense all by themselves, to not require other beliefs for support or epistemic credibility. Take, for example, seeing and consequently believing that there is a purple book on the table. It might seem that other beliefs simply are not needed to support this belief. But the coherentist asks you to consider the matter a bit more closely. You remember your brother mentioning that the color of the book cover matches his shirt; you remember seeing him leave the book there; you believe that there is nothing unusual about the situation. Indeed, you probably would not be so confident of this particular belief *unless* you also believed that your vision was quite normal and that you could certainly perform the routine perceptual

task of identifying the type of object and its color.[14] Not only do you know a book when you see one, but you know purple when you see it! As you begin to see that the belief about the color of the book fits with so many of your other beliefs, you also begin to see the *source* of your epistemic confidence. Your recognition of the way in which this belief is tied to other beliefs at the very least increases the visual belief's epistemic credibility.

This support is, in a sense, a two-way street.[15] Your belief that you know a book when you see one is itself supported by all the particular occasions like this one in which you saw individual books—whether purple books, blue books, or an intriguing little black book. Even your belief that your vision is normal is supported by all the individual occasions on which you have managed to navigate your way through a room or reached for an object you thought you saw and, indeed, found an object there to be grasped. Just as in

14   Lehrer 1997, Chap. 1; also Chap. 3.
15   Lehrer 1997.

a web, each node is supported by other parts of the web, and each node also contributes to the support of the whole.

The metaphor of the "web of belief" has become commonplace in recent decades. Notice that a web has no real starting point; no one place in the web is more basic than any other. This is precisely what the coherentist has in mind. No individual belief, and no type of belief, is epistemically basic. Rather, each belief has a role to play, but that particular role makes sense only in the context of the whole set of beliefs. The web of belief hangs or falls together.

Different coherence theorists view this support—this coherence—in different ways. Indeed, there are several different "takes" on how to understand the nature of the coherence. Two should be mentioned, since we cannot consider them all. The first is the idea of *explanatory coherence*. Some particular belief coheres with our other beliefs if it is either *explained by* those beliefs or that belief helps *to explain* our other beliefs. Recall Julia's belief about the cantaloupe—what other beliefs could it explain? For example, it might help explain Julia's "tactile belief" that when she pushed on the stem end of the cantaloupe is was still quite firm. The general point about this example is that even perceptual beliefs might stand in an "explanatory relationship" to other beliefs.

Keith Lehrer argues that it is sufficient for some belief to cohere with a person's other beliefs when that belief coheres with only some beliefs or a set of the person's beliefs. He understands the coherence relation as evidential or "making more likely to be true." This version of coherence is interested in the *epistemic aim* of acquiring the truth. Justification as coherence, in this version, takes as its theoretical starting point that a person is primarily interested in believing the truth. Now it is perhaps easier to see what coherence is in this version. A belief coheres with a set of beliefs if that set makes the belief more likely to be true.[16]

Recall the circular picture of justification that we considered earlier. Each belief is connected to another belief, which in turn, is connected to another belief.... until the path leads, in circular fashion, back to the original belief. In a sense, this is a kind of coherentism; but it is widely rejected by coherentists, who think of our system of beliefs as a "web," rather than as a "big circle." If the "big circle" view of justification fails to provide a satisfactory answer to the regress argument for foundationalism, perhaps the "web" view does.

---

16   Lehrer 1974, Chap. 8; Lehrer 1997, Chaps. 1–3; Lehrer 1990 and 2003.

Isolation Objection: Beliefs and the World

C.I. Lewis offered this observation about coherence theory: "I think the whole system of such could provide no better assurance of anything in it than that which attaches to the contents of a well-written novel."[17] Lewis's observation is animated by a central objection to coherence theory: In coherence theory, there's nothing to tie a person's beliefs to the world (or reality). A person might have a "well-written" store of beliefs; all the person's beliefs might "hang together" or cohere. Yet that set of beliefs might for all that be just a cleverly constructed fiction, *isolated from the world*. The isolation objection claims that coherence theories of justification cut justification off from the world. In other words, the coherentist can explain why a person's beliefs cohere, but can't explain why those beliefs are likely to be true. In one form or another this objection has been endorsed by many theorists in epistemology.

In coherentism, justification arises only from the relation between beliefs. A belief is justified, according to the coherentist, if it is connected in the right way to other beliefs. And that is all—justification depends on the connections between beliefs. Now the isolation objection is that, if coherence appears as an "internal" relation among beliefs, then there's nothing that assures any connection to what's actually happening in the world. Thus, for example, consider Sara's belief that a pineapple upside down cake is in the oven. Coherence says this belief is justified if it's connected in the right way to other beliefs. It coheres, and is hence justified, if, for example, she believes that she put the cake in the oven 25 minutes ago, that the aroma in the kitchen is that of cake baking... etc. What is apparently ignored here is how any of the beliefs in this "family" are connected to what's happening *in the world*.

In determining whether a belief is justified, then, there can be no appeal, according to the critic, to anything outside a person's beliefs. Yet, the *truth* of a person's beliefs depends on more than just other beliefs. It depends on a connection or a relation to the world. Sam's belief that there is a Jamoca® Almond Fudge ice cream in the freezer may *fit* very well with all his other beliefs. But whether that belief is *true* depends not on other beliefs—but on what is actually in the freezer! More to the point, if we think of "being justified" as connected to or aimed at truth, the coherentist seems unable to explain this connection. How is it that simply appealing to other beliefs gives us any reason to think the original belief is true?

---

17   C.I. Lewis 1970, p. 328.

Both coherentist and critic agree that our normal way of learning about the world is perception. Some feature of the perceptual process "injects" a bit of truth about the world, and this bit of truth is subsequently reflected in the person's beliefs. Julia lifts the cake cover, sees nothing but crumbs and comes to have the perceptual belief "*no more cake.*" She then adjusts her other beliefs accordingly, including beliefs about who might have had a hand in the cake caper. So, here we have a case of things out in the world affecting a person's belief. And foundationalists are happy to claim that their view is very good at explaining what's going on here and that foundationalist justification reflects this connection between world and belief.

Coherentist and foundationalist alike see the isolation objection as suggesting that coherence views cannot properly explain the role of perceptual beliefs. Recall Lewis's suggestion that coherence would say *an entirely fictional set of beliefs* is nonetheless justified, so long as those beliefs "cohere." But coherentists think this is quite wrong. First, many coherentists doubt the possibility of the sort of scenario envisioned by Lewis. More important is the general idea that runs through coherentist responses, that their view in fact accounts for the role of perceptual beliefs.

Coherentists have different ways of going about this. One view holds that coherence includes, not just coherence among beliefs, but also among sensations or sense impressions.[18] Another coherentist view[19] holds that the "content" of any belief is given by its causal connection with the world; so any interpretation of what someone's beliefs are "about"—any way of understanding their content—that makes most of them false must be mistaken about how they are to be interpreted. This then guarantees that most of our beliefs about the world are true.

Another approach is to suggest that a person's beliefs should be responsive to or sensitive to new information, and this is part of our evaluative capacity.[20] Julia's beliefs that she will soon be enjoying a piece of cake with a scoop of Jamoca® Almond Fudge ice cream and that she can trust her friends not to have eaten all of it are revised in light of her perceptual belief that there is no more cake. Julia then evaluates the epistemic situation, in light of this new information (crumbs only, no cake). Of course, this evaluation can be quite complicated, involving not only perceptual beliefs, theoretical beliefs, memory

---

18   Kvanvig and Riggs 1992.
19   Davidson 1986a.
20   Lehrer 1997.

beliefs, beliefs about perceptual beliefs, even "metaphysical" beliefs—that cake didn't just get up and walk away by itself. This evaluative aspect, coherentists claim, is the real substance of "connecting" truth to justification.

Perhaps, in the end, coherentists have a problem tying justification to truth. But, as we have seen, perhaps foundationalists are in no better position in this regard than they are.

No doubt more can be said here, on behalf of both foundationalist and coherentist. The isolation objection points to a number of distinct and difficult issues. We should not lose sight, however, of the key issue that lies at the center of this dispute: how best to explain how our beliefs came to have the epistemic credibility we take them to have.

Evidentialism

So far, we have been talking about "reasons for belief," and about "evidence," as if they're the same thing; and more or less assuming that one must have reasons/evidence for all of one's beliefs. But we need now to look into these matters more deeply.

In an 1877 essay entitled "The Ethics of Belief," William K. Clifford (1845–79) made the following comment: "... it is wrong always, everywhere, and for anyone, to believe anything upon insufficient evidence."[21] In Clifford's view our "epistemic duty" is to believe only if we have sufficient evidence. Indeed several of the hypothetical cases Clifford offers and his subsequent analysis suggests that this is not only an epistemic duty, but a moral duty as well. In one of his examples, a ship owner, disregarding strong evidence to the contrary, believes falsely—with disastrous results—that his ship is safe. Of course, failing our epistemic "duties" can have morally bad consequences. Clifford argued, however, that belief without sufficient evidence was always bad in itself, even when there were no morally relevant consequences.

Some years later, in 1896, in an address to two university philosophy clubs, William James (1842–1910) took issue with Clifford's view, offering an account of when belief might be justified, even if it did not satisfy Clifford's standard. James was particularly interested in explaining how religious belief might be justified.[22] His argument, in a nutshell, was that it had good psychological consequences, so it is justified despite lacking evidence.

---

21   Clifford 1999.
22   James 1951c.

Evidentialism, holds that justification should be seen as dependent on the evidence one has.[23] It is Clifford's position, and a familiar one in philosophy. Hume similarly endorsed evidentialism over a century earlier than Clifford, remarking that "A wise man proportions his belief to the evidence."[24]

This position may seem obvious, but, as we shall see, there is much to think about here. It should be noted first that the two positions we have been concentrating on earlier in this chapter—foundationalism and coherentism—are both compatible with evidentialism. Those two positions disagree with the basis of justification, but both can agree that justification is necessary, and depends on the evidence one has.

The version of evidentialism presented by Richard Feldman and Earl Conee holds that a person's belief is justified if two conditions are met: first, the person has evidence that supports the belief; second, the person believes on the basis of that evidence. Again recall Julia's belief that her good friends have had a hand in the disappearance of the cake. How is this belief justified, according to the evidentialist? We can think of her evidence as her beliefs that the cake was there this morning and that only her good friends, Deirdre and Sara, have been in the kitchen since then. *And* Julia comes to have her belief about the disappearance of the cake *based on* or *because of* these other beliefs. Then, according to evidentialism, Julia's belief is justified.

Evidentialists see the motivation for their view in our notion of justification. A belief is justified, we suppose, only if there are good reasons for it. And those good reasons are reasons to think the content of the belief is true. It is then easy to see these "good reasons" as evidence.

Evidentialism does not discount the possibility that other evidence may count against a belief. Julia may be aware that once in a while Sam comes to visit Sara. The evidentialist view, however, only requires that the balance of an agent's evidence support the belief.

The concept of evidence is easily seen as central in epistemology, especially in our understanding of knowledge and justification. Earlier we used "reasons" and "evidence" almost synonymously. Citing reasons for a belief is citing the evidence—evidence justifies belief. Yet there are different ways to specify the concept more precisely. Some see a very close, almost definitional connection between justification and evidence—(positive) evidence is whatever increases

---

23   Feldman and Conee 1985 and 2004.
24   Hume 1975, p. 110.

justification.[25] A somewhat broader understanding suggests that evidence is anything—some sensation or experience, some proposition, or some belief—that tells us something about the truth or falsity of a belief.[26] On some occasions, we may have an argument for a belief; on others, our evidence might be something more like "it seems to me that ..."

We will adopt this broader notion of evidence being whatever indicates something about truth or falsity, in line with the view developed by Feldman and Conee, with the proviso that the evidence involved in justification is evidence a person *has*. A bit more technically, a person is considered to have evidence if that evidence is reflected in a person's beliefs or other mental states, and the person could access or become aware of having this evidence. Thus, if Sara has the sensory impression or sensory experience of a ruby-colored glass, she has evidence for her belief that the glass is on the counter. Though we generally do not reflect on our sensory impressions, Sara could become aware that, yes, she is having a sensation or visual experience of a ruby-colored glass. Similarly, if Julia learned last fall that the Battle of Shiloh was fought in Tennessee, just a little east of Memphis, then she has evidence for her belief that there are Civil War monuments in that that state, even though she might not currently recall the information about that battle. Should we require that in some sense she *could* become aware of it or remember it? Suppose that she has completely, irremediably forgotten. Perhaps it is enough that she once knew about that battle, and based her belief about monuments in Tennessee on it, and only the second belief remains. That appears to be enough for justification of the second belief: as long as the believer has *or had* good enough evidence.

The motivation for the insistence that the justified belief *be based on* the evidence the believer either *had* or *has* is seen in this sort of example. Sally's brother, whom she knows to be reliable, told her last week that he'd be leaving his house first thing on Saturday morning to drive to her house. She knows it takes him a couple of hours to get to her place, but she simply didn't put two and two together at the time, and figure out that he'd be arriving at Saturday noon. She guesses—with no basis at all—that her brother would be arriving around noon. Her guess turns out to be true, and there is good evidence for it—what her brother told her—and she remembers what he told her, but her belief is not based on that evidence. She didn't know he'd arrive at noon—it was just a guess.

---

25   Kim 1988.
26   Feldman 1993.

Now consider this example. Sara and Sam are planning to see a movie. Sam has *in his hand* today's movie listings, but remembers that yesterday the movie started at 8 pm and so does not check today's paper. The two arrive at the theater to discover that the movie started twenty minutes earlier at 7:30. Disappointed, they complain to the manager, who points out that the revised time was published in today's paper. Sara suggests that Sam should have checked the paper, and thus, she might claim, he was not justified in believing the movie started at 8.

First, note that the information that Sam based his belief on was pretty good justification (because movies at that theater usually start at the same time each night). Remember that a false belief can nevertheless be justification.

Second, note that what would count as justification does not, if it is overruled by stronger contrary evidence. Sam's mistaken belief would no longer be justified if he had read today's schedule in the newspaper, but somehow just not managed to adjust his belief in accord with this stronger evidence.

Third, note that justification is about what evidence one has, not what one might acquire. Clearly it would have been very easy for Sam to acquire the evidence about the movie's start time; the paper was there in his hand. And we can understand Sara's frustration ("Why didn't you look?"). Yet—despite not checking the paper—Sam was justified, according to Feldman, in believing the movie started at 8. Thus, *evidence* comprises only what the person has (or had). Such mental states include beliefs as well as other mental states, such as sensations.[27]

But fourth, consider what was in fact Sam's justification for his false belief. Was that justification enough? Should Sam have gotten stronger evidence than he had, as Sara suggested? There is no general answer to how strong evidence needs to be before one commits to a belief. It depends on the situation: how bad is it if one gets things wrong? how important is it to get things right?

In Chapter 1 we considered whether we have enough evidence that global skepticism is wrong. That is, are our experiences or other beliefs sufficient to justify our thinking that, yes, we have knowledge and justified beliefs about the world? Common sense—and a typical reaction on first encountering, say, the Dream Argument—tells us that we are justified in believing that there is a cup on the table or that $2 + 7 = 9$. Yet, some have suggested that we do not have evidence for this; we don't have the evidence to defeat the skeptic's challenge.[28]

---

27   Feldman 2003, pp. 47–48.
28   DeRose 2000.

The evidentialist might reply that in ordinary contexts, and applying a commonsense notion of evidence, we are justified in believing that the skeptic is mistaken. That is, we take it that our reasons for believing are sufficient justification even if they might not be able to deflect every skeptical challenge. Such ordinary contexts seem especially amenable to the evidentialist view. In ordinary contexts, a person's evidence is just what we would expect. Ask Andy why he believes that Jack will not be at the party, and Andy will offer his recollection of a perceptual belief: he overheard Jack saying that he plans to do some vacuuming and to read a book instead. Often this ordinary use of evidence is *good enough*. Or Sara comes to believe that the essay's due date has been extended because she receives a text from Julia. Again, good enough. As we shift to more demanding notions of *being justified*, it might be less clear how the evidentialist responds.[29] If the skeptic insists on more than just the normal, everyday sort of justification, what evidence might we have, according to the evidentialist, that would refute the skeptic?

Belief without Evidence

We have been considering what it is for there to be evidence for belief, but we have not yet touched on a central claim of the evidentialists: that beliefs always require sufficient evidence. Recall the argument above between James and Clifford. James, as we noted, was especially interested in religious beliefs; he argued that they were entirely acceptable, even desirable, despite their lack of support by evidence.

James's argument was that some beliefs unsupported by evidence, such as the belief in God, can make a difference in our lives, and thus we are justified in holding them on *pragmatic*—that is, practical—grounds, if not epistemic ones. If a belief has good effects, helps us get along better, then we are justified in believing it.

The evidentialist does not deny that there are often pragmatic or moral reasons to believe that might incline belief in one proposition rather than another. But *epistemic justification*, the evidentialist claims, points to the truth of a belief, not its practical or moral value. James, however, went so far as to claim that a belief that had practical value—good consequences for the believer—was therefore true, because practical value *was* truth. "The true

---

29   Mittag 2013.

is the name of whatever proves itself to be good in the way of belief."[30] This, of course, is an odd view of truth. But might we abandon truth-production as the point of justification, and count a belief as justified when it is good for the believer?

Perhaps it is impossible to marshal evidence against thoroughgoing philosophical skepticism. But we might find the rejection of skepticism to have psychological value, and maybe even practical value (because we would trust our inductions, expect things still to remain there when we're not looking, and so on).

David Hume acknowledged in the conclusion to Book I of the *Treatise* that he had no answers for his theoretical skepticism, but he recognized that he is *naturally disposed* to carry on as he normally had:

> Most fortunately it happens, that since Reason is incapable of dispelling these clouds, Nature herself suffices to that purpose, and cures me of this philosophical melancholy and delirium, either by relaxing this bent of mind, or by some avocation, and lively impression of my senses, which obliterate all these chimeras. I dine, I play a game of backgammon, I converse, and am merry with my friends. And when, after three or four hours' amusement, I would return to these speculations, they appear so cold, and strained, and ridiculous, that I cannot find in my heart to enter into them any farther.[31]

But Hume is not claiming that our unavoidable habits of belief constitute justification.

Justification and Truth: A Brief Conclusion

Eddie Haskell is an (infamous) character on the oft-derided 1950s sitcom *Leave It to Beaver*. A cursory glance at but a few episodes reveals the following truth: the fact that Eddie Haskell said something is never a good reason to believe it. Why (the main character is asked) did you not do your history homework? Eddie Haskell told me the teacher would become spoiled and expect too much from the class. Of course, listening to Eddie's views rarely got one closer to the *truth*. Reasons to hold a belief are reasons to think a belief is true. Many hold that the connection between justification and truth

---

30   James 1975, p. 42.
31   Hume 1978, p. 629.

is implied in the definition of justification: the more justified our beliefs, the more likely the truth of those beliefs.

Each of the three accounts of justification tells us something about how we ought to view this connection between justification and truth. The coherentist, for example, takes it that the greater the coherence among our beliefs, the better our chance of acquiring truth about the world. The foundationalist holds that basic beliefs are the interface between us and the world and the link between belief and truth. And one way to judge or to evaluate the three views is to ask which of the three provides a better understanding of how our beliefs fare as representations of the world.

Key Concepts

- foundationalism
- coherence theory (or coherentism)
- regress argument
- fallibilism
- isolation objection
- evidentialism

Reading/Discussion Questions

1. Explain how the regress argument can lead to a foundationalist view of justification.
2. Describe the differences between strong and modest foundationalism. Which of these two views seems the better account, in your opinion? Explain.
3. History and science provide us with justified beliefs (at least, that is the widely held view). Is foundationalism or coherentism the better view to explain the justification of historical beliefs? of scientific beliefs? Give an example of a historical or scientific belief (e.g., that Hannibal crossed the Alps in 218 BCE, or that water is made up of hydrogen and oxygen) and explain why either the coherentist or foundationalist view offers a better account of the justification for that belief.
4. What is the isolation objection? What is your evaluation of the objection—that is, does it succeed in showing that coherentism is wrong?
5. First, explain evidentialism. Between foundationalism and evidentialism, which view do you think gives a better response to the skeptic? Explain.

For Further Reading

Of course Descartes 1968a is perhaps the historically most important presentation of strong foundationalism. Lehrer 1974 and 1990 criticize the notion that we have infallibly justified beliefs. Also see Crumley 2009 for further discussion. Two of the leading contemporary proponents of modest foundationalism are Robert Audi 1993 and William Alston 1989.

Keith Lehrer's account of coherentist justification has undergone modification over the years, while the main ideas have remained. Two "middle" accounts are Lehrer 1990 and 1993; his 2003 presents a more recent view. Donald Davidson 1986a and 1986b provide Davidson's view of coherence, both of knowledge and truth. The *locus classicus* for W.V.O. Quine's holism is of course "Two Dogmas of Empiricism," reprinted in Quine 1961.

Discussions of the debate between foundationalism and coherentism can be found in Matthias Steup and Ernest Sosa 2005, Steup 1996, Richard Feldman 2003, Audi 2005, and Crumley 2009. Although it is specifically about knowledge, Ernest Sosa's "The Raft and the Pyramid: Coherence versus Foundations in the Theory of Knowledge" is a classic statement of the differences between coherence and foundationalist views; see Sosa 1980.

For Feldman's and Conee's view of evidentialism, see Feldman and Conee 2004 and Feldman 2003. James, "The Will to Believe" (1896), is reprinted in Fisch 1951.

Discussions of virtue epistemology can be found in most of the epistemology surveys noted above. Also, Code 1987 develops a version of virtue epistemology, as does Pritchard 2009 and Sosa 2007. Sosa expands and further extends his view of virtue epistemology in Sosa 2011. Also discussions of virtue views can be found in Steup and Sosa 2005.

CHAPTER FOUR

NEW DIRECTIONS

Whether we imagine Descartes, attired in his dressing gown, seated by the fire in his seventeenth-century "lazy boy" chair, or we imagine some more somber pose, such as that struck by Rodin's *The Thinker*, we cannot help but be struck by this idea: in many ways traditional epistemology is "armchair epistemology." Descartes supposed that once and for all he would discover the basics of what we know simply by sitting and thinking. The practice of epistemology—the science of knowledge—would be unlike what we now take to be that of other sciences. Its "laws," its bedrock principles, could be discovered just by thinking. Neither Descartes's meditations nor Hume's radical empiricism required a laboratory.

Rethinking the nature of epistemology is a prominent theme of the last three decades of the twentieth century—reconsidering not only its connection to the sciences, but also its connection to people. This chapter tells two of those stories. The first—the story of naturalized epistemology—envisions epistemology, not as separate from the sciences, but as a part of them. The second story, closely connected to the first, is that of feminist epistemology, which claims that epistemology has had at best an unfortunate relationship with a good part of the human race. Both of these approaches seek to reconfigure or "reconceptualize" the discipline. They seek to take epistemology in new directions.

Naturalizing Epistemology

In the seminal "Epistemology Naturalized,"[1] W.V.O. Quine articulated and argued for an alternative to traditional epistemology: **naturalized epistemology**, a view that sees epistemology as part of natural science, with the principal aim of discovering, not the justification link, but the *causal link* between evidence and theory. Different versions of naturalized epistemology have of course emerged, some more dramatic than others. Our focus is naturalized epistemology's rejection of certain traditional tenets, and the main features shared by many versions of this new alternative.

Tenets of Traditional Epistemology

Naturalized epistemology is a reaction against what its proponents see as the legacy of Descartes: traditional epistemology is Cartesian epistemology. Some tenets of this Cartesian legacy are more central to the criticism of naturalized epistemology than others. That is, naturalized epistemology sees certain of these tenets as more "culpable" and thus requiring rejection. Quine outlines these disputed tenets in his 1969 essay.

Perhaps the two central culprits are a commitment to foundationalism and a commitment to *a priori* reasoning. Foundationalism is traced back to Descartes's *Meditations*, where he insists that we find those beliefs that will serve as the foundation for the rest of our knowledge. Of course, the foundational belief of the *Meditations* is "I think therefore I am" (although Descartes does not put it this way in the *Meditations*), but foundationalists since Descartes argued for various classes of beliefs counting as basic or foundational. For some, beliefs about sensations or perceptual beliefs are epistemically basic; introspective beliefs about one's own thoughts or certain *a priori* justified beliefs have also been counted among the broader class of foundational beliefs. Whichever beliefs these might be, whether they were counted as infallible or

---

1   Quine 1969, Chap. 3.

fallible, the aim of the traditional epistemologist was always the same: find those beliefs that served as the basic justification for all our other beliefs. No matter how mundane or theoretical the belief—e.g., Sam's perceptual belief about the blueberries on the plate or Einstein's view of the nature of time—we could trace the "justification source" of each and every "nonbasic" belief back to one or more of these foundational beliefs.

The second central tenet is the commitment to epistemological theory as essentially an *a priori* endeavor. That is, we discover the conditions of justification and knowledge by means of *a priori reasoning*. Traditional epistemology typically counts perception or induction as providing, on many occasions, instances of knowledge, and thus does not discount instances of *a posteriori* knowledge. But the traditional view holds that we arrive at the conditions for, and the principles of, *a posteriori* knowledge by means of a kind of reasoning that does not depend on empirical research. This gives rise to the notion—perhaps pejorative—of the "armchair epistemologist." Descartes's nightly meditations, his most famous arguments, were solitary ruminations, made by the fire, in his dressing gown, without recourse to experiment or observation. We can, in this picture, find out about the nature of knowledge and justification just by the right kind of thinking. No need to imitate the sciences, whether natural or social. Everything we need to know about the nature of knowledge can be found by the appropriate *a priori* reasoning. And the truths of epistemology are conceptual truths.

The *a priori* nature of traditional epistemology leads to two further features. First, it leads to the conception of epistemology as distinct from the sciences. That is, epistemology is an autonomous discipline. We can't, in the traditional understanding, kick epistemology out of our intellectual repertoire and replace it with some theory from cognitive neuroscience or some psychological theory about vision. Nor can we "reduce" these truths of epistemology—we can't, as it were, translate our epistemological concepts into the theories and terms of some scientific discipline. To say that epistemology is autonomous is to say that it tells us something unique; it gives us a knowledge that cannot be gained through some other discipline.

Closely related is the thought that epistemology is logically or conceptually *prior* to the sciences. Epistemology, in the traditional view, reveals the nature of knowledge, and hence, shows which claims of other disciplines are indeed instances of knowledge. That is, epistemology draws the boundary of legitimate inquiry. It tells us which of our cognitive endeavors yield genuine instances of knowledge and which are mere pretenders.

There are thus four features of traditional epistemology that Quine holds that naturalized epistemology ought to reject—the foundational structure of knowledge; the *a priori* basis of our epistemological principles; the autonomy of epistemology; and the logical priority of epistemology.

Naturalism and Epistemology

Facts and Values

Philosophers have sometimes distinguished between facts and values, suggesting that the former, but not the latter, are the province of the sciences. Judgments about facts are thought to describe the way things are. But evaluative judgments, or judgments about the value of something, express the way things ought to be or that a certain thing satisfies some standard of what ought to be. For example, calling a sculpture a work of art is thought, at least by some, to be an evaluative judgment. The significant feature of the distinction is that there are no factual judgments that "add up to" the judgment that the sculpture is a work of art. Factual and evaluative judgments are different in kind, according to this view.

Analogously, it might be thought that epistemology aims to explain the conditions for evaluative judgments, or judgments about certain epistemic properties, such as being justified in believing. In one sense, the topic of this chapter is whether the evaluative judgments of the epistemologist can be explained in terms of some set of factual judgments or properties.

Naturalized epistemology does not see the sharp dividing line between facts and values; values, especially epistemic values, are to be seen as naturalized. There are of course different ways to go about this naturalization, as is seen both in the different approaches to naturalizing epistemology and feminist epistemologies.

Quine's commitment to naturalized epistemology springs in part from his commitment to **naturalism**. This is the doctrine that everything that exists is natural. Objects and their characteristics and relations are real precisely to the extent that they are natural objects or properties or relations. And we discover the natural objects and properties *through science*, which tells us which objects and properties are the natural ones: the ones that are talked about or referred to in the explanations and theories offered by the natural sciences.Quine claims that naturalism is "the recognition that it is within science itself, and not in some prior philosophy, that reality is to be identified and described."[2] The methods of the natural sciences include observation, hypothesis and prediction, and experimentation. And these methods are distinctively empirical: they depend on experience.

According to Quine, traditional epistemology carries an insurmountable burden in its foundationalism, starting, as Descartes does, with what are supposed to be indubitable truths, revealed by the unmistakable contents of one's own mind. But Quine thinks that neither the rationalist nor the empiricist is able to show us the way from *in here*, in our minds, to *out there*, the natural world. Quine thinks this is a misbegotten process. If we start "inside," with the contents of our own minds, we can never find a *logical* connection to get us outside. On the other hand, if we start—as some foundationalists are inclined to do—with beliefs about external objects, then we are already in the realm of science. Thus, we should start with science—physics, chemistry, biology, psychology, and their allied disciplines.

This thought—that we are better off starting with science—leads Quine to claim that we are better off replacing traditional epistemology with psychology.

---

2   Quine 1981, p. 22.

If we cannot identify and legitimate the principles that tell us what we *ought* to believe, then we should begin with finding out *how* we came to believe what we in fact believe. "Better," Quine says, "to discover how science is in fact developed and learned than to fabricate a fictitious structure to a similar effect."[3] Even with this replacement, Quine claims, perhaps surprisingly, that epistemology, "or something like it," would still continue.

Notice first a significant consequence of accepting that we must begin with science. We abandon the foundationalist aim, of course, since there are no certain first principles or starting points. But there is more than that. We should not look to *a priori* reasoning to tell us about knowledge. We learn about the nature of knowledge *within* science. All justification is in the end scientific justification. And Quine thinks this has an important consequence for our understanding of skepticism. He remarks that "the Humean predicament is the human predicament."[4] We should recognize, however, that once the skeptic offers the challenge, we are free to make use of science in responding! Quine says:

> *Skepticism is an offshoot of science.* The basis for skepticism is the awareness of illusion, the discovery that we must not always believe our eyes. Skepticism battens on mirages, on seemingly bent sticks in water, on rainbows, afterimages, double images, dreams. But in what sense are these illusions? In the sense that they seem to be material objects which they in fact are not. Illusions are illusions *only relative to a prior acceptance of genuine bodies* with which to contrast them.... Rudimentary physical science, that is, common sense about bodies, is thus needed as a springboard for skepticism.[5]

Surprisingly for the traditional outlook, Quine sees skepticism as presupposing science. Making sense of even dreams, much less sensory illusions, depends on a kind of "rudimentary physical science," in Quine's view. The way we understand dreams or illusions depends on our accepting the existence of bodies, *real objects*. And like a lawyer cross-examining a witness who has just brought up a subject, the naturalized epistemologist is now free to "cross-examine" the skeptic about the assumptions the skeptic makes.

---

3   Quine 1969, p. 21.
4   Quine 1969, p. 72.
5   Quine 1975, p. 63; emphases added.

We might have reached a bit of an impasse here. Friends of traditional epistemology think this strategy begs the question against the skeptic: the naturalized epistemologist unfairly *assumes* what is at issue, namely, the "epistemic credibility" of science. The Quinean naturalized epistemologist, however, thinks that skepticism is trying to have its cake and eat it, too! When skeptics rely on dreams or illusions, they are *assuming* the objects of a "rudimentary science." Naturalized epistemology thus claims there's nothing question begging at all, since the skeptic opened the door to this response.

Suppose we follow this path and set aside any worries about the skeptic; how are we to proceed? That is, what does this new naturalized epistemology look like? Quine tells us it is now a "chapter in empirical psychology." But what could this mean?

The central idea is that we are to set aside the project of trying to justify our theoretical beliefs by an appeal to foundational beliefs. Don't try to explain, say, our theories about the nature of light or heat or magnetism by tracing these beliefs back to, and justifying them on the basis of, some set of basic beliefs about what our senses tell us. Instead, we should look to "empirical psychology" to tell us this story—how do we get from what our senses tell us to our more sophisticated beliefs? That is, empirical psychology (now we might think of something like cognitive neuroscience or cognitive science) will show us the causal link from senses to theory. Empirical psychology answers the question "how did I come by this knowledge?" What *cognitive* steps took me from seeing a nail attracted to a magnet to a theory that invokes quarks?

Two other differences between traditional and naturalized epistemology are now apparent. First, the naturalized story is a causal story. That is, modern "brain science"—the family of neurosciences—tells us (not yet completely) how light of certain wavelengths striking the retina leads us to believing "Oh, that's where I left the Santa Claus cup!" It tells us *how*, in the brain, it happened. It does not tell us, however, "And, oh, by the way, since it involved this cortical sheet, this group of neurons, this belief is *justified*." At least not in the traditional sense of "justified" inherited from Descartes.

As noted earlier, scientific justification still remains. We have good reason to claim to know that certain areas of the brain process information about color. But that is "good reason" as science sees it, not the way the "armchair epistemologist" sees it.

But this leads to the second difference. Traditional epistemology is a fundamentally *normative* discipline. It tells us what we *ought* to believe. Yet as a chapter in empirical psychology, naturalized epistemology seems to tell us only what we in fact believe. The normative character of epistemology seems to be lost in Quine's alternative conception. And this leads us to one of the most significant criticisms of naturalized epistemology.

Critics of Quine's naturalized epistemology point to the descriptive character of science and the intrinsically normative character of epistemology. Science describes *what* happens and *how* it happens. But traditional epistemology asks "Should we count these scientific beliefs as justified?"—a question science seems not to address. Jaegwon Kim insists that psychology studies the *causal* relation between the information provided by our senses and our consequent beliefs. But this causal story, which interests the naturalized epistemologist, is not the story of justified or reasonable belief. Yet it is this "justificatory story" that interests the traditional epistemologist.[6] Kim reminds us that Hume gives us a type of causal account of our beliefs: nature has deemed the explanation of our beliefs about the world too important an affair to leave to our meager abilities, so imagination fills in the cognitive gaps. But Hume insists that such causal relations are not justificatory relations. And it is this latter feature that characterizes epistemology, according to Kim. Knowing *how* we come to believe what we do does not yet tell us whether we *ought to* believe the way we do. By emphasizing the descriptive task of something like empirical psychology, naturalized epistemology forsakes its normative ancestry. Naturalized epistemology gives up on the fundamental challenge—explaining why our beliefs are justified. In Kim's view, as for others, an epistemology that is not primarily about this normative task—explaining why our beliefs are justified—has no right to the name. In giving us only an account of "how we got here," how we came to have these beliefs, naturalized epistemology fails to be *genuine* epistemology.

Various responses to this criticism have emerged from the naturalists' side. Quine holds, in opposition to Kim, that science is itself normative. Scientific method, he argues, tells us what we *ought* to believe. Unlike traditional epistemology, however, science has arrived at this method, not by *a priori* reasoning, but by empirical research. For example, we now subject new drugs to "double blind" trial. Neither doctor nor subject knows whether the patient is being given a placebo or the subject drug. And why is this? Because *observation and testing* showed that the doctor knowing which was which biased the results. Scientific

---

6   Kim 1988.

method corrected its own method! In a sense, science "bootstraps" its way into telling us which beliefs are justified: the ones reached through the use of the scientific method. Again, for Quine, all justification is scientific justification.

Other proponents of versions of naturalism have urged that we see the normative aspect of epistemology as depending on natural processes or properties—the properties or processes that science in some sense sanctions. Thus, they, argue, the normative is compatible with the natural. In this way, the evaluative features—the *ought* features—need not be counted as something extra-natural, or non-natural. Epistemology can see these evaluative features as natural because they depend on natural processes or properties. For example, Alvin Goldman's reliabilist account of justification holds that we ought to have those beliefs that are brought about by reliable belief-forming processes. In other words, the evaluative property *is justified* depends on very natural, albeit complicated, physico-psychological belief-forming processes. Determining these processes, in Goldman's view, is a task for cognitive psychology, an empirical, not an *a priori* discipline.[7] This particular example of a naturalized account of the normative aspects of epistemology differs from Quine's, but Goldman and others insist that it still naturalized epistemology.

Three Options

This view of the relationship between the natural and the evaluative leads us to seeing three different ways of thinking of the relation between traditional and naturalized epistemology. These ways as outlined by Richard Feldman are *replacement*, *substantive*, and *cooperative* naturalism.[8] Replacement naturalism holds that our traditional epistemology should be replaced by an empirical discipline, that is, some science or combination of sciences. This is a very strong view of the sort Quine presents.

Goldman's view is an instance of *substantive naturalism*. In this view, there are no extra- or non-natural facts. Epistemic properties or processes are not some distinctive kind, separate from the natural world. *Being justified* or *being rational* or *being evidence for*, or any other epistemic property, are one and all traceable, to or ultimately just, natural processes or properties or facts. Another way to put this is that *being justified* is a property that depends on natural

---

7   Goldman 1986.
8   Feldman 2012.

features. Consider Sara believing that the Northern Cardinal is found in the eastern half of the United States. That belief is justified if it is produced by certain types of *natural* psychological processes, such as vision or deduction (see Chapter 2, "Reliabilism"). Epistemology is not replaced by natural science in this view, but epistemic properties are ultimately natural properties.

Finally, *cooperative naturalism* perhaps sees epistemology as more nearly autonomous from the sciences. Traditional epistemology continues to have its distinctive questions—for example, "In virtue of what are our perceptual beliefs justified?" But the epistemologist will take into account the results of the sciences. These results can influence the nature and direction of epistemological theory, perhaps ruling out or supporting some theory as inconsistent or consistent with scientific findings. Epistemological theory, according to the cooperative naturalism view, must then be *consistent with* science.

While Quine's version of naturalized epistemology might not be widely held, there is no doubt that this conception of epistemology has had significant influence. Theories in epistemology must in some way address the claims of the naturalist. And in some sub-disciplines of epistemology, naturalized epistemology has served as a model for other new interpretations of epistemology, as is seen in the following section.

Feminist Epistemology

Cartesian epistemology paints a picture of the *practice* of knowledge in which the would-be "knower" is an individual, dispassionately pursuing all and only the truths about our world, guided by reason, free of emotion, not worried by historical situation or social context, and free of the influence of values. Recent critics—especially feminist philosophers—argue that this pictured ideal is a bad one, in that it both misrepresents science as it is actually practiced, and is a mistaken and harmful ideal to pursue.

Feminist epistemology comprises several different outlooks and approaches; here we can do no more than sketch its general outlines. In a sense, feminist epistemology begins as a critique of the practice of science. Two principal targets of the feminist critique are the conventional understanding of reason and objectivity, and of their privileged place. Brief outlines of two of the more prominent feminist theories of knowledge conclude this chapter.

Two ideas are worth noting initially. Feminist theorists have emphasized the thought that *gender* should be used as a category for analyzing the pursuit of knowledge and our theories about that pursuit. An explicit concern thus arises concerning androcentrism, the practice of seeing things exclusively from a male point of view, ignoring the activity and concerns of women. Feminist epistemology is thus in part motivated by what it sees as critical reflection on political and power relations, which include the relationship of women to the dominant cultural groups.

A second notion, not wholly unique to feminist epistemology, is that knowledge is social, both in its production and its nature. We will see this idea in a subsequent section. First, we begin with an outline of what Philip Kitcher calls "The Legend."[9]

Traditional Epistemology, Science, and "Knowledge Products"

Feminist theorists objected to aspects of both the institution and practice of science, and consequently to the epistemology they presuppose.

Our commonsense outlook is that science produces—discovers—or gives us knowledge. It is commonly taken as the paradigm for good epistemological practice. A more or less standard account of the scientific production of knowledge has four principal features: (1) this production of knowledge is guided by reason—science is a rational enterprise; (2) science is an individual enterprise; (3) the knowledge enterprise is essentially foundational, meaning there are basic or foundational items of knowledge from which other knowledge proceeds; (4) the "knowledge products" correspond to the world; that is, science leads us to objective truths.

THE "LEGEND"

When scientists adopt a theory, they are *realist* about it. They think the theory describes actual—real—features of the world. Accepting atomic theory is accepting that protons, neutrons, and electrons are part of the world, independently of anyone's theory. And those little atomic and subatomic bits were part of the world long before anyone ever believed in a proton or an electron. Our scientific theories then purport to tell us about *real* natural objects and their features.

These theories—despite their sophistication and "theoretical complexity"—are based on some very basic observations. No one sees an electron, of course. But arriving at the atomic theory, arriving at beliefs about theoretical

9   Kitcher 1993, pp. 3 ff.

objects, begins with the evidences of our senses. We see a piece of litmus paper turn from red to blue; we see a needle point to a number on a counter; we hear the crack of thunder. These elementary observations are the foundations of our scientific knowledge. And we can, it is thought, be certain of these foundations; at least about the foundational elements our knowledge, we couldn't be wrong.

Although a scientist may have colleagues or rivals or both, in this standard account, science is still thought of as an individual enterprise, in two senses. Individuals make discoveries, whether it is Newton describing gravity or two individuals working together, such as Watson and Crick describing the double helix. More importantly, it is individuals who come to have beliefs or adopt a theory. To say that a community of scientists accepts the theory of relativity is only to say that each of the individual scientists of the community has, on the basis of good reasons, accepted the theory.

SCIENTIFIC METHOD AND VALUES

Perhaps the most important aspect of this standard account is the idea that scientific method and reason go hand in hand. The method of science assures us that we will adopt only those theories or hold only those beliefs that are rational; it will prevent the scientist from being misled by superstition, pre-conception, emotion, bias, or external historical or social circumstances.

Here we come across an important consequence—for some, a benefit—of adhering to the scientific method. As long as we follow the method, we can be assured that the results, the knowledge we obtain, are *value-free*. Scientific method embodies only "epistemic values" such as comprehensive truth or being able to explain new things. Science doesn't depend on bias or the attitudes of a particular social class or on the values of a particular culture, or on the values of a particular scientist. Even less does it depend, according to the standard picture, on a scientist's *gender*.

Of course, if the method of science is value-free and objective, its deliverances—the products of scientific method—will themselves be objective. Science discovers empirical truths, truths rationally acceptable by all who will only avail themselves of the scientific method.

This commitment to method brings with it the distinction between the context of discovery and the context of justification. An apple falling on Mr. Newton's head is part of the context of discovery: the set of circumstances that lead to the formation of a hypothesis or theory. But science works—progresses—because of the context of justification, the continued experiments that either support or do not support Newton's conception of gravity. The justification of a hypothesis—its validation—matters. It does not matter how the hypothesis was discovered. And it is the method that tells us how to justify belief, how to justify theory. Notably, testing requires experiment. And experiments produce evidence—value-free evidence.

It is this sketch that the noted philosopher of science Philip Kitcher called the "Legend." And in the Legend, we see a commitment to reason and to objectivity, two of the main critical targets of the feminist critique. This set of beliefs are part of the epistemology of science—that there is a rational method and following that method leads us to objective, value-neutral results.

Objectivity

Objectivity has two dimensions that interest us here. The first is an explicitly epistemological aspect; let us call it "point-of-view independence."

Everyone has a point of view stemming from many things, including a person's historical place and time, the person's experiences, values, and beliefs, all of which lead to "This is the way I look at things; this is what my experience is like." Science, however, and the approach recommended by most of traditional epistemology, is not supposed to be like that. Knowledge is objective; it is from no point of view or, as it is called, "the view from nowhere."[10]

Closely tied to this independence of point of view is a metaphysical supposition: that scientific objectivity is supposed to give us the facts about the way the world actually is. We are not making them up. When we use objective methods, we discover aspects—real ones!—of the world.

Science's commitment to objectivity is criticized on two counts. First, feminist theorists point to cases of "bad science," cases in which research clearly was far less than objective, in which the research failed to live up to the norms of science practiced according to the scientific method. Bias and androcentric values can be found in research design, in the language used in analyzing data and explaining certain phenomena, and in the development of hypotheses. Here are some examples:

· In an often cited essay, the Biology and Gender Study Group illustrate that the language used in describing fertilization of the egg in reproduction is

---

10 Nagel 1989.

hardly "objective," instead relying on stereotypical and biased descriptions of interactions between men and women.[11]

· Studies in primatology mating strategy in recent decades focused only on that of males. As one researcher in the field notes, "No one will ever again be permitted to make pronouncements about primate breeding systems after having studied only one sex or after watching only the conspicuous animals." She also remarks that it is "by now undeniable" that research in various fields has been male-centered.[12]

· In another set of often cited studies researchers noted the impact of male hormones on brain development, but neglected to study the impact of female hormones. Consequently, the study reached unsubstantiated conclusions, such as that males possessed better visual-spatial skills and mathematical abilities.[13]

After examining a range of scientific theorizing and investigation, feminists have come to think that failure of objectivity is widespread in science. Sandra Harding, an American philosopher who has pioneered much of feminist theory, as well as epistemology and philosophy of science, has remarked that "feminist researchers in biology and the social sciences have shown in convincing detail the sexist and androcentric results of research...."[14]

Some feminists go beyond pointing out instances of the failure of objectivity; they deny *the very possibility of purely objective science*. Their claim is twofold. First: Science invariably reflects the values and beliefs of its researchers, and hence the values and beliefs of the social setting of its researchers. Second, the products of science—the theories, the knowledge claims—are not simply reflections of the way the world is, independently of us. Instead, the theories and results of science are *social constructions*.

Social constructivism, like feminist epistemology generally, not only has various manifestations, but it is very controversial. Indeed the "Science Wars" of the 1990s was in part a reaction of some scientists and philosophers against postmodernist and social constructivist views.[15] Constructivism is

---

11   Biology and Gender Study Group 1999.

12   Hrdy 1986, p. 141.

13   Bleier 1986, especially pp. 156 ff.; Nelson and Nelson 1994, especially pp. 502–03; Longino 1990, Chap. 6.

14   Harding 1991, p. 57.

15   See, e.g., Andrew Ross 1996 and Ashman and Barringer 2001 for collections of essays which mostly defend the postmodern and constructivist critique of science.

widely thought to be relativist, rejecting the existence of a mind-independent reality and truth. However, not all constructivists hold this sort of a view. As an example, we might briefly consider Melinda Fagan's view of social constructivism and its relation to scientific practice.[16]

Fagan notes three different ways we might understand the idea of the social construction of scientific knowledge, including the claim that scientific facts and truths are socially constructed. Her focus, however, is that the standards of justification are constructed. She argues that the standards for justification arise from the historical settings in which inquiry takes place and that these standards "develop by means of social structures, interactions, or values."[17] After surveying various alternatives to this constructivist view of justification, she concludes that effective critique of science requires constructivism.

Because the results of experiments don't dictate which theory to hold, if we want to see why scientists accept specific claims, we need to understand the complex interactions that underlie the adoption of particular standards. And part of these interactions are the values, including non-epistemic values, that guide inquiry. As Quine insisted, there is no "deductive proof" that leads from our evidence, our observations, to a theory. There are indefinitely many theories consistent with any particular set of observations. Theory, in other words, is "underdetermined" by evidence. Well, how does the gap between observation and theory get filled? What gets us "over the hurdle" from evidence alone to theory?

Feminist critics of the "Legend" claim that *values* supply the link. But these are not just the traditionally accepted epistemic values. According to the feminist critique, the cultural values of the researchers influence the application of the epistemic values. Various "extra-scientific" beliefs and cultural biases influence the choice of theory.[18] As Ruth Hubbard remarks, "There is no such thing as objective, value-free science."[19] Science then is not value-free; nor will scientific method guarantee objectivity. The idea then that scientific method is value-free is, according to feminist critics (and others), little more than a myth.

Boghossian 2007 and Hacking 2000 are two of the better known and widely cited critiques of postmodernism and constructivism.

16 Fagan 2010.

17 Fagan 2010, p. 97.

18 For other versions of this argument see, e.g., Longino 1990, especially Chaps. 4, 5, 9, 10; Fricker 1994, pp. 95–109.

19 Hubbard 1983, p. 47.

Fagan does not in this essay defend all of constructivism's views, such as the metaphysical claim that reality is socially constructed. Yet she is intent on illustrating the way in which social construction impacts the actual practice of science and its epistemic norms and considers these impacts open to investigation.[20]

As noted above, social constructivist views often claim that scientific facts and truth are reflections of or determined in large part by the categories, values, social relations, and views of a community. Moreover, these social relations can and do differ from society to society and historical setting to historical setting.[21]

Constructivists claim that the concepts we use to describe ourselves and the world reflect our society and its structure. In one sense, of course, this seems uncontroversial. We can only use the conceptual resources available within our particular society and historical circumstance. The claim becomes a bit more controversial when it is understood that the conceptual resources reflect the arrangements and structures in society. The interactions between male and female, between educated and uneducated, between poor and rich, between those in different political classes, determine the ways in which the society conceptualizes itself and the world. This may seem very plausible for concepts like "structural unemployment" or "middle class," but the social constructivist asks us to consider that concepts like "natural" or "factual" or "mental illness" also depend on social structures.[22]

More to the point, concepts like "woman" point not simply to some independent part of the world, but to a complicated set of social relationships:

> [O]ne is a woman, not by virtue of one's intrinsic features (for example, body type), but by virtue of one's part in a system of social relations which includes, among other things, men. Gender is a relational or extrinsic property of individuals, and the relations in question are social.[23]

It is now perhaps easier to see why the constructivist thinks that our concepts refer to objects and properties that *we* have made. Our concepts draw the frames, as it were, through which objects come to be. Social constructivists are not claiming that there is nothing physical or material, that all that exists

---

20 Fagan 2010, pp. 110 ff.
21 E.g., Schutte 1998, pp. 87–95.
22 Hubbard 1999.
23 Haslanger 1993, p. 88.

is our own concepts and ideas. We interact with a real world; we can't make the world do whatever we desire. Yet constructivists claim that the world's objects and properties depend on our concepts and beliefs, and thus in a real sense are structured by us. Of course, these are contentious views, and our current concern is how social constructivism is related to certain aspects of feminist epistemology.

Joseph Rouse, in reviewing the work of feminist author Karen Barad, suggests that according to Barad nature is "normatively constituted." In part this means that nature does not appear wholly independently of our ways of thinking, of our standards, and our concepts. The phenomena to be studied in a sense come to be and are made intelligible through our experimental inquiries.[24]

Louise Antony suggested that some sort of constructivist account lies behind all feminist theorizing.[25] To be sure, some feminist epistemologists seem to endorse a view that is decidedly and avowedly constructivist. Harding, for example, notes that nature never comes to us "naked." We encounter nature only as it is already structured by "social thought." She is even more explicit:

> [I]n fact scientists never can study the trees, rocks, planetary orbits, or
> electrons that are "out there" and untouched by human concerns.... Trees,
> rocks, planetary orbits, and electrons always appear to natural scientists only
> as they are *already socially constituted* for the social scientist.... Scientists never
> observe nature apart from such traditions [discussions by earlier generations
> of scientists].[26]

Not all feminist epistemologists find social constructivism quite as unavoidable. But once the notion of objectivity is challenged in this way—that scientific practice is not objective in the sense that it is value-free—the way is open for the social constructivist.

And Harding too thinks we can attain a kind of objectivity, which she calls "strong objectivity." This "requires that the subject of knowledge be placed on the same critical, causal plane as the objects of knowledge."[27] In her view, the scientists are not exempt from the scientific method. Harding holds that they

---

24   Rouse 2004, especially pp. 150 ff; for a "nonfeminist" account of reality being shaped
      by our concepts, see Schwarz 1986.
25   Antony 2002, p. 471.
26   Harding 1993, p. 64; emphasis added.
27   Harding 1993, p. 69.

too should be subject to the same critical scrutiny that is normally reserved for nature. This scrutiny will reveal the underlying assumptions that scientists bring to their research. Scientists—contrary to the "Legend"—are not and cannot be value-neutral. The best we can do is bring to light the values that guide scientists. In this way we can see the role *social causes* play in science.

We cannot, in the view of many feminist theorists, "turn back the clock." There is no way to screen out the importance and relevance of the social context of inquiry. Still, various theorists, such as Evelyn Fox Keller,[28] worry that treating science *simply* as a social product will mean that science will come to count as little more than a kind of ideology. Such theorists wish to preserve a kind of objectivity as an attainable goal, while also recognizing the different beliefs and values that structure the search for knowledge and the outcome of that search.

Reason

The matter might seem a bit different when it comes to reason, or our capacity to reason. Reason is, after all, a capacity we possess as human beings. Perhaps we learn to reason in a way that need not involve us in the values implicit in our social structure or the social relations that might seem to define us. Indeed the hope that reason can bring us to the truth—an objective truth—depends in no small part on reason being "bias-free."

Feminist theorists again do not have a single view of how gender relates to reason. Yet many share a concern about the nature of reason and how it has been used to support androcentric views. The concept of reason is then sometimes described as a *gendered* concept. To say that a particular notion or concept is a gendered concept is to say that its meaning arises from some social or cultural structure or set of relations, in particular those that reflect relations between sexes, rather than from some "natural" fact or property. Thus, our concepts of male and female might be held as reflective of certain physical features, whereas what properties or features count as feminine or masculine are tied to social or cultural relations.

In one of the early and more important works in this area, Genevieve Lloyd argues that the history of western philosophy and its reliance on reason is a story of an extremely androcentric account of reason.[29] Lloyd's principal

---

28   See, for example, Keller 1985.
29   Genevieve Lloyd 1984.

claim is that "Our trust in a Reason that knows no sex has, I will argue, been largely self-deceiving."[30] Reason, according to Lloyd, is a gendered concept. Most important, masculine bias influences our understanding of "what reason is." Her analysis of Descartes, of course a central figure in modern philosophy, provides a sense of her view.

Initially one might object to the idea that Descartes's view of reason is biased. Didn't he carry on a quite detailed correspondence with Princess Elisabeth? Didn't this correspondence evidence a *woman* very capably discussing metaphysical issues of mind and body, as well as advanced mathematical issues? And Lloyd recognizes that Descartes thought women might employ reason as ably as men. But she also holds that the consequences of his view of reason were not so impartial.[31]

Lloyd thinks there are certain consequences of identifying reason, as Descartes had, as the chief capacity of the nonphysical, incorporeal mind. Aspects of thought that are influenced in some way by the body—the senses, imagination, feeling—are not to be trusted. In a view like Descartes's, reason alone, undistracted by the body, deserves our complete cognitive faith. Reason tells us that body and mind are wholly separable, and that it—reason—is a capacity of the mind. And this insistence, according to Lloyd, already biases the concept of reason in a certain direction.

Lloyd points to the way in which the reality of women's lives, as evidenced in Princess Elisabeth's letters to Descartes, made it difficult for women to participate significantly in the endeavors of science. She also argues that Descartes's insistence on reason untainted by the body as the way to achieve truth—common in Descartes's time and still influential today—reinforced the idea that the reasoning abilities of women are seen as connected with emotion and the sensuous aspects of thought.

This view that women are associated with a less than ideal form of reason is not unique to Lloyd. Sally Haslanger argues that women are seen as guided by emotion or intuition, or worse, as incapable of the kind of abstract and formal thought required by the ideal of reason. She further argues that the fact that the feminine is so often characterized as being in opposition to the ideal of reason suggests that the concept of reason is a gendered notion.[32] Of course, we have not far to look if we want to find examples, whether in scientific

---

30   Genevieve Lloyd 1984, p. x.
31   Genevieve Lloyd 1984, pp. 45–50.
32   Haslanger 1993, pp. 85–125, especially pp. 95 ff.

writings or pop culture. Ruth Hubbard gives several illustrative quotations from Darwin, including this one: "The chief distinction in the intellectual powers of the two sexes is shown by man's attaining to a higher eminence, in whatever he takes up, than can women—whether requiring deep thought, reason, or imagination ..."[33] This idea is presented, in exaggerated parody, in the song "The Hymn to Him," sung by a decidedly biased male in *My Fair Lady*: "Women are irrational, that's all there is to that / Their heads are filled with cotton, hay, and rags ... Why is logic never even tried?"

There are other understandings of reason in our intellectual history. Margaret Atherton argues that the "Cartesian influence" is the other way around: Descartes's view of reason helped shape our concept of masculinity. The ideal man can willingly engage in impartial, abstract thought, or Cartesian reason.[34] Nonetheless, a central point remains: reason is a gendered concept, according to many feminist critics.

As with the concept of objectivity, we see different attitudes toward reason, its nature and status. But this perhaps serves to underscore the general feminist claim that what we have taken for granted, what we have assumed as obvious, objective, or applying to all, needs to be the subject of a critical inquiry.

Two Theories

Postmodern Feminist Epistemology

The term *postmodernism* has its origins in a family of artistic movements, especially in architecture and literature, in the 1960s and 1970s. As the name of a family of philosophical views, the term is often traced to a report, *The Postmodern Condition* (1979), written by Jean-François Lyotard for the Québec government on the technological future; Postmodernism is a critique of "totalizing" views, especially that of science. According to postmodernism, we have inherited from the Enlightenment project the idea that science, guided by impartial reason, provides a unique, privileged perspective from which everything is to be understood. This total perspective is a metanarrative—a narrative about narratives—an overall account of the world, our relation to that world, our relation to each other and our practices and methods. This sort of grand narrative is in a sense "self-certifying": it provides the criteria for determining which claims are acceptable, and these criteria

---

33   Hubbard 1983, p. 55.
34   Atherton 1993, pp. 19–34.

sanction the grand narrative itself. There are no external criteria by which to judge the legitimacy or validity of the grand narrative.

A **postmodern epistemology** rejects the idea that there are any grand narratives or totalizing views, and in doing so, rejects the assumptions and values of traditional epistemology. A postmodern epistemology sees all knowledge as practical: the values and methods manifested in the local, fragmented narratives are values and methods for negotiating one's way in a particular social and historical setting. And negotiation is a practical matter. Moreover, the objects of knowledge are largely constructs of these local narratives. Their nature, their identity, is determined by the particular narrative that is their setting.

This is not to say that the world is wholly imagined or just a compilation of our ideas. There is a world that pushes back against our activity. But the knowledge we gain of this world is very much a localized, narrative knowledge, and we should thus be circumspect of any view that tries to identify an appropriate "standpoint" for theorizing.

Postmodern feminist epistemology agrees that we should abandon the idea of a single meta-narrative that is at once the standard for epistemological adequacy and provides its own justification. But postmodern feminists also suggests that we abandon certain categories, including "women's ways of knowing," as a way of thinking about knowledge. We should abandon traditional epistemology and any view that seeks some category that applies across different narratives or perspectives. And this implies that we have but a plurality of perspectives.[35]

Madan Sarup 1993, Chap. 6, provides a nice summary of the various terms, e.g., modern, modernity, postmodern, postmodernism.

The feminist critique of the notions of objectivity and reason has led to alternative conceptions of epistemology. We can draw our brief survey of feminist epistemology to a close with a quick sketch of two of the more influential conceptions.

Feminist standpoint epistemology, championed by Harding, sees knowledge as the outcome of a social process. Knowledge is itself a social product. More dramatically, feminist standpoint epistemology claims that we must give a privileged position to the understanding and perception of women.

Standpoint theory claims that the starting point of theorizing ought to be women's lives. Not only does this view begin from a different place than

---

35   Anderson 2000/2007.

traditional epistemology, its goal is both different and more modest. The epistemic goal of the tradition was attaining truth or acquiring comprehensive truth while avoiding error. But standpoint theory has a different thought: work to be less biased. Notice the assumption of this new goal—our inquiries are products of our beliefs and values, and we cannot achieve a value-free inquiry. We can, however, be vigilant about trying to identify the assumptions that form the background of that inquiry. Standpoint theory thus sees its aim as the ability to identify and acquire those beliefs that are less distorted by the implicit values and assumptions of the social setting in which they occur.[36]

Feminist naturalized epistemology draws together the lessons of naturalized epistemology and the feminist critique of traditional epistemology. In this view, as in standpoint theory, our inquiry is always situated—it always starts from or within a particular historical and social context. The aim, in this view, is to determine the causes of our hypotheses and theories—what leads us to a given conclusion based on a given body of evidence. This starting point and this aim thus require that the social context and the social values are also part of what science investigates. It is only through this sort of inquiry that we can answer an important empirical question: which of our biases and values serve our inquiries well and which do not? As Louise Antony remarks, "*We must treat the goodness or badness of particular biases as an empirical question.*"[37] Feminist naturalized epistemology thus sees epistemology as an extension of our empirical investigations. It shares this with naturalized epistemology, of course. But it also requires that we see the way in which cultural bias and cultural values affect inquiry; and we are to understand the nature and extent of these precisely by studying them in the same way that we would investigate any other empirical phenomenon.

Feminist epistemology—like other areas of epistemology—is diverse and complex. When it is committed to empiricism, it widens the empiricist outlook into areas not previously considered to be areas of inquiry. In general, it aims to draw our attention to the assumptions of traditional epistemology and what feminists argue are the intrinsic flaws of those assumptions. Our *knowledge* always reflects, according to feminist epistemologists, our cultural and social background, with its implicit values and bias. More specifically, this "situatedness," this value-laden character, influences scientific method and the outcomes of scientific inquiry.

---

36 Harding 1991.
37 Antony 1993, p. 115; emphasis in the original.

Key Concepts

- naturalized epistemology
- naturalism
- androcentrism
- social constructivism
- gendered concept
- postmodern epistemology

Reading/Discussion Questions

1. Can you explain how naturalized epistemology is "naturalistic"? Do you think philosophical theories should be naturalistic?
2. Why does Quine think that naturalized epistemology adequately addresses skepticism? Do you agree with this view?
3. In what sense can feminist epistemology be a "naturalized epistemology?"
4. Why do some feminists think that objectivity and reason are gendered concepts? Do you agree?
5. Can you explain why feminist standpoint epistemology is an example of feminist epistemology? What is your assessment of this view?
6. As the text indicates, Quine is a realist about science, but feminist epistemology, especially as seen in someone like Sandra Harding, stresses the social constructivist nature of our theories. Which of these approaches do you think is more in keeping with naturalism? Which do you think has a better understanding of the nature of science? Why?

For Further Reading

In naturalized epistemology, the seminal text is Quine's "Epistemology Naturalized," in Quine 1969. Another very accessible essay is his "The Nature of Natural Knowledge," in Samuel Guttenplan 1975. Several important essays, including Quine's and Kim's, are collected in Hilary Kornblith 1985. A very nice and accessible survey is James Maffie 1990. The essay not only recounts major themes and perspectives in naturalized epistemology, but it draws a number of important and useful distinctions between views. *A Companion to Epistemology*, edited by Jonathan Dancy and Ernst Sosa, contains several entries relevant to this chapter.

Rosemary Tong 2013 is an excellent overview of feminist thought, and Alessandra Tanesini 1999 is an excellent introduction to feminist epistemology.

A number of the essays noted in the text, along with several others, may be found in Linda Alcoff and Elizabeth Potter, eds. 1993. Sandra Harding 1986 and 1991 are both important moments in feminist epistemology, as is Genevieve Lloyd 1984. Simone de Beauvoir's *The Second Sex*, first published in 1949, is often considered a foundational moment in modern feminism; see de Beauvoir 2011.

For an interesting history of the notion of objectivity, see Lorraine J. Datson and Peter Galison 2010.

CHAPTER FIVE

PERCEPTION

Our most basic information about the world comes from our five senses—touch, taste, smell, hearing, and sight. Our senses tell us about the objects around us—what those objects are, what they are like, what properties or characteristics they have. We smell popcorn as we walk by a store in a mall; we see a cake sitting on the counter; we taste the chocolate in a special truffle; we feel the warmth of the sun on our back; we hear a car door close. Most of us could tell a rather simple story about how this information is conveyed. Take, for example, seeing the cake on the table. Light strikes the cake, some of that light bounces off it, striking our retinas; and that light (or energy) is somehow transformed into signals moving along various passageways in the brain, until finally we have the visual image of the cake.

There are some very basic assumptions in this simple story. First, we take it that there are physical objects. We take physical objects as *independent* of us and as *publicly accessible*. What do we mean by "independent"? Again, consider the cake sitting on the table. Even if no one were around to see the cake, smell it, or touch it, even if no one "sensed" the cake, it would still be there. And the cake is a publicly accessible object: any normally sighted person could see it. A related characteristic, one that is especially important for this chapter, is that the qualities we sense are *in* the object. The simple story has it that if we see dollops of red or green frosting, then that's merely because the dollops of frosting are *really* red or green. The green is part of the frosting, no less than the red is part of the skin of an apple. Were the apple not red or the frosting not green, we wouldn't see those colors. This important point is fully general. These *sensible properties*—the reds and greens, the smells, the textures—they really are *part of* the object. Take observers away—us, with our senses—and those sensible properties would still be there as properties of the objects.

Common sense—our untutored, non-theoretical way of looking at the world—finds all this unremarkable. But according to some, it is very difficult to hold onto this simple story after a little further reflection. In this chapter, we look at this matter in more detail; that is, we will examine the philosophy of perception. Actually, this is a bit misleading, for following a long tradition, we look primarily at but one of our senses—vision—on the assumption that arguments we make about vision can also be applied to the other senses.

Three theories of perception are of interest to us in this chapter: representative realism, phenomenalism, and direct realism. We begin with a version of direct realism called naïve realism—the simple, commonsense narrative of perception—and with the arguments against it. The challenge to naïve realism leads to views such as representative realism and phenomenalism, as well as "less naïve" versions of direct realism.

The Simple Story: Naïve Realism

The simple story—often called naïve realism—has it that we directly perceive physical objects and their properties. Perceiving, as it were, gives us an immediate contact with or awareness of objects and their properties. But what does it mean to say that we "directly perceive" or are "immediately aware" of physical objects?

Perhaps this can be best explained by a couple of examples in which awareness is not immediate. Suppose, as you finish cleaning the kitchen one evening, you note a single piece of pie, which you promise yourself will later make a nice snack. You return a couple of hours later to find only a smattering of crumbs and infer that your roommate has forsaken her diet. Now, you did not actually witness the pie eating, but you are confident that she is the guilty party. Or consider showing a photograph of a sibling and yourself to one of your friends. Clearly, your friend does not actually see your sibling; what she sees is a picture, or a representation, of that person.

In both examples, there is an intermediary of sorts—the crumbs in the first case and the picture in the second. We become aware of the actual thing by first being aware of something else. That is, we infer the occurrence of the event (the eating of the pie) from the crumbs or existence of the object (your sibling) from the photograph. Similarly, arguments against naïve realism hold that "direct" perception is actually not immediate—that, for example, when there's a red apple that you see, you are actually inferring the existence of the apple. You might be wondering what it is that could possibly come between us and the objects we perceive. The answer, which we will see below, may surprise you.

A second feature of naïve realism is that, according to this view, the properties we perceive are located *in* the object. These properties, things such as color, scent, taste, shape, and size, are sometimes referred to as the *sensible qualities* of the object. And the object doesn't "need" us; were no one around to see or smell them, roses would still be red and fragrant; apple pies would still be sweet; silk would still be soft.[1]

Again, this might seem unremarkable to you. Just where else would the sensible qualities be if not in the object? Consider for a moment the sort of reddish tint the sky seems to you to have after you take off sunglasses with a particular color of lens. We understand that the apparent redness of the sky is an artifact of wearing the sunglasses—that is, it's not part of the sky itself. But, despite counterexamples like this, naïve realism is committed to the claim that, normally, sensible properties are not artifacts of the perceptual process; they really are features of the objects we perceive.

These aspects of naïve realism have epistemological significance: if we perceive objects directly, then, normally, if you see a red rose, you are immediately justified in believing that there is a red rose. That is, seeing that the apple is red is sufficient, or provides enough evidence, for believing that there is a red apple. Indeed, this is, according to naïve realism, how we arrive at *perceptual knowledge*. We know that the apple is red because *we see that it is red.*

The reason for the qualifier "normally" is that there are clearly conditions under which seeing something may not yield sufficient justification. You may be too far away, the lighting may not be good, or there may be something

---

1   Crumley 2009, Chap. 10; also Smith 2002, Chap. 1.

wrong with your eyes. So, we might say that under *normal conditions*, if you see an object as having a certain property (the apple is red; the cake has green frosting), then you are immediately justified in believing that there is an object that has that property.

Naïve realism is generally taken to be a form of **direct realism**. Like naïve realism, direct realism holds that we perceive independent and publicly accessible physical objects. But direct realism, as we will use the term here, differs from naïve realism in that it does not hold that physical objects are necessarily what we perceive them to be. The direct realist accepts that science may present facts that are at odds with our prescientific or "naïve" views about the objects we perceive, and thus may alter our view of the nature of the objects of perception. The important point is that direct realists hold that we directly perceive physical objects. (We should note that among philosophers there seems to be no consistent usage of the two terms. Some treat direct and naïve realism as equivalent; others consider naïve realism to be one type of direct realism.)

Naïve Realism—An Illusion?

A family of arguments known as the **arguments from illusion** are designed to undermine the naïve claim that objects possess the sensible properties or qualities that our senses tell us they have, or our commonsense idea that "what you see is what you get." Moreover, illusion arguments are sometimes used to bolster views opposed to direct realism. These views hold that the direct objects of perception are something quite different from the roses, cakes, tables, and chairs we assume them to be.

Bishop George Berkeley (1685–1753) offers a version of an illusion argument. He suggests that you first put one hand in cold water and the other in hot, and then put both hands in lukewarm water. In the lukewarm water you will have two different sensations. The water will seem hot on the hand that was previously in cold water and cool on the hand that was in the hot water. Now, clearly, the water in that container cannot be both cold and hot. The sensible qualities of hot and cold cannot both belong to the water at the same time. Experiments of this general form can be used for other senses, as well.

Berkeley has his own account of perception, which we will see later. Notice, however, the apparent lesson to be drawn from this little experiment. Since one and the same thing cannot be both hot and cold at the same time, and since we are sensing *something*, it would appear that it is not the water that has the properties of hot and cold. The sensible properties don't seem to belong to—they don't seem to be *in*—the water.

Initially, one might think that naïve realism can be saved by appealing to normal conditions and that Berkeley's case is not one in which conditions are normal. Yet other critics of the view have more ordinary cases in mind. The British philosopher Bertrand Russell (1872–1970), for example, drew attention to the fact that one and the same object might yield very different appearances. Looked at from one perspective, a table might appear rectangular, from another somewhat diamond shaped, and from still another as some sort of irregular quadrilateral. From certain angles the table may appear brown, and from others white.[2] Similarly, golfers have learned, even in normal circumstances, that the color or the "look" of the grass can differ according to where one is standing. Intensity of light, too, can make a difference in the color perceived; the grass will look different on a cloudy day, or a sunny one.[3]

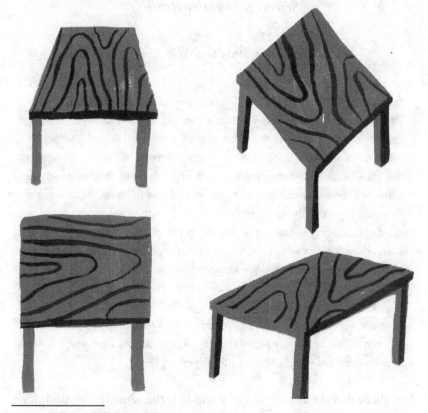

2   Russell 1959, Chap. 1; Smith 2002, Chap. 1.
3   Hardin 1986, especially Chap. 2.

Again, examples such as this are designed to show one thing. Those properties we sense that objects have may not be *in* the objects, since different perspectives yield different sensory properties. Unless we think the object is changing—e.g., that the grass is changing color or the table is changing shape—then we seem forced to draw this conclusion.

Apart from examples like these, specifying "normal conditions" is sometimes problematic. "Normal" doesn't exactly mean "usual." Color scientists, for example, use conditions very much unlike our normal, everyday perceptual conditions in order to identify standard red or standard blue, making use of specialized fluorescent lights for illumination. The color of the water in the harbor is quite different when it's cloudy and when it's sunny. If the harbor weather is cloudy most days, is that "normal conditions" for what the sea color is?

Science and Naïve Realism

Blindsight?

One of the interesting and controversial issues in recent work on perception is the phenomenon of "blindsight." Subjects who are blind in one area of their visual field are presented with a certain stimulus, typically a simple drawing such as an X or an O, in the blind portion of their visual field. Now, the subjects do not claim to be able to "see" the stimulus. However, when they are asked to guess whether there is an X or an O there, their answers are correct considerably above the chance level. Some interpret this to indicate that they have beliefs—perceptual beliefs—even though they do not have the corresponding sensations. A similar sort of phenomenon is reported in some individuals in whom the two brain hemispheres have been partially or completely separated. These individuals cannot say what they are seeing, but they do sometimes have appropriate behavioral responses to the objects before them. As noted, the interpretation of these cases is extremely controversial. But some have suggested that they lend support to the idea that sensations or sensory experiences are not necessary for the acquisition of perceptual beliefs. (See "For Further Reading.")

It might be thought that science could settle whether sensed properties belong to an object, or, in other words, are *intrinsic properties* of the object. Of course, it is the various physical properties of an object that produce in us sensations of red or sweet. But can we equate the shapes of the molecules in the apple with "redness" or "sweetness"? The apple's physical properties are undoubtedly the source of these sensations, but these may not be the properties naïve realism wishes to defend.[4] And what science tells us is that a sensation we have depends in complicated ways on physical properties of the object, plus numerous and variable conditions of sensing, and of the observer. Does that mean that colors, odors, etc., are not really in the object?

A Brief Journey into the World of Sense Data

A historically strong competitor to naïve (and otherwise) direct realism theories claims that we never directly encounter external physical objects in perception; rather we have internal sense-experiences that represent external objects, and from which we infer the existence and nature of externals. This sort of view is indirect realism.

Indirect Realism

Perhaps this will motivate this view for you. Close your eyes for a moment and try to imagine as vividly as you can looking across a valley toward snow-covered mountains. Imagine the vivid greens of the countryside, perhaps the red-tile roofs of buildings, the blues of the sky, and the white, snow-covered peaks in the distance. Perhaps you can even imagine feeling a certain coolness on your skin. Obviously, you aren't perceiving anything; you are merely imagining. But according to some, your "imagining experience" is very much like what happens when you sense some object. When you open your eyes and focus on your actual surroundings, don't think about the objects you see or feel or the events you hear. Focus—or try to—instead only on the sensations, on the colors, the sounds, the felt qualities. In the early twentieth century, these sensations were called *sense data*. Sense data are thought of as what we are immediately or directly aware of in the perceptual process—they are the internal images we have (typically) when we are perceptually encountering external objects. To give perhaps a better idea of what is meant by the term, here is how Bertrand Russell characterized it in 1912:

---

4   Robinson 1994, Chap. 3; the text combines two separate arguments.

Let us give the name of "sense-data" to the things that are immediately known in sensation: such things as colors, sounds, smells, hardnesses, roughnesses, and so on. We shall give the name "sensation" to the experience of being immediately aware of these things. Thus, whenever we see a color, we have a sensation of the color, but the color itself is a sense-datum, not a sensation. The color is that of which we are immediately aware and the awareness itself is a sensation.[5]

Sense data prove to be difficult entities to define. But Russell tells us two things about them: they are what is immediately known in sensation, and they seem to be the familiar sensible properties—colors, sounds, smells, etc. Sensation is an awareness, Russell tells us, an awareness of sense data or sensible properties. This process is sometimes described as *sensing sense data.* We are, it's claimed, immediately aware of sense data, before we become aware of our familiar objects. I am immediately aware of the red sense datum, for example, not the red candle.

Theories that invoke sense data are varied; still some features are constant among them. First, sense data theories typically divide the perceptual process into two parts, which we can call *sensing* and *perceiving.* The first part of the process, at least logically (and in some views, temporally) is sensation, in which we encounter sense data. The second part of the process we might call perception proper. It is here that we can be said to perceive objects, but we seem to do so *indirectly.* We perceive objects, e.g., the candle or the cake, by means of the sense data. Notions of how exactly such perception occurs, and in exactly what it consists, vary.

A second aspect of such theories is that sense data are typically counted, though not uncontroversially, as *mental objects.* Sense data are thus mind-dependent. Were there no minds, there would be no sense data.

One further aspect can be mentioned here. Some hold that there is a distinction between the experience or sensation which is *unconceptualized,* and the consequent classification or categorization of the experience as a certain type of object. In this view, sensation gives us "unclassified" information, whereas in perception that information is classified or organized, so that we can then be said to *perceive* some type of object or property.

To illustrate this, imagine there is a red book on your table. In sensation, in the first stage of the perceptual process, all you have is a red, rectangular

---

5   Russell 1959, p. 12.

patch surrounded by other color patches of various shapes. You haven't yet categorized or classified these sense data as being books, tables, computer printers, cardboard boxes, or gifts from admirers. All you have at the level of sensation are the different sense data. Only when you draw on the concepts or ideas that you have learned and begin to identify the red patch as a book, the gray patch as a printer, the white patch as a gift, and so on, do you get objects. According to this line of thinking, perception is the conceptualization of our sensory experience.

The existence of sense data is a matter of some dispute. The main objection to sense data theories turns on the difficulty of specifying the nature of sense data: What kind of things are they? Whether we count them as purely physical items or as mental, non-physical items, it's hard to understand how they have their alleged *sensory* properties. If we take them as physical, they would seem to be some aspect of the brain, some brain state. But brains aren't colored red and they don't have the taste of cake. On the other hand, if we think of these sense data as somehow "non-physical," matters seem even worse. How could something non-physical have a color or a taste? We will leave aside this complex question of the nature of sense data, however, since it is time to consider two prominent theories of perception.

Accounts of perception address two important questions. First, what is the connection between our sensations and the properties that objects actually possess? Second, can this connection tell us anything about what we are justified in believing about the world around us? If we only have *immediate* access to our own mental experiences of sensory information, how do we ever *justifiably* get from in here, in the mind, to knowledge of what's out there, in the world? Do we get back to our physical objects as we ordinarily think of them?

Representative Realism

Representative realism is the view that our sensations somehow represent external objects, and we are immediately aware only of the sensations. Those objects cause us to have the sensations—we have the sensations *because of* the objects—and it is via these sensations that we know of the objects. Our perception of objects is thus indirect. Hence, representative realism is a kind of indirect realism. Because it is also a causal view, it is also known as the *causal representative theory*.

We begin with a version of representative realism presented by John Locke. Our primary interest here is to present the general outlines of this view, using

Locke (1632–1704) as a point of departure. Later, we will see how Locke's view might be generalized to give us a more contemporary version of representative realism. Though some have questioned whether he in fact subscribed to this view, it is still widely held that Locke supported it and thus can serve as a kind of model of representative realism.

Primary and Secondary Qualities

What Color Is That?

*"We once asked a scientist who performs research on color vision why people think that most opaque objects have a **real** color. His answer was, 'They do? How odd.'"*[6]

Common sense is typically *realist* about colors. Colors are out there in the world, belonging to objects, *and* there is a right answer to the question, "But what color is it *really?*"

Bulls do not see that cape being waved at them as red. They are color-blind. Man's best friend sees mostly grey, but also some blues and yellows. But we take that as a reflection of their limited capacity, not of ours. Or, a little more precisely, we take it that such creatures are simply unable to detect the real colors of things. On the other hand, birds see red, green, and blue, plus ultraviolet light, invisible to humans.

It turns out that there are a number of different views about color. Some philosophers, for example, argue that there are no colors at all, while others claim that there really are colors, but *no one right answer* to the question "What color is that?"

One type of *realism* identifies the color of an object with its reflectance properties, that is, the nature of the light reflected from the object. The conversation between critics and defenders of this view is ongoing.

Representative realism is a type of *relativism* about color—the color of something is determined by the physical circumstances, the object, and the unique type of sensory mechanisms of the perceiver. Locke's view is sometimes considered a type of *dispositionalism*—objects have a power, a tendency, a disposition to cause perceived colors. Berkeley's view could be considered an instance of *phenomenism*, the view that color properties are just special sorts of mental properties.

---

6   Boghossian and Velleman 1991, fn. 23; emphasis added.

Eliminativism holds that there is nothing in objects that could be identified with color; in such a view, our ordinary color terms do not refer to anything real.

Perhaps *pluralism* is one of the more intriguing options—things are colored, but there is no one right answer to the question, "What color is that?" In a sense, this is a kind of realist view; but it says that there's more than one right answer to the question. Eli Mark Kalderon notes that color pluralists can avail themselves of an argument from analogy: just as there is interspecies variation—the colors dogs see and the colors we see—so there is the possibility that Norm and Norma perceive different colors—and *both are right*.

Various further issues arise here, but perhaps this is enough to suggest the intriguing possibilities of the different views. Kalderon's 2007 essay examines several different views, and at length explains the defense of pluralism.

Three brief quotations from Locke's *Essay Concerning Human Understanding* will serve to get us started. The first quote presents us with Locke's official doctrine concerning the use of two important terms:

> Whatsoever the mind perceives in itself or is the immediate object of perception, thought or understanding, that I call *idea*; and the power to produce any *idea* in our mind, I call *quality* of the subject wherein the power is.[7]

For Locke, the immediate objects of perception are *ideas*, not objects or their properties. (Today we might instead talk of sensations rather than of perceiving ideas. But Locke speaks of perceiving ideas, notably in Book II, Chapter viii, Section 8 of the *Essay*.) Thus, if we are to be able to perceive objects, such perception will clearly have to be indirect. Locke also sees a causal connection between the objects and our ideas: objects have the power to cause ideas in us. And this power Locke calls *quality*. So, a quality is the power of an object to cause ideas in us. Locke has in mind two kinds of quality: primary and secondary. Although this distinction was not original with him, it plays a pivotal role in Locke's view:

> *The ideas of primary qualities* of bodies *are resemblances* of them, and their patterns *do really exist in the bodies themselves*; but the *ideas produced* in us by these *secondary qualities, have no resemblance* of them at all.[8]

---

7   Locke 1975, Bk. II, Chap. 8, Sect. 8; emphasis in original.
8   Locke 1975, Bk. II, Chap. 8, Sect. 15; emphasis in original.

Primary qualities are thus in the objects, and our sensations in fact resemble them. Secondary qualities are the powers of objects to produce in us certain sensations, specifically sensations of color or taste or feel. But our sensations do not resemble those secondary qualities.

Interestingly, the primary qualities—solidity (impenetrability), extension (takes up space), figure (shape), motion or rest, and number—are just the sort that could be treated by a quantitative science. Locke regards primary qualities as inseparable from the objects—that is, whatever change an object undergoes, Locke thinks it will still have some shape and size. So, an object's particular shape (figure) may change, but there is no shapeless object, nor is there an object that is neither at rest nor in motion. Locke makes a further important claim: our ideas caused by the primary qualities are "resemblances" of those qualities themselves.

This last point is important. Locke is saying that our ideas of primary qualities tell us something about properties that are actually in the object. When I see a round penny, roundness is a feature of the penny itself. When I have the sensation or idea of a running puppy, motion is part of, is in that object. When Deirdre stubs her toe against the rock, her idea of solidity "resembles" the rock's solidity.

Two questions arise here. Does Locke have a good reason for thinking that the ideas of primary qualities *resemble* some feature or property of the object? Do our ideas of secondary qualities resemble the objects? Deirdre's idea of solidity resembles the rock, according to Locke, but does her pain resemble anything in the rock? Or, Deirdre's idea of the roundness resembles the apple, but does her idea of the redness resemble the apple?

Locke's answer to this second question is "no." Our ideas of secondary qualities—colors, tastes, scents, sounds—do not resemble the objects themselves. In fact, Locke claims that secondary qualities are "nothing in the objects themselves but powers to produce various sensations in us by their primary qualities."[9]

When we have ideas of the primary qualities, we know, in Locke's view, what the object is like in itself. The primary qualities of an object can "combine" in certain ways to produce in us other types of sensations or ideas, sensations that in no way resemble the object. Just as the pain that is produced when we cut ourselves in no way resembles the knife, so the fragrance of the rose in no way resembles the actual makeup of the rose.

---

9   Locke 1975, Bk. II, Chap. 8, Sect. 10.

Perhaps Locke's view can be explained by a simple and more or less familiar scientific story. When we catch the scent of the rose, what has happened?
Certain molecules of the rose "broke off," mixed with the molecules of the
air, struck our sensory surfaces, and set off a physiological process, which
results in our sensation, the scent of the rose. (Locke of course did not know
of molecules, but he guessed that "insensible particles" were involved here.)
Yet the scent itself bears no obvious resemblance to the molecular structure
that is the impetus for our sensation. A lemon tastes sour, we learn, because
of the structure of the "lemon molecules" and the physical structure of our
gustatory system ... our taste buds. The "sour" sensation tells us nothing about
what to expect from the lemon *as it is all by itself,* in Locke's view. So, our ideas
of secondary qualities do not resemble the objects. Rather they are a reflection
of interaction of the physical structure of the objects and our own sensory
system. We can't count on our ideas of the secondary qualities to reflect the
way objects really are.

If we can't count on our ideas of secondary qualities to reflect the real
properties of objects, why should we trust our ideas of primary qualities?
This next brief passage lays out the somewhat difficult task of answering this
question:

> It is evident the mind knows not things immediately, but only by the interven-
> tion of the ideas it has of them. Our knowledge, therefore, is real, only so far
> as there is conformity between our ideas and the reality of things. But what
> shall be here the criterion? How shall the mind, when it perceives nothing but
> its own ideas, know they agree with things themselves?[10]

The first sentence of this passage is a clear statement of representative realism.
And the previous two passages have made it clear that this representative
realism is a causal view. But Locke himself recognizes the most difficult question such a representative view must face. First: What justifies the primary/
secondary quality distinction? Why think that primary qualities resemble the
ideas they cause in us, but secondary qualities do not? But the more general
problem it faces is this: Why think that either of these sorts of ideas give us
any knowledge of the actual objects which they are supposed to represent?
We suppose that all sensation-ideas are caused by external properties (which
may or may not resemble them), but where can we get any justification for

---

10   Locke 1975, Bk. IV, Chap. 4, Sect. 3.

that supposition? Why are we not locked forever only in the web of our own ideas or, as some have characterized it, behind a veil of perception?

A Lockean Response or No Way Out?

Locke thought that he could answer both of these questions. He draws our attention to the apparent fact that our ideas, our sensations, of primary and secondary qualities seem to be *contravolitional*, that is, imposed on us against our will. As such, they do not seem to be caused by our own minds, so they must be caused by something external to our minds—namely, the objects to which our sensations refer.

Having established the notion of an external object as the causal source of ideas, Locke thinks that we can make sense of the further supposition that these ideas, in some way, "conform to" or "agree with" the objects. That is, the fact that on one occasion we may have the idea of red and on another blue can be explained by different qualities of objects producing these different effects. In other words, Locke supposes that different sensations come about, or are caused by, different features of an object.

This makes some sense. If at one time I taste coffee and it tastes "normal," but a few minutes later I detect a noticeable sweetness that was not there before, I might reasonably conclude that something has changed about the coffee. This fairly simple inference can be thought to be at work in Locke: distinct sensations are caused by distinct features of the object.

But the problems remain. The causal inference is dubitable. After all, we can infer from the existence of X that its cause Y must exist, only if we have experience of X's coming about because of Y's. But in this case, for Locke, there is only experience of internal ideas, never of their causes. Similarly: because we perceive only our own ideas, how can we ever determine that any of our ideas resemble their objects? Resemblance or conformity is *a claim about a relationship that is external to our ideas*. You can find out that a portrait of Sara resembles her by looking at the portrait and looking at her. But in the case Locke is talking about, all that's available to us for inspection is one of the two things.

Recall that we are interested in answers to two questions: We want to know something about the nature of the objects of our perception, *and* we want to know what sort of justification we have for our perceptual beliefs. To the first, Locke gives an answer that we can make some sense of and that has tempted many. We are directly aware of only our own sensations. Further,

Locke gives us at least the outline of how we might view physical objects as the source of those sensations, as what the sensations are sensations *of*. The problem, however, is that we are left without any justification for the claim that we are at least indirectly perceiving physical objects. Once we confine ourselves to only what's inside our heads, there is no way to get outside.

Science to the Rescue?

Despite the difficulties associated with Locke's representative realism, the framework has not been abandoned. There are some who think that the merits of representative realism outweigh its defects. Contemporary representative realists hold that scientific theory can help to fill out the causal story outlined by Locke. Though ordinary physical objects are not directly encountered in perception, this view suggests, they are inferred from our sensations and the theoretical—the scientific—framework that explains those sensations.[11]

Let's remind ourselves first of how science frequently works. Scientists postulate the existence of *unobserved* phenomena, which have certain properties that explain observed effects. Electrons—unobserved—explain electricity; chemical bonds explain the rigidity of ice and the liquidity of water; heat is explained by the rapid movement of molecules. Scientists *infer* the existence of some type of object or process to explain what we observe. Contemporary particle physicists do not directly observe subatomic particles; yet they rely on them to explain observed effects. Appealing to these unobserved "objects" allows us to predict consistently over a wide range of circumstances what other sorts of phenomena we might observe.

Could we use something like this method of inference to overcome the difficulty encountered in Locke's version of representative realism? Suppose that our ideas of primary qualities—shape, motion, and the like—could be quantified, and then suppose they could be used to make predictions about our future experiences. Using these primary qualities, we could make predictions about other ideas that we might subsequently come to have.

So it seems that the supposition that external objects exist could be tested—if only in a roundabout sort of way. As science performed its task, it would tell us what sorts of ideas or sensations we should expect if physical objects are the sort of thing we think they are. As we've noted previously, our rudimentary knowledge of some of the sciences—physics, optics, and the like—gives us

---

11   Maclachlan 1989, Chap. 10; also Mackie 1976, Chap. 2.

just such a story of our perception of physical objects. Physical objects disrupt light waves, for example, and this results in our having certain kinds of visual sensation. What Locke surmised turns out to be correct according to this story: different kinds of sensations are correlated with different kinds of objects. I see a red book instead of a blue book precisely because the red book selectively reflects light waves in a (complex) way different from a blue book. I taste a certain sweetness when eating chocolate but a certain tartness when biting a lemon because of a difference in the kind of object. The difference in each case is also due to the structure of my sensory apparatus, but this is as much a part of the story as the inferred structure of the objects.

Although details may vary, a general form of this view is discernible. Here is a passage from a book on perception that gives us some sense of the general outline of the view:

> Well, suppose we seem to see a table. How do we get to the table? The first step in bridging the relevant epistemic gap seems to involve referring that sensation [seeming to see a table] to an external cause. But if my earlier arguments were correct, belief in the table's existence involves far more than belief in the existence of a cause of that sensation. Rather it involves belief in the existence of something occupying a place in a complex nomological network, something that underlies and explains not a sensation in isolation but complex connections between possible sensations.[12]

Several of the points we have been making about representative realism are apparent here. In the first instance, we have a sensation or Locke's "idea," the "seeming to see a table." And, quite obviously, an important epistemological gap must be bridged *before* we can justifiably claim we see a table. Just how is this to be done? By invoking a belief—a hypothesis—about objects governed by a "complex nomological network"—a system of objects that behave according to a set of interlocked physical laws Relying on these laws we are able to make predictions about the way in which all the various sensations we have, as well as possible sensations we could have, are connected. The existence of external objects like tables is thus inferred from our sensations, relying on the theory that explains them. In this sense, our familiar objects turn out to be not all that much different philosophically from other kinds of objects like molecules, neutrons, and magnetic fields. All are underwritten by belief in a vast, very complicated causal story.

---

12   Fumerton 1985, p. 176.

We can quickly mention two kinds of reaction. The first challenges the idea that we are only immediately aware of our own sensations, rather than being immediately aware of external, physical objects. This response questions the idea that, somehow, we initially view our sensations *only*, and from these private viewings construct the world of objects and properties with which we are most familiar. Instead, a critic of representative realism might suggest that we perceive objects first, and only afterward can deconstruct this perception into separate sensations.[13]

Representative realism might also raise a question about the relation between our familiar objects and properties and the objects and properties discovered by science. The *real* world, for Locke, is a world of objects that have only what he called bulk, figure, texture, and motion. Similarly, the world of contemporary physics is a world that lacks Locke's secondary qualities. The scientific world eliminates the properties that fill up so much of our familiar world. As I look across at the boulder-strewn hill outside my window, I see expanses of shades of green, gray, brown, red, and blue; I hear the sounds of cars and the bark of a dog; I catch the scent of the late spring bloom. But the scientific story that might save Locke and his representative realist kin takes the qualities that fill our experience of the world and replaces them with forces, particles that are nothing like the matter we encounter, and, mostly, empty space.

The difficulty seems to be this: representative realism might leave us without knowledge of anything more than our own experiences. We are seemingly rescued from this by appealing to a kind of scientific theorizing. The main leap here is from the existence of our sensations to any sort of external cause; but if that is scientifically justified, as the best explanation of what we sense, then the more familiar scientific enterprise of telling us what that external world is, in itself, can take over. But the world that science restores seems very much unlike our familiar world—and some might protest that it is this familiar world that we were hoping to secure.

Phenomenalism

Both naïve and representative realism seem to leave us with certain difficulties. Our direct realist inclination is that we perceive our familiar objects directly. Naïve realism seems unable to explain how that might work, and representative realism seems to say, at most, that those objects are indirectly perceived, but runs into a skeptical problem about what they're really like, or

---

13   Heil 1983, p. 70.

even if they really exist. A very different approach might occur to us, however. Maybe the best way to "save" our familiar objects is to say that objects are nothing but our ideas! All there is to an object is our sensations. This view is known as phenomenalism. (The name derives from a philosophical term for our sensations: "phenomena.") It claims that all we are ever directly aware of are our own sensations. And since objects are nothing but our sensations, then ... we are directly aware of objects! At first glance, phenomenalism can seem not phenomenal, but incredible. Yet it has had some interesting defenders through the centuries, including some scientists.

There are two main versions of phenomenalism. The first identifies physical objects with our sensations and thus holds that it makes no sense to think of physical objects existing independently of minds. So, objects are mind-dependent. This we will call *factual phenomenalism*. A second version of phenomenalism is *linguistic* or *analytic phenomenalism*. In this view, our ordinary talk of external, physical objects is but a kind of abbreviation or shorthand way of talking about sense data. Unlike factual phenomenalists, linguistic phenomenalists need not deny the mind-independence of physical objects. Rather, linguistic phenomenalists are making a claim about the meaning of our talk about physical objects. Interestingly, elements of both these views can be seen in George Berkeley's writing, along with a dose of theism. As we did with Locke, we use Berkeley's view as a departure point for a broader consideration of phenomenalism.

Berkeley's Factual Phenomenalism

Why might anyone be tempted by factual phenomenalism? After all, what could be more obvious than that objects are *not* dependent on us, much less that they are not just groups of sensations or ideas? The phenomenalist, however, wants us to slow down a moment and think about how we really conceive of physical objects.

So, think about any arbitrarily selected physical object. The phenomenalist claims that we are likely to cite exclusively its sensible properties. This is our principal cognitive grasp of the notion of a physical object—its sensible properties. Now, peel away these properties, one by one. Take away the sensible properties—take away what we sense or what is in principle sensible—and we are left with something that looks a lot like, well ... nothing. There is nothing to our idea of "object" other than these sensible properties.

Our only understanding of a physical object thus hinges on identifying it with its sensible properties. And the inference now comes rather easily: sensible properties depend on some mind or other; physical objects are nothing but these sensible properties (our ideas or sensations); so, physical objects are mind-dependent. A physical object exists then only to the extent that it is an idea (or complex of ideas) in the mind of some perceiver.

Neither Berkeley nor phenomenalists in general deny the *reality* of what we normally refer to as physical objects. My computer is real, just as is the book you are currently reading. Berkeley instead denies that an object could exist independently of its being perceived. In particular, Berkeley argues that any claim we could make about an object existing independent of perception would make no sense. This is because, when we talk about a physical object existing, we can only mean something quite specific: in Berkeley's view, physical objects are simply complexes of sensed qualities. As Berkeley phrases it,

> [I]t seems no less evident that the various sensations or ideas imprinted on the sense ... cannot exist otherwise than in a mind perceiving them.... The table I write on, I say, exists, that is, I see and feel it; and if I were out of my study I might perceive it, or that some other spirit actually does perceive it.... Their *esse* [Latin: *to be*] is *percipi* [Latin: *to be perceived*], nor is it possible that they should have any existence out of the minds or thinking things which perceive them.[14]

We see here one of the reasons why Berkeley held that his phenomenalist view is much more in line with the view of the ordinary person than is the representative realist's view. In that view, objects are perceived only indirectly. In the phenomenalist view, however, since we perceive our sensations directly and since objects are just complexes of sensations, we perceive objects directly. Berkeley agrees with the naïve realist on this score! He differs from the naïve realist, however, in that he denies the existence of a mind-independent matter. He denies its existence because he thinks it would put objects outside our grasp; mind-independent matter leads to skepticism, in Berkeley's view. We could never know about such mind-independent matter because all we know are our own sensations. This he thinks is the obvious lesson of Lockean representative realism.

---

14   Berkeley 1965, I, Sect. 3.

Still, Berkeley's factual phenomenalism puts him at odds with the commonsense view. Although he does not deny the existence of our ordinary everyday objects, he clearly denies that these could exist independently of being perceived. In Berkeley's view, physical objects are simply complexes of sensible qualities, or in more modern terminology, sense data or sensations. (We can continue to call them "physical objects." As complexes of sensible qualities, they are ideas. There is disagreement over whether they are basically "mental" in nature.[15]) But the commonsense view, of course, holds mind-independence to be a necessary feature of external, physical objects. And this raises questions for the phenomenalist, to which Berkeley offered some interesting answers.[16] Here we consider two.

It might be thought that for the phenomenalist, reality appears all too dreamlike. What's the difference between these mind-dependent objects and just a bunch of ideas in our heads, as we see in dreams? Berkeley responds that reality is distinguished from dreams in the same way we normally distinguish fact from fiction—by the stability and orderliness of those complexes of ideas we call *real*. Indeed, this stability and orderliness are what science studies—what gives rise to our ability to predict that one type of sequence of sensations will most likely be followed by another type.

While this may seem a bit reminiscent of the representative realist's position, Berkeley doesn't think of causes in the same way. According to Berkeley, causes and effects are only the regular succession of types of sequences of sensations. Fire does not *cause* pain, nor does my pounding on the table *cause* noise. The fire and the pounding are merely signs—signs of the pain and the noise to follow. For Berkeley, both these signs and that which they signify are authored—caused—by God.

It is worth noting that Berkeley claims that things—or collections of ideas—continue to exist, even though we may not currently sense them because those things are nonetheless perceived by some other spirit, and he remarks in various places that "things" continue to be perceived by God.[17]

---

15   Compare, for example, Luce 1941 and Foster 1985.
16   Berkeley 1965, I, Sects. 16, 36, and passim.
17   Berkeley 1965, *Dialogues*, III, 5; for a complex view of God sustaining things, see Mabbott 1931.

God in the Quad

The theistic philosopher would happily agree with the following limerick, written by Msgr. Ronald Knox, plus the reply following it, which Knox jokingly attributed to "Anonymous."

There once was a man who said: "God
Must think it exceedingly odd
If he finds that this tree
Continues to be
When there's no one about in the Quad."

Dear Sir,
Your astonishment's odd;
I am always about in the Quad;
And that's why the tree
Will continue to be,
Since observed by
Yours faithfully,
God.

(First published in Langford Reed, *The Complete Limerick Book* [1924].)

This leads, however, to perhaps the deepest problem for factual phenomenalism. In Berkeley's view, there are no unperceived objects or complexes of ideas because God perceives all. But suppose one wishes to dispense with this theistic phenomenalism. (Berkeley did not—he was, after all, a bishop.) How might a factual phenomenalist explain unperceived objects or properties without theological backing? How might the phenomenalist explain, for example, the existence of dinosaurs, which existed when nobody was around to be looking?

Berkeley asked a somewhat similar question. What sense, he asked, might be given to the statement "the earth rotates"?[18] (It was widely agreed in Berkeley's day that the earth rotates, but obviously no one had yet perceived its rotation.)

---

18   Berkeley 1965, I, Sect. 58.

Berkeley's suggestion is intriguing. Suppose you were transported to a certain place in the heavens. Then you would have the perceptual experience of the earth rotating. The fact that you *could* perceive the earth rotating is proposed as sufficient for the earth's rotation to exist—that is, "God" is replaced with the possibility, *in principle*, of someone witnessing the rotation of the earth. Dinosaurs roamed much of the earth, yet no one sensed them. In what sense are they real? In principle, had one been located at a certain place at a certain time in some part of Montana, one would have sensed a dinosaur.

Now, this seems a plausible response. But it is suggested that the phenomenalist faces a difficulty with this answer. This "place" or "location" that will allow us to sense these objects or phenomena—does the place or location itself need to be perceived in order for it to exist? And if that's true, don't we need to conceive of still another place from which to perceive the first? Of course, this question about places or location could go on for some time. In fact, it is claimed that either we must appeal to some mind-independent place, or we are caught in an unending regress of "locations."[19]

As noted, Berkeley provides responses to a number of potential objections; he thinks in doing so that he provides an adequate defense of a view of perception that avoids both skepticism and atheism. Factual phenomenalism may still seem outlandish, yet Berkeley may have succeeded in removing some of the "incredible" aspects that critics attack. Some of Berkeley's remarks can also be considered to suggest linguistic phenomenalism. In the early part of the twentieth century, a number of philosophers took this latter view quite seriously; we turn to it briefly.

Linguistic Phenomenalism

Recall that linguistic phenomenalism is a view about the meaning of terms employed in our accounts of perception. Our references to objects are nothing more than a shorthand way of talking about our sensations. The central tenet of linguistic phenomenalism then is that, in principle, we could take all the references to physical objects and "translate" them into terms or sentences that mention only sensations. Any time I refer to an object, such as a table or a pencil, I could, in fact, simply describe the succession of sensory states I had during a certain span of time. Moreover, this succession of sensory states is all that there is to my talking about, say, the pencil on the table.

---

19   Fumerton 1985, Chap. 5.

In some ways, we might find this even more "incredible" than factual phenomenalism. How is it that all this time—eons and eons, to exaggerate a bit—we thought we were saying one thing, but really meant another? It was in part inspired by a view about science, about how it works and how it should work. Linguistic phenomenalists were impressed by the idea that in scientific theory, one term or a phenomenon could be "reduced" or explained in terms of other terms. "Heat," as we mentioned earlier, gives way to versions of "motions of molecules." In a parallel way, this type of phenomenalism drew on sensations as the logical and epistemological building blocks for our notion of objects; hence, references to physical objects were really about references to sensations, so statements about physical objects could be reduced to statements about sensations.

An obvious difficulty soon appears: no one has ever provided a hint about how, in general, to meet the requirements of linguistic phenomenalism! No one has told us the general procedure for "translating" all our references to physical objects into "sensation talk." How could we? Imagine: here's a banana. What sequences of sensations are to be associated with it? Oh, of course, the obvious ones, like yellow and slightly curved. This cannot be all, however. We sometimes mash bananas, split them and make banana splits out of them, slip on them; Andrea might even be exasperated with Andy and bash him with a banana! So, just what are the sensations that are to be associated with "banana"?

Roderick Chisholm captures the essence of these worries in a more rigorous way. He offers the example of "There is really a door in front of me." Presumably, this sentence implies that if I had certain kinds of visual experiences, then I would have certain kinds of tactile experiences (if I saw my hand reaching for the doorknob, I would then have the feeling of touching the doorknob). But this "prediction" need not actually come about. As Chisholm points out, I may be the victim of certain perceptual abnormalities, such that when I have certain visual sensations, my tactile sensations are somehow blocked or altered.[20] Of course, other theories of perception must worry about such abnormalities. But linguistic phenomenalism claims, unlike the other views, that "There is a door in front of me" *implies* certain sensation statements. And that is a very different claim than that made by other views.

20   Chisholm 1957, Appendix.

Linguistic Phenomenalism and the Skeptic

Linguistic phenomenalism was a popular theory among some epistemologists in the early and middle twentieth century. It is not difficult to see why. Suppose for a moment that one accepts the skeptic's challenge of showing how, on the basis of our sensory experiences, we could arrive at our beliefs about the world, which typically involve reference to physical objects and their properties. Linguistic phenomenalism promises that reference to physical objects is nothing more than reference to a set of sensory states, perhaps a complicated set. We could "rationally reconstruct" our claims about the physical world by providing the linguistic equivalents of such claims.

Thus, we would have sufficient evidence for our beliefs about the world—and a reply to the skeptic—because such beliefs are simply shorthand ways of talking about our sensory states. Indeed, as Berkeley claimed, one advantage of his phenomenalist view is that it avoids the skepticism engendered by representative realism.

Of course, the difficulty lies in showing how to create such a reconstruction. It is very difficult to explain how we might take all of our references to objects—our ordinary talk about cars and Cadbury eggs, about tigers and tables and Twix bars, about rocks, raccoons and rocky road ice cream—and "translate" or "reduce" all of those ordinary sentences into very complicated sentences that use only sensory terms.[21]

This worry of Chisholm's points to still another worry. When Chef Andrea sends Andy out to fetch some bananas for tonight's dessert, we normally think—our commonsense view is—that she is talking about an actual existing clump of objects. Yet no sentence or set of sentences describing sensations seems to imply the existence of some object. That is, our talk about physical objects seems to imply something that our talk about sensations does not.

Reviving Direct Realism

Facing the difficulties of representative realist and phenomenalist views, the latter part of the twentieth century has seen attempts to move away from reliance on internal mental states as the direct objects of perception and to recapture the core insights of direct realism, but without the apparent defects of naïve realism. Two kinds of direct realist view have been especially prominent.

---

21   Crumley 2009.

Adverbial Theory

Adverbial theory attempts to recapture the idea that we see or perceive objects directly. But it also wants to retain the idea that our sensations or sensory experience plays a key and basic role in our seeing or perceiving objects. The fundamental thought of the adverbial theory is this: We see objects by experiencing them in a certain way. Sensations are not themselves objects of awareness, but rather are *ways of being aware* of physical objects. Compare: when we run fast, "fast" is not the name of something we do, but rather a way we do something—running. So "fast" here is an adverb.

A simple example will help illustrate. I sit with my keyboard across my lap, and I see a blue book on the desk. Like most books, this book has a generally rectangular shape. But because of my particular perspective at the moment, the shape of the book seems to me a bit more diamond-shaped. That is, the kind of visual experience I am having is in part characterized by its "diamond-shapedeness." I am seeing the book, but the *way* in which this rectangular book *appears* to me is diamond-shaped. Similarly, another part of the way in which I am currently visually experiencing the book is in a somewhat Columbia-bluish way.

Philosophers sometimes describe this adverbial view in this way. Julia sees a shirt that is chartreuse. She is thus *appeared to chartreuse-ly*. Or Sam takes a bite of an apple, and he is appeared to *sweet-ly*. Adverbial theory gives us a way of talking about *how* we sense, and the subsequent belief that arises from sensation.

We can see from these examples that sensations are not mental objects, but the ways the mind reacts to sensory stimuli. Analogously, consider "a warm smile" and "smiling warmly." The latter makes clear that it is a *way of* smiling. The "warm" is not something separate. There is then no "intermediate mental object" that is the object of perception. We perceive objects directly, experiencing them in certain kinds of ways.

How does the adverbialist diagnose those cases of illusion that motivated indirect theories in the first place? When Macbeth hallucinates a dagger, there is nothing in front of him, so he is clearly not seeing a dagger. But his sensory experience is just what it would be if there were a dagger in front of him. There is nothing that might be said to be *appearing daggerly*. The adverbialist might suggest that in such a case, Macbeth is indeed having a kind of sensory experience, but he is not having a *visual* experience. He merely believes he is.[22]

---

22   Audi 1988, Chap. 1.

Recall the problems that the indirect view faced. Sense-data were strange objects, and the inference from their existence to externals was problematic. The adverbial view returns to direct realism, but attempts at the same time to save our idea of sensations that don't have to correspond to what we perceive. Thus, adverbial theory is both a direct realism and a causal theory.[23]

But the previous example of the blue book leads to what many have considered to be a decisive criticism of adverbial theory. The *many-property problem* suggests that the adverbialist cannot distinguish two different complex sensory experiences of similar properties. Suppose Deirdre sees a blue book and a red ball. In the adverbial account, she is sensing bluely, rectangularly, redly, and roundly. But this would also be the adverbialists' description of what is going on when she sees a red book and a blue ball.

The difficulty for the adverbialist might be brought out in the following way. Our experience has a complex nature involving objects and spatiality and "belongingness"—the redness belongs to the ball, which is over there, not here where the book is. Adverbial theory needs to offer a means for distinguishing which part of our sensing goes with which object. And as yet, there does not seem to be a consensus about how the adverbialist should reply.

The Doxastic View, or Acquiring Belief

Recent developments in the philosophy of mind have led to a quite different sort of view of perception. Instead of viewing the perceptual process as primarily producing sensations or sensory experiences, some now claim that perception is, in essence, information-conveyance—the generation of beliefs, of mental states with content. Thus, we get versions of the *doxastic view*. ("Doxastic" means related to belief, from the Greek word *doxa*, which means opinion or belief.) In this view, seeing is coming to believe. We need not talk of sensations at all then. This view, especially as it is represented by David. M. Armstrong, holds that perception as the *acquiring of beliefs* by means of our senses. Such views deemphasize the experiential (sensory) character of perception.[24]

The doxastic view is less interested in the experiential features of the perceptual process, but it does not deny that our senses are the mechanism by which information about the world is conveyed to us. Instead, the view stresses

23   Chisholm 1957; Tye 1984.
24   Armstrong 1988, Chap. VII; also Crumley 1991 offers outlines of the view.

that the information conveyed by our senses is important for our acquiring beliefs, and this latter is the essential feature of perception. Thus, sensory processes—involving retinal images, optic nerves, striate cortexes—transmit and process information, which eventually produces beliefs. According to this view, there is no denying that our perceptual beliefs often are accompanied by sensory qualities. Unlike the representative realist, however, the doxastic theorist holds that the experiential character of these sensory qualities does not determine the content of our perceptual beliefs.

This is both a direct realist and causal view. It is causal because it holds that perception is a process that takes physical signals, like light waves, and transforms them into "brain information," and eventually into "mental information," or beliefs. It is a direct realist view because it holds that we are directly perceiving objects, which actually have many of the properties we perceive them to have.

Perhaps one thing that has struck critics as odd about this view is the idea that the character of our sensory experiences somehow derives from the informational aspects of our perceptual beliefs. That is, critics claim that we obviously might have sensory experiences, that we might see things, without having perceptual beliefs about those experiences. As I sit in front of my computer, I am seeing a great deal; there is a richness of detail to my sensory experience that is not obviously included in any perceptual beliefs that I have. The extreme version of this objection is that I could have sensory experiences without having any perceptual beliefs at all.

The doxastic theorist needs to explain the apparent non-belief-like character and richness of our sensory experience, and to give an account of illusions. In response, some doxastic theorists suggest that more of our sensory experience is represented in our beliefs than is assumed. And they suggest that illusions might be handled by appealing to certain physiological facts together with the idea that certain other beliefs may prevent the agent from acquiring a belief she would have acquired otherwise.[25] Perhaps also of some help to the doxastic view is the claim that the sensory aspects of perception are *representational* in nature; that is the sensory qualities are attached to objects and interpreted in light of those objects.[26]

We should note why this sort of response has not appeased critics. The doxastic view appears to provide at best an incomplete account of the nature

---

25   Fish 2010, Chap. 4.
26   Tye 1992.

of our perceptual experience. Sensory experiences do not seem to be readily construed as beliefs. Noting, for example, that I believe that there is a blue jacaranda tree in front of me and that I believe that those sounds are the distinctive music of the jazz fusion band Return to Forever does not quite capture the difference between the two experiences. There is something that it's like to hear jazz fusion; there is something quite different that it's like to see a blue jacaranda. We cannot account for this difference by appealing simply to the difference between seeing and hearing. Hearing a Patsy Cline recording is a different experience from hearing a Reba McEntire recording. It's not simply that my beliefs are different in each situation. The *experiences* are different. At least, this is the point of the critics.

Yet to the extent that one thinks naïve realism cannot be maintained, and given the number of difficulties subsequently encountered in other views, it might be worth revisiting the issue of whether a form of direct realism can be suitably revived.

Key Concepts

- naïve realism
- direct realism
- arguments from illusion
- indirect realism
- representative realism
- phenomenalism
- adverbial theory

Reading/Discussion Questions

1. Why are arguments from illusion thought to undermine naïve realism?
2. What is Locke's distinction between primary and secondary qualities? Why is this distinction important for Locke?
3. Do you think the representative realist can explain how we might have knowledge of the world by means of perception or that there are mind-independent objects?
4. How would you evaluate the factual phenomenalist argument that objects are nothing more than "sensible properties," and hence mind-dependent?
5. How does Berkeley respond to the objection that there seem to be objects or properties that we suppose exist, even though they are unperceived?

Does the factual phenomenalist have a viable way of dealing with this without invoking the notion of God?

6. Why might someone consider adverbial theory to be better than phenomenalism or representative realism? What are its weaknesses?

For Further Reading

Fish 2010 is a detailed but accessible survey of theories of perception.

A defense of a version of naïve realism can be found in Cornman 1975; he considers other theories of perception as well. Russell 1959 is a very accessible introduction to arguments from illusion and the notion of sense data. More recent is Smith 2002; some of the arguments are perhaps more challenging for the beginner.

Austin 1962 is a classic discussion and critique of sense data theory. Some classic critical essays are in Swartz 1965. See, for example, Paul 1951 and Barnes 1945. For more recent criticisms, see BonJour 2001/2007 and Huemer 2001.

Maclachlan 1989 defends a representative realist approach, as does Fumerton 1985.

Tipton 1977 contains a number of essays about Locke's theory of perception, including Tipton's introductory essay. Mackie 1976 provides a closely argued account of Locke's view. Berkeley 1965 is very readable.

Two contemporary defenses of phenomenalism are Robinson 1994 and Dicker 1980.

Price 1932 and Chisholm 1957 are classic works on perception. Chisholm's is one of the first statements of the adverbial theory. Also of interest with regard to adverbial theory is Hardin 1986.

Hardin 1986 is a comprehensive and intriguing start to the study of color; his 2003 is a critique of a realist view. Also Boghossian and Velleman 1989 defend a representative view of color, again critiquing the realist position. Mark Eli Kalderon 2007 surveys various options but also explains a defense of color pluralism. Byrne and Hilbert 1997 is an interdisciplinary collection on color. Barry Maund 2011 presents a detailed account of color eliminativism.

CHAPTER SIX

UNIVERSALS

The noted American humorist Will Rogers once remarked, "If there are no dogs in Heaven, then when I die I want to go where they went." About a quite different subject, C.S. Lewis, the Christian apologist and author of *The Chronicles of Narnia* and *The Screwtape Letters*, along with many other works, noted, "Courage is not simply one of the virtues, but the form of every virtue at the testing point."

A common linguistic occurrence is found in both these quotations. We sometimes think about a particular dog or talk about a particular character trait or note a particular color on a particular object. We sometimes say that a particular action was an instance of courage. Often enough we do more than that. Some thoughts are about *all* dogs or are about *all* mammals. Sometimes we want to say something about *all* compassionate or brave acts. Our language enables us to refer to all members of a certain group or kind or to refer to the kind itself: dogs are mammals; dogs are four-footed; wisdom is a virtue; compassion is a virtue.

Closely related to this sort of ability to think and talk *generally*, we find occasion to distinguish between an object and its properties. This can lead to thinking or talking about the *property itself.* Not only do we notice "this red over here" or "that red over there," but we often identify all these occurrences as *instances of the same color.* That is, we distinguish at times—in thought and language—between *red* and all the particular occurrences or *instances* of red. Someone who says "Red is my favorite color" is not talking about any particular colored surface. A small, local coffee shop chain once used magenta for the color of the upholstery in its booths—here a magenta, there a magenta, separate occurrences of *the same color.* No need to confine ourselves to talking about color; consider *courage.* This soldier is courageous, that bystander is courageous in helping someone out of a burning vehicle, and many years ago, a young Chinese man blocked a tank at Tiananmen Square. These and other numerous acts are *particular instances of courage.* All these particular behaviors are grouped together because they evidence the *same attribute*—courage. Moreover, we take the concepts of courage or beauty or magenta as *predicable of* many different objects. That is, we often say—or think—that a particular property or characteristic is possessed by many different objects; we attribute or *predicate* a property of many different objects.

These examples point to two phenomena, which require two technical terms. We refer to—talk about—some kind or property. This type of linguistic reference is known as *abstract reference.* While the term might be unfamiliar, there is nothing out of the ordinary about abstract reference. Our ordinary way of talking apparently makes use of abstract reference in sentences like "Magenta is a color" or "Patience is a virtue." Notice that in such examples we appear to be talking about some quality or property. The other technical term, *attribute agreement*, refers to different instances of the same property. This American Eskimo pup, that piece of paper, and this napkin "agree" in having the same attribute: they are all white. Attribute agreement is our primary concern in this chapter.

These technical terms should not distract from the main point. Our ability to think and talk about an entire class of objects or to recognize the same property occurring in a lot of different places constitutes our ability to think and talk in general terms. And this ability is tied to an important and longstanding metaphysical problem: the problem of universals.

Universals, Particulars, and Instantiation

Aristotle and the Essence of Human Beings

Aristotle clearly had an interest in terms referring to a particular *kind*, such as "human" or "animal." And he had a quite specific account of the nature or essence of human being: an essence he argues is captured by the term "rational animal." The Aristotelian terminology of genus and species enables us to see the role of each part of the term in identifying human nature. Humans are in the genus *animal*, while their "specific differentia"—the quality that defines their species, and differentiates it from others in its genus—is *rationality*. In other words, while we are similar to other animals in many ways—and thus part of the animal genus—we differ from other animals because of our rational ability, and thus constitute a unique species. The universal *animal* is in each of us, just as it is in the gray wolf or the koala bear. But another universal is immanent in each human, a universal not had by other animals, and that universal is rationality.

Start with attribute agreement: instances of the same property occurring in many different places at the same time. All the different instances are grouped together because—some believe—they share a common element. Indeed this booth is magenta because it shares in some sense the element, *magenta*, with other objects, just as this act is courageous because it shares the element, *courage*, with other acts. We say that the booth *instantiates* magenta or this act of pulling someone from a burning vehicle *instantiates* courage. Courage or magenta is something over and above—separate from, but shared by—all the particular instances. Such an element, if it exists, is a *universal*. A universal then is that which can be instantiated—shared—by many objects or particulars at the same time; it can be predicated of or attributed to many things.[1] This gives us a way to think about particulars, as well. Particulars—or, synonymously, what we have been calling "objects" or "individuals"—cannot be instantiated. In this sense, every particular is unique.

Plato, the first to identify universals, used the term *forms*:

Socrates: We speak of many beautiful things and many good things, and we say that they are so and so and so define them in speech.

---

1   E.J. Lowe 2002, Chap. 19.

Glaucon: We do.
Socrates: And Beauty itself and Goodness itself, and so with all the things which we then classed as many; we now class them again according to one *Form* of each ...
Glaucon: That is so.[2]

Socrates identifies the form as existing separately from the "many" instances.

Philosophers disagree about whether or not universals exist and, if so, what they are. There are three main views on this subject. Realism holds that universals exist. "Realism" is the view held by Plato and others that universals are a special kind of object, which exist separately from the many occurrences or instances. At the other end of the spectrum is nominalism, the view that universals do not exist; only particular things or particular occurrences of properties exist. It turns out that there are several nominalist options. There are also two middle views that call for consideration. One, called *moderate realism*, holds that there are universals, but not as separately existing objects. This view is often attributed to Aristotle. (Some call a Platonic view, by contrast, "extreme realism.") Another view, first articulated (according to some) by the French philosopher Peter Abelard (1079–1142), is conceptualism, the view that universals are just concepts, located in the mind, that are universal because they refer to many individuals.

Universal: A Special Object

Words and Universals

As we've noted, realists hold that a property, such as *redness* or *courageousness*, is a universal. Words that name properties are typically called *predicates*, a term that you might have seen in the context of grammar, or computer or formal languages (e.g., "predicate logic").

As we will see, some nominalists hold that all predicates are just words.

But another question arises: does every predicate name a property? Clearly the question is more pressing for realists, and some predicates seem obvious. "Is a candle" counts as a predicate, as does "is red" or "is cylindrical." Other predicates less obviously name properties, e.g., "is a book returned to the store" or "is a color liked by logic students." In Plato's *Parmenides*,

---

2   Plato 1974, *Republic*, 507b; emphasis added.

Parmenides asks the young Socrates if "hair" or "mud" names a form. Socrates seems uninclined to think so.

Different theorists of course give different answers. One possibility is to recognize as *real* properties only those required for science. And the most extravagant view is to say that, yes, there is a property named by each meaningful predicate. Allowing the unrestricted view, however, can quickly run into problems, seemingly inviting contradictions. Michael Loux discusses this "unrestricted predication" in his *Metaphysics* (2006), Chap. 1.

The realist view holds that universals are independent, existing apart from their instances. A ruby red glass goblet sits on the table. Here is an instance of the universal *red*. Destroy this goblet; smash it to smithereens! You will have destroyed *this instance*, but you will not have destroyed the universal *red*, which exists independently of particulars. Indeed, even if all red things were destroyed—even if there never were, or never will be, any red things—the universal red would still exist.

This independence raises a difficult point, however. Although instance and universal are distinct, *the universal is wholly present in each instance*. This coffee shop booth is no less magenta than that one. And courage is wholly present in this Medal of Honor recipient, just as it is wholly present in this Victoria Cross recipient. By contrast, compare, in this respect, a class—a collection—of things, for example, all the states of the US. Wyoming is one of them, but that class of states is not wholly present in that state. That state is just a part of that class. Similarly, the coffee shop booth is only a (very small) part of the class of magenta objects, past, present, and future.

Thinking of a universal as a kind of pattern or archetype might help us to understand how a universal is wholly present in each instance. Many shirts may instantiate *the same pattern*—shape, form, style. The pattern is wholly present in each individual shirt. (We're not talking about the sewing pattern—the paper shapes that guide construction.) Make as many shirts as you wish of this pattern. Each shirt is an instance of the pattern, and the pattern is wholly present in each shirt. Thus, note two slightly embarrassed individuals who arrive at the social event only to find that they are wearing *the same shirt*! And the pattern never gets used up. No matter how many instances, the pattern is never exhausted. Perhaps this metaphor helps with understanding how the entire universal is present simultaneously in many different objects. We can also note that this "not getting used up" feature is a consequence of their immaterial or nonphysical nature.

Those who believe in the existence of universals mostly agree that they are not physical. They aren't made up of elements listed in the Periodic Table; they aren't electromagnetic fields or very special plasmas. Perhaps the most important aspect of this immateriality is that universals don't take up space. And this has an interesting consequence: Lots of different universals can be instantiated by the same object. Not only can one and the same universal be *multiply instantiated*, but multiple universals are or can be in the same place. Consider again that ruby red glass. It instantiates several universals at once: cylindrical, red, and glass. All these universals are simultaneously "in" this particular ruby red goblet. How many universals can be present in any given object? An indefinitely large number. Each genuine property possessed by an object is an instance of a universal. And for each *kind* that this object belongs to, it instantiates that universal.

While universals are instantiated in spatial objects, the separately existing universals—e.g., *beauty* or *magenta* in themselves—are not located in space, the way a chair or a table is. And non-physical, non-spatial objects are not discoverable by the senses; they are discovered instead by reason or thought. (In the *Republic*, according to some translations, it is "understanding" that enables us to grasp or discover universals.) As nonphysical objects, universals are one type of *abstract object*—members of a category that, according to some, includes a variety of other kinds of nonphysical entities, such as numbers.

(We leave aside the issue of whether universals are "in time" or temporal objects. In calling them "abstract," we simply note that they don't have the other attributes or properties associated with physical objects.) Realists about universals accordingly are realists about abstract objects.

Realism

The Transcendentals

Thirteenth-century medieval philosophy saw a heightened interest in a very special kind of universal: the *transcendentals*. These are those properties or qualities that are true of everything. According to Jorge Gracia 1992, a transcendental includes or "covers" not only other objects and properties, but all categories as well, whether substance or quality or quantity. In a sense, transcendentals run through every category. The property of *being* was held to be the highest or most fundamental transcendental; it is true of everything that *is*.

Other predicates, such as unity, good, and truth—and for some, including Aquinas (1225–74), beauty—are "convertible" with being. To say that the predicate "true" is convertible with the predicate "being" (or "is" or "to be") is to say that we have two names for one quality. If something *is*, it is always also *good, unified*, and *true*. Or as Aquinas remarks, true, for example, and being "differ in idea," but are the same in reality.

How can it be that beauty or goodness are properties of everything? Here is Aquinas: "Nothing exists which does not participate in beauty or goodness, since each thing is good according to its proper form.... Created beauty is nothing other than a likeness of the divine beauty participated in things." Setting aside for now the reference to a "divine" beauty, Aquinas also seems to acknowledge a "natural" beauty. Everything is composed of form and matter, and the proper form of an object is inherently beautiful.[3]

Realists incline toward two principal arguments for the existence of universals, and versions of both these arguments appear in Plato's dialogues. Socrates asks Meno, in the eponymous dialogue, to provide the *common element* or *characteristic* that all virtues share. In response, Meno offers a list of several different virtues for different types of people, and Socrates remarks:

---

3   Aquinas 1953, p. 88

I seem to be in luck. I wanted one virtue and I find that you have a whole swarm of virtues to offer. But seriously, to carry on this metaphor of the swarm, suppose I asked you what a bee is, what is its *essential nature*, and you replied that bees were of many different kinds. What would you say if I went on to ask, And is it in *being bees* that they are many and various and different from one another? Or would you agree that it is not in this respect that they differ....

Then do the same with the virtues. Even if they are many and various, yet at least they all have some common character which makes them virtues.[4]

Socrates' remarks rely on the notion of attribute agreement. We group different particular dogs as one and all *dogs* because they all share a common attribute or characteristic. (They may be different colors, sizes, weights, etc., but they all share the common attribute *being dogs*.) Similarly we identify different virtues (e.g., courage, moderation, wisdom) as one and all *virtues*. Socrates asks for the shared common attribute. Socrates asks the same question in *Laches*, but here about courage:

And I will begin with courage, and once more ask *what is that common quality, which is the same in all these cases* and which is called courage?[5]

Notice that Socrates claims we need some explanation about why we group all these things together. Why do we count all these various actions as one and alike "brave"? Or why do we group Helen of Troy, Renoir's *Sunset at Sea*, a melody, and a rainbow as all beautiful? Socrates is arguing that there is "something" common to each, and our grasping that common element leads to grouping these things together. In other words, attribute agreement, according to Socrates' argument, requires acknowledging the existence of universals.

Abstract reference of words seems to provide another reason for asserting the existence of universals. We take the common noun in "Traveler is a horse," or "Donald is a duck" to be referring to the kind *horse* or the kind *duck*. Those nouns pick out or refer to a class of neighing or quacking creatures. "Courage is a virtue" or "patience is a virtue" are similarly cases of abstract reference.

The realist claims that the best explanation of the *meaning* of such sentences is that "virtue" or "color" refer to *universals*. Similarly the meaning of

---

4   Plato 1961b, *Meno*, 72b, d; emphasis added.
5   Plato 1961a, *Laches*, 191e; emphasis added.

familiar sentences, such as "The authors of the Constitution had wisdom," is explained by claiming that "wisdom" refers to a *universal*.

We have, then, two related arguments for the realist view of universals. Let us call the first argument the *argument from attribute agreement*; that is, universals are necessary to explain attribute agreement. This is also sometimes called the *problem of the one over the many*. That is, the "many"—the particulars—are grouped together because they all fall under the universal—the one. The universal is thus "over" the many. The latter is the *argument from abstract reference*; universals are needed in order to explain the meaning of certain sentences that make use of abstract reference.

Third Man Argument

Undoubtedly the most famous argument against Plato's view and against realism generally is provided by Plato himself. This objection is known as the Third Man Argument, which holds that accepting the attribute agreement argument for universals in fact leads to an infinite regress of universals. The argument is presented in the first part of the dialogue *Parmenides*, as one of several objections to the theory of forms that the philosopher Parmenides makes in a conversation with the younger Socrates.[6]

The literary encounter leaves us with one of the more famous objections in the history of philosophy. Remarkably simple in design, the objection targets the idea that universals provide an answer to the one over many problem. Consider two large objects. The realist claims that these objects are both large because they each instantiate the universal *largeness*. Indeed, the realist claims attribute agreement between any two objects—here, that both objects are large—is best explained by appealing to a very special object, a universal. The universal is the one over the many large items. Parmenides now asks the young Socrates:

> Parm: But now take Largeness itself [the universal] and the other things which are large. Suppose you look at all these in the same way in your mind's eye, will not yet another unity make its appearance—a Largeness [another universal] by virtue of which they all appear large?

---

6   The conversational encounter is purely a literary construct. Though the historical Parmenides was a well-known "pre-Socratic" philosopher, and probably met the youthful Socrates, there is no real evidence that the two ever held a philosophical discussion.

Socrates: So it would seem.

Parm: If so, a second Form of largeness will present itself over and above Largeness itself and the things that share in it; and again, covering all these, yet another, which will make all of them large. So each of your forms will no longer be one, but an indefinite number.[7]

Parmenides' line of questioning is very simple. The problem Parmenides is raising is this. Universals are supposed to explain the likeness of attributes between individuals. If you need the universal to explain how all the particulars are alike, will you not need still a second universal to explain the apparent likeness between the individuals and the first universal? And if we need this second universal, won't we still need a third universal? And won't this process of needing another universal continue indefinitely?

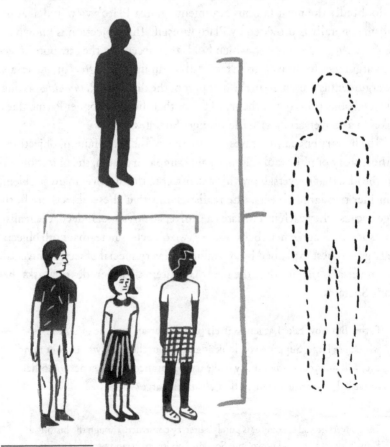

---

7   Plato 1951, *Parmenides*, 132a, b.

Realists invoke universals to solve the problem of the one over the many, the problem of attribute agreement. Parmenides' objection, however, suggests that the one over the many problem arises *even for universals*. An explanation that keeps introducing new things that need to be explained hardly seems an adequate solution to the problem.

Explanations, interpretations, and assessments of the Third Man themselves have filled books. While most scholars agree that there is a challenge to the realist position, they disagree over how to understand the argument. The twentieth-century Plato scholar Gregory Vlastos claims that the argument is Plato's "record of honest perplexity,"[8] that Plato knew there was a problem but was unsure of the best way to address it. Some commentators have identified the problem as "self-predication," or the idea that the form itself has the property or attribute it's supposed to explain—so the form *largeness* is itself large, or the form *man* is somehow "manlike," or the form *beauty* is itself beautiful. We may not be able to cover all of these difficult issues, but we can look at some important aspects of the problem.[9]

It might seem that the Third Man Argument threatens only Plato's version of realism. But various "regress arguments" challenge any realist who holds that universals exist separately from their instances.[10] Cynthia Macdonald casts the challenge in the form of a dilemma for realists. Here we modify her presentation a bit. The dilemma is this: either the universal is *like* the particulars, or it is *not like* the particulars. To put it a little differently, the universal "unifies" the instances—makes them all instances of red or instances of beauty—either because it is *like* the instances, or is unlike them, but has some other relation to them.

Well, if we take the first—the universal is *like* its instances—we are on a very quick ride to the Third Man Argument. (But this doesn't seem right: the form *largeness*, for example, is not itself large. In general, universals aren't instances of themselves.) But let us take the second—focus instead on the *relation* between universal and its instance. Now we have the relation between universal and this instance, and the relation between the universal and that instance, and so on. This relation is the same in each case. But now we seemingly need a universal that "covers" all these *particular* relations between universal and instances.

---

8   Vlastos 1954, pp. 343–49.
9   Meinwald 1992 addresses the self-predication problem and suggests a resolution.
10   Loux 2006; Macdonald 2005; Donagan 1963.

The following particular instance of the Third Man Argument may make it a little clearer. Consider a large pile of different hats: a derby, a top-hat, a balaclava, a beanie, a baseball-cap, a fire-fighter's helmet, and so on. Each hat is different from every other one, but they're all *hats*. So that means (according to realists) that they all participate in the form of hats—each of them is related to a single *Ideal Hat*. Now, the ideal hat cannot be made of silk or knitted wool or cotton, or any other particular material, because real hats made of any one of a large number of different particular materials are all related to it. So what is in common between all those real hats and the Ideal Hat? Well, there must be another form that all those real hats and the Ideal Hat participate in. But now we can run the same line of reasoning concerning this additional form and the Ideal Hat and the real hats, and conclude that still another form exists. And so on, multiplying forms infinitely.

Whichever way we choose, then, to understand universals, a version of Third Man—a regress—seems to pop up. We continually see the need for yet another universal to explain a new group! And that is just Macdonald's point.

A common thread runs through many realist responses to the dilemma. They insist that the initial relation between universal and particular is both explanatory *and basic*. Appealing to the universal tells us something about the world, about the things in the world, and about our ability to think and talk about various kinds of objects. But they also claim that we can't analyze this concept of "instantiation" further. It's a basic essential fact about red or beautiful particulars, for example, that they instantiate a given universal.[11] It is perhaps worth noting that, as we will see, this notion of *basic and unanalyzable* appears in both realist and nominalist views—though the views differ over what counts as basic and unanalyzable.

Universals a Precondition for Thought and Communication

A further passage from the *Parmenides* is also relevant. Parmenides' series of criticisms of the theory of forms, at least in the dialogue, seem to leave Socrates at a loss. Yet Parmenides seems disinclined to discard entirely the theory, as he says:

> But on the other hand ... if, in view of all these difficulties and other things like them, a man refuses to admit that the Forms of things exist or to distinguish

---

11   Macdonald 2005; Donagan 1963; A.E. Taylor 1949. Armstrong 1989 suggests that there is no real regress problem for realism about universals.

a definite Form in every case, *he will have nothing on which to fix his thought*, so long as he will not allow that each thing has a character which is always the same, in so doing will completely destroy the significance of all discourse. But of that consequence I think you [Socrates] are only too well aware.[12]

A necessary condition of thought and language, according to Parmenides, is that something "anchors" our thoughts. If we are to make any sense of our many references to beauty or to courage or all the various properties we ascribe to things, something fixed, something unchanging must exist. We suppose, for example, that Sara is thinking the same thought, about the same thing—courage—when she says on Tuesday that the soldier is brave as when she says on Wednesday that the teacher showed courage. Julia may disagree with Jack that the painting is beautiful, but they presume that there is something over which they disagree. Parmenides suggests that without forms, without the "anchor," Sara's thought about courage could mean one thing one day, and another on another day; Julia and Jack would not really be communicating at all, since nothing ties one thought to the other. If Julia and Jack are to engage in genuine discourse, there must be something that is the *same* in their conversation. Thinking and meaningful speech require a unity, Parmenides suggests, something that binds together separate thoughts or different utterances. Without the theory of the forms we are unable to account for the apparent fact that thought and language are meaningful.

This view is shared by contemporary writers, as well. C.A. Baylis makes a similar point:

> The existence of communicable knowledge requires shared meanings. Such knowledge, in its simplest form, is knowledge of the *common characters* exhibited by various objects and events.... Our problem is to explain [universals'] nature and their function in knowledge in terms that are neither mystical nor false to the facts of conscious communication.[13]

Baylis underscores the recognition expressed in Plato's dialogue: universals are required to explain successful communication. This perhaps helps us to see the realist insistence on the need for universals. Universals explain not only our *individual* ability to think and talk generally; they also "anchor" the possibility of shared, common knowledge about the essence or nature of things.

12　Plato 1951, 135c; emphasis added.
13　Baylis 1951, p. 636; emphasis added.

Nominalists, of course, think that their view also provides an explanation of the meaningfulness of our language and our thought.

Nominalism

Nominalism comprises several different views, but they all have this in common: they deny the existence of universals. Only individuals or particulars exist. The word "nominalism" comes, via French, from the Latin *nominalis*, meaning "pertaining to a name or names." Nominalism seems to many to have the commonsense advantage of recognizing only individuals and rejecting the need for any special type of object. Instead, nominalism asserts that nouns that apparently pick out or designate universals in fact are words only and can be "rephrased."

The celebrated medieval English philosopher William of Ockham (1285–1347) was a champion of nominalism. He is also responsible for a principle that underlies many nominalist arguments: the principle now known as "Ockham's razor." That "razor," now expressed as "do not multiply entities beyond necessity," tells us to prefer the simpler of two explanations.

Michael Loux provides an instructive contemporary account of this notion of simplicity as a standard for evaluating theories.[14] Loux notes that the aim of a theory, whether in the natural or social sciences or in metaphysics, is *to explain*. A theory is judged to be better because it better explains those phenomena being investigated. But simplicity is one way an explanation can be better. So, given two theories, each explaining the desired "facts," we are inclined to prefer the simpler of those theories. One quick example might help to illustrate. Let's take the example of Newton's laws of motion, which became the basis for classical mechanics. Newton's laws explain motion from the behavior of billiard balls on a table to the motion of a train approaching a station—or, as the former football commentator John Madden liked to point out, the force exerted by a player on an opposing quarterback. The beauty of Newton's law is that, with just three simple principles or laws, it explains so many varied instances of motion and rest. The theory explains, and it has the virtue of being simpler than its rivals.

Here's an example of its use in medicine. When confronted with a patient with a collection of different symptoms, doctors first look for a single underlying condition that would explain them all.

---

14   Loux 2006, Chap. 1.

Nominalists think their view is simpler because they rely on only one kind of entity—individual objects—to provide explanations of abstract reference and attribute agreement. In their view, acknowledging the existence of universals is a multiplication of entities beyond necessity.

In his writings about nominalism, Ockham went a step further, arguing that appeal to universals inevitably led to contradiction. Like others, Ockham believed that anything that exists is an individual, and that to claim otherwise is obvious folly. So, if a universal exists, it too must be individual: "It ought to be said that every universal is one particular thing and that it is not universal except in its signification, in its signifying many things."[15] Nothing could be both universal and individual at the same time

It's important to be clear about Ockham's complaint. Anything that exists, he says, is individual. By definition, individuals cannot be in two places at once. Yet universals—supposedly—are in many places at once. So it seemed to Ockham and others that realism bordered on self-contradiction: Something that can't be in many places at once was held by realists to be in many places at once.

Yet this still leaves us with questions. If we are not to rely on universals, what then can we say about, for example, why we call all these things magenta or all these acts courageous? If nominalists claim to offer a simpler theory than realism, how do they propose to explain the apparent fact of attribute agreement? Of the many types of nominalism, we look at the answers provided by two.

Strict Nominalism

Strict nominalism insists that all our apparent talk of attribute agreement, apparently implying the existence of universals, in fact refers to nothing more than individuals. (David Armstrong, an enemy of this view, called it "ostrich nominalism."[16]) Realists, recall, invoke universals to explain the truth of various assertions, such as "Socrates is wise": Socrates instantiates the universal *wisdom*. Similarly "Boethius is wise" and "Pascal is wise" are true because both Boethius and Pascal also instantiate the same universal. The strict nominalist claims, instead, that there is nothing to explain here. We have three individuals, each of which is wise. There is no exemplifying or instantiating to be explained.

---

15   Ockham 1974, p. 78.
16   Armstrong 1978, Vol. I, pp. 12–16.

There is just this individual, and he happens to be wise, and that individual, and he happens to be wise.

Along with the realist, you might be waiting to ask about all these individuals that are wise. Haven't we come across a case of attribute agreement? That is, aren't we grouping these three individuals—Socrates, Boethius, and Pascal—together because they *share the same property*? In other words, isn't there *agreement* between their *attributes*? We know the realist explains that the attribute agreement which allows for this "grouping together" occurs precisely because these three individuals share in or instantiate the same *universal*.

But how will the strict nominalist explain attribute agreement without relying on universals? The strict nominalist insists that there is nothing here to explain because we have come across a basic metaphysical fact. These facts—that there are different objects described using the same predicates—are primitive; they cannot be analyzed further. This thing is magenta, and that thing is magenta, and that's all there is to it. You don't need a third thing to explain this.

In a famous essay titled "On What There Is," the twentieth-century philosopher Willard Van Orman Quine straightforwardly expressed this idea:

> One may admit that there are red houses, roses, and sunsets, but deny, except as a popular and misleading manner of speaking, that they have anything in common. The words "houses," "roses," and "sunsets" are true of sundry individual entities which are houses and roses and sunsets, and the word "red" or "red object" is true of each of sundry individual entities which are red houses, red roses, red sunsets; but there is not, in addition, any entity whatever, individual or otherwise, which is named "redness".... That the houses and the roses and the sunsets are all of them red may be taken as ultimate and irreducible, and it may be held that [the realist] is no better off, in point of real explanatory power, for all the occult entities which he posits under such names as redness.[17]

To say that facts are "ultimate and irreducible" or "primitive" or "unanalyzable" is a way of saying that a particular theory or view takes certain facts or items as basic or as starting points; there is no prior point of explanation. When Newton proposed his view of gravity, critics asked for an explanation of the attractive force of gravity. Newton, however, insisted that there was no

---

17   Quine 1961, p. 10.

further explanation. Matter attracts. Period. There isn't any further explanation of how or why it does it. Strict nominalists thus make two claims. First, they can explain just as well as the realist. Second, that there are numerous *individual* red things or *individual* wise persons is just a fact about the world. An *ultimate* fact—it requires no further explanation.

But Realists of course hold that attribute agreement—counting different objects as having the same property—requires some explanation. If Danny has a red rose and Deirdre has a red rose, our ordinary sense is that the two roses *share* the same color. These are both *instances of red*, realists say, because they share a common element, the universal. Realists hold that strict nominalism simply ignores these apparently obvious facts without *explaining why* our "normal sense" about attribute agreement is mistaken.

Despite the fact that their explanation is more complex because it requires a second kind of thing—universals—realists think they still offer a *better* explanation than strict nominalism. Why? With the claim that it is just a brute fact about the world that there are only individuals, *and* no explanation why our ordinary view is mistaken, strict nominalism seems incomplete or arbitrary. The realists think they explain our normal intuition, accommodating our sense of the metaphysical makeup of the world.

Nominalism and Resemblance

Another less "strict" version of nominalism, resemblance nominalism, claims that we classify together certain individuals or use the same word to describe multiple objects because they *resemble* each other. Still, resemblance nominalists hold, there are only individuals in the world. But like members of a family, some individual objects may resemble one another, while another set of individuals resemble each other in a different way.

In the view of resemblance class nominalism, there is no need to bring in universals to explain attribute agreement. There are just individuals, grouped together. When Julia says "this book is blue," according to the resemblance class nominalist, she is talking about nothing more than individuals. She is saying, in effect, that this individual book is one of many objects that constitute a resemblance class—the class of blue things. Similarly, Deirdre's applauding the *courage* of the men and women of the armed forces does not invoke the idea of a universal. Instead she is referring to that group—that *class*—of individuals that are brave. Again, there is no need for the universal.

We've been slipping in the quasi-technical term "class" as a synonym for "group." This use of "class" is not in the socioeconomic sense, but the mathematical sense. A class is just a specified group: the class of people invited to Julia's party on Saturday, the class of books owned by Deirdre, the class of *wise* individuals, the class of *red* individuals. So, according to resemblance class nominalists, when we say that Deirdre bought a *blue* dress, we are simply noting that the dress belongs to a particular group.

Moreover, a single individual might belong to many different classes. An individual book can belong to the class of individuals that are red, to the class of individuals that are rectangular, to the class of individuals that are expensive, and to the class of individuals that are books about physics.

Thus, according to the resemblance class nominalist, there are only individuals. Individuals belong to different sets, such sets being specified or described by one of our linguistic terms. The realist is then wrong to think that universals must exist in order to explain our apparent reference to or thought about some common or shared element. This appeal is both unnecessary and a mistake, in the resemblance class nominalist's view.

The realist worries, however, that a resemblance class nominalist will get the wrong classes. A simple example might help. When I *think about* dogs—e.g., that they are descendants of the gray wolf—I am thinking about all and only those things that are dogs. My thought is about *everything* that instantiates the universal *being a dog*. Thus, my thought "includes" American Eskimos, Irish setters, shelties, puppies at the animal shelter, puppies I've seen, and puppies I will never see. Pick any two members of this class and here's what is guaranteed: they both instantiate *being a dog*. Instantiating the relevant universal determines the class of things included in my thought. That's how the realist gets the "right" class.

But some have noted that the resemblance nominalist can get some very odd "groupings." Our resemblance class can be a very motley crew—an Irish setter, which resembles a golden retriever, which resembles a bulldog, which resembles the Terrytoons cartoon character, Deputy Dawg, which resembles creatures from the infamous *Star Wars* bar scene, one of which resembles a Yorkshire terrier, which resembles a cat a former neighbor once owned ... A cat?

WITTGENSTEIN AND FAMILY RESEMBLANCE

Various versions of resemblance theory provide different accounts of the nature of resemblance. One development of this view suggests that paying attention to our ordinary ways of talking and thinking—the way ordinary language works—may provide some relief to our perplexity.

Ludwig Wittgenstein had influential views about the problem of universals. First, it seems that he should be classed as a nominalist, not a realist. It is the rules of our language that determine when we group objects as falling under the same general term, or as showing the same characteristic. And the language, he argued, does group things by resemblance, but he thought that the usual view of resemblance was often too simple. Often we group things by their "family resemblance." This sort of grouping is an ordinary aspect of daily life. Observe a group of close relatives. What you see is that there is no characteristic that they all share; rather, there is a chain of overlapping similarities. Albert's eyes may be like Betty's, whose nose may resemble Cliff's, whose mouth and chin resembles unmistakably his brother Dexter's, whose.... no doubt you can continue the pattern.

Wittgenstein uses this everyday concept to explain why we take various items and call them by the same name. One of his favorite examples is "game," but we might use any common noun, say "chair." We identify all chairs as chairs, not because they possess some common element, but because we recognize

ALBERT   BETTY

CLIFF   DEXTER

overlapping similarities. (It won't do, for example, to say that all chairs are fit for sitting—so are sofas and loveseats and benches. But we want "chair" to refer to *only* chairs.) Overlapping similarities are the basis of resemblance, and hence enable us to group things together under the same term.

Renford Bambrough argues that in appealing to the notion of family resemblance, Wittgenstein solved the dispute between realism and nominalism.[18] According to Bambrough, Wittgenstein's concept of family resemblance explains why various items are "collected together" in language and thought, thus responding to the realist argument that our intuitions about groups of objects require explanation. Wittgenstein would not count as a realist, however, since family resemblances do not involve universals. There is no such thing as the "ideal chair" whose characteristics are true of all and only chairs.

TROPES

Resemblance nominalism explained how two individual things are both (for example) blue by saying that they are both members of the same sets of things, and that these sets are constituted by individuals that resemble each other. But the problem with this is that individuals, each with a complicated collection of characteristics, can resemble each other in many ways. Well, we can specify that the appropriate resemblance is with regard to color: they're all blue. But that just puts us back where we started.

Trope nominalism[19] hopes to solve the problem here by seeing individual things as bundles of tropes. What is a trope? Sam's blue shirt has a particular blue on him, and the sky has a particular different blue up there. Even though we can imagine that they are precisely the same shade of blue, there are two tropes here: the one that is in Sam's shirt, and the one that's in the sky. These aren't instances of a universal; they're particular "things"—individuals. Borrowing the term from one of America's more famous philosophers, George Santayana (1863–1952), Donald C. Williams named these individuals *tropes*.[20] Now think of ordinary things, like Sam's shirt, as being constituted by a bundle of different tropes, and nothing but them. The suggestion is that they are the basic entities of reality!

---

18 Bambrough 1960; also Nammour 1973.

19 This is a very recent position, but some think that versions of it occur in Aristotle and William of Ockham. See Lahey, 1998.

20 Donald Williams 1953, pp. 5–6.

But now let us try to see how this is supposed to help with the problem of universals. What we want trope theory to do is to answer the question: why are Sam's shirt, and the sky, both blue? The answer proposed by trope theory is not the realist answer: that they both "participate" in the thing that is the form of blueness. Neither is it the resemblance-nominalist answer: that they are both members of a class of things that resemble each other. The answer they propose is trope-resemblance-nominalism. One of the tropes constituting Sam's shirt *resembles* one of the tropes constituting the sky. The class of blue tropes (for example) resembles each other more than any of them resembles any trope not in that class. So the relevant resemblance class includes all and only the resembling tropes. We avoid the problem of "in what respect" the members of the resemblance class resemble each other. In this class, they're all reds.

And what of nominalism's promised "simpler" view? It's true that there are only particulars in the trope view. But admitting tropes—particularized properties—might not be all that simple. Note that tropes are not physical objects; they are, instead, what some call "abstract particulars."[21] So, while the trope view may not require us to posit the existence of universals, the realist might doubt that it is any simpler to think of ordinary objects—a table or a dog or a glass—as bundles of abstract particulars.

But consider an argument Bertrand Russell made in favor of universals: it raises a problem about resemblance nominalism, and also about the trope-resemblance proposal. Russell asks whether the relation of *resemblance* and all its instances require a universal. In the context, how else should we explain our calling all the particular resemblings by the same name? Why do we count these as *resemblance* classes? We apparently count them, Russell says, as instances of the *same relation*. Russell argued that the nominalist is thus unable to escape invoking universals. All the individual resemblings can be treated as the same only if we see them as instances of the universal *resemblance*.[22] Some trope theorists reply that there is a *resemblance trope*. Otherwise, the resemblance-relation is not explained. So is trope-theory an advance?

More can be said about trope theory, and indeed, about the unabating dispute between realism and nominalism. But two "intermediate" views are worth noting.

---

21   Campbell 1991.
22   Russell 1959, Chaps. IX and X.

Moderate Realism and Conceptualism

Immanent or Scientific Realism: David Armstrong

David M. Armstrong, an Australian philosopher who has been extremely influential in metaphysics, epistemology, and the philosophy of mind, argued for a version of moderate realism that is sometimes called *immanent realism*.

Like Aristotle, Armstrong held that universals exist, but not separately from their instantiations; universals always and only exist in the objects. A distinctive feature of his view is that determining which universals exist is an *empirical* matter. That is, science tells us which properties exist. And the relevant properties are those that are reflected in scientific laws; for example, the charge of an electron is a property of electrons, and therefore a universal. Hence, this moderate realism is a scientific realism.

Armstrong thought that the ontology of the world—its structure—was a conjunction of all the states of affairs, that is, all the objects and their properties. Immanent universals are necessary to explain the structure of the world, and the physical necessity that we see in scientific laws.

His two-volume work, *Universals and Scientific Realism*, examines the various nominalist views in the first volume and develops his own version of moderate realism in the second volume. *Universals: An Opinionated Introduction* is a tour of his objections to nominalist views and a briefer account of his own view. Interestingly, in the concluding section, Armstrong suggests that a version of trope theory and his immanent realism may both be right, simply alternative ways of talking about the same set of issues.

Perhaps there is a different way to understand the "universal" element in our thinking. Two different views suggest just that. Moderate realism holds that our "kind concepts" refer to universals, but universals are "in" the objects. Conceptualism holds that each concept itself is universal because it stands for or refers to a number of individuals. Aristotle is often considered a moderate realist, as are various thirteenth-century philosophers, such as St. Thomas Aquinas, while Peter Abelard's view is often thought of as conceptualism (but different commentators have variously associated him with moderate realism or different versions of nominalism).

Understanding and comparing views such as Aristotle's moderate realism or Abelard's conceptualism is challenging because each uses its own terminological framework. While the intricacies of the terminological framework frequently nuance the views under consideration, it is possible to provide general outlines of moderate realism and conceptualism using the terminology employed elsewhere in this chapter.

Moderate Realism

A sketch of Aristotle's moderate realism emerges in his *Metaphysics*, in a criticism of the realist view he attributes to Plato. In *De Interpretatione*, Aristotle defines "universal" as "that which is of such a nature as to be predicated of many subjects, by 'individual' that which is not thus predicated."[23] For our purposes, we can interpret "can be predicated of many" to mean "can be multiply instantiated."

Aristotle, like the realist, holds that different individuals may manifest the *same property*. This chartreuse shirt and that chartreuse blouse both exhibit the property "chartreuse." Chartreuse can thus "be predicated of many" and so denotes a universal. To put it another way, chartreuse is a universal because it is instantiated in this shirt and this blouse.

Aristotle, the *moderate* realist, disagrees with the realist's view that the universal exists *separately* from its numerous occurrences. For the moderate realist, universals always exist in the objects that manifest them or possess them. (The technical term is that the universals are *immanent*, existing only in particular objects.) This has an interesting consequence: there are no *un*-instantiated universals. We have a concept of the universal, but this concept is not a universal itself—it just "stands for" the universal. If we think *chartreuse*, we are thus referring to the universal, wherever and whenever it occurs in one or many individual objects.

It's important to be clear on a major difference between moderate realism and trope theory: in moderate realism, it is the universal occurring in each object. These "chartreuses" are not merely similar. *They are one and the same chartreuse* occurring in different places at the same time. (The chartreuse tropes in those two pieces of clothing are distinct things. Tropes in two distinct places are never one and the same: they are always distinct tropes.) We group objects together—that is, we recognize attribute agreement—when we recognize that the same quality is instantiated in more than one object. But, though the moderate realist agrees with the realist that the best way to explain attribute agreement is reference to a universal, moderate realism also differs

---

23   Aristotle 1941c, Sect.1, Pt. 7.

from realism in that the moderate realist rejects the idea of independently existing universals. Instead, moderate realism sees universals as a distinct type of entity, multiply and simultaneously occurring in various objects.

The moderate realist view then looks like this in simple outline. A group of blue objects are classified as *being blue* because the same universal exists in each. This is how the moderate realist explains attribute agreement. While the universal can exist in many objects at once, there are only "immanent occurrences," never existing apart from those individual objects. Hence, for the moderate realist, the universal *blue* is occurring here, now, in this book, in that book, in this glass, in that shirt—and when we think *blue* we are thinking about all and only these "immanent occurrences" of blue. The moderate realist keeps universals, but they're "pushed inside" the objects.

(The idea that one and the same thing exists at two different places at the same time is not as bizarre as it at first might seem. Consider a university with two campuses: it exists downtown and in the suburbs simultaneously. The difference, however, is that we should say that part of the university is here, and the rest of it is over there; but *all* of the universal *blue* is supposed to be both in the sky and in Sam's shirt.)

Why does Aristotle think that the universals don't exist separately from their occurrences? His principal criticisms of Plato appear in the *Metaphysics*, one of Aristotle's more difficult works, which examines not only Plato, but his other predecessors as well. Two objections to Plato are worth noting.

First, Aristotle claims that invoking the Ideas, or Plato's forms—our universals—is an unnecessary duplication. Aristotle likens those who affirm the independent existence of universals to a man who wanted to count the things that existed, but thought the counting might be easier if there were more things to count. But the metaphysical task of "counting" or cataloguing the types of objects is hardly made easier by adding more. Aristotle wonders why we should add to or complicate our "counting task," by supposing that there is a whole class of objects undetectable by the normal means. This criticism leads quickly to the second, more important thought behind Aristotle's criticism.

Aristotle apparently held that Plato's view is not explanatory because it's not clear how the *independent* existence of universals contributes to the nature or essence of particular things. How can something *outside* the object be a part of its essence?[24]

---

24   A.E. Taylor 1949.

Perhaps Aristotle's point might be explained in this way. We sometimes want to know what makes something a given *kind* of thing. For example, we want to know what is that special characteristic or group of characteristics that makes something a dog, and not, say, a coyote. Today we might rely on the genomic differences to tell us their different natures or essences. Having the "dog-gene-structure" is the essence of being a dog. But the essence is something *in* the object. Once we know that essence, does it tell us any more to say, "Oh, by the way, this essence also exists by itself"? Aristotle thinks not. A universal "off by itself" seemingly has no effect on the essence of some individual object. So, Aristotle thinks that if our aim is to understand something about *particulars*, knowing something about a universal *removed from* particulars seems an unlikely path to the desired understanding.

On two counts then, Aristotle thinks separately existing universals don't help: they don't help with explaining the essence or nature of objects, and they don't help with explaining our knowledge of individual objects.

Two points might be made on Plato's behalf. Some have pointed out that the forms as Plato viewed them are not really unnecessary, since they allow him to give a unified answer to ethical, epistemological, and metaphysical questions. That we call widely different actions all by the same name, e.g., "courageous," that we are able to explain differences between opinion and knowledge, that we are able to explain the nature of the objectivity—all of these matters can be given a consistent, unified account by appeal to the forms. Identifying courage as a universal explains why we call "courageous" widely disparate acts, e.g., the act of the bystander who steps in to prevent a mugging of an elderly citizen or the soldier who sacrifices his life. And we are able to explain the differences between believing and knowing about the nature of courage, which in turn is explained by a metaphysical theory, the theory of the forms. We *know* what courage is when we have grasped the form. This theory at once gives us an understanding of the connection between attribute agreement, knowledge, and objectivity. Thus, there is an "economy" to Plato's view.[25]

Second, Plato might agree that it's only when a universal is instantiated in an individual that it makes a difference to the sort of individual it is. Yet Plato might—and arguably did—dissent from the idea that independently existing universals do not contribute to our understanding of individuals

---

25 Cherniss 1936.

or particulars. For example, in the *Phaedo* Socrates argues that we can come across two items that are said to be equal, but we recognize that they are not quite *exactly* equal. This implies, Socrates claims, that we are comparing the apparently equal objects to some independent standard, which Socrates says is the universal *equals*, or the relation of equality.[26] Responses to these objections might be made on behalf of Aristotle, but there is not room to discuss them here; instead, we will move on to one more important facet of moderate realism.

Aristotle held that we acquire our concept of a given universal by a process of abstraction, which is an intellectual rather than a sensory process. But abstraction begins with the sensory process. Imagine that as Deirdre surveys her back yard, she notices several American finches perched on the various trees and bushes. Of course, Deirdre has "sensings" of each of the finches. But something else also happens. Deirdre's intellect extracts or *abstracts* the *intelligible form* of the common nature or essence of this kind, American finch. The intelligible form itself is not something sensible. Rather it's something apprehended and known intellectually. Deirdre doesn't see or smell or taste the intelligible form, but she does cognize or apprehend or think it. In virtue of possessing this abstracted intellectual form, Deirdre now has the concept *American finch*, a concept standing for or referring to all and only American finches.

Moderate realism thus holds that universal concepts—concepts that refer to many instances—are formed by an intellectual process of abstraction. The universal concept refers to all particular individuals possessing the universal because the abstracted form is the intellectual aspect of that essence. And this provides the moderate realist with an explanation of abstract reference: the concept refers to the universal. When Deirdre says that finches are birds, she is referring to the immanent essence of any and all finches.

The Aristotelian in particular and the moderate realist in general thus think that their view possesses all the advantages of a realism like Plato's, but none of the disadvantages.

Moderate realism is closely related to conceptualism, but, as we will see, they differ in an important respect.

---

26 Copleston 1946, Vol. 1, Pt. II, Chap. 29.

Conceptualism

Heloise and Abelard

The twelfth-century relationship between the philosopher Abelard and his student Heloise could scarcely be rivaled by Hollywood. In fact, Hollywood saw fit to make *Stealing Heaven* in 1988—the story of their romance, perhaps the most famous of the medieval period.

In Paris Abelard achieved considerable fame: his attractiveness, his intelligence, and his skill in argument, all contributed to his reputation. When he was hired by Heloise's uncle to tutor her, the two fell in love. Abelard's poems to her and their affair became well-known among the populace—and eventually by Heloise's uncle, who tried to separate them. The lovers continued to meet secretly, however, and when Heloise became pregnant, Abelard offered to marry her. Only after a time did she accept, and the two attempted to keep the marriage secret to minimize the damage to Abelard's career.

Heloise's uncle began to spread information about the secret marriage, and Heloise retreated to a convent to escape the situation. Her uncle, believing that Abelard was trying to end the marriage by forcing Heloise to become a nun, had him beaten and castrated. Abelard retired from public life, entered a monastery and eventually founded a convent that Heloise later headed.

Out of touch with each other for ten years, the two began a correspondence, initiated by Heloise. The letters are a famous moment in romantic literature (Levitan 2007). They range over various topics, including morality, the nature of love, Heloise's and Abelard's feelings about their relationship, and Abelard's request to her that he be buried at her convent. Heloise honored his request.[27]

Peter Abelard contributed significantly to the medieval debate about universals. While most commentators recognize the importance of his work, there is some controversy about how to interpret and categorize it. He is described as a moderate realist, as a nominalist, and as a conceptualist. Here, we will interpret Abelard's view as a form of conceptualism—but clarifying this account will perhaps also illustrate why Abelard's view is sometimes classified in other ways.

---

27   Wagoner 1997; Marenbon 1997; Gilson 1960.

To put it simply, Abelard's view is that universals are concepts that exist only in the mind but can refer to many individual non-mental objects. In other words, concepts are particular "things," which exist only in individual minds and enable us to think about objects. Concepts, of course, are not things the way a coffee cup or a camellia bush or a cloud are things; they differ both from each other and from things like camellias and clouds. Contemporary vernacular might call them "mental particulars." Here Abelard holds a view not unlike other nominalists, namely, that everything that exists is particular (or individual). Concepts, too, are particular. Yet, some concepts are also *universal* in the following sense: they refer to more than one individual. As in moderate realism, these universal concepts are reached through intellectual abstraction.

Abelard's view requires us to be careful about the nature of these universal concepts. As mental phenomena, they do not exist apart from the mind. Indeed this is part of what differentiates Abelard's view from realism. The universal concept enables us to talk and think generally, yet it does not exist outside the mind.

Understanding the process of forming a universal concept is central for Abelard. On encountering a particular horse, Dobbin, I form a concept *of that particular horse*. This concept includes the various aspects of *this horse*. It's brown, with a black mane, not very tall, but friendly.

After seeing several horses, after collecting several sensory images of particular horses, Abelard says that I abstract a common form. This form, or "image" as he sometimes says, is not tied to any particular horse. The image is generalized, so that it stands for all horses. This differs from Aristotle; I don't abstract the intellectual form from the universal or the essence contained by the individuals. Abstraction for Abelard is more like neglecting the individual differences, or *abstracting away* from the particular differences of each of the individual concepts and "seeing" what is left. This abstracted or generalized concept *horse* is universal in the sense that it has been "de-particularized" sufficiently so that it stands for all the various particular horses. The word "horse," when it names this universal concept, is a universal name or word. So, the word names the concept, and the concept stands for all the particulars. As a generalized and hence universal concept *horse* now refers to any and all horses.

The universal concept *horse* stands for all horses. The English word "horse" and the Latin word "*equus*" refer to all horses, since they name the same universal concept. But does the universal concept stand for many particulars because there is something *the same* or *common* in the individuals? Or is this just a matter of convention or arbitrary grouping, such as "Well, it seems to me that these individuals are alike ..."? Abelard holds the former, that a universal concept is formed because of something in the objects; there is an *objective* reason for universal concepts. We didn't just manufacture the concepts based on nothing. Instead we group or classify individuals because of some common element, or "common cause," as Abelard called it. Abelard further seemed to suggest that it's more than just similarity or "being a lot alike" at work here. But conceptualism rejects also the idea of moderate realism, which holds that a universal exists *in* many different particulars. Thus, Abelard says "Since there is no *thing* in which things could possibly agree, if there is any agreement among certain things, [that is, if they are both of the same sort,] this must not be taken to be some *thing*."[28]

To put it more succinctly, universal concepts are generalized images, intellectually abstracted from the particular sensory images. The generalized image thus explains our ability to refer to many individuals by a universal word, e.g., "horse." And this standing for or referring to many individuals explains why we have a *universal* concept. Such concepts are universal because they stand for a plurality of individuals.

Two principal differences between moderate realism and conceptualism may then be noted. While there is a "common form" that is the basis of the universal concept, Abelard rejects the idea that there are immanent universals. And while both views acknowledge a process of abstraction, the moderate realist believes that it is the universal (or the form) that is abstracted. For the conceptualist, the intellect abstracts by generalizing, by ignoring the differences between particulars.

While conceptualists reject the moderate realist's claim that a universal exists in each object, they also reject the nominalist claim that what might look like a universal essence is just similarity or "being a lot alike" in some respect. There really is something common to the various individuals, says the conceptualist—just not a universal.

To its critics, this seems like an uneasy intermediate view, occasionally flirting with realism, then with nominalism. For it might seem a simple step from "common element" to "immanent universal." And, in the other direction, it might seem a simple step from the conceptualist emphasis on naming a universal concept to the nominalist dismissal of categories as "just names." In its position on this issue, conceptualism occupies a central fault line between realists and nominalists. In attempting to find generality in our thoughts

---

28   Abelard 1969/1992, p. 26; Marenbon 1997, pp. 190 ff.

rather than in the world, conceptualism attempts a delicate balancing act. In doing so, it inherits special problems of its own. And these problems perhaps illustrate why most theorists are today either realist or nominalist.

Key Concepts

- universal
- particulars
- realism
- nominalism
- conceptualism
- Third Man Argument
- strict nominalism
- resemblance nominalism
- tropes
- moderate realism

Reading/Discussion Questions

1. In your own words, explain the attribute agreement argument for realism. How would you assess this argument? Do you agree with Plato or other realists that there is something like an objective standard for beauty or courage? Explain.

2. In the dialogue *Parmenides*, Parmenides asks the young Socrates if he accepts universals for things like mud or hair. Socrates says that he is unsure. (The problem here seems to be that a universal is an ideal form, and how can there be an ideal form of something that is nasty?) And in the *Republic*, Socrates mentions the form of "bed." Do you think a realist about universals ought to accept that universals for these sorts of things exist?

3. Do you agree with the strict nominalists, like Quine, that we don't need to explain why we group red houses, red books, red glasses together? Why or why not?

4. Which form of resemblance nominalism do you find more defensible, the resemblance class view or the trope view? Why?

5. Abelard held the view that it is only words or concepts that are "universal." A word or term is universal because it is used to refer to many individuals. Do you agree with this view? Why or why not?

For Further Reading

Three surveys of metaphysics contain chapters on universals. E.J. Lowe 2002 and Loux 2006 are perhaps a bit more advanced. Loux has separate chapters on universals and nominalism. Carroll and Markosian 2010 also contains a chapter on universals. Two worthwhile collections of essays/selections on universals and particulars are Loux 1970 and Schoedinger 1992. The shorter work by Armstrong 1989 presents his assessment of other views, primarily forms of nominalism, and also presents his own moderate realist view, which identifies universals with scientific properties. W.T. Jones 1969b contains a section explaining the medieval thinkers' debate on universals. There are several accessible treatments of Aristotle's view; Copleston 1974 is particularly helpful and readable. The interpretation of Plato's views on universals (forms) is still contested. White 1976, which is readily accessible, and Rosen 2008, perhaps a bit more challenging, offer important and interesting interpretations.

Gracia 1992 is an accessible and careful presentation of the medieval view of transcendentals.

CHAPTER SEVEN

THINGS

Metaphysics aims to describe the nature of reality, of all that there is. Perhaps the single most obvious feature of that reality is the existence of *things*, of objects, of individuals. Philosophers often call them "particulars." Particulars range from the very large—the planet Jupiter, for example—to the very small—the molecule or the atom or the neutron or the single cell. Now philosophers are not usurping the role of scientists when they attempt to explain the nature and structure of all things. When philosophers ask about the nature of things, they are trying to understand something about their metaphysical nature. They are not trying to reveal the genome of the *canis lupus familiaris*—man's best friend—but they are interested in finding out what it is to be an individual object, whether a dog or a ball or a building, or any *thing*.

It may seem odd to think that metaphysics could tell us about the general structure and nature of things. After all, isn't that the business of the sciences—to tell us what makes up things and how they are put together? Notice, however: we can still ask a few very general questions, which the sciences seemingly don't answer. We distinguish between a thing (or object) and its characteristics (or properties). Just what is the relationship between the thing and its characteristics? (This question will become clearer in a moment.) And a related question: is there something more to an object than just its characteristics? What more is there to this hollyberry candle than its color, scent, shape, and its other features? Are some properties more important than others for an object to be that object or that *kind* of object? That blue footed booby—it couldn't be a *blue footed* booby without its blue feet (could it?), but what if it didn't have the characteristic of performing a mating dance? The "metaphysics of things" aims at answering these types of question.

Notice that the metaphysics of things distinguishes between the *type* or *kind* and an individual instance of the kind. No doubt your early science classes taught you that mammals are warm-blooded vertebrates with hair that produce milk for their young. The kind *mammal* has various individual instances, including Millie, the echidna (a relative of the duck-billed platypus), a mascot of the 2000 Summer Olympics. And Millie has characteristics that distinguish or *individuate* her from other echidnas. The metaphysics of things considers both the identity of the kind and the individual.

First Thoughts: Individuals as Substances

Many perhaps take for granted an intuitive picture of individuals or things. We think of cats and dogs, or people and chimpanzees; we think of rose bushes or cherry trees. At some point, we may come to think of molecules. We may wonder if mountains or clouds are things in the same way as chairs or golf balls. No matter our answer to these latter examples, we continue to think of the world as a world of things. And we think of these things—each one having its uniquely identifying characteristics or properties—as the ultimate constituents of the world. We may nonetheless recognize a thing as made up of various components. Yet the puppy's tail, the cat's whiskers, a person's hand—these are parts of the whole, of the individual. The *individual* thing is basic.

Notice that it is not the type that is basic, in this view; it is the individuals. And the individuals or basic things of course have characteristics or properties. The dog is growling, or the rose bush is blooming. Julia is wise, or Jack is frugal. The kitten is calico, the puppy energetic, or the chimpanzee curious. Such characteristics or features are features that *belong* to the individual, not to some part. We don't think, for example, that there goes "Jack's brain again, being frugal." Springtime visitors to Washington, DC, during the Cherry Blossom Festival, don't think that a branch is blooming, but rather that the tree is blooming. Moreover, setting aside the Cheshire Cat in *Alice in Wonderland*, we don't think there are disconnected, independent grinnings. We think that we always experience "frugal-ness" as someone or other being frugal, the smile or the grin as belonging to someone or other. It is a cherry blossom or a shirt that is pink; we don't experience pink "all by itself." Our experience of pink is always an experience of the color as *belonging to* some individual thing.

There are then three aspects of this intuitive picture of the makeup of the world: individuals as basic, individuals as being of a certain kind of thing, and features or characteristics or aspects as belonging to or depending on the individuals.

Aristotle's *Categories* provides one of the earliest attempts to describe systematically the picture of the things that make up our world; it is a view that is in many respects similar to the intuitive picture just described.[1] Aristotle identifies the basic things or individuals of the world as *substances—primary substances*, as he calls them—the puppy, the palm tree, the proton, or any other individual thing. Primary substances "underlie" everything else. We can note two senses in which they underlie everything else. First, they are the ultimate constituents of the world, which is made up of individual dogs, trees, and planets (rather than being made up of qualities like "brownness" or of categories like "Chihuahuas"). Second, the properties of these individuals, including relations to other individuals, depend on the individuals or primary substances. You can't have just brown, by itself; you have to have a brown something—a brown dog, for example.

Things Change: Substance, Essence, and Accident

Aristotle's substance view continued to serve as a metaphysical framework much discussed by medieval philosophers, discussed in relation to a wide range of topics including the nature of individuals or things in general, human nature and the soul, and even the nature of God.[2] Reliance on the concept of substance, variously defined, continued through the early modern period.

---

1   Aristotle 1941a.
2   Gilson 1940 surveys many of these issues.

More recently, despite serious criticism offered by Berkeley and Hume, and twentieth-century process philosophy, substance views have seen something of a revival by some contemporary defenders.[3] The notion of substances with attributes—called the substance view or the substance-attribute framework—is a fundamental framework for thinking of individuals, one that has been used to explain a number of features of things or individuals.

First, consider the thought that individuals, for example, belong to kinds. This plant is a begonia, that animal is a white-tailed deer. The kind has an *essence* or a *nature*, some defining property or properties that each member of the kind possesses. You're not a mammal unless you're a vertebrate, for example. In the early twenty-first century, we might appeal to DNA, for example, to distinguish the kind *rhesus macaque* from *lemur*. Sometimes it is an easy matter to identify a defining characteristic—e.g., one defining characteristic of a tricycle is that it has three wheels—while listing those defining characteristics

---

3   Loux 2006; E.J. Lowe 1998, Chaps. 5–7; Macdonald 2005, Chap. 3.

for some objects may be more complicated. Often we note the kind as a way of identifying the essence. Bucephalus is a horse and what makes him a horse is possessing that characteristic of *being a horse*. Alexander the Great is a human being in virtue of his having a certain essence, a certain defining characteristic, namely, *being a human being*. Of course, if we thought that what makes something a human being or a horse is simply having the DNA definitive of a human being or horse, we might say: Bucephalus is a horse because he possesses the attribute of *having the DNA definitive of being a horse*. Notice, however, that identifying the essence of more complex objects—say, human beings—simply by noting the molecular makeup can be controversial. Various thinkers—among them philosophers, but also theologians, artists of various types, and social scientists—have held that the defining characteristic, or *attribute*, of the *nature* of human beings is more than just some common molecular structural pattern.

Aristotle, for example, thought that the defining characteristic of human beings is the ability to reason, as did Descartes and Kant, each with their own take on this ability. Julia and Sam are of the kind *human being* then because they both possess this rational ability. On the other hand, the twentieth-century German philosopher Martin Heidegger suggests at times that the defining nature of human beings is that we are the being that speaks—we are language-using creatures.[4] The interest here is not to adjudicate between rival conceptions of *human being*. The point rather is to note that an essence or nature comprises certain properties, certain attributes. And two individuals belong to the same kind if they both have the same general nature or essence.

Leibniz: All Our Attributes Are Essential

G.W. Leibniz held an unusual view of substance. In his view, the basic individuals are immaterial, indivisible entities called *monads*. Our familiar objects are composed of monads or societies of them. Monads are characterized as "windowless": because of their nature, they are not affected by the outside world. The apparent interaction between monads or societies or collectives of monads is only apparent. That is, when Andrea tells Andy to close the door and he does, or when one billiard ball hits another and the second takes off, this looks to us as though there is some causal interaction between the two. But this is merely apparent. What we take to be cause-effect sequences are

---

4   Heidegger 1976; also see Heidegger 1965.

rather unrelated; any change in a substance comes solely from the nature of that substance itself. Observed regularities—the second billiard ball *always* moves when hit by the first—are due to the coordination of the natures of things by divine plan, known as *pre-established harmony*.

Leibniz held that persons possess only essential attributes; there are no inessential or accidental attributes. According to him, apparently accidental attributes are so only from *our* perspective. From God's point of view, those attributes are necessary parts of who we are. Thus, God knows a complete description of each individual from eternity, and there is no changing any item in that description. Hence, Alexander acquiring Bucephalus at the age of thirteen is an essential feature of Alexander the Great, even though it seems to us to be an accidental or inessential property of Alexander.

Not all attributes are essential, however. Some attributes are inessential or *accidental* to being a particular kind of thing. While both Julia and Sam are human beings, her light-colored hair differs from his dark-colored hair; similarly, their eye color may differ, or their height. Characteristics such as height or eye color or age are *accidental* attributes. Changes to these—Sam dyes his hair; Julia becomes a year older—do not change the kind of thing, only some of its properties.

The substance-attribute framework thus provides an answer to a more general question: what is change? For the substance theorist, change is simply a change in attributes. Lose an attribute, gain an attribute—a thing changes. And with the distinction between essential and inessential attributes, we also have a way of understanding two different types of change. Paint the dining room table a light red. The table has changed. Yet it's still a dining room table, because the altered attribute is inessential. The cherry tree loses its blossoms, but it's still a cherry tree. Sara now sports a tattoo—changed, yes, but still Sara.[5] On the other hand, supposing for a moment that cellulose is an essential characteristic of wood, burning a spruce log in the fireplace "changes" the essence of the wood. This is essential change, also called substantial change.

Any substantial change involves destruction. The individual becomes a new kind of thing, and the old individual exists no more. During cases of "radioactive change," for example, an atom of one kind can change into a new kind of atom.

---

5   See, e.g., David Ross 1971, pp. 81–83; also Aristotle 1941e, Book V.

Hierarchy: Animal, Vegetable ... or Artifact

Dogs belong to different (pure or mixed) breeds, but they all belong to the same species. And here we have a simple example of a hierarchy of kinds. Perhaps somewhere along the way, reading a book in botany or biology, you came across a more complete hierarchy: species, genus, family, order, class, phylum, kingdom. We talk about the *animal* kingdom, for example. Is there an analogous hierarchy for objects?

Sort of. Aristotle identified three kinds of primary substances, or things: animals, including human beings; plants; and the basic individuals or elements acknowledged by science. Of course, Aristotle knew nothing of hydrogen or carbon atoms, even if certain kinds of "stuff"—of say, iron, gold, and silver—were well-known. But Aristotle thought there were four "basic elements" composing all physical things. (For modern substance theorists, there are far more elements in this category; a standard version of the modern Periodic Table recognizes about 120 basic elements.)[6]

To these three kinds of individuals or things, let us add a fourth—artifacts. We might think of an artifact as something which requires the skill or intervention of some animal. Thus, we might think of beaver dams or bird nests as artifacts, and hence a type of individual (though some philosophers argue that artifacts are not individuals[7]). Still there seem to be clear cut cases of artifacts, such as things we make or build.

We might then think of our hierarchy like this. Every individual thing is a member of some kind. And every kind is a member of some "family"—animal, plant, basic scientific element, or artifact. Each of these then is a kind of object; each belongs to the "object kingdom."

To recap: a substance is our familiar individual—Bucephalus, Alexander, the rose bush, the table. And the *kind of individual* is determined by the essence or the defining attribute(s) that each possesses. Substance theory enables us to explain the nature of change too, as well as to distinguish essential from inessential or accidental change. It also enables us to classify individuals according to the type of object they are.

---

6   See Aristotle 1941e, Book II.
7   E.g., van Inwagen 1990, Chap. 13.

Things = Substratum + Properties

Sally is a tall read-headed Mid-westerner. The rug is brown, oval, and fuzzy. In each case, we think of a *something* plus its properties; the *something*—the substances—holds its properties together.

Some might think that the notion of a primary substance doesn't quite explain all that we need to know about things. So what holds the properties together? What's the Sally or the rug here?

In response, some have urged a different notion of substance, that of substratum—*that which supports or holds together the various properties of an object*. Substratum theorists distinguish between the properties of an object and what it is that holds the properties together. Importantly, this theory does not identify the substratum with any group of essential properties. Moreover, for the substratum theorist, the substance *as* substratum is not the individual, as it is in the Aristotelian substance-attribute view.

Locke on Substance as Substratum

Observing that we find groups of qualities or characteristics occurring together, John Locke, the seventeenth-century empiricist and political philosopher, argues in *An Essay on Human Understanding* that we naturally suspect that something *holds them together*. Qualities aren't "free-floating"; they don't exist alone, by themselves. I now experience or sense individual qualities—red, solid, glass, Christmas-tree shaped—and I sense them as occupying this same little space. This Christmas decoration comprising these qualities has "something" that holds all these properties together, so that I can talk about *this* Christmas decoration rather than just a number of individual qualities. Locke's explanation of these qualities being joined together is that "we accustom our selves, to suppose some *Substratum*, wherein they [the qualities] do subsist, and from which they do result, which therefore we call *Substance*." If any one were to reflect on the notion of substance in general, Locke says that person would find that this notion is only "a supposition of he knows not what support of such qualities."[8]

It is worth noting that Locke's view of a substratum is simultaneously a critique of the Aristotelian notion of substance and a distinct view about the notion of substance, understood in the only reasonable way we can, as *substratum*.

---

8   Locke 1975, Bk. II, xxiii; E.J. Lowe 2005, Chap. 3.

Aristotle thought we experienced or sensed substances directly; but Locke suggests that the notion of substance is an inference. We *infer* the existence of this substratum, based on our "sensible ideas," or our experiencing of apparently "grouped together" sensible properties. As I look at the book lying on the table, I have various sensations, among them orange, rectangular, a certain feel. I find these properties "together" on numerous occasions: I found—experienced or sensed—them together last evening, this morning and now again this afternoon. And I suppose or *infer*—as you might also—that there is *something that holds them together.*

At least initially this seems a reasonable inference. We don't experience properties disconnected from objects. I find this orange and this rectangular together, or I observe the yellow and a slightly curved, cylindrical shape together; and the red, slightly sweet-smelling, and spherical stay together. That is, something seems to hold together the properties of this book, of that banana, of this apple—something that properties are *of.* This something—*we infer*—is the substratum, which we call "substance," according to Locke.

So far we have been thinking of the particular substratum of a particular object. When we ask what the idea of "substance in general" is, we find, according to Locke, that we can give nothing other but this sense of *support* to the idea. This is all we are left with if we take away all the qualities or characteristics that apply only to specific objects. *Substratum* is, he says, we know not what. If we take away our ideas, which arise through our senses, caused by things' qualities or characteristics, we are left only with this idea of support.

Substratum theorists tell us that the metaphysical structure of things is that they are "compounds." The pup at my feet, the book on the table, the cup, the crickets outside are to be understood as things, each comprising two kinds of components or constituents. Things are constituted by, made up of, a substratum and various properties. Michael Loux characterizes this as a *reductionist* picture of objects: the substratum theorist *reduces* objects to this general structure of substratum and property.[9] While the substance-attribute view agrees that a thing has properties, that view, at least as understood by Aristotle, takes individual objects as basic. Instead substratum theorists find something more basic than individuals or our ordinary objects, namely, the substratum and the qualities attaching to a substratum.

Substratum theory also provides a way of distinguishing two objects. Imagine that Danny and Deirdre have the same book—same color, shape,

---

9   Loux 2006, Chap. 3.

markings, etc. What is it that distinguishes the two books? According to the substratum theorist, each has its own unique substratum. The particularity or individuality of any object derives from the substratum of that object.

So the substratum view tells us what it is to be an individual thing and how individual things may be discerned. Individual things are "composed of" substrata and qualities. And each individual thing has its own unique, identifying substratum.

But What's It Like? Worries about Substrata

Very quickly, however, we confront a difficult question. A substratum holds the qualities or properties together; it supports the qualities. Does the substratum itself have any qualities? It would seem not. How could it? If the substratum had its own properties, something would be needed to support or hold together those properties—another substratum, which would presumably have its own properties as well. So we would need another, and another.... This would seem to lead to a never-ending regress.

But then what? We seem forced to the conclusion that *substrata have no properties whatsoever*. Pointing out that a substratum has the property of *holding properties together* does nothing to dispel the difficulty, since this is but another way of describing the *property-less* "we know not what" that holds properties together. Following the substratum theorist's idea leads us to a very peculiar metaphysical entity. All we can say about this "thing" is that it holds properties together somehow. Bishop George Berkeley would later suggest that this substratum looks a lot like, well, nothing.

A related difficulty emerges. Substrata were supposed to serve to distinguish or uniquely identify objects, but we cannot use them for this. And this seems to lead to an odd conclusion: if we accepted this view, we would not be able to distinguish what common sense tells us are two objects with all the same properties. How could we? Imagine, for example, apparently two identical books—same size, color, markings, etc. The properties are the same, so those do not *individuate* them. And now the substrata won't help either—they don't have any properties that would serve to say "here's one and there's the other." How can a "featureless" substratum accomplish the uniquely distinguishing or individuating function? It would seem substrata can't. Substratum theory is thus unable to explain a very basic metaphysical intuition of ours. It does not tell us why what appear to be two identical items are in fact *two*. So, there seems to be something fundamentally wrong with the substratum view.

Indeed, it looks even worse! It's not just that substrata aren't able to differentiate similar objects, but that the substrata of very different kinds of thing seem to be interchangeable. The substrata of the pie and the piano, of the piano and the pup, of the pup and the palomino, would all also seem to be wholly interchangeable. Nor does there seem to be any difference between the substrata of Julia and Jack. How could this be? Differences, notice, apparently come from having different properties. But there can't be any *difference* between substrata because substrata don't have any properties!

(You will notice that we aren't relying on where an object is located, or its "space-time" location, to differentiate between objects. We would like our "identifying feature" to be something *internal* or *intrinsic* to an object, not its location, which is an extrinsic property.)

The metaphysical picture of substratum theory seems to have collapsed because of two apparent problems. First, a substratum is itself without properties; it supports properties but does not itself have properties. So, we are seemingly unable to explain anything about substrata. What are they? Well, they hold properties together ... but that's all we know about them. Apparently we are led then to a second problem. If substrata are themselves "property-less," it is not at all clear how objects are to be distinguished from one another—not only very similar objects (this book and that one) but even wildly different ones.

To be fair to substratum theorists, some contemporary thinkers have defended versions of this view, under the heading of "bare particulars," or sometimes "thin particulars." For example, it is argued that "thin particulars," while not themselves things, are nonetheless of a special ontological or metaphysical type. A bare particular "makes" an object *this individual*. Thus, to ask what sort of properties they have is a mistake. Worrying about the property-less aspect—and assuming that they need to have qualities in order to be distinct from one another—is to misunderstand the claim that thin particulars are distinct.[10] This version of the substratum view then suggests a different way of thinking about what it is to be a real individual object. There are particulars—bare or thin—that are without properties and unlike the particulars of our normal acquaintance, yet are what makes some object an individual object, distinct from any other. Property-less yet real.

A different approach to this problem is rather abrupt: dispense with substrata! and just keep the properties! So let's see what things look like if we get rid of substrata and keep just the qualities ... objects are *bundles* of qualities.

---

10   Sider 2006.

Bundle Theory

Fictional Objects

In an 1897 editorial in the *New York Sun*, Francis Church famously penned the line, "Yes, Virginia, there is a Santa Claus," answering an eight year old girl's question about whether Santa Claus exists. He wrote, "The most real things in the world are those that neither children nor men can see." But even many children nowadays think of Santa as fictional.

We often refer to fictional characters. How are we to understand what—if anything—we are referring to in this ordinary practice? Are fictional characters *objects*? If so, in what sense? Do they "exist"? If they don't exist, in any sense, what are we talking about, when we talk about them? How can we say true things about them? One widely held view is *abstract artifact* theory, and a recent elaboration and defense is that of Amie L. Thomasson.

In her 1999 *Fiction and Metaphysics*, Thomasson argues that fictional objects, including fictional characters, are abstract artifactual objects. Like other artifacts, fictional objects are created by one or more human beings. And they are created *in* the literary work penned by the author(s). Oedipus, Romeo and Juliet, Don Quixote, and Sherlock Holmes, are one and all *creations* of their authors. In this, they "existentially depend" on both the author and the literary work or works.

But they are also *abstract* objects. They are not concrete objects, having some location in space and time. Do they exist? Yes: they exist as much as any other artifact. But they exist only in those possible worlds where the elements on which they existentially depend also exist—Iago exists, but only in the possible worlds where Shakespeare exists and wrote the play *Othello*.

R.M. Sainsbury's 2010 *Fiction and Fictionalism* critically examines a number of views about the nature of fictional characters, including abstract artifact theory. Sainsbury also explains and defends *irrealism*, the view, which he opts for, that we should not think of fictional characters as objects.

Empiricism moves in a dramatic direction after Locke. Locke's empiricism led him to invoke the notion of a substratum as our best understanding of the idea of substance. A more trenchant empiricism, however, insisted that the evidence of our senses simply did not entitle us to invoke any notion of substance or substratum at all. The senses reveal no hidden substance or substratum, but only qualities: the lavender of a late spring lilac bloom, a summer scent of cantaloupe or watermelon, the orange of a carrot, with its crunchy texture—no substratum, just a bundle of qualities.

Berkeley and Hume on Bundles

In 1710, George Berkeley gave an early version of the bundle theory:

> As several of these [qualities] are observed to accompany each other, they come to be marked by one name, and so to be reputed as one THING. Thus, for example, a certain colour, taste, smell, figure and consistence having been observed to go together, are accounted one distinct thing, signified by the name apple.[11]

But Hume is often credited with the full and explicit version of the theory. In the opening pages of his *A Treatise of Human Nature*, Hume writes:

> I wou'd fain ask those philosophers, who found so much of their reasonings on the distinction of *substance and accident*, and imagine we have clear ideas of each, whether the idea of *substance* be deriv'd from impressions of sensation or reflexion [introspection—observation of one's own mind]? If it be convey'd to us by our senses, I ask, which of them? and after what manner?[12]

Hume continues that if substance *were* discovered through the senses or through subsequent introspection, it could be nothing more than a quality itself. And this leads to the conclusion, according to Hume, that we encounter not substances and their attributes but bundles of qualities: "We have therefore no idea of substance, distinct from a *collection of particular qualities*, nor have we any other meaning when we talk of reason concerning it."[13]

Berkeley's skepticism about material substances and Hume's skepticism about the notion of substance in general led them to a view, still held by many in one form or another, known as the bundle theory—the view that objects are nothing more than collections, or "co-locations" of qualities. There is no substance, no essence; nor is there any property-less substratum that holds together or supports an object's qualities. For example, two candles sit in

---

11   Berkeley 1965, Sect. 1.
12   Hume 1978, I, i, 6; first emphasis added.
13   Hume 1978, I, i, 6; emphasis added.

front of me. Each cylindrical, each six inches high and three inches in diameter. But one is red and the other green. The qualities *constitute* or *make up* the candles. That's all there is to these two candles. A certain, shape, height, weight, scent, color. And what is true of the candles is true of every object, animate or inanimate.

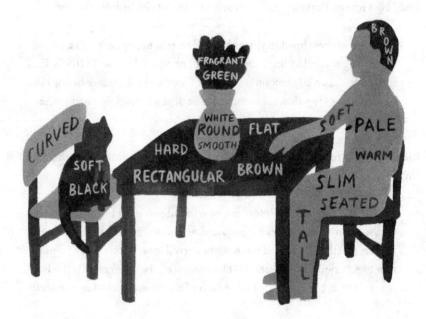

But wait—if things are only their qualities, and nothing but their qualities, there is a surprising consequence: *any change of quality changes the identity of the object*. An apparent advantage of the substance view is that it explains how an object changes but remains the *same* object. Yet, according to bundle theory, if Julia paints the bookcase red, we have a different object from the white bookcase we had before!

Why this counterintuitive but apparent consequence of bundle theory? In the bundle theory view, all qualities are "equal": there is no distinction between essential qualities and accidental qualities. Every quality is just as important as any other quality. In fact, *every quality is essential to the object* because that's what it is to be an object—to have a particular group of qualities. To be *this* object is to have *these* qualities. So, any change in quality yields a very similar, but a brand new, object. To put this a bit more formally, the identity of an object is determined solely and wholly by *all* its qualities.

This of course differs dramatically from our two previous views—and from our intuitions about the identity of an object. When we see Julia's newly painted bookcase, we don't think that Julia has created an entirely new object. This was the apparent advantage of the substance kind and substratum views: we could continue to think of the bookcase as the *same* bookcase because either the essential properties remained or the substratum remained. Bundle theory then departs considerably from our more commonsense view of objects.

Someone like Hume has a response to this apparently extreme consequence. The bundle theorist notes that when we pause to consider the notions of substance or substratum, we cannot get a clear sense of such a notion. Our sensory experience simply fails to reveal anything in the world that corresponds to our commonsense notion of objects. And reflection on our actual sensory experience reveals that objects are comprised solely by their properties, and by *all their properties*. This object—whether bell, book, or candle—is all and only this group of qualities. Consequently, any change in properties yields a new object. Hume accepted this highly counterintuitive consequence of bundle theory, saying that a series of very similar things does not constitute one continuing object, and that we merely imagine some unseen continuing substance.

Further, we do not experience any select properties as *essence*. As Berkeley suggested, take away the qualities, and we are left with ... nothing! Hence, in this sort of empiricism's view, it's not surprising that my knowledge of objects is knowledge of nothing more than a bundle, a bundle of qualities. Of course, not all advocates of bundle theory accept Hume's version of empiricism. Nonetheless, versions of empiricism much like Hume's often motivate such a view.

Bundle theory seemingly differs from substratum and substance kind views in another respect; we might wonder how it is that the bundle theorist identifies *kinds* of things. Imagine two dogs, say, Snoopy and Spot. All of Snoopy's properties make him this dog and not some other. That's the point of bundle theory: to be Snoopy is to be this bundle. Similarly with Spot. Without a distinction between essential and accidental properties, however, bundle theory doesn't provide us with a way of identifying what makes Snoopy and Spot this *kind* of thing, namely, a dog. According to bundle theorists, however, we can choose a set of properties ourselves and simply decide that so long as a bundle has these properties, it is a dog. Thus, the radical nominalism discussed earlier.

This need to decide that certain properties define the kind *dog*, or any other kind, varies from our typical view. We tend to think there is something internal or intrinsic about the fact that "dog-defining qualities" are found together. That is, we commonly think of these qualities as *essential*, and as internally unified, regardless of our decisions or beliefs. Bundle theory rejects this notion of essence or of "kind-defining" properties and directs us only to all the properties equally. This gives us little guidance as to how to determine the kind, apart from whatever customary or conventional decisions we make.[14]

Critics of bundle theory have also noted the problem of distinguishing between two (or apparently two) objects that have all the same qualities. Common sense seems to say that two objects can have exactly the same properties, yet remain distinct. Bundle theory seems to lead—mistakenly, critics contend—to a different result. Again, imagine two candles, identical in all respects: same height, color, diameter, weight, scent. They have the same properties. Now ask the simple question: according to bundle theory, what makes them two things instead of one?

You might suggest that we can distinguish objects because of their spatial location. Could we imagine two distinct objects sharing every characteristic, and occupying exactly the same space at the same time? Wouldn't that really be one object?

This may seem unsatisfying, however. If Deirdre and Sara are identical twins, we don't think they are two *because* they occupy different spaces. They are two because *internally* or *intrinsically* something differs. Similarly for objects: critics argue that there must be something "inside," as it were—an intrinsic "thisness" that makes this thing and that thing two different things ...[15]

Various replies have been proposed to this problem. Unfortunately we cannot follow most them here since following the ins and outs of the replies and objections to those replies requires a technical framework that we leave aside. There is still doubt about the success of the bundle theory replies to the "identity problem."[16] But a brief sketch of one possible solution is available.

A Bundle of Tropes

Normally we think that this red of the candle and that red of the book are but instances of the same kind of quality. (See Chapter 6: Universals.) Trope theory, on the other hand, claims that there is no kind *red*, but only different,

---

14   Macdonald 2005, pp. 91–95.

15   Loux 2006, Chap. 3.

16   Loux 2006, Chap. 3.

"particularized" reds—different ones for every object. These particularized qualities are called *tropes*. We distinguish the two candles because each has its own particular properties, and these particular properties occur nowhere else.[17] Similarly Julia's book differs from Jack's seemingly identical copy because hers is nothing but this "one-time only" group of particularized properties—tropes. So, the trope theorist can explain how objects are individuated.[18] It is not surprising, however, to find that one of the standard questions posed to trope theory is the same as that posed to bundle theory in general: "what holds the bundles together?" Substratum and substance theorists already have an alternative they prefer. Rather than re-explore this terrain, perhaps we might look in a different direction ... some very different directions.

Different Directions: Whitehead and Heidegger

An ancient Chinese tale tells of a teacher and a young student. One moonlit night, the teacher points to the moon, and proclaims, "That is the moon." The young student moves closer and begins to inspect the teacher's finger. No, protests the mentor, "you've mistaken my finger for the moon." Some twentieth-century philosophers became convinced that the history of metaphysics, with its emphasis on things and substance, had mistaken the finger for the moon. Traditional metaphysics, whether rationalist or empiricist, missed the real nature of reality in focusing on things and substance. Two of the more dramatically "counter-traditional" metaphysical views looked to *process and event* and the *Being-ness* of things or beings.

Whitehead: Process and Reality

Alfred North Whitehead (1861–1947) was a British philosopher, logician, and mathematician, co-author with Bertrand Russell of *Principia Mathematica*, a work that was very important for the fields of both mathematical logic and the foundations of mathematics. As a Harvard philosophy professor, he supervised Quine. A justice of the United States Supreme Court once remarked that he knew of no one that had more influence on American university life than Whitehead.[19] Perhaps his most lasting philosophical influence in metaphysics is a view known as process theism, the view that God is not an eternally fixed

---

17 Donald Williams 1953.
18 But see Casullo 1988 for a contrary view.
19 Irvine 2013.

being, but one that undergoes changes through various interactions with creatures and creation. He writes:

> That "all things flow" is the first vague generalization which the unsystematized, barely analysed, intuition of men has produced.... Without doubt if we are to go back to that ultimate, integral experience ... the flux of things is one ultimate generalization around which we must weave our philosophical system ...
>
> But there is a rival notion, antithetical to [this] ... The other notion dwells on permanencies of things ...[20]

Here we see contrasted two views of the essence of things.

Whitehead thought that the essence of things was their *becoming*, that things essentially flow. Reality, for him, was *process*, as suggested by the title of his most important treatise in metaphysics, *Process and Reality*. It is the *event*, not the thing, that is the most basic aspect of reality. The instant or the moment is an abstraction. *Duration*, not instants or moments, is the nature of reality, and duration is how we experience the world. In fact, throughout *Process and Reality*, Whitehead refers to his philosophy as the "philosophy of organism": what we think of as a "thing" is not static, and so is better described as an organism. The *being* of the organism is a process, a process of growth, of development, of *becoming*.

Our interest here is his view of the nature of reality generally. Whitehead thinks there is a better way to understand the world than as relatively static individual substances. He thus conceptualizes or "frames" reality differently than the substance-attribute views of Aristotle or Descartes do. Reality comprises the "creative flow" of actual entities, the basic units of reality. All our familiar objects are made up of "societies" of actual entities; that a rock or this rabbit consists of a society of actual entities. Understanding actual entities in their creative flow will help us to understand Whitehead's view.

We can use an understanding of the self as an analogy for understanding actual entities and their "creative flow." My self is fundamentally an *experiencing* self. But let's think about where this self of mine has been, and where it's going. Right now—its present—is a *duration*—not an instant, but a very short length of time. To be experiencing is to be experiencing through a "space" of time, a duration. If we are to understand our world, we must understand it through

---

20   Whitehead 1929, pp. 240–41.

the notion of duration.[21] My present experiencing is the *novel expression* of my past experiencing. In other words, this present experience takes over and takes from and unites those past experiences, but it does so in a way that is novel—different from all of my previous durations of experiencing. Because every experiencing is new, it is creative. Because every experiencing expresses past experiences, experiences are not isolated or "atomistic" bits separate from other "experience-ings." Whitehead's notion of experience differs from Hume's in an important respect. Any particular experience is always part of a process, which includes as an essential part a "re-expression" of our previous experiences.

This novel expression of past experience only lasts for a brief duration, however. It gives way to still another, future experience. And that future duration of experience will be a taking over of this and all other past durations and a novel expression of this flow of experience. This flow of experience continually manifests itself in novel experiencings. And the "me" in all this, the subject, is these novel experiencings, or the "flow" of these experiences. In a moment, we will see the sense in which they are united, according to Whitehead.

Whitehead's notion of an actual entity as a novel experiencing subject shares some kindred aspects with William James's view of consciousness.[22] James, one of the most important American pragmatists, is considered by many to be the father of American psychology. James holds that moments of consciousness last only for a brief duration, but are taken up or subsumed by the next moment—that is "All real units of experience *overlap*."[23]

Affinities—Ralph Waldo Emerson

Ralph Waldo Emerson (1803–82), the nineteenth-century American philosopher, essayist and poet, has been called both the father of American literature and the father of American religion. Emerson's principal occupation was the writing of essays and lectures which he presented throughout New England. His writings reflect diverse influences—from Plato to the German idealist F.C.S. Schelling (1775–1854) to Hinduism.

His essay "History" reflects his view that no thought of one person is "foreign" to anyone. Seemingly this is because all minds are interconnected and that all can share the same thoughts. Plato's and Euclid's thoughts are

---

21 Whitehead 1925, pp. 71 ff.
22 Flanagan 1992.
23 James 1951a, p. 162; also 1951b.

my thoughts, reflected in my thinking, and of course, reflected in all minds. This view has obvious affinities with the Hindu doctrine of Atman, according to which individual egos are but particularized manifestations or reflections of the whole. In other essays, Emerson notes the interconnectedness of conscious minds and nature. Though there are significant differences between Whitehead's and Emerson's views of nature, the themes of interconnectedness and of individual as reflection of the whole are discernible in both thinkers' work.[24]

In Whitehead's view these temporally extended bits of experience—the durations—are actual entities. Each is a welling up or an upsurge of a prior flow. And each new actual entity expresses that prior flow in a novel way. The actual entity wells up, and it will fall away—cease to exist—only to be creatively "re-expressed" in still a new novel bit of experience, a new actual entity. Thus, every actual entity is a novel expression of the actual entities that preceded it. Because of this, Whitehead claimed that "each actual entity is a locus of the universe."[25] This reflects Whitehead's view that any actual entity is in fact a microcosm of the universe, and understanding that actual entity is to understand the interconnections between all actual entities.

One further aspect of this creative flow of experience, which is my *self*, needs notice. Any experience takes in, or is related to, all of the other novel experiences, out there, "outside" of me. My self, in any chosen duration, is related to all the other experiencings. My experience is interdependent with those of others, just as it is interdependent with my prior and future experiences. Sam's experience takes in Sara's experience, just as hers takes in Deirdre's. As Whitehead notes, "we must say that every actual entity is present in every other actual entity."[26] Why does he think this? Since all actual entities are interconnected, Whitehead apparently thinks that a "complete picture" of any actual entity necessarily includes all other actual entities. You can't grasp some actual entity without seeing its "relations," its "family." And its family is all other actual entities.

The becoming of an actual entity is a complex process, involving both *eternal objects* and *feelings*. Eternal objects are very similar to universals,

---

24   Emerson 1987.
25   Whitehead 1929, p. 97.
26   Whitehead 1929, p. 65.

although Whitehead wished to avoid the controversial history of that topic, and so chose the term "eternal objects." These are qualities that determine the character of some actual entity. And the actual entity has *come to be* when it takes on this determinate character, that is, when the eternal objects have "combined"—Whitehead calls this "ingression"—to make the actual entity.

Whitehead's terminology is unfamiliar, in part because he is trying to describe a *metaphysical* process, and he wants to avoid the "baggage" of the more common terms in the history of philosophy (e.g., substance, universal). Yet we can get some sense of Whitehead's view of the "coming to be" of an individual. Every individual, whether cup or coconut or koala bear, has specific qualities. Cup, coconut, and koala all manifest "roundness" to some degree, while the koala is furry, the coconut hard, and the cup fragile. (Whitehead's notion of eternal objects is roughly that of our universals; and roundness appears to be an eternal object.) Like tributaries coming together to form a river, an individual finally *comes to be* when all its qualities are there. The cup *becomes* because a variety of streams of influence or streams of qualities now come together in a particular way. The cup becomes because it reflects particular qualities in a novel way. Also, the koala bear becomes because it now reflects the qualities that "make it up" in a novel way. It is perhaps a little easier for us to think of the koala bear as *becoming* or *in process*, than it is to think of a cup as a process. But in Whitehead's view, all actual entities are in process, whether they are animate or inanimate, animal, vegetable, or mineral.

It may seem that Whitehead suggests that an actual entity is but a combination of eternal objects, without any unity, and thus his concept is similar to bundle theory. Whitehead, however, thinks that there *is* unity to the actual entity, but we must look for it somewhere different from where substance-attribute theorists would look.

Central to Whitehead's view is abandoning the substance view of essence that we find in Aristotle or Descartes or Kant: "It is fundamental to the metaphysical doctrine of the philosophy of organism that the notion of an actual entity as the *unchanging subject of change* is completely abandoned."[27] In the substance view, the *essence* of a thing—its essential qualities—remains the same, or else the object becomes a different thing. For Whitehead, unity of an actual entity is to be found in *process*. More specifically, the essence

---

27   Whitehead 1929, p. 65; emphasis added.

of an actual entity is the final end or aim of the process, the becoming.[28] Whitehead calls this end "the subjective aim." The unity of an actual entity is the unity of the process: "Process is the growth and attainment of a final end."[29] It's important to note that Whitehead does not mean that there is some final stage to this process, as graduation is to the process of receiving a college degree. Rather the whole of the process, the becoming itself, is the subjective aim. (Perhaps the education analogy is useful here: we think of our education as an ongoing, continuing process, one that does not end with the awarding of a degree. Similarly the subjective aim is continually ongoing, as is the "developing" process of any actual entity. As long as the actual entity exists, it is in process; it is *becoming*.)

Indeed the actual world itself is a process, one made up of the actual entities. And here is perhaps one of the most remarkable features of Whitehead's view: *feeling*. Every actual entity is a *drop of experience*. This experience manifests itself as *feeling*.

Given that all our familiar objects comprise "societies" of actual entities, that a rock or rabbit consists of actual entities, does this mean that feeling is everywhere? And Whitehead's answer is "yes," but we must realize that not all feeling is conscious. Sam may sense the rose or be aware of his feeling of sadness. These are paradigms of feeling, as conscious events. But Whitehead holds that the feeling is "two-way": the rose "feels" Sam, just as Sam feels the rose. The difference in feeling is a difference in degree, not in kind.

We can get a sense of this similarity of feeling by thinking about Sam and his experience. Sam is an experiencing creature. A full understanding of that experience requires understanding all Sam experiences, including the rose. Sam's experience reflects the *actual world*. Whitehead claimed that every actual entity "houses" the world within itself. And it does so because of its feeling, its feeling of the actual world.

But how are we to understand the rose *grasping* or feeling Sam? Or for that matter, any actual entity? The rose reflects an actual world *that includes Sam sensing the rose*. The feeling of the rose is thus an expression of the relatedness of the rose; it expresses its connection to the world. The rose, no less than Sam, houses the actual world in itself, as any actual entity does. Its feeling is a reflection of the actual entity in its relation to the world. Notice also that

---

28   Whitehead 1929, p. 65.
29   Whitehead 1929, p. 65.

feeling will thus sometimes be a physical feeling, since the relations between actual entities are physical. Indeed, Whitehead identifies physical feeling as one of the two most basic types of feeling.

And this leads us to another important difference between the "categoreal scheme" of Whitehead and that of the substance theorist. For the substance theorist, substances are related to each other primarily extrinsically. A substance is still itself apart from its connection to any other substance.

Whitehead sees the matter differently. All relations—that is, the *connectedness* between actual entities—are intrinsic. In other words, the actual entity is what it is precisely because of its feeling. It comes about because of the prior flow of experience, and that prior flow is manifested in its feelings, its relation to the other actual entities.

Whitehead thought that we had a better *metaphysical* understanding of the world if we abandoned the substance view and instead turned to a view of process, in which actual entities are what they are because of their becoming. *Process and Reality* not only presents a very different metaphysic that can be difficult to grasp, but it is also very terminologically challenging. And we have barely indicated the depth of that work. Nonetheless, we might leave this section by noting just a couple of questions. Whitehead acknowledges that he wants to stretch the language. We might wonder, however, whether using the notions of feeling or experience to describe the interconnectedness of things is the best way to go about it. More precisely, we might wonder what more Whitehead has told us about the *cause* of something by talking about feeling or reflecting the relatedness of things. Whitehead also stresses the novelty or creativity of actual entities. But does suggesting that every entity has its own "point of view" capture the essence of creativity in the universe? And finally, we might wonder about the building blocks of the system, the actual entities themselves—are we really clear what an actual entity is? At one point, Whitehead suggests they are like the monads of Leibniz, only "becoming." And he says there is nothing more to the actual entity; it's as basic as you get. Knowing that it is a drop of experience may still leave us puzzled a bit, in light of the above.

Despite these questions, Whitehead—in both *Process and Reality* and *Science and the Modern World*—raises a number of challenges to a long held tradition and to the assumptions underlying much of western metaphysics. For now though we turn to another twentieth-century challenge to traditional metaphysics.

Big "B" Being: Heidegger and the Metaphysics of Being

Mahāyāna Buddhism and Heidegger

Some have found similarities between Heidegger's view and the metaphysical views explicit in particular Asian philosophies. One place to see such a similarity is in Mahāyāna Buddhism.

One difference between Hinayāna and Mahāyāna Buddhism is the ontological status of elements of our experience. For the former, these are passing, temporary phenomena, yet real. The Mahāyāna view differs. In this view, there is an underlying reality, but the world of our experience is not real.

As Heinrich Zimmer says in his classic work on Indian philosophy, "This one reality, in its ontological aspect, can be termed only *bhāta-tathatā*, 'the suchness of beings, the essence of existence.'" Zimmer notes that the Mahāyāna philosophers distinguished three aspects of things: quintessence, attributes and activities. While the latter two might change, the quintessence of a thing is indestructible.

Thus, the "final truth," as Zimmer calls it, is the "being thus," the "suchness."[30] In this "being thus," we might see some similarity between the Mahāyāna Buddhist notion and Heidegger's concept of Being.

Martin Heidegger (1889–1976) thought that metaphysics had forgotten an important question, the question of the meaning of Being. Heidegger's project, as he saw it, was to rethink the traditional metaphysical categories, thus overcoming the historical oppositions in metaphysics and epistemology, such as subject-object and mind-body. More than that, he wanted to enable us to ask again the question of Being—to come to understand Being.

Heidegger insisted on our recognizing the difference between beings and Being. (Or as William Lovitt, both a translator and interpreter of Heidegger, once said: "little 'b' beings and big 'B' Being."[31]) Our everyday preoccupation with things "hides" from us the *Being* of these beings. We are preoccupied with the *ontic* level—the level of individual physical things—rather than an *ontological* understanding of Being. Philosophy, too, shares this preoccupation; the metaphysics of substance is also restricted to the ontic level. But Being *as such* is not some further thing, nor should it be understood as the most general universal. In Heidegger's view Being is that which "gives"

---

30   Zimmer 1951, p. 517.
31   Heidegger 1977; also Lovitt and Lovitt 1995.

the things of our every day world their being. It is the "presence-ing" of things. In a sense, the more fundamental ontological question for Heiddeger, is not the nature or the essence of things, or even with the question of what should be identified as a thing or "primary substance," but rather that things *are*.[32]

Understanding Being is the peculiar task of human being or *Dasein*, as Heidegger called it. It is only through Dasein that Being can be understood. This understanding is not a purely intellectual understanding that humans can achieve themselves by "figuring out" Being, but is better conceptualized as a *disclosing* or the *revealing* of Being that humans can be open to. In an early essay, "On the Essence of Truth," Heidegger notes that our naming of things draws them out so that they can be present to us, where we can let them be.[33] Indeed, a function of the poet, according to Heidegger, is this naming. Truth, then, is not the corresponding of sentences to the world, but is this drawing out of the presence of things. Better perhaps, it is letting be of the world, so that the Being-ness of things can reveal itself or become present.

In Heidegger's view, as Being discloses or reveals itself to us, it also withdraws. This is because we always engage Being through a framework, through a particular style of representation. Perhaps the account of the poet Petrarch climbing Mont Ventoux in 1333, with his "only motive ... the wish to see what so great an elevation had to offer," comes close what it means to letting the Being of the world reveal itself. Yet even Petrarch inevitably relied on some frame or style of representation. These are not styles of representation or frames for encountering Being that we devise ourselves. Instead Being presents itself in different ways in different epochs. Our modern period is "technological," a period characterized by the domination of nature.[34] (Indeed, Heidegger's views have led to Heideggerian interpretations of environmental ethics.[35]) Heidegger often used the German word "Gestell"—a frame or shelf—to highlight the way in which we frame or understand things. Since we encounter things through a particular style of representation, Being withdraws. In other words, we grasp Being only partially, failing to grasp Being as such, Being as it is in its "pure" presence.

In his seminal work, *Being and Time* (1962), Heidegger's primary concern is with Dasein, as this is, by definition, the type of being that can ask about the "meaning of Being." At our most basic ontological level, human beings are the *only* type of being that can ask about this most general characteristic

32 For more, see Wisnewski 2011, Chap. 2.
33 Heidegger 1965, pp. 317–52.
34 Again, see Lovitt and Lovitt 1995.
35 E.g., Zimmerman 1997.

of the world.[36] Heidegger calls this sort of inquiry into our finite essence "fundamental ontology."[37] He describes human beings as Dasein—as essentially finite creatures, who are always tied to some context.

Our basic mode of encounter with things of the world is as "ready-to-hand." The hammer, like anything we might use for work or play, is ready-to-hand when it is there for us as we are engaged in our projects, in a world. But when we approach things as philosophers, scientists, or observers, we experience them more distantly, as present-at-hand. We also see things in this mode, as present-at-hand, when we cannot engage with them as we normally do—when the hammer breaks, for example, and loses its function. Our most basic encounter with things is not as "knowing" them or "theorizing" about them, but engaging a world with them. Heidegger thought that seeing things as part of our interaction in the world overcame the untenable separation between subject and object, between knower and known.

In later works Heidegger places more stress on language, both how language hides Being from us and how we can come to see or engage Being by getting clearer about how our language operates. More precisely, we have to follow the cues language gives us. Done correctly, this can help us get closer to seeing the true meaning of Being or Being as it is in its original revealing.

In *What Is Called Thinking?* (1976) an early work from his later period, Heidegger attempts to trace the meaning of "thinking," back through language, to its pre-Socratic origin. He hopes to find the source or the "originary" understanding of Being. Before Plato's categories of "form" and particular, or Aristotle's notions of substance and attribute gave shape to the style of thinking that dominated western metaphysics, Heidegger finds a different style of thinking. Seeing thinking in this earlier setting, especially in the few extant fragments from Heraclitus, before our thought was shaped by the categories of traditional metaphysics, we find thinking, which is not first and foremost theorizing. It is rather a kind of "thanking," a primordial way of acknowledging or encountering Being.

It is easy to see a religious sensibility or background in his later work. Being gives us, gives human ("little b") being, its fundamental gift, the encounter with a world. In some more challenging works, there seems to be the suggestion of a coming Event, an appropriation of Dasein by Being. This event strikes some as a kind of redeeming act. Others have resisted this religious interpretation

---

36   Heidegger1962a, especially the Introduction.
37   Heidegger 1962a, especially the Introduction and 1962b.

of Heidegger. Yet there is little doubt that the mystery of the relation between Being and Dasein evokes a spiritual atmosphere.[38]

Heidegger's critics have sometimes suspected that there is less to his work than the often difficult vocabulary makes it seem. Defenders object that Heidegger viewed himself as overthrowing the metaphysical tradition, thus requiring a new vocabulary, a set of terms, which made it possible for him to "think the unthought," to see what was underneath or behind the layers of centuries-old conceptual categories of western metaphysics. Heidegger thought we saw *things*, but missed *Being*.

Granting this, there is still room for question. For example, in the essay on truth noted earlier, Heidegger seems to think that the "disclosing" or "revealing" of Being is the essence of truth. This, however, does not follow from his argument. A functioning oven is part of the required background for baking a cake. But it does not follow that an oven is the essence of what it is to be a cake. Similarly the presence (or presence-ing) of beings—of things—may be part of the requisite background for us to talk meaningfully of truth. It does not follow, however, that this disclosing is the essence of truth.

Conclusion

Things are the most familiar part of our world. Natural and social scientists, artists, and writers have all offered viewpoints for understanding things. Yet those viewpoints perhaps do not settle the metaphysical questions as much as invite them. And as the various positions indicate, how we understand the nature of things cannot be divorced from our understanding of the world as a whole—or from an understanding of ourselves.

Key Concepts

- substance view or the substance-attribute framework
- substratum
- bundle theory
- actual entities
- Being

---

38   E.g., Philipse 1998. It is also worth noting that Heidegger thinks that a basic mistake of Western metaphysics is to mistake *Being* for a being, namely, God. Being, however, is ontologically more fundamental than God.

Reading/Discussion Questions

1. The substance view holds that certain properties constitute the essence or nature of a kind of thing. Explain what this means. Do you think things have "essences"? If so, what is our best guide to identifying these essences? Science? Philosophy? Something else?

2. Explain the similarities and differences between the substance-accident view and the substratum view. What do you see as the main criticism of this latter view? Do you agree with this criticism?

3. Try to explain the connection between Hume's empiricism and bundle theory. Explain and evaluate one criticism of bundle theory.

4. Why is Whitehead's view thought of as a *process* view? In a few sentences, explain the importance of the notions of creativity and feeling in Whitehead's metaphysics.

5. Do you think Heidegger is right to claim that beings and Being are different, and we always understand the latter from some incomplete particular perspective?

6. Which view presented in the chapter gives the best account of *change*? Explain.

Bonus round: Meinongianism, eponymously named for Alexius Meinong (1853–1920), roughly holds that for every possible combination of qualities or properties, there is a corresponding object. A gold mountain just west of Fresno is an object as is the fountain of youth in Florida ... objects, but they just don't exist. What do you think—does any consistent combination of qualities constitute an object? Are there "nonexistent" objects?

For Further Reading

Aristotle's most important works on substance are *Categories*, *Metaphysics*, and *Physics*, 1941a, 1941b, and 1941c, respectively. There are many useful and accessible introductions to his work: A.E. Taylor 1949 and 1955, Veatch 1974, and more recently, Irwin 1989. And Jones 1969a and Copleston 1946 remain excellent sources.

More recent accounts and defenses of the substance-accident framework are Lowe 2002, Macdonald 2005, and Loux 2006. Each of these also includes accounts of both the substratum view and the bundle view. Lowe 2005 is a very clear account of Locke, including his views on substratum and personal identity, and is easily accessible to the beginner. The two criticisms of bundle theory noted in the text can be found in various places, but a good place to start is James Van Cleve 1985. Macdonald contains those and additional criticisms of the bundle view. A defense of bundle theory is Albert Casullo 1988; Casullo develops a view, not discussed in the text, of objects, as momentarily existing. Loux 2006 explains the conceptual route between bundle and substratum views. Donald Williams 1953 defends the trope view and is generally credited with "baptizing" modern trope theory. Campbell 1991 is a detailed presentation and defense of tropes as abstract particulars; some of the arguments may be a bit advanced for the beginner, but it repays the extra effort that might be required.

In addition to the two works already noted, Martinich and Stroll 2007 offers a theory of fiction, examining other theories of fiction as well, and broadly connecting the theory to recent issues in philosophy of language.

Whitehead 1929, *Process and Reality*, is the *locus classicus* for a systematic statement of his metaphysical views. His 1925 presents a number of these ideas and places them in the broader context of the history of philosophy and scientific developments. Both are challenging, especially *Process and Reality*. Two classic secondary works are Sherburne 1971 and Victor Lowe 1962; the more recent Mesle 2008 is a relatively brief and very accessible introduction to Whitehead's view.

Heidegger 1962a is of course the main work; his 1976 and 1977 provide generally accessible accounts of his "later" view. 1965 is an important, if earlier, statement of his view of truth. Lovitt's commentary in Heidegger 1977 is helpful, as is Gray's in Heidegger 1976, for understanding the later view. Zimmerman 1986 and 1990 are very helpful book-length treatments of Heidegger's views. The 1986 notes the parallel between Christian views and Heidegger's view of authenticity. A somewhat more recent work, which also notes the "Christian connection," is Philipse 1998. Wisnewski 2011 is also a helpful introduction to both Heidegger's early and later works.

Heinrich Zimmer 1951, edited by Joseph Campbell, is a readily accessible account of the philosophies of India, as the title indicates. D.T. Suzuki 1963 is also a classic and accessible study of Mahāyāna Buddhism; Chap. V is a consideration of the doctrine of suchness.

CHAPTER EIGHT

THE NATURE
OF MIND

Thoughts, wishes, hopes, fears, emotions and sensations—these we take as part of the facts of life, as part of the world. Of course, we aren't always "paying attention" to our mental life, cataloguing every thought or feeling as it happens. Still we often notice some features of our mental lives. Danny notices that the pain has diminished since he took the aspirin. Sara thinks this is the best tasting cake her mother has ever made. After being pressed by friends, Julia "becomes aware" that she really is angry at Jack. When asked— perhaps asking ourselves—we can catalogue or identify our thoughts or our beliefs, our desires or wishes, what we know, or what we fear. All of these mental states—beliefs, desires, hopes, fears, sensations, emotions—make up our mental life. And for many, these mental states seem very different from ordinary physical happenings or states.

It Takes Two

Why do we think these two—the physical and the mental—are different? And why do some of us think that they aren't? Perhaps a good place to start is the different ways we describe and experience them in everyday life.

Getting Physical

Notice the sorts of things that we say about the physical. Julia is wearing a *blue* dress; the cake *tastes* sweet; the desk is too *heavy* to move; that music is too *loud*. In addition, we notice the *location* of things, their *shape* and *size*, or their *motion*. Or we might notice the absence of motion: "Sam hasn't moved from that chair since dinner."

Two sets of characteristics define the physical for us. Our senses give us one: color, sound, taste, feel, smell, shape, motion (or lack of it). And from science we learn a second set: electrons and protons have a charge; quarks have flavors; there are not only "particles" but "fields" too. From an early age we learn a simple scientific account of those sensory characteristics, e.g., sound—"vibrations" in the air that cause vibrations in the ear; or color—light waves of a certain length striking our retina; or smells—molecules traveling through air, striking our olfactory organ.

These observations provide us with a general way of characterizing the physical: the physical is what science studies. Physicalism is the view that everything is ultimately physical; only physical things and properties exist. Physicalism is sometimes called *materialism*.[1] It is a type of monism (i.e., a system that holds that everything that exists is the same type of thing).

Dualism

Propositional Attitudes

"Propositional attitudes" are an important type of mental state. As creatures with minds, we have beliefs, desires, hopes, fears. We know things and doubt things. All these (and others) are identified as propositional attitudes.

Why *propositional*? This type of mental state has a distinctive feature: content. Such states are *about* something. For example, you believe *that* the

---

1   This philosophical term does not mean what it does in ordinary language: a preoccupation with money and ownership.

Declaration of Independence was signed in 1776 or *that* the blue-footed booby is found in the Galapagos. Or you hope *that* the blue-footed booby will perform its mating dance; you know *that* 1776 was an important year. The content of the belief or the hope or the fear is given by a sentence or a proposition; these are sometimes called "that clauses."

As noted, there are different types of *attitude* one might have toward a proposition—e.g., belief, desire, hope, fear, wishing, knowing. Two of the more important attitudes are beliefs and desires, since we frequently appeal to a person's beliefs and desires to explain behavior. Epistemology focuses especially on *knowing that* and the justification of or rationality of *belief*.

Our mental life, however, can seem like a different kind of thing from a table or a coffee cup. Dualism is the view that the nature of the mental is indeed something very different from the physical; the mental is nonphysical. The dualist holds that a complete inventory of the *physical* world would leave something out. Science provides an understanding of the behavior of quarks or the nature of the Big Bang, but no matter how much we learned about physical things, we would still not have a story about a very important part of the world, the mental. So, we might ask the dualist to tell us a little more about these "mental things."

We've already said what, according to the dualist, the mental is not—it's not physical, not colored or fragrant, without shape or extension. My *belief* that the Radiators are playing on Decatur doesn't have a shape or a velocity, any more than my *desire* to have Julia drive us to the Quarter is loud or colored. Of course, we might say, "I'm thinking as fast as I can how to do it," or "Deirdre seems to be feeling blue," but dualists count these as metaphors. Similarly, we might characterize a pain as "sharp" or "burning." These also are metaphors for the dualist; you can't cut anything with a pain, and a burning sensation is no fire hazard. Physical characteristics don't describe or characterize the mental. But, then, what features does the mental have?

The two principal characteristics of the mental are content and feeling. Many of our mental states are *about* actual or possible events or states of affairs; that is, they have content. Jack fears that Julia won't drive; the content of that fear is that Julia won't drive. Sam believes that Twitter is better than email. The content? That Twitter is better. Thus, one quality or characteristic of some of our mental life is that the mental is *about* something, or mental states have content. Willing and choosing, thinking and judging are states with content as well. Danny wills (chooses/decides) going to Baskin-Robbins; the content is that he goes to Baskin-Robbins.

Do all mental states have "aboutness"? Some philosophers think so. But maybe not: for example, you feel sort of sad, but not about anything in particular. Similarly a pain, say, a headache, doesn't seem to be about anything.

Being about something doesn't seem to capture everything about our mental life, however. Some of our mental life is better described as a "felt" quality or as having a qualitative aspect. It is difficult to describe this aspect, but for some mental states, *there is something that it's like* to be in that state. A bit of chocolate tastes a certain way, which can be distinguished from the taste of a strawberry. Anger feels different from frustration; being a little blue can feel much different from depression. Most are very aware of the difference between liking something and loving something. It just *feels different*. These qualitative aspects of the mental, the felt quality, are often referred to as qualia, a term meaning a state or condition or property. Qualia, or the synonym "raw feels," are the felt quality or the qualitative aspect of some mental occurrence.

The two principal aspects of the mental then are its *aboutness* or its content and its *what it's like* or *qualitative* character. Some try to understand one in terms of the other; here it's enough to observe that both of these properties seem to describe the mental.

Two Types of Dualism

Epiphenomenalism and the Knowledge Argument

Epiphenomenalism is a type of property dualism, but for some time was not widely countenanced in the philosophical world. It holds that physical events cause or bring about mental states and properties, but mental phenomena are just *epiphenomena*. They don't cause anything; the mental is just an accompaniment of the physical.

Frank Jackson's "knowledge argument" (referenced in the text) thrusted epiphenomenalism back on to the philosophical scene. In an argument that occupied a very small portion of an essay (1982), Jackson asks us to imagine a neuroscientist who has learned everything physical there is to know about vision. The hook: she only sees in black and white, until one day, surgery enables her to see in color. Jackson claims she learns something new by virtue of her color-experience. She now has knowledge that physical theory was unable to give her. And if this is right, Jackson claims, there is more to the mental than what physicalist scientific theories can tell us.

Dualism comprises two main types, a dualism of *substance* and a dualism of *properties*. Substance dualism is the view that there are two distinct kinds of substances in the world: bodies—the physical—and minds—the mental. Property dualism is consistent with substance monism; it might claim that there is only one kind of substance—the physical—but distinctly mental properties emerge from particular physical arrangements.

Substance dualism tells us that we encounter two *types* of things or entities. There are not only physical objects, but mental objects or entities. But what sort of thing are mental objects? I know what makes an iPad or a peach ... but what makes a mental object? Can I bite one? Do they go bump in the night? Clearly not.

You've probably guessed: mental objects are individual *minds*. We may eat a peach—or even a brain—but never a mind. We are nonetheless aware of minds, or at least aware of what's going on "in" our own. This ability to "look into" our own mind is typically called *introspection*. Introspection reveals content (I just realized *that darn Sam is late again*), attitude (I fear *that he is late*), sensation (that stings), and process (assenting or affirming). And we know our minds by our awareness of them, or our awareness of having a particular thought or a particular sensation or an awareness that some mental process is occurring.

Non-Cartesian Dualism

Does substance dualism need to hold that mental substance is *immaterial*? Of course Descartes thought so, arguing that the mind possesses only nonphysical mental properties. The *essence* of a mental substance is these mental properties—and mental substances have no extension or mass or velocity. Many contemporary nonphysical substance dualists similarly argue that minds are immaterial or nonphysical.

Not all contemporary substance dualists, however, are committed to the immateriality of the mind. For example, E.J. Lowe, the author of several books and many articles on metaphysics, argues for a *non-Cartesian substance dualism*. A self or *subject of experience* is the subject of all and only its own mental states. This self, however, is not identical with the body or any significant part—such as the brain—of the body. This subject of experience is, in Lowe's view, a *human person*.

It may be true, according to Lowe, that a person could not have such experiences or mental states without also having a body; hence his *non-Cartesian* view. Unlike Descartes, Lowe insists that the "mental substance"—the person—may also have physical properties. But it is the person, not the body, that has the experiences. And the person is not identical to the body.

Lowe argues for this view by showing that the *identity conditions* of the body—the conditions that make a body *this* body—differ importantly from the identity conditions of the person. One of the principal arguments Lowe offers is the "replacement argument": "I"—the subject—could survive the replacement of all parts of the body, but clearly the body could not. Thus the subject of experience is not identical to the body.[2]

Minds—mental objects—of course do not have physical properties. We sometimes say they are "located"—Sara's mind is where she is, Sam's where he is—but not all substance dualists agree about that. But this leads us to a catch. One to a customer! Doubtless some of you want to note that it's easy to see what makes one body separate from another. But what makes this mind different from that one? And why are these *my* thoughts that I'm thinking, and not my neighbor Gloria's?

Substance dualists make the plausible assumption that if there are thoughts or sensations or processes, those thoughts or sensations must be had by some *subject*. And that "subject" is the mind; it is what holds all thoughts and sensations together. While there are arguments to this effect that we could follow, we will content ourselves with this assumption: if you are aware of it, it's your thought, and it's in your mind. Of course Sam and Sara could share the same type of *thought contents*, e.g., they both believe that Abigail Smith was married to the second president of the United States. But Sam and Sara have their own individual thoughts. And in general all persons possess a unique and individual mind, and this is a particular and unique mental substance.

Property dualism draws the line between physical and mental in a different place. Property dualists often hold that there is only physical substance, and hence every object is a physical object.[3] Some physical objects turn out to be rather special, however, in that they have not only physical properties, but *mental properties*, too. Brains, for example. (Or the nervous system, including the brain.) Because of the complex configuration of approximately 100 billion neurons, especially the 20 billion or so in the cerebral cortex, mental properties (or features) arise. In addition to possessing physical properties,

2   E.J. Lowe 2006; Foster 1991; Swinburne 1997; Baker 2000.
3   Jacquette 1994, Chap. 1.

like weighing about two pounds, being sort of gray and white in color, the structure and functioning of human brains also gives rise to another kind of property, mental properties. But unlike the color or the weight of the brain, which could be explained by appealing to more basic physical properties, mental properties cannot be given an ultimately physical explanation. We can tell an evolutionary story of how they came to be. We can know that certain physical arrangements in the brain are associated with certain mental states. But the mental state is *more than* something physical. The right "dopamine arrangement" and we're *feeling* fine. But you can't say everything there is to say about that mental property simply by talking about the underlying physical structures and processes. Hence, we have in mental properties a distinctly different *kind* of property.

Both substance and property dualism share the idea that the mental is *irreducible* to even a very complicated neurophysiological story or theory. You can't explain the nature of the mental by explaining the physical; inevitably the physical account leaves out something essential about the mental.

Arguments for Dualism

Why believe in dualism? There are two principal arguments, the *introspection argument* and the *conceivability argument*, which we will discuss in a moment. Some have found dualism is preferable for the reason that it is necessary for survival after death or free will.[4]

Lying behind this thought that dualism is necessary for free will is the assumption that a wholly physical world is purely mechanistic—a world in which things happen "automatically" because of the laws of physics and of what occurred before. And such a mechanistic world leaves no room for free will. Similarly, the claim that a person survives death is held to require dualism, most likely substance dualism. We know that the body doesn't survive after death; if something survives, it must be nonphysical.

The free will debate is itself vexed—we shall go into this in detail in Chapter 10—and it is not obvious that free will requires the truth of dualism. Nor is it obvious that the truth of dualism would preserve free will. There is nothing inconsistent about thinking that a nonphysical world is as determined and law-governed as the physical world. Let your beliefs and desires be as nonphysical as you choose: still mental laws governing those beliefs and

---

4   Crumley 2006.

desires may "dictate" subsequent action just as physical laws "dictate" certain subsequent events in the physical realm.

A physicalist might also hold that a person could survive the death of one's body. Supposing that the mind is simply the brain and its trillions of neural connections, the physicalist might find nothing inconsistent in our learning to write the computer program for all the neural connections in the brain, and running that program on a very special computer and that this could constitute survival after death. We just move "you" from one physical system to another. Perhaps this is not what some have in mind by survival after death. (We shall consider what constitutes a continuing person in Chapter 9.) But it is questionable whether survival requires the existence of a *nonphysical* soul. (But is substance dualism *sufficient* for survival after death? The Reading/Discussion Questions at the end of the chapter ask this question.)

Two other arguments—the introspection and conceivability arguments—are more important for the dualist. The broad outlines of the first, the introspection argument, are already in front of us. Our senses tell us about the world of physical objects. And introspection tells us of the world of the mental, revealing a world of meaning or content, of feeling or "what it is like" to experience this or that. But introspection does not reveal a world replete with physical properties—it reveals a world *devoid* of physical properties. Physical descriptions seem out of place. Leibniz claimed that were we somehow able to walk around inside a brain that we would see moving parts, but we would not see thought or memory; mental "things" just don't seem physical.[5]

Of course, if something doesn't have physical properties, then it seems very reasonable to think that it isn't a physical object. So, introspection reveals that the mental is *nonphysical.* The substance dualist will go on to note that minds, as the subjects of these mental events, are not physical, while the property dualist will be content with noting the nonphysical nature of mental properties, such as having content or being a sensation of a certain type.

The appeal of the argument is undeniable. It fits with our everyday experience: it certainly appears from our own introspection that my feeling or your belief or Danny's emotion is very different from physical things and their properties. But does this argument make a compelling case for the nonphysical character of the mental? Critics press a crucial point: this introspective power—why should we think that it's so good at telling us what is really there? And critics point to this analogy: perception.

---

5   Leibniz 1979, p. 536.

Look around you, they invite you. Notice what you see: people, trees, tables, cups, and water. In other words, you see medium-sized physical objects. Now they ask, what don't you see? That's right: you don't see protons and neutrons and leptons and hadrons; you don't even see the bigger things that make up our world, like water molecules. So, these critics claim, maybe your introspective power is like your visual power. Just as your visual power doesn't reveal the real, deep-down nature of physical objects, maybe introspection doesn't reveal the deep-down nature of the mental. Maybe once you get "down there," you find that the mental is, after all, millions and tens of millions of neurons, in wonderfully coordinated symphonies of excitation and inhibition, reaching out and touching other neurons. My *thought* that if Julia doesn't come soon, the riverboat will leave without us, and my *sadness* that we'll miss the Rads last concert is *nothing but* complicated brain activity.

This challenge by critics doesn't show that dualism is wrong. But it highlights a plausible reservation about the introspection argument. Accepting the dualist conclusion requires more assurance of the correctness of the dualist view of introspection. That is, we need some further argument from the dualist that introspection reveals all there is to know about the mental.

The *conceivability argument* deserves to be called famous. To many, it is *the* metaphysical argument for dualism.

The physicalist is making a claim about the necessity of the physical or the impossibility of having anything exist that isn't ultimately physical. The physicalist is saying that *it has to be this way*, not simply that it just happens to be this way. The claim is that it's the nature of the world to be ultimately physical. It's *necessary*.

This makes the dualist objective very clear: undermine the physicalist claim by showing that it's *logically possible* for minds to be nonphysical. This "showing" constitutes the conceivability argument.

How do you show that a claim of impossibility or necessity is false? By showing that its contradictory—its opposite—is *possibly true*. Recall that logical possibility is a much more general notion than physical possibility. It's *physically* impossible to travel faster than the speed of light. It is not, however, *logically* impossible. My father used to ask why something couldn't go faster than the speed of light; why couldn't you get something going 300,000 km/sec, and just give it a little push? That push to get it going faster is logically possible, but the laws of nature in this universe prevent speeding, and speeding counts as anything faster than 300,000 km/sec.[6]

---

6   This example also appears in Crumley 2006.

We rely on a variation of the conceivability argument given by Descartes. For convenience, the steps are listed singly:

I can conceive of a mind existing separately from a body.
If I can conceive something, then it's conceiv*able*.
If it's conceivable, then it's possible.
So, it's possible for a mind to exist separately from any body.
If it's possible for minds to exist separately, then physicalism is false.
If physicalism is false, then dualism is true.
So, dualism is true.[7]

This argument is sometimes met with incredulity: how can you prove that minds exist and are nonphysical just from some ideas about possibility and necessity and some definitions? You can't prove that something exists just by thinking about ideas!

There is some point to this objection, but some context is needed to evaluate it. Notice first that only two options—physicalism and dualism—are in play. If someone believed that only spirits or minds, and not physical objects, existed—a view sometimes called *idealism*—they wouldn't accept considering only these two options. But Descartes and most contemporary substance dualists admit the existence of physical objects. So, the issue separating dualist from physicalist is whether there is something *other than the physical*.

More important—and a bit harder to grasp since it is a *metaphysical* issue that is disputed—the conceivability argument takes the physicalist view to involve a "necessity claim": *it's not possible for "you"(some object) to exist at all and not be physical*. (In other words, *it's necessary that any existing object is physical*.) So, showing *that it is possible for a non-physical thing to exist* is enough to show that physicalism is false. And the only other option—dualism—is true ... that is, the mental is not physical.

Critics point to the pivotal moment of the argument—the move from conceivability to possibility. Conceiving something does not imply that it's logically possible, according to the critic. I was once told by a logic student that she could conceive a square circle. Granting for a moment that she could

---

7   For examples of the conceivability argument, see Chalmers 1996; Campbell 1984; Crumley 2006.

have such a conception, a "square circle" is a self-contradictory notion and hence, by definition, not logically possible.

Something similar, according to the critic, is going on here. It *seems as though* a mind separable from a body is conceivable. You may consider the *idea* of a mind as much as you like and never find the *idea* of a body or brain. Yet your inability to discover the necessary connection may reflect only a *cognitive limitation*. Centuries ago, people knew about static electricity discharge (call that SED) from shuffling across rugs and touching doorknobs, for example. But they didn't know that lightning was (high-powered) SED, and were able to conceive lightning that wasn't SED. But this argument for the falsity of the lightning = SED theory is obviously no good:

Lightning that's not SED is conceivable.
If it's conceivable, then it's possible.
So, it's possible for a lightning to exist separately from SED.
If it's possible for there to be lightning without SED, then the lightning = SED theory is false.
The conceivability argument is then not compelling.

[handwritten margin note: equation for arguments]

It took scientific experiment to prove the lightning = SED theory. (Remember Ben Franklin and his kite?) Similarly, physicalists would presumably need science to prove their theory right. They have tried to make good on this promissory note; we will see how below. First, though, we will pause at one problem that has bedeviled dualists for some time. A princess even took up the matter with Descartes!

How Did I Do That? Mental Causation

Minds move matter. Danny wants to let Deirdre know he thinks her talk is going well, and he believes he knows how to let her know—he leans his head to the side, and when he thinks she's looking, he winks. Sam decides that the coffee needs warming so he puts it in the microwave. Julia intends to wave at Jack: her arm raises, her hand opens, and her fingers begin to wiggle. All these believings and intendings and decidings are mental in nature, according to the dualist. But they have physical effects: they move bodies.

How can something that has no physical properties whatsoever suddenly *bring it about* that hands move, feet shuffle, fingers wiggle, eyes wink?

This problem is the *causal interaction problem*. How do two completely different substances interact?

In 1643, after reading Descartes's *Meditations*, Princess Elisabeth of Bohemia (1618–80), the granddaughter of James I of England, raised the interaction problem in a letter to Descartes:

> Excuse my stupidity in being unable to comprehend, from what you had previously said concerning weight, the idea by which we should judge how the soul (nonextended and immaterial) can move the body; nor why this power ... ought to persuade us that body can be pushed by something immaterial any more than the demonstration of a contrary truth (as you promise in your physics) confirms us in the opinion of its impossibility.[8]

Note that Elisabeth asks how an immaterial substance could move a material body. Later she is more explicit: how might something immaterial impart *motion* to material objects, e.g., parts of the body.

To put the matter slightly differently, we tend to think of causes producing certain effects by means of a mechanism or a series of steps. Critics insist that in many cases we have a pretty good understanding how one physical event might cause another. A cue-ball causes another billiard-ball to move by bumping into it, transferring kinetic energy into it. A burner produces boiling water in a pot by transferring heat energy to the pot, which then transfers it to water molecules. Similarly, we have a pretty good understanding of the sequence of electrochemical steps that lead from neural activity to the contraction of muscles in the arm, hand, and fingers, and the subsequent wave.

We have no clear understanding, however, of the series of steps that might lead from thought to physical change in a body. Critics think it is utterly mysterious how a set of nonphysical thoughts and desires could bring about Jamoca® Almond Fudge neural signals that lead to body movements.

Different dualist responses to this problem are available. One scholar suggests that Descartes had the "opposite" understanding of mind-body causation. That is, Descartes thought our understanding of the mental causing physical events is our basic and fundamental understanding of what it is for one thing to cause another. In a sense, we take our experience of the mind causing behavior and apply that to the physical world.[9] A twentieth-century philosopher,

8   Cited in Tollefsen 1999, p. 70.
9   Garber 2000, Chap. 8.

C.J. Ducasse, held that the way that the mental brings about bodily changes or movements is basic and unanalyzable.[10] It is a fact about nature, just as is gravitational attraction. More recently, John Foster argues that so long as there are laws governing mental-physical interactions, there is nothing mysterious.[11] That physicalists are suspicious of these claims is perhaps best revealed by looking in more detail at physicalist views of the mental.

Physicalism

Physicalists hold that everything, object or property, is ultimately physical, differing, however over exactly how the mental and physical are related. The most basic ontological distinction within physicalism is that between those who think that at least some mental things we talk about are *real*, and those who think that our usual "mental talk" is about something *unreal*. Call this latter group *eliminativists*; they hold that it's best to eliminate or get rid of the mental from our best theories about the world.

But many, if not most, contemporary physicalists think that the mental is something real. Within this group, the most active fault line is between *reductive* and *nonreductive* physicalism. We begin with the currently most widely held version of reductive physicalism.

Reductive Physicalism—The Brain Version

At the beginning of the twenty-first century, a work that received some attention in the popular media, *Why God Won't Go Away: Brain Science & the Biology of Belief* (2001), identified religious and spiritual experience with *brain activity*. The authors "took pictures" of the brains of subjects undergoing mystical experiences.[12] Of the many sorts of experience people have, spiritual experience may seem the paradigm of something nonphysical. Unsurprisingly the book proved controversial.

At about the same time, a neuroscientist said in an interview, "That's what the brain is: just a piece of meat that has chemicals and electric charges. The mind, of course is just a special version of that."[13]

---

10   Ducasse 1960.
11   Foster 1991, Chap. 6.
12   Newberg, D'Aquili, and Rause 2001, p. 5.
13   Dreifus 2002.

What is asserted here is that the mental *just is* what happens in the brain. This gets us to the heart of the central version of reductive materialism, generally referred to as the type identity theory. This is the view that every type of mental state is nothing more than some *type* or pattern of brain activity. That is, if Sam and Sara both believe that Li Po is a great poet, then the very same pattern of brain or neural activity is occurring in each of them. Deirdre and Danny both desiring to read Emerson's essay "Self Reliance" is *nothing more than* the same type or pattern of brain activity occurring in each.[14]

We then have two ways of talking about one thing. Our commonsense use of mental terms—belief, desire, love, pain, hope, fear—designates the same thing that a sophisticated neuroscience will talk about using its theoretical terminology. Whether Lois Lane says "Clark Kent" or "Superman," she is referring to the same individual. Similarly, something like the terms "visual awareness" and "synchronized neural firings in the visual cortex" name the same thing (at least according to certain researchers).[15]

But why is it called *reductive* physicalism? Identity theorists tell us we have two theories of the mind, our familiar commonsense view and the increasingly rich and sophisticated neuroscientific theory of the brain. As this latter theory becomes more complete, we will be able to replace the commonsense explanations of our behavior with more comprehensive and detailed neuroscientific explanations. *Wants* (*desires*), along with *beliefs, hopes, fears,* etc. figure importantly in our commonsense explanations of ordinary behavior. An adequate neuroscience will explain the very same behavior, perhaps by describing different sorts of neural networks.[16] This *replacing* of one theory's explanations with another theory's—that is *reduction*. And we don't lose our ability to explain anything in the process. Indeed, identity theorists claim that in the end we will be able to explain more! It's not that common sense about the mind is wrong, any more than it's wrong to say that the water in the pot gets hotter. But, in each case, there is a scientific theory that gives us a more accurate, precise explanation of the phenomenon or behavior we wish to explain.[17]

The origins of identity theory can in part be traced to ancient Greece, but Thomas Hobbes is probably the first modern philosopher to hold a version of the view. For a long time it was observed that the location of brain injuries or

14   For influential statements of this theory, see Smart 1959, 2004.
15   Smart 1959.
16   E.g., Paul Churchland 1988, 1996, 2013.
17   Smart 2004; see also Crumley 2006, Chap. 3.

surgery corresponded to types of mental impairment. In the mid- and late-1950s, Ullin Place and his professor J.J.C. Smart published papers explaining and defending versions of the identity theory; the two are generally credited with originating the modern identity theory.[18] (The version explained here, however, is more in line with Smart's 1959 and 2004 view.) Interestingly, Place bequeathed his brain to the University of Adelaide, where he had been Smart's student, and his brain is on display at the university! Advances in brain research have exploded in the last 20 years.

Apart from the evidence offered by various surgical and experimental procedures, identity theorists invoked two basic ideas for accepting their view. First, it is simpler: A world that is through and through physical is "ontologically simpler" than a world that has either two kinds of substance or two kinds of property. This leads to perhaps their more important argument. Science continues to explain more and more of our world. If some form of dualism is true, however, then the mental would be scientifically inexplicable. But given the extent of scientific success and explanation, it's more reasonable to believe that *the mental is scientifically explicable*. So, dualism—it's reasonable to believe—is false, and physicalism *à la* identity theory is true.[19]

This is an important but controversial argument. The ancient Greek philosopher Heraclitus wrote that "nature loves to hide"; perhaps the nature of the mental loves to hide, as well ... even from science. The dualist suspects that the identity theorist's optimism is at best quite premature. Below we will get some idea why.

Identity claims are very strong claims. And identity claims can be falsified—shown to be incorrect—simply by finding some difference between those things claimed as identical. If Sam brings Sara a book and tells her "This book is your book," Sara can reject this identity by pointing out a difference: "No, it isn't; the author signed my book; this one isn't signed." Similarly finding some characteristic that applies to minds (bodies) but not bodies (minds) is enough to show that the alleged identity does not hold.

Various differences have been suggested, and we have already seen some of them. Mental states don't take up space or have a size. On the contrary, says the identity theorist, it may seem a bit odd, but it's true: Sam's belief occupies a certain space, and if you take its "size" to comprise the relevant neurons, then it has a size. Or to the claim that physical things aren't *about*

18   Place 1956.
19   Smart 1959.

anything, or don't have a meaning, the identity theorist says, "Again: odd, but, yes, relevant brain activity *is about something*."

Surely, however, brain activity isn't introspectable, but we can introspect our mental states. Doesn't that serve to distinguish the mental from the physical? The identity theorist replies that we are in fact introspecting neural activity. We may not have the language (yet) to describe it as such, but it is still neural activity.[20]

You might suspect that "what it is like" or "how it feels" truly describes the mental, but these descriptions aren't true of patterns of brain activity. Isn't this a difference then—tell me all you want about neurons and electrochemical changes in the brain; tell me all you want about a flood of the neurotransmitter dopamine, but that just isn't the same as *feeling* happy or *feeling* sad, is it? So, mental, states have qualitative aspects; brain states don't. Alternatively, *qualia* can't be explained just by explaining complicated neural activity. (The knowledge argument, discussed in the box "Epiphenomenalism and the Knowledge Argument," trades on just this point.[21])

Perhaps it is sufficient to point out that qualia arguments highlight this question: Is it plausible to think that we might have a scientific theory so detailed that even the felt qualities of various experiences—tasting ice cream, feeling a tickle, being angry or joyful, having the visual sensation of magenta or indigo—could be fully explained by understanding the physical? It took a while, but we finally understood why water is *wet*. It took a while, but we finally understood how just by the right (complex) physical arrangement, rather than by some *élan vital* (vital force), we could say "It's alive." So, is it plausible to think that after we learn (much) more about the brain, we will finally be able to say, "Oh; so that's why it feels this way"? In fact, this challenge arises, not just for reductive physicalism, but for any version of physicalism that acknowledges the reality of qualitative states.

Nonreductive Physicalism

A Mental Code

In 1975, Jerry Fodor's *The Language of Thought* brought a seismic shift to philosophy of mind.

---

20   For example, Paul Churchland 1988; also 2013.
21   Jackson 1982.

Fodor—drawing on philosophy, linguistics, and psychology—argued that the mind is essentially *computational*. The "mental basis" of our beliefs and desires and other propositional attitudes is not whatever spoken language we use, but a *language of thought*, or "mentalese." Unique mental symbols and rules for combining and "transforming" them into new sequences, similar to the rules of syntax that structure a spoken language, are the computational basis of our propositional attitudes. *Thinking* is a series of unconscious computations. To have a belief that the Rads start playing at 11:11 is to be in a certain computational relation to an inner string of symbols, a mental sentence. Unlocking this "mental code" is a task for cognitive science and allied disciplines.

Fodor allies this representational or computational theory of mind with functionalism. It has stalwart adherents and equally stalwart detractors (e.g., Daniel Dennett 1978, Chap. 6).

If you've seen the original *Star Wars* movie, you perhaps recall a scene in which R2D2 is about to be left behind, and the little "fellow" lets out a mournful R2D2-cry. Could a complicated machine think at all, much less think "hey, don't leave me"? What about those fantastic creatures in the bar? Jabba the Hutt? Those creatures don't have anything like a human brain!

Almost as soon as identity theory began to gain credibility, other *physicalists* were expressing doubts. Their complaint was this. Identity theory seems extraordinarily *chauvinistic*; it limits mental states to human beings. But that can't be right. There's no reason to think that some other sort of nonhuman, even extraterrestrial, creature might not think. My dog and I may both believe, after watching it roll, that the ball is under the deck; we may both lie on the ground, seeing the ball under the deck. How likely is it though that we have the same type of brain activity? In principle, with the right arrangement of neurons or some other physical "stuff," almost any physical thing might think. So, identity theory would be wrong about *reducing* the mental to patterns or types of brain activity. You couldn't reduce the mental to one type of physical pattern *because there are too many physical ways for any particular sort of mental event to come about*. Puppies desirous of their toys; robots and Transformers thinking; dolphins and gorillas believing; E.T. being sad; Vulcans being logical—and the list *in principle* goes on. This objection to identity theory is known as the *multiple realizability objection*. As a result of this objection, many physicalists are functionalists.

Functionalism is the view that we classify—name and describe—mental states by their *function*—what leads to or causes them, what they're connected to, and what happens as a result. (Most functionalists are physicalists, although functionalism does not require this; a dualist too might specify mental states by their *functional role*.)

In a simple case, my belief that the ball is under the deck has three types of connections. It's caused by my senses; it interacts with my other beliefs (e.g., well, for sure I'm too big to crawl under there, and I can't reach it); and it leads to some other state or behavior (I grab the garden rake and use it to pull out the ball).

It is important to be clear why functionalism is thought of as a *nonreductive* theory. If the ultimate nature of the mental is ultimately functional, many different physical bases might serve. Consider a rough example, my pup and I coming to have the belief that dinner is ready and our subsequent behavior. Upon hearing someone in the next room say "Dinner's ready," we each have the same input. This input interacts with various memory beliefs, together with the common desire "let's eat, I'm hungry." And for both of us, there is a common resultant behavior: both of us rouse and head to the kitchen. Functionalists claim that it's the *functional role* of this belief that tells us what it is to be this type of mental event. Now notice. My pup and I share the same belief despite having different brain activity. Extend this idea to many different kinds of physical systems. So long as the physical "stuff" is something that can support the functional role, the *kind* of physical "stuff" doesn't matter, whether it belongs to computer-driven robots, other terrestrial animals, or other extraterrestrial creatures. Consequently—and this is the key point—there is no way to *identify* some mental state with a *unique* type or pattern of physical activity. *Wanting to go home* is a type of mental state, but it cannot be uniquely identified with a type of *human* neural activity. The physical type may vary, even within our own species. Desiring to see the rock band Radiators on the riverboat may be realized by one type of brain activity in Julia and a different type in Jack. And if we don't have identity between mental pattern and physical pattern, then we can't *reduce* the mental to the physical.

As stressed above, functionalism is compatible with physicalism. A functionalist might well hold (in fact, many do) that each mental state in an individual at a particular time (identified as to type by its functional role) is identical with some physical state of the individual. But the functionalist will insist that *types* of mental state need not be—most probably are not—identical *types* of physical states. So this physicalism is not type-identity theory. Philosophical jargon distinguishes between a type of things—e.g., dogs—and a *token* of a type—e.g., Fido. A functionalist who is a physicalist, then, would advocate not type identity theory, but rather token identity theory.

An interesting but controversial consequence of functionalism is that in principle computers could think. This is analogized by thinking of the brain as the hardware and the mental as the software or the program. An actual R2D2 would really think, as would an actual Data (the android in *Star Trek: The Next Generation*). HAL of *2001: A Space Odyssey* and "Skynet" of the *Terminator* movies are examples of computer systems having mental states, as is Optimus Prime. The computer "brain" has some means for receiving input (analogous to our senses), processing or transforming it, and producing some output. Given this rough view, a suitably embedded computer *really has* mental states.

If the possibility of a thinking computer is a conceptual consequence of functionalism, would showing that you can't have thinking computers imply that functionalism is wrong? Many have thought so. John Searle's famous— some would say infamous—*Chinese Room argument* attempts to show that computers could never think, no matter how sophisticated the hardware or program.[22] Having a mental life, according to Searle, requires content or meaning. Thinking is more than the mere manipulation of symbols; it's *recognizing* the connection between a symbol and the referent of the symbol. But no computer does this. No computer, according to Searle, does anything other than "process" symbols by means of certain rules or instructions. The computer never "sees" what the symbol is about. On the other hand, the symbol string "Jamoca® Almond Fudge" has a meaning for Deirdre precisely because she recognizes a connection between that symbol string and that stuff in that five-gallon drum there.

Searle illustrates the argument by asking you to imagine being in a room, with an instruction book containing rules (in English) for sending out cards with various Chinese symbols on them, given certain inputted cards with Chinese symbols (and Searle imagines that "you" in this example can't speak or read Chinese). The rules only tell what to do when you see various symbols and their combinations, not what the Chinese symbols mean. A Chinese speaker outside the room passes in a card that says, in Chinese, "What is the world's longest river?" and after a while, a card comes out that says, in Chinese, "It depends how you measure river length, but by usual measuring methods, it's the Amazon." From the outside, it might look as though there was a competent speaker of Chinese inside the room. But you know nothing of Chinese, and won't learn anything. Searle invites you to agree that if all you had was the rule book, together with the stacks of Chinese symbol cards, *you would never come to understand Chinese.* Since you don't know what the symbols are *about,* you'll never grasp the Chinese language.

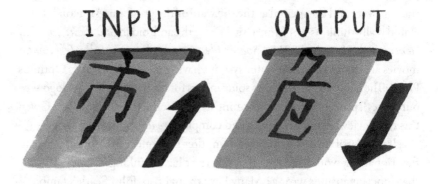

INPUT   OUTPUT

---

22   Searle 1984, Chap. 2.

Disagreements over this controversial argument have continued for over a quarter of a century. Critics insist that Searle misunderstands the nature of programs, that his "Chinese room" is too oversimplified, or that he's looking for meaning in all the wrong places. For example, it is argued that it is in the causal interactions between a robot and its environment that meaning would arise. You don't understand what the symbols mean, but the whole Chinese room, including you and the rule book, do. Searle, however, continues to insist that neither anything in the room, nor the whole room and its contents, understands Chinese.

This argument is relevant to functionalism because the Chinese room, as a whole, can exhibit language-related functional states just like those in humans have; yet, he insists, there's no language-related mentality in the box. If Searle is right about this, functionalism would be false. And this accounts for part of the controversy surrounding the argument.

We'll close this section by briefly revisiting the dispute between functionalists and identity theorists. Many turned to functionalism because of the multiple realizability objection. But identity theorists think there's a way around that objection. Their idea is that reduction is possible within a restricted range. Thus, there is, for example, human pain and Vulcan pain and lobster pain.[23] So, there is "pain-in-humans" or "pain-in-Vulcans" or "pain-in-lobsters." And these types of pain can be identified with *restricted* patterns of physical activity. Of course, functionalists insist that this cedes their point—even though the mental is tied to the physical, it's not the physical stuff that tells us the nature of mental. We discover the nature of the mental in its *function*. In other words, we only know that "pain-in-humans" and "pain-in-Vulcans" should be treated as mental states because of the function of these states.

But functionalism too faces a fundamental criticism. Function seems to mischaracterize or miss entirely a whole aspect of mental states—their qualia. In a recent radio ad, a doctor is asked about pain. He responds that pain is the body's way of telling a person that something is wrong. This is of course a very nice *functional* definition of pain; it tells us the purpose pain serves. And of course, this functional view seems to leave out the most important feature of pain: pain *hurts*! Function cannot capture feel. And, indeed, pains, sensations, emotions are normally defined by how they feel. And qualia—the "how it feels" of particular mental states—appear to be an intrinsic feature of those mental states, not a feature determined by functional connections to

---

23   Spector 2013 (on lobster pain).

other elements. The pain Danny feels because of his toothache, is not captured by his subsequently desiring relief or inferring that he should call the dentist or asking Deirdre to bring him an aspirin. Critics of functionalism—and physicalism generally—insist that the real nature of pain is simply that it hurts. Functionalism defines mental states extrinsically; yet the nature of some mental states—qualitative states—seems to be intrinsic.

Critics—noting the "how it feels" aspect of some mental states—have some eye-catching arguments. One thought experiment asks us to imagine the one billion citizens of China *functionally organized* just like a human brain, attached to a bionic body, with appropriate devices for sensory input and motor output. When something heavy is dropped on the body's toe, information is sent to various members of the Chinese population, and they send other information to others (according to the instructions of the organizers), and eventually these vast networks of information-passing result in motor output from the bionic body: it says "OUCH!" and quickly pulls back its foot. Of course, it is claimed, despite its having the "same functional organization," no one would think that such a "brain" is conscious.[24] Defenders insist that, technical difficulties aside, yes, it would be. The emphasis on the huge size of this operation makes it difficult to see the forest for the trees. If it were not so big, we'd have no problem attributing consciousness, complete with qualia, to this thing.[25] Critics are thus wrong to suppose that there would be *absent qualia*, the name of this type of objection.

Still another striking thought experiment called *inverted qualia* or *inverted spectra* is intended to show that an intrinsic feature of some mental events simply cannot be captured by functionalism. Imagine Sam and Sara looking at a rose. Sara has the sensation of red, while Sam, who suffers from "qualia inversion," has the sensation of green. Similarly, when Sarah looks at the clear sky, she has the sensation of blue, but Sam has the sensation of yellow. Otherwise their behavior and their thinking is exactly alike. Both admire the beauty of the rose; both want to leave it on the plant. Both stop at red lights and go on the green. Crucially, both call the color of the rose "red," because that's the word both have learned to use corresponding to that sensation. Functionalism seems to require saying they are having the same sensation. Yet this seems counterintuitive—there's a difference between green and red sensations.

---

24 Block 1978.
25 E.g., Lycan 1987.

Functionalists' responses are quite varied and detailed. One prominent functionalist grants the qualia objection, acknowledging that functionalism only explains the nature of mental states like beliefs and desires, not qualitative states. Others attack the idea that Sam and Sara are really functionally the same, if they are indeed having different sensations. That is, defenders claim that if there really are two different sensations here, then there is a functional difference.[26]

Does function have a feel to it? This blunt question perhaps captures the contentious point of these arguments. Some would be inclined to say that there are feeling states, qualitative states: the issue is whether or not identifying the function of such states can capture this feeling aspect.

Eliminativism

Dualism, identity theory, and functionalism each agree that there really are mental states and mental properties. They just disagree about the ultimate nature of those real states and properties. But not everyone shares this position: various philosophical arguments and empirical findings have led some to adopt a view known as eliminative materialism. The central position of this view is that some significant class of what we might think of as mental phenomena do not exist.[27] Some eliminativists claim that states like belief and desire—states that are claimed to exist in our commonsense view—are in fact not real. "Folk psychology"—what they call our commonsense view of our mental states—is, they claim, a radically false and misleading theory.[28] Other eliminativists suggest that our notion of sensation is at best confused, and sensation terms do not pick out a clearly defined kind of state.[29] And at least one prominent theorist has claimed that all of our everyday references to the mental are mistaken, whether talking about a hope or a wish or a thought or a sensation.[30]

As startling as such views might initially appear, eliminative materialists have offered a number of arguments that, while disputed, are not easily dismissed. Suppose for a moment that our view of the mind is an *empirical* theory.

---

26   Harman 1999, Chap. 14.
27   For more, see Crumley 2006, Chaps. 6 and 10.
28   Paul Churchland 1981.
29   Dennett 1991.
30   Skinner 1990.

Like any other theory of the world, it's susceptible to confirmation or refutation by evidence or experiment or by considerations of what makes for good theory.

Eliminativists note that other "folk theories" have not had a good track record—the theory of witches, for example, or "folk physics" (e.g., the sun moves round the earth, is smaller than the earth). Here's a bit of folk science you probably believe. In the same room, touch some ceramic tile, and then touch some wood. You'd say that the tile is colder than the wood, right? Wrong. Science reveals that real temperature is the mean kinetic energy of molecules, and if both wood and tile have been in the same room for a while, then they have the same temperature. (The difference is in heat conductivity: tile conducts heat away from your finger much faster.) Your folk theory of temperature includes radically false beliefs. There is no such thing as the "temperature" of something, that you can feel.

But why think that folk psychology should be grouped with other folk theories that have been definitively refuted? Empirical approaches like cognitive neuroscience explain even more of our mental life, while folk psychology, which has hardly changed since Socrates' day, seems to give us very little that we expect from a good theory. Using folk psychology, which features entities like belief or hope or desire, we still can't predict anyone's behavior better than they could centuries ago, and neither we nor the ancients could predict very well. Neither does it provide much in the way of explanation: "Why did you paint the living room that color?" "Well, I like it." If we take seriously findings in neuroscience, it becomes harder to see how belief-desire psychology turns out true.[31] For example, eliminativists suspect that understanding brain activity will require sophisticated theoretical and mathematical tools, and consequently, notions like belief and desire just won't be all that helpful in explaining human behavior. This is unsurprising, they think, since our talk about hopes and fears or beliefs and desires evolved largely as a result of ignorance of the real—neural—causes of our behavior. A science that starts at the "bottom" with synapses and neurons and neurotransmitters may develop theories that ignore descriptions like "Danny fears that the taxi will be late," just as modern chemical theory ignores phlogiston or modern thermodynamics ignores caloric[32] ... *because there aren't any such things!*

---

31   Paul Churchland 1981.

32   The fluid substance that was thought, during the eighteenth and part of the nineteenth centuries, to be responsible for heat, and to flow from hotter to cooler things.

Similarly some have thought that our notion of sensation is at best unclear; moreover, some think that there is no way to settle whether a sensation is of one type or another—there is no "fact of the matter" about such sensations. Thus, for example, Daniel Dennett argues that we have no way of identifying whether one sensation is the same as another. You simply don't know whether your "spectrum" is the inversion of someone else's. Maybe it doesn't even make sense to think that it does. Dennett draws on various empirical findings that suggest that our conscious life is not always a reliable guide to what is actually happening in the world and "inside" us.[33]

One version of eliminative materialism, developed by Paul and Patricia Churchland, accepts the idea of sensation, insofar as it is reducible to complicated neural states, but rejects the existence of mental states, such as beliefs and desires. They acknowledge that the brain takes in and processes information or content; our brains indeed have a representational function. That is, our brains give us a "picture" of the world around us. But they reject the idea that "Jack believes the ball is under the deck" is an accurate way to describe or explain the content of the neural representations or the way our brain employs such representations. The Churchlands disagree with the suggestion that understanding our cognitive life is best accomplished by utilizing a folk psychology that depends on a notion of propositional attitudes—beliefs, desires, hopes, and the like, whose content is given by sentences. Our brains represent the world around us, but not as described by the commonsense view of the mental.[34]

Perhaps you are familiar with behaviorism (or at least with a well-known aspect of it, behavior modification or behavioral conditioning). Although historically its development came before other physicalist theories—Ullin Place was looking for an *alternative* to behaviorism when he began developing identity theory—there is a reason we have postponed its discussion. Depending on the version of behaviorism, it can be viewed as reductive or eliminative.[35] A definition that encompasses both views might run as follows: behaviorism is the view that the best explanation of behavior is to be found in environmental causes (stimuli) in our environmental history, and the subsequent conditioning that leads to patterns of behavioral response.

---

33 Paul Churchland 1981, and Dennett 1991.
34 Patricia Churchland 1986; Paul Churchland 1988, 1996, and 2013.
35 Crumley 2006, Chap. 2.

Reductive behaviorism, sometimes called analytic or logical behaviorism, is the view that the causes of behavior are environmental stimuli; mental terms refer to *tendencies or dispositions to behave in certain ways under certain conditions*. In this view, mental terms, such as "belief" or "desire," are reducible to descriptions of complicated behavioral dispositions; hence our commonsense conception of the mental turns out to be scientifically respectable.

Eliminative behaviorism, or "ontological behaviorism," similarly adopts a view about stimulus and response, but it rejects the existence of the mental. B.F. Skinner (1904–90) rejected the idea that we might understand the causes of behavior by invoking beliefs, and even expressed a skepticism about sensations. Even as neuroscience was developing rapidly, he argued that the study of the brain would be useless for good psychology.[36]

Skinner was behaviorism's most prominent proponent, although John Watson pioneered the view.[37] Skinner's *Walden Two*, a "scientific novel" published in the 1940s, imagined the benefits of behaviorism by imagining a small society, Walden Two, structured according to the principles of behaviorist psychology. And Watson famously claimed that with a fully mature behaviorist psychology, we could take ten infants and produce musicians, ship captains, scientists, or any other personality type desired. Deirdre's writing talents, Sam's passion for poetry, Sara's scientific abilities are only the consequence of being exposed to certain stimuli and conditioned to respond in certain ways. This is no different from any other animal behavior; indeed "conditioning" birds to play a piano or dogs to run in a particular direction is no different in principle than producing Sam's or Sara's unique interests.

Perhaps the most important motive for behaviorism is the thought, shared with eliminativists, that appealing to mental states simply isn't explanatory. In trying to explain terms like "wants" or "loves" or "believes," we are caught in a circle, always appealing to still other beliefs or desires. We are never really able to explain intelligent behavior—our ability to operate successfully and in sophisticated ways in the world—if we rely on our mentalistic view. Behaviorists think that the real causal explanations are to be found instead in one's genetic makeup plus—and especially—one's environmental history, the sum total of a person's interactions with the environment. Indeed, Skinner thought it was futile to look inside a person. No matter what inner state one

---

36   Skinner 1990.
37   Watson 1930; Skinner 1974.

might find, tracing the history of that state led outward, to the environment. If you want to understand why Deirdre goes to the opera and Julia hangs out at the Dream Palace, awaiting the Rads' next show—all you need to look at is their respective past histories.[38]

While behaviorism was the dominant psychology paradigm in the United States for the first half of the twentieth century, by the mid-1960s, the information processing paradigm—or cognitive psychology—had more or less replaced it. In part, this was due to serious criticisms of behaviorism, which, according to many, did not receive adequate answers.

Many suspect that replacing mental terms with references only to behavioral dispositions is an impossible task. The behaviorists wanted to interpret assertions that S likes X as something like this: "Under conditions C, when presented with X, S will do A." So we might understand "Sam likes SpaghettiOs" as "If you put SpaghettiOs in front of Sam, he tends to eat them." You may already see at least one problem: what if Sam *wants* something else? What if he's simply not hungry? What if he *wants* to hide from Sara his craving for SpaghettiOs? What if he *wants* to consume less iron? What if he *fears*...? The problem is that process of filling out the schema seems (a) endless and (b) to involve still other uses of mental terms. We are unable to get away from our references to the mental.

Next, turn to the claim that inner causes are not explanatory, even if those inner causes are various types of brain state. We can accept the claim that brain states result in part from environmental influences. This claim, however, is not enough to demonstrate that brain states are never the cause of behavior. Because there was some prior, external cause of brain activity, it does not follow that the brain activity is not a cause of subsequent behavior. Indeed, we often cite *causal chains*—a series of causes—as leading to some event. Yet those more *proximal* causes are no less causes because some cause brought them about. Analogously, consider the "cause" of Julia, namely, her parents. Imagine now the claim that Julia's parents are not themselves causes since they themselves are the result of some earlier cause, namely, grandparents. This claim is at least open to skepticism on the grounds that it misunderstands a series of causes. Yet Skinner's claim about brain states seems just as suspect.

Skinner does not, of course, deny that brain states exist, or that they have a causal role to play in the body. What he does deny is that a scientific

---

38   Dennett 1978, Chap. 4; also see Crumley 2006.

explanation of *behavior* (not just muscle-contraction, for example) doesn't involve brain-states. Whatever brain states are involved when someone has a conditioned disposition to behave in some way, that plays no part in real explanation.

But here is an objection that is perhaps more important: environmental conditioning seems unable to explain *novel behavior*. Past history may explain why Jack is waiting at the corner bus stop every morning at 7:37. But how are we to explain an entirely new experience? Perhaps on the way to the bus stop he notices a small dog limping, with no one else around, and he picks up the dog, carries it home, and calls the owner? Of course the behaviorist can say "Well, there's *something*, some set of interactions; some set of 'pet-compassion interactions' in his past...." This seems, however, explanatorily unhelpful. The behaviorist doesn't really tell us how this current behavior was produced, but rather notes "something" must have done it. But this seems much too easy, and perhaps a bit empty. Imagine that you want an explanation of why Pauline is addicted to Queen Anne milk chocolate cherry cordials. The behaviorist tells you that there must have been "Queen Anne" addicting interactions in Pauline's history. Yet we might wonder whether the behaviorist has really explained anything. Again, this type of explanation seems a bit too easy, and perhaps a bit empty.[39]

What's a Belief?

What is it to have the belief that *this chapter is coming to a close*? The dualist tells us that to believe that this chapter is coming to a close is to have a non-physical mental property. For the substance dualist, the belief is property (or state) of an immaterial mind. Property dualists, on the other hand, tell us that this belief is a mental property had by some brain.

Identity theory, a version of reductive physicalism, tells us that this type, this pattern of mental state, is at bottom nothing more than a type or pattern of neural activity. Pushed by the multiple realizability objection, identity theory concedes that the human pattern of neural activity identical to the pattern *believing that this chapter is coming to a close* likely differs from the Vulcan Mr. Spock's type of "brain activity," which in turn clearly differs from R2D2's or Optimus Prime's types of *physical activity*. Each different type of

---

39   Dennett 1978, Chap. 4.

physical activity is the belief type *that this chapter is coming to a close*. There are beliefs, according to the identity theorist; they are just patterns—(perhaps restricted) types—of neural activity.

Functionalists—as nonreductive physicalists—are at ease with all these different types of physical bases for the mental. For them, a belief is not to be identified with the physical "stuff," but with the functional or causal role: what typically brings about this sort of belief, what other mental items does it interact with, what kind of behavior—output—does it typically produce? The belief that *this chapter is coming to a close* is a special type of functional state, connected to sensory inputs (e.g., your visual impression of the words on the pages), other mental states (e.g., your belief about the length of this book's previous chapters), and of course behavior (e.g., putting down the book).

Reductive behaviorists think it's a bit misleading to talk about a belief as some sort of inner state. For them—the logical or analytic behaviorists—the belief that *this chapter is coming to a close* is just a way of talking about a tendency to act in a certain way, and it is likely manifested in an arbitrarily large but finite number of behavioral dispositions.

Eliminative materialists claim there isn't any such type as *your belief that this chapter is coming to a close*. Appeal to beliefs and desires is an old, tired, retreating folk theory that will eventually be replaced by the theories arising from the new cognitive and neuroscientific disciplines.

And that brings this chapter to a close.

Key Concepts

- physicalism
- dualism
- qualia
- substance dualism
- property dualism
- type identity theory
- functionalism
- token identity theory
- eliminative materialism
- behaviorism

Reading/Discussion Questions

1. Explain the difference between substance and property dualism.
2. Do you think there is an adequate *dualist* resolution of the mind-body interaction problem? Explain.
3. Is substance dualism necessary or sufficient for survival after death? Why or why not?
4. What do you think is the best argument for identity theory? What do you think is the biggest problem for identity theory?
5. What are qualia? Explain the problem qualia present for physicalist theories, like identity theory and functionalism. Do you think there are aspects of the mind that cannot be explained by appealing only to the physical? Explain.

For Further Reading

Over the last several decades philosophy—and other disciplines—witnessed an explosion of interest in questions related to the mind. There are too many introductory texts to list here. Paul M. Churchland 2013 has doubtless become a classic; Jaegwon Kim 2010, John Searle 2005, John Heil 1998 are comprehensive introductions to the field, each examining the various positions and each explaining the author's own views. Dale Jacquette 1994 surveys the issues and defends a property dualist view. Also Crumley 2006 surveys the several theories considered here. Borst 1970 contains several of the seminal papers in development of philosophy of mind. Fodor 1981 is still a nice overview of the twentieth-century history of philosophy of mind, explaining the issues and problems that motivated competing theories. Two valuable collections of essays are Rosenthal 1991 and Heil 2004. William Lycan's anthology, which first appeared in 1990, and now in its third edition with Jesse Prinz, 2008, is a classic anthology. Sterelny's 1990 is still one of the best accounts of the representational theory of mind. And Chalmers 1996 is still very influential, not only for its defense of a form of dualism, epiphenomenalism, but also for opening new concerns and areas of research in philosophy of mind.

CHAPTER NINE

PERSONAL IDENTITY

"I haven't changed. I'm the same as I was before—only in a different way."
Judy Holliday (as Gladys Glover), *It Should Happen to You*

In Lewis Carroll's *Alice's Adventures in Wonderland*, the title character tumbles down a rabbit hole to some strange adventures. She happens upon the Caterpillar, who inquires, "Who are you?" This question leaves Alice at a loss: "I—I hardly know, Sir, just at present—at least I know who I *was* when I got up this morning, but I think I must have been changed several times since then." Alice's puzzlement about her present *identity* raises an interesting topic in metaphysics.

Metaphysics aims to identify both the things that populate our world and their nature. There is one type of very familiar "thing" whose nature we often take for granted. And that "thing" is persons. Like Alice we might under various circumstances be led to ask exactly what features constitute the identity of persons. What is it that makes some-"thing" *this* person, rather than some other? For some the identity of a person is to be found in having a soul. For others it—personal identity—is found in having a particular unique configuration of DNA. For still others it is having that body. Answers to the question of *personal identity* are not limited to these three, however.

We might also be led to ask whether some particular person *at this time* is the *same* person as that one, earlier. For instance, you might wonder whether that woman you saw in the supermarket today is the person whom you briefly met at a party a year ago. The issue here is not what we think when we say, "Fred has changed so much since high school that he's not the same person." Fred now and Fred then are literally the same person. What is meant here is whether this person, Fred, is literally the person also called Fred that you knew in high school.

The imagined technology of television programs such as *Star Trek* raise the question in more dramatic fashion: When you flip open your communicator and command "Beam me up, Scotty!" not everyone is so sure that it is *you* that reappears moments later in the starship Enterprise. So, we might then ask about not just how many changes, but also exactly what kind of changes you might go through and still be you. Forget about Alice and *Star Trek* for a moment: scientists are hard at work developing new microchip implants for the human brain—in addition to the implants that have already been developed![1] Microchip implants could extend the range of our senses, allowing us to detect more than our "normal" senses allow.[2] Would you now with a normal functioning brain, and the you, say, 20 years from now—with a head-full of microchips, replacing your brain—be the same person?

We can distinguish several sorts of questions about identity, corresponding to several senses of the words "identity" and "identical."

When we say "X and Y are identical," we might mean one of two things. We might mean that X and Y, despite being two separate things, have exactly the same characteristics. Two new dimes are in this sense (just about) identical. But we might also mean that "X" and "Y" are two names for one thing. In this second sense, George W. Bush is identical with the forty-third president of the United States, and Fred, whom you have just bumped into, is the person you sat next to in third grade. To distinguish the two kinds of "identity," philosophers call the first kind qualitative identity (X and Y have the same qualities) and the second kind numerical identity (X and Y are one and the

---

1   Snyder 2012.
2   Moyer 2013.

same). And—to make things more confusing—there's a third use of the word "identity" that means the qualities or personality or whatever it is that constitutes the important nature of an individual—make you what you are, as in "My Italian roots / love of music / work with dog rescue are basic to my identity." Notice that this sort of "identity" can change over time in what is numerically the same person: a few years ago, Ella wasn't interested in dog rescue. Let's call this sort of "identity" individual identity. And, more confusing still, we can ask about what makes for personal identity, where this question is about what counts as a *person* (as opposed to some other sort of being). An answer to this might imply that we count—or don't count—fertilized human eggs, or chimpanzees, or robots, or silicone-based aliens from the planet Zarkon, as persons. We'll call this personhood identity.

Persons and Identity

Two obvious and very broad characterizations of persons come very quickly to mind. We think of persons as having a mental or psychological life. More generally, we might characterize this as a conscious life, or simply, consciousness. People have memories, desires, opinions, wishes, fears, sensations, and emotions. They know things, make plans, have hopes and goals. All of these, and others, we tend to think of as mental, as psychological. So, we might identify persons with some aspect of their mental lives, or perhaps the sum total of their mental or psychological life. This sort of idea about identity may have implications for what makes for identity in several of the senses listed above.

But a different point of view produces different sorts of multiple implications. No doubt our most immediate and default means of *identifying* people is by their bodies. Indeed we can tell at a glance that this is Julia because she has Julia's body; we can tell that this is Jack because he has Jack's body. And we know that this is the same Julia we spoke with last Sunday because it's the same "Julia body." No need to investigate mental lives. Thus, one might think of identity as fundamentally body identity.

These two views are familiar to common sense, to our ordinary way of thinking. *Hylomorphic* accounts, or "form-matter" views, are another historically prominent view. In these views, a human being is a combination of the matter, or the physical "stuff," and a form, some organizing principle or arrangement of the matter. Such views might differ whether the "form" or the hylomorphic composite is the locus of identity.

A variation of the psychological view, proposed by John Locke, provides a starting point for examining these different views.

I Remember Me: A Psychological View

John Locke is perhaps best known for his *Second Treatise on Civil Government* and its influence on the thinking of the framers of the US Constitution and other advocates of the rights of the governed. His contributions to metaphysics and epistemology are significant, too, including his memory criterion of personal identity. Locke argued that a person's identity consists in the chain of remembered experiences. Here, we should note, he was speaking about numerical identity. In particular, he was worrying about what features account for a person remaining the *same* or *identical person* over time, even through various changes. But a second sort of question can be raised about numerical identity: What constitutes the identity of a person; what features or properties make some being *this* person and not some other? These two questions are sometimes characterized as a **persistence question**: what makes this the same person as that one earlier; and an **individuation question**—what makes someone this person and not someone else at the same time.[3]

My remembered experiences make me who I am; your remembered experiences make you who you are. (They are important, perhaps, to all senses of "identity" listed above.)

Now this needs a little clarification, but first consider the intuitive motivation for adopting Locke's memory criterion for persistence. Normal growth or changes in the body do not affect or determine who one is, we suppose. Changes in size or hair color, loss of some body part, we think, still leaves you *you*. Your body keeps discarding old tissue, and building new, so after one year, virtually 100% of the atoms in your body have been replaced. But you are still there. We suspect, therefore, that something else determines persistence identity. In a movie early in Tom Hanks's career, *Big*, Hanks plays a character who is magically transformed from a child into an adult. The "big" version of his character persuades his closest friend that he—in his "big" form—is the same person, by recounting—*remembering*—various experiences. Similarly, the 2000 movie *Bedazzled* imagines the hero—after a bargain with the devil—occupying successive, very different bodies (in some very different circumstances), in order to win the heart of his true love. A bit more recently,

---

3   These designations due to Macdonald 2005, Chap. 4.

13 Going on 30 imagines the dramatic change in a teenager who wakes up to find herself in the body of a 30 year old woman—yet her "psychology" remains the same.

A less fictional and a more heartbreaking example is perhaps illustrated in later stages of Alzheimer's. Those suffering from the disease no longer *remember*—family members, friends, or even what they were doing a few moments ago. Indeed it's not too far amiss to say that they don't remember themselves. Some suspect that as the memory of personal experiences disappear, the earlier *person* disappears, as well. We might want to say then that *in a literal sense* this Sally, deep into Alzheimer's problems, is not the Sally we knew—is not numerically identical with her.

Locke argues for this idea: a person's memory is determinative of personal identity. The *person* is whatever the person's memory encompasses. We have then a psychological or memory criterion of persistence identity: a person's identity is determined by conscious memories, or a little more clumsily, by the memories contained in consciousness. Locke himself was not intent on distinguishing between one's memories and one's consciousness. He notes, for example, that a person's identity "extends" as far as consciousness extends. Thus, he seemingly intends memory and consciousness to be indistinguishable, at least as far as personal identity is concerned. Perhaps this works for individuation identity as well. Deirdre then is a different person than Sara insofar as her memories differ from Sara's. Deirdre remembers jumping off Rainbow Bridge into the American River the day before graduation; this memory, however, is not "shared" by Sara. They are thus two different persons. Similarly my current memories constitute my identity, just as your memories constitute your identity. And if, for example, Sam's memories include those of Nestor—an ancient Greek king who participated in the Trojan War, according to Homer—then Sam is indeed *the same person as* Nestor. (What is meant here is not merely that Sam *remembers that* Nestor met Telemachus after the Trojan War; what is meant here is that Sam *remembers* meeting Telemachus after the Trojan War.) Thus, there seem to be some puzzling implications of the view. Locke himself acknowledged that some of his "suppositions will look strange to the reader."

Locke dismisses the idea that *substance* plays a role in determining identity. Locke seems to consider substance, in this context, as the "whole particular," a combination of physical and mental. In ordinary cases, consciousness is a part of the whole particular. But a person goes wherever that consciousness goes. So in Locke's view, my consciousness might find itself attached to the body that we recognize as Carrie Underwood, yet my identity is unaffected. So long as consciousness extends or includes the memory of any past action, it is the same person:

> For it being the same consciousness that makes a Man be himself to himself, *personal identity* depends on that only, whether it be annexed only to one individual Substance, or can be continued in a succession of several substances.

The same consciousness, in Locke's view, can occur in different bodies, different substances. What matters for identity is consciousness:

> For it is by the consciousness it has of its present Thoughts and Actions, that it is *self* to it *self* now, and will be the same *self* as far as the same consciousness can extend to Actions past or to come....[4]

So in Locke's view, if Sam wakes today and remembers the French toast he had for breakfast yesterday, the "Sam remembering" is the same person as the "French toast-eating" Sam. Personal identity is not dependent on the body or some immaterial thing. I am me because of the thoughts and memories that I have when I am conscious. Period.

Our ordinary view considers that temporary losses of consciousness, including sleep, are no threat to one's identity. But if Locke is right and my identity is determined by my consciousness, when my body falls asleep and there is no consciousness, I temporarily cease existing.

There is a more challenging worry about the memory view: we are of course forgetful. I remember but a few things from my experiences in second grade. Indeed for most of us, experiences from but a few weeks ago are no longer remembered; they are no longer part of consciousness. Yet we are inclined to think that, yes, it is us that did these things, even if the experiences have been forgotten. Deirdre no longer remembers her going with her cousins to see *The Lion King*, but we think she is still that same person. A person *persists continuously over time*, we think, even if that person has forgotten certain events or experiences. But Locke's view seems to disallow this. This is but a version of one of the earliest criticisms of Locke.

---

4   Locke 1975, Bk. II, Chap. XXVII, Sect. 10.

Thomas Reid: The Brave Officer and Locke

Thomas Reid (1710–96), associated with the Scottish school of Common Sense, and one of Hume's earliest critics, thought he saw a consequence of Locke's view of identity that he suspects Locke did not see:

"It is, that a man be, and at the same time not be, the person that did a particular act."[5]

Reid supposed a brave officer, who as a boy was flogged for stealing from an orchard. In his first military campaign, he acted bravely, and later became a general. Now Reid supposed that the brave officer remembered his childhood punishment. But later as a general, he remembers only those military actions, not the childhood punishment.

Notice the apparent consequence for Locke's view: The general *is* the brave officer, and the brave officer *is* the young boy. But the general *is not* the young boy. The general remembering the younger brave officer makes the general the *same person* as the brave officer. And that brave officer, because he remembers the punishment, is the same person as the youthful offender. Seemingly then, the general is that offender—he is the brave officer who is the young thief. Yet the general has no memory of the theft. So, he is not the thief. And now the general is and is not the young thief.

Reid's puzzlement is now clear. Locke's memory criterion conflicts with our normal "transitivity" intuition about identity. It leads to apparently self-contradictory claims.

This type of criticism led defenders of a psychological criterion to a *continuity* view.

Indeed, in Locke's view, it looks as if there may well be multiple persons occupying Sam's body! For example, suppose that Sam now remembers walking through Aldo's, while visiting New Orleans five years ago. Call Sam's body then BODY X. Now, body X contained someone who was remembering playing in a little-league baseball game 15 years earlier. So body X contains the person who played in that game. But since Sam doesn't remember playing in that game, that person is not Sam. It appears to follow that body X contains both Sam and someone else!

---

5 Reid 1975, p. 114.

Perhaps an obvious solution to some of these difficulties is to suggest that it is *continuity* or overlapping sets of memories that determines personal identity. A *chain* of memories—overlapping sets of memories—enable us to trace the connection between earlier and later memories. Thus, Reid's general is the same as the young boy because the general remembers his actions as a brave officer, and as a brave officer, he remembered the orchard thievery. This *continuity* version of the memory criterion of personal identity—overlapping sets of memories constitute the identity of a person—has prominent defenders.[6]

But consider Alzheimer-afflicted Sally, mentioned above, who has no memories of any past, is numerically identical with no earlier person. There's no overlap between her and any earlier person. Of course, her earlier individual identity is now, we might think, totally destroyed; but still, that person back then, with the different individual identity, was numerically Sally. She's just changed a whole lot.

The memory continuity criterion invites a branching or **fission objection**, that is, we can imagine a person "dividing" into two equivalent beings. The fission objection is a version of the *duplication* problem. Imagine that someday we can transfer the "mental life" of someone near death (call this person U) into a complicated cybernetic system.[7] Suppose further that for some reason, the "transfer engineer" is overly cautious and makes two cybernetic "homes" for U's mental life. U suffers bodily death, but two creatures remain that lay claim to U's memories. Call them U-1 and U-2. You can see the problem. U's mental life, is continuous with both U-1 and U-2. But 1≠2! Identity means one ... and only one! How are we to decide? Can we?

Bernard Williams suggested this "branching problem" many years ago:

> It is logically possible that some other man ... should simultaneously undergo the same changes ... What should we say in that case? They cannot both be Guy Fawkes [our U] ... Moreover, if they were both identical with Guy Fawkes, they would identical with each other, which is also absurd.[8]

Advocates have two types of response to his fission problem. Roderick Chisholm (1916–99), extremely influential in both metaphysics and epistemology, claimed that U is *in fact* identical with one of U-1 or U-2. We just can't tell which. That, is suppose that you somehow undergo fission: U "branches"

---

6   E.g., Shoemaker and Swinburne 1984, pp. 67–132.

7   Daniel Lyons 1998.

8   Bernard Williams 1973, p. 8.

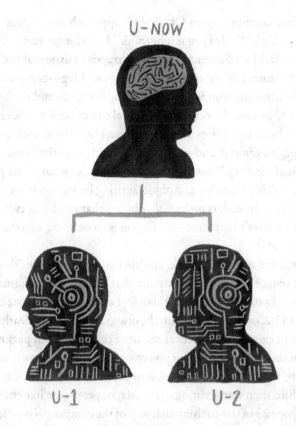

into U-1 and U-2. Chisholm claimed U are *in fact* one—and only one—of those branches. The other is someone mentally very much like U, but not *identical* to U. We will just never know which one. So, in Chisholm's view, there's a metaphysical answer to the question. It's just that the metaphysical answer brings with it an epistemic problem, namely, that we can't tell which of U-1 or U-2 U now is.

This response sometimes strikes people as arbitrary. Yet Chisholm held that we are not identical with a body, but rather a "self" that continues in some one of the bodies. That we are unable to *decide* which body "contains U" does not lead to the conclusion that U is not one of them:

> In such a case there may be no sufficient reason at all for deciding that you are
> or that you are not one or the other of the two different persons. But from
> this it does not follow that you *will* not in fact be one or the other of the two
> persons.[9]

***

9   Chisholm 1976, p. 112.

Others are less sanguine about Chisholm's approach and suggest that neither U-1 or U-2 is U. Sadly (you might think), U no longer exists. These two branches are in fact two different people who happen to share many of the same memories. This leaves but one option. Fission—branching—brings an end to U.

Occasionally some wonder why branching brings an end to the original U. Why can't U be two? It seems fundamental to our notion of identity that a person can't be in two places at once; one can't be both at home, watching reruns of *Gilligan's Island*, and simultaneously sitting in the library, reading about personal identity.[10] But someone might urge: what if the person is a nonphysical thing? Can't a nonphysical thing be in two places at once? (Another chapter considers *universals*, objects that can be in two places at once.) But that won't help here—to be you is to be some *particular* thing, not some universal.

Still some are tempted to ask, couldn't some person be "distributed" throughout space? Consider a company that outgrows its original offices and moves into two new offices (call them O-1 and O-2) in separate buildings. Does O-1, or O-2, or neither, contain the original company? Clearly both do. A company can exist in two places at the same time. (Note, in passing, that a company can also be an intermittent object—a status that was worrisome when it appeared to follow from Locke's view of persons. A company can cease to exist for a while, then start existing again. Maybe people are like companies?)

But perhaps it's better to think that *part* of the company is now located in each new office. We are not wondering about U dividing into *two parts of one thing*. The branching problem concerns U-1 and U-2 are each *two whole persons*.

We have then three options available to us upon branching: 1) U comes to an end; 2) U is one of U-1 or U-2, but we can't tell which; and 3) the unattractive "option" of saying that U, U-1, and U2 are all the same person.

These difficulties have led many to think that in the end we should abandon a memory criterion of personal identity. And they turn to the other seemingly obvious criterion of personal numerical identity: that of having the same body.

Same Body, Same Person

Identifying and re-identifying persons by means of their bodies is no doubt the everyday norm. Sara sees that *Sam* is walking towards her because she recognizes the body. Yet she doesn't think "Oh, here comes Sam's body"; she just sees Sam.

---

10   Parfit 1986, p. 199.

This routine practice suggests a view of personal identity as consisting in having the same body: same body, same person. This is the body criterion of personal numerical identity, and perhaps it answers both the persistence and the individuation questions. Of course, we should be reluctant to interpret "same body" in some ways. Bodies change over time. Bodies grow—and shrink—in various ways, in height or weight. Hair color changes, sometimes naturally, sometimes helped along. A person may lose a toe or a finger, an appendix or even a limb. In order to understand "same body, same person," we need to understand what exactly is meant by this "same body" criterion of identity. One thing it can't mean is *exactly the same physical stuff*. It's almost certain that not a single atom of a person's body stays there for more than a few years.

Same Body—Having the Right History

Bodies come from somewhere. The body that each of us has right now has a history. The history of the body that is "me," or that body that is "you," can be traced. Initially this history leads to a body of a few hours ago or a few days or months. A complete history will of course lead back to the originating zygote. This body then, like any other human body, has a continuous history, beginning with its origin. Of course, we don't tend to think of zygotes as bodies. Still from whatever point at which we are willing to say that we have a human body, "this body" has a continuous history.[11]

Perhaps we can use this idea of a continuous history to give us a clearer sense of "same body." Intuitively, we think that a body is the same body as before because it is *continuous with* all the previous moments or times in that body's history. We can trace back successive moments of Sam's body to the first moments in the history of Sam's body. *Continuous* implies that there is an uninterrupted chain of "moments" of Sam's body. Indeed if we could somehow draw a line on a graph or chart, a line representing the history of Sam's body, it would be a continuous or uninterrupted line. We might impose a grid on that graph of Sam's "body line," which allowed us to talk about Sam's body today or last week or last decade. We should not be misled, however: Sam's body remains continuous.

How does this help us with an account of personal identity as same body? First, we have an idea of what makes me *me* and you *you*—our respective and different bodies. Second, it also gives us a way of answering the persistence question: it provides a way of explaining or defining continuous identity

---

11   E.g., Forbes 1986.

through the *same body*. That is, a body now is the same body as a body then, if they are both "located" in this continuing, uninterrupted "body history." Julia's identity is determined by her body, and *you* are your body. And Julia is the same person today that she was six days or six months or six years or six decades ago because of this continuous, uninterrupted "body history." It doesn't matter which two points we choose from this body history; we get a definitive answer to the persistence question.

You might worry that this can't be the "same body" simply because a body has a shape and size, along with other physical attributes. Change the shape and size, you might ask, and haven't you changed the body? Wouldn't this be a different body? Doesn't "identity" mean "exactly the same"?

An analogy might help allay this sort of worry. Suppose Andy returns to Graeagle to revisit his childhood home on Chilula St. The paint color of the house may have changed; a room might have been added; the living room window might have been replaced by a larger window; the roof might have different shingles. Despite these changes in color, shape, size, "décor," we could trace this house back to the very same house of Andy's earliest days. In principle, some group, making an odd documentary, could have taken turns with their iPhones video-recording every moment of that house, from the time cheap wooden stakes and twine first marked out its foundation until now, as Andy pulls up alongside the curb. And time-lapse video would show that Andy is now looking at a house *continuous with the origin* of the same house of those bygone baby bassinet days. We might even suppose that a large number of small renovations have resulted in a house which has no material in it that was there in the old days.

Similarly Andy's body now is continuous with the origin of the body that—let us put it like this—was first Andy. Something may have been added, something taken away. Still we can trace the continuous, uninterrupted history of this body. And this body is Andy. And as long as this "body history" remains continuous and intact, we'll know where to find Andy: go find Andy's body.

We have some understanding then of "same body, same person." Still, even if we accept that bodies persist over time, we might still want to know if there are good reasons for thinking of a body as determinative of identity. Two natural suggestions occur to us almost immediately. The first is already suggested: we count and distinguish persons by their different bodies. That's all we see. A second natural suggestion is that we engage with the world as bodies. Julia's acts—visiting a library, watching a movie, showing a child how to do long division—are the actions of a body. It might be further claimed that our fundamental orientation in the world is a bodily orientation. Directions, spatial relations, perceptual relations are part of our bodily connection with the world. The French phenomenologist, Maurice Merleau-Ponty, explored this idea at length in one of his seminal works, *The Phenomenology of Perception*.[12] Some would go further, insisting that our psychological lives, our thoughts and feelings are tied to our bodies (which, of course, include our brains and the rest of our nervous systems). In recent decades various authors on consciousness and our emotional and mental life have argued that even our mental life must be understood as tied to the body.[13]

"Beam me up, Scotty?"

Should you be willing to walk into that transporter of the fabled starship *Enterprise*? Even if someone that looks, walks, and talks exactly like you shows up at the other end of the transporter travel, perhaps it isn't you after all.

Suppose the transporter works by making a "blueprint" of you at this end, and at the other end, that blueprint is used to assemble "you" out of completely different matter. Would you still think it's you? Derek Parfit first imagined a transporter case like this.[14]

Or suppose that the transporter disassembles you into sub-atomic particles which it whisks to your destination, and again, a blueprint is used to put you back together out of those particles. Why would you think it's you at the other end, rather than just a duplicate?

According to one expert,[15] the writers on Star Trek were inconsistent about how the transporter actually worked. In some episodes it appears that the transporter sends the person's actual matter through space; but in others, it appears that it just sends a blueprint. This might make a difference about whether you'd like Scotty to beam you up to the *Enterprise*, or you'd rather just be left to face the Klingons on the surface of the planet Wombax.

Perhaps you might insist instead that none of this matters because you are nonphysical—but then that might make you wonder whether Scotty's transporter beam could lock on to "you" at all.

---

12   Merleau-Ponty 1962.
13   Damasio 2000; Edelman 1992.
14   Parfit 1986, Chap. 10.
15   Krauss 1995.

The above illustrates that your view of the transporter depends, at least in part, on your view of personal identity—and that thought experiments involving the transporter can help clarify these views.[16]

If I Only Had a Brain

In the movie *The Wizard of Oz*, Scarecrow wishes his head weren't just stuffed with straw:

> I could while away the hours, conferrin' with the flowers
> Consultin' with the rain.
> And my head I'd be scratchin' while my thoughts were busy hatchin'
> If I only had a *brain*.

Brains play a significant part in our lives, as Scarecrow tells us. Despite the apparent simplicity of the same body criterion, various considerations suggest to some that it's not the body, but the *brain* that matters for personal identity. Once again science fiction may not outrun real possibility by that much.[17] But to prevent our discussion from seeming a bit "creepy," let's treat this as a bit of science fiction—one that illustrates a rationale for a view of personal identity in the real world.

Can we imagine losing parts—even significant parts—of the body, yet still being ourselves? Not only might we lose a limb or an eye, imagine losing the whole body, except for the brain. If we could find a way to preserve the brain—to allow it to continue functioning—then we might think that our identity is still preserved. Recent philosophy sometimes describes this preservation *sans* body as a "brain in a vat." As long as our brains continue functioning, we continue. Our identity therefore is determined by or constituted by a functioning brain: persons remain the same over time, if their brains continue. Deirdre is the same person today as she was yesterday if she has the *same brain* she had yesterday. And here we can understand "same brain" in like manner as we understood "same body."

We see the brain as constituting personal identity, again, because it is fundamentally implicated in that "part" of us that seems to matter most, namely,

---

16   These and other similar transporter cases are outlined in Carroll and Markosian 2010, Chap. 5. See also Merricks 2001 and Corcoran 2001b.

17   Tyson 2010.

our psychological life. Emotions, desires and goals, actions and their motivations all seem inextricably tied to a functioning brain. Thus, it is claimed, personal identity is determined by the brain.

MORE SCIENCE FICTION

As before, we can test the thought that the brain really carries what we think of as personal identity—versus the same-body account—with a science-fiction story. Imagine that Sam's brain and Sara's brain are swapped. Now consider the Sam-body with the Sara-brain. This person has Sara's memories and personality traits, but Sam's body. Is this person Sam or Sara?

Here's a more complicated science-fiction thought-experiment, this time with a bit of connection with reality. The reality: In the 1950s, neurosurgeons began performing a special kind of brain surgery, commissurotomy, in order to help patients suffering from debilitating epileptic seizures. This operation severed the corpus callosum, a network of fibers that allows normal communication and coordination between the two brain hemispheres. Roger Sperry and Michael Gazzaniga studied extensively the effects of this surgery on the patients, finding that the two halves of the brain, when separated, could function independently.[18]

Now to let reality meet science fiction: Imagine for a moment that we can not only "split" brains, but do so in such a way that each hemisphere retains the same psychological life—same memories, same knowledge, same hopes,

18   Godwin and Cham 2013.

desires, goals, wishes. And now combine this idea with that of transplanting the separate hemispheres. Again—not entirely disconnected from reality: some very young patients can have half their brain removed, but grow up functioning almost normally.

Let us imagine first that Kiersten, through some medical emergency, is told by doctors that, along with the rest of her body, half of her brain is dying, but that they have been able to "reconfigure" the other hemisphere so that it contains her entire mental life. This half will be transplanted into a new body. If Kiersten is an advocate of the same brain view of identity, she should not be particularly alarmed about whether or not *she*—Kiersten—will continue to live. After all, she will continue as long as her brain continues.

Same brain theorists typically do not require that the *entire* brain continue. Rather they require first that the "new" brain is a continuant of the original brain. Same body theorists and same brain theorists are alike in this respect. It is the *same* if there is a continuous history. Second, same brain proponents assume that the relevant functional aspects of the brain, such as memories, cognitive abilities, and values, continue. Kiersten survives then so long as the brain (or brain hemisphere) is continuous with her "original" brain and the relevant functioning remains.

Now imagine a variation. Kiersten is dying from cancer that has spread all over her body except for her brain; the doctors decide that they can save her by transplanting her brain into another body (brain-dead, but with the rest of the body okay). But they'll make sure she survives this risky operation by having a "backup": one separable functioning hemisphere into each of two bodies—another case of "fission." So Kiersten's medical emergency will produce two independent yet psychologically equivalent hemispheres. (Imagine that doctors desire a "backup" in case one of the transplants fail.) Now suppose that prior to the surgery Kiersten wonders what will happen if both transplants succeed. What should Kiersten think is about to happen to her?

One thought, widely held, is that Kiersten is about to cease to exist! Just as we saw above with the case of U-1 and U-2, a fundamental principle of identity is that $1 \neq 2$. And we now have Kiersten-left and Kiersten-right. But she can't be both. So, Kiersten ceases to exist, and is replaced by these two new "Kierstens." So fissioning of the brain can also lead to identity problems.

(Cases such as this and others are variations of a case originally imagined by Sydney Shoemaker.[19] Considerations of the "Brownson" case—the name given by Shoemaker to one transplant recipient in his original scenario—can even be found in the pages of *Psychology Today*.[20])

Notice: the same brain view encounters the same problem as the memory criterion: we can always imagine there being two beings that have exactly the same identity-determining characteristics, each of which comes into being at the same moment.

We have been concentrating, for the moment, on persistence identity, but the split-brain phenomenon also raises questions about a person's individuation identity. Because the right hemisphere of the brain controls the left side of the body, and the left hemisphere the right side, real people who have had the split-brain operation sometimes exhibit strange behavior. One, for example, was observed to be pulling up his pants with one hand, and pulling them down with the other. Does one of these actions represent the real intentions of that person? Or do we now have two persons in one body?

Does Being Me Depend on the Absence of Competition?

The duplication problem (or fission or branching), along with the various responses to it, highlights an important issue for identity. Identity should, it seems, depend on internal or intrinsic features of an object or person.[21] Continuity of psychological states or continuity of a body or brain require

---

19 Shoemaker 1963, pp. 24 ff.; also Shoemaker and Swinburne 1984.
20 Burton 2012.
21 For example, Wiggins 1967, Chap. 1.

only that we look at some feature of the person. We don't need to check and see what is happening in the vicinity.

Yet the two hemisphere transplant case seems to raise the suggestion that identity can depend *extrinsic* or *external* conditions. If both transplants are successful—if there are post-transplant *competitors*—there's reason to think Kiersten ceases to exist. On the other hand, Kiersten continues if but one transplant survives; so her identity is preserved.

Now imagine that after the operations, one of the transplants, the right hemisphere, awakes before the other. What should she think? Well, she will certainly recall herself as Kiersten. But whether she really is Kiersten seemingly depends on the success or failure of the other transplant. Kiersten must wait to find out who she is! She is either Kiersten or "Kiersten-right." This seems odd that the "first-awake, post-transplant" Kiersten should have to see what happens to *someone else* to find out who she is! Fission cases produce competitors. And the notion of competition seems to lead to the idea that identity depends on extrinsic features, which seems to have odd implications.

Survival vs. Identity

Faced with these sorts of difficulties some wonder whether numerical *identity* is what we really care about. Might we care about something else that does not require identity? Some philosophers have wondered whether what we really care about instead is survival.

Survival

This survival view first became prominent in Derek Parfit's influential *Reasons and Persons*.[22] And this novel suggestion attempts to avoid the difficulties of identity while retaining something important.

How does survival differ from identity? A person, according to Parfit, is constituted by beliefs, goals, and values, around which actions and projects are organized.[23] Sometimes the person envisions these goals and values in some detail. Or they may only be drawn in broad strokes, such as wanting to be a millionaire, or wanting to be your own boss, or wanting by the time you're 30 to know more about poetry than anyone else. Here Parfit seems to be talking about individual identity, and perhaps personhood identity.

---

22   Parfit 1986.
23   Perry 1976.

A person cares rather that *this set* of beliefs, goals, values, and projects continues. Personal numerical persistence identity doesn't matter. That is, when we shift the emphasis from identity to survival, the persistence question gets a very different answer. *I survive*, in some sense, if these projects of mine, together with my beliefs and values, continue to exist, and in some way, my "survivor" can continue to carry out these projects or fulfill these aims or act according to my current beliefs and values. Or as David Lewis describes the view:

> When I consider various cases in between commonplace survival and death, I find that what I mostly want in wanting survival is that my mental life should flow on. My present experiences, thoughts, beliefs, desires, and traits of character should have appropriate future successors.[24]

Suppose then that Deirdre wants to major in mathematics to become an actuary, raise a family, and help rescued animals. She identifies with these projects and values. As long as she is able to pursue fulfillment of those projects, she might well be indifferent to whether *this* body or *this* brain continues.[25] In this survival view, Deirdre should be unfazed by the possibility of multiple survivors. Still a critic might note, as Lewis does, that prior to any transplant operation, Deirdre might reasonably—and compellingly—wonder which *one* will be *me*? But a more central question is this: if Deirdre's goals and values survive—say, in her children—but she dies, is that all she should be interested in? No, say critics: she wants to survive.

Substance and Souls

Animalism

Recently a view intriguingly known as *animalism* has attracted a number of defenders, most notably Eric T. Olson.

Olson holds that human persons are fundamentally animals; we are not essentially persons. The concept of person describes a characteristic of humans, but not a defining characteristic. The kind of being we are is determined by our biological properties, and the continuing of some individual is coincident with the continuing of various biological processes. As animals, we temporarily have certain psychological characteristics, but

---

24   David Lewis 1976, p. 17.
25   Perry 1976.

these are ultimately due to our biological or animal nature. Our identity is not determined by our psychology, as the subtitle of Olson's book indicates: "*Personal Identity without Psychology.*"

Animalism insists that *person* is not a kind of substance. This view is considered to be opposed to Lockean or psychological continuity views. Indeed there has been considerable exchange over the past decade or so on the rival virtues and vices of Lockean and animalist views.[26]

Perhaps you wonder why we have not considered a view that has been around, in one form or another, for a long time: that sameness of *soul* determines sameness of person? Of course, if we are to accept it, it will help to know what a soul is, and when we have the same one.

Plato, according to many commentators, held that persons are their souls. In the *Republic*, several of the arguments apparently identify a person with a soul and its characteristics. The *Phaedo*, Plato's dialogic and literary recounting of Socrates' last hours, explores several ways to think of the soul and whether those accounts of the soul might support a notion of immortality or survival after death.[27]

Aristotle's view of the soul depends on his more general view of form and matter. As we will discuss in more detail below, matter and form provide a way of thinking about the nature or structure of each individual object, including persons. In his view, various objects—living ones—have a special type of form, namely, a soul.

These ancient philosophers' views of the soul have had substantial influence on subsequent metaphysical views. Plato influenced early Christian thinkers, such as St. Augustine. Aristotle influenced St. Thomas Aquinas, who relied on and synthesized the Aristotelian metaphysics to provide a coherent framework for Catholic thought in particular and Christian thought in general—a framework still very much in evidence in present day views.[28]

Form and Matter: "Stuff" and Organization

In thinking about an object, we might adopt one of two perspectives. We might think about the "stuff" of an object, asking, for example, "Where's that wooden candle holder you used to have?" Along the same lines, we might

---

26   Eric T. Olson 1999; Shoemaker 2008.
27   Plato 1961c; see discussions in Burger 1984 and Rosen 2008.
28   Gilson 1940, especially Chaps. IX and X.

naturally ask of Michelangelo's masterpiece sculpture, the Pietà, "What is it made of?" We do not marvel, however, at the mere fact that the statue is made of marble. We marvel at the marble stuff because of the way it is shaped or carved—*because of the way it's organized*. There is an "organizing principle" to this rather large clump of marble. Similarly the candle holder: it's not just that it's made of wood, but that the wood is shaped or structured in this particular way. This piece of wood might have been organized or shaped in some other way; for example, it might have been fashioned into a small bowl.

We have only one object in each case: a marble statue and a wooden candle holder. Yet we "analyze" each object as comprising what it's made of—the "stuff"—and how that stuff is put together. By now you have likely surmised that these two aspects are the matter and form in Aristotle's view, which we discussed at length in Chapter 7. Here is a bit of review of the parts of that view that are relevant here.

Hylomorphism is the view that any individual object or substance can be analyzed as a unity of form and matter. The "stuff" of an object is its matter. The form is the organizing principle of the object, or how the stuff is arranged or put together. Not just the candle holder, but the candle too is a "unity" of form and matter—the matter is the wax, while the form is the structural arrangement of that clump of wax. Again, it is important to emphasize that candle, candle holder, and statue are each *one* object composed of matter and form. And this is true of any object—it is constituted by its matter and its form.

Soul as Form

Some objects, like the statue or the candle holder, have their forms given to them, imposed by an artisan or a sculptor. We are interested in living things, however. And these seem to have their form *intrinsically*. Living things are of a certain type because of their form. The matter of the lilac bush or the matter of a monkey or the matter of a person is organized according to an innate principle. To be a monkey, to be a "monkey kind of thing" is to have a monkey form. The form *informs* or organizes the matter and guides the development of the matter. Aristotle called the form of any living thing a "soul." Although he distinguished the types of soul characteristic of plants, animals, and people, our focus is the human soul or the form of persons.

The kind of soul distinctive of people is the *rational soul*. Rational souls guide both the physical development and sentience—our sensory ability—of human beings. More importantly, the rational soul structures our rational features, our cognitive or intellectual characteristics. We are thinking creatures in virtue of our having a rational soul. Indeed people are *rational animals*, according to Aristotle. They belong to the genus of animal, but are a distinctive species, namely, thinking animals. (Aristotle understood thinking as an attribute of people, not of nonhuman animals.)

So a person is a basic or primary substance, a single object composed of soul—that is, form—and matter. If we ask, however, what makes a person *this* person and not *that* one, we get an interesting answer from Aristotle. His view might be more easily understood if we return for a moment to our simple candle holder.

Imagine that a candle holder company machines many teak candle holders of the same size, shape, finish, and weight. The form—the shape, the arrangement—of the teak clumps is the same. The form doesn't distinguish one candle holder from another. So, it must be the wood, the matter, that distinguishes. That is, *this* candle holder is made from *this clump* of teak and *that* candle holder is made from *that clump* of teak. More technically, it is the matter that *individuates* candle holders. Matter, not form, individuates.

Analogously, Sam and Sara are of the same type: rational creature. Thus, they are alike in form. Sam and Sara differ, however, in their matter. Then while persons are basic or primary substances, a unity of matter and form, the individuating principle is the matter of the person. Perhaps what we have here is a body criterion for individuation numerical identity. Yet Sara remains the same person over time because she remains *this unity* of matter and soul. Then, it seems, we have a different test for persistence numerical identity.

You might wonder why the sameness of person over time is not also determined by the matter. Were this same matter to lose its organizing principle, to lose its form (soul), we no doubt would be disinclined to call this the "same person." Indeed it's not just the calcium, water, and other chemical elements and compounds that make a *person*. It's that these chemicals—this stuff—are organized in a particular way, by a form—a soul—of a certain kind.

Summarizing then, in Aristotle's view a person is the body plus soul. Different matter distinguishes individuals, but a person persists because the unity of form and matter remains. What we want to know from Aristotle, then, is: Is this how we tell it's the same person? Fred now and Fred-as-a-child back then do not have the same matter (though there is a spatio-temporal continuity, with small changes, as we've noted). But do they have the same form? If form is rationality, then every human is endowed with this universal characteristic. But if we're looking at individual types of rational thought, then it's for sure that Fred now and Fred-as-a-child are wildly different.

Medieval and Contemporary Understandings of the Soul

Plato's view may seem a little more typical: namely, soul constitutes identity. Jack goes where his soul goes, just as Julia goes where her soul goes. And Julia is the same person today as yesterday if and only if she has the same soul. In a widely held and well-known, if controversial, set of views, persons continue in the after-life if and only if their souls continue. Thus, no amount of bodily change or even "bodily disintegration" damages personal identity. How are we to think of this type of soul? We look—as a start—to Thomas Aquinas.

Aquinas utilized the Aristotelian framework for understanding the soul: the soul, as form, organized the matter. Like Aristotle, Aquinas too held that the person was a basic substance, a unity of form and matter.[29] Of course Aquinas, as a Christian, was also concerned about an issue that troubled Aristotle far less. Aquinas needed a metaphysical understanding of persons and personal identity that guaranteed not only survival after death, but that it was *this person* that survived.

Aquinas, like Aristotle, held that persons are numerically individuated by their matter. We have different ways to characterize this matter—flesh and bones or a continuing genetic structure—but the matter is the body as physical. Whether we describe it in modern or medieval terms, it is the matter that is the individuating principle. And, to an extent, Aquinas followed Aristotle's view about the numerical persistence of individuals: He would say that Sam, for example, persists as long as there is a continuing unity of soul and matter.

Now, however, consider Sam's eventual death. Aquinas held, consistent with the Christian view, that his soul continues to exist, even though his body ceases to function or even disintegrates. He further held that eventually the soul would be reunited with a "resurrected" body. Christian thinkers continue to puzzle over the nature of this resurrected body.

But another question arises for Aquinas. We know that the *person* Sam is "restored" when soul is reunited with the resurrected body. What becomes of Sam while soul is separated from body? In the Thomist[30] view, Sam is distinguished from Deirdre by virtue of his matter. And Sam remains the same person as long as the unity of soul and body continue. There seems to be a gap, however, in Sam's existence between the time the soul slips his mortal coil and the time it is united with a resurrected body.

---

29   E.g., Leftow 2001, p. 137.
30   "Thomist" is the conventional adjective form for St. Thomas Aquinas.

Recognizing the difficulty, Aquinas seems to admit that it is *not* Sam that exists while his disembodied soul exists: "The soul, since it is part of man's body, is not an entire man, and my soul is not I."[31] Of course, this runs counter to the views of many Christian thinkers, as Goetz and Taliaferro observe. Similarly Brian Davies, a noted Thomist scholar, also holds that "my soul is not I" for Aquinas. Davies argues that, in the Thomistic view, the survival of the soul is not the survival of a human being. It is only an *intellectual* being that exists.[32] Yet Aquinas' view that Sam is not his soul does not seem to bode well for *Sam's* existence post-mortem, at least during that time that body and soul are separate."[33]

If Davies is right, then a consequence of Aquinas' view is that there is a gap in the existence of the person, from death until the soul is united with a resurrected body. (By analogy, imagine that a house burns down, and nothing is left for a while except the original blueprints, from which the same house is reconstructed later.) Perhaps Davies's interpretation helps Aquinas. One might still wonder what it is that is special about the soul and not some other part of the person. Would preserving all, or even some special part of the body, be sufficient, as well? Clearly, Aquinas would reject this possibility. Otherwise, Sam would have become a "split person," existing both wherever his soul is and wherever the preserved parts of his body are. Indeed, Davies notes that for Aquinas, the *human person* Sam exists only after the soul is reunited with the body.[34]

A different view of personal identity as constituted by the soul, and one that seems closer to the conventional religious view, is found in Richard Swinburne's *The Evolution of the Soul*. Swinburne has written extensively about theological and related philosophical issues (see Chapter 11). Swinburne argues that, while the soul is *part* of a person just as the body is part of a person, a person's soul constitutes personal identity.[35] Souls individuate persons, and the continued existence of the soul explains the persistence of persons over time.

Swinburne views souls as immaterial, as nonphysical subjects. Those items we typically identify as mental, such as beliefs and desires, or intentions and hopes, are in fact *states of the soul*. The beliefs and desires give a structure to the soul. The way in which beliefs and desires are related, how they affect

---

31   Aquinas n.d., Sect. 924.
32   Davies 1992, pp. 216–17.
33   For a different view, see Stump 2003, Pt. II.
34   Davies 1992, pp. 217–19.
35   Swinburne 1986, p. 147.

our acquisition of other beliefs and desires, how they affect the judgments a person makes, and consequently, the person's behavior—this complex network of belief and desire determines the structure of the soul.[36] This evolved structure constitutes a person's character. Swinburne summarizes the nature of the soul thus:

> Souls are immaterial subjects of mental properties. They have sensations and thoughts, desires and beliefs and perform intentional actions. Souls are the essential parts of human beings, and humans have sensations etc. and perform intentional actions in virtue of their souls doing so.[37]

This description of what souls are, however, does not yet answer the question of personal identity—what makes a soul *this* soul, and how *this* soul constitutes *this* person. Swinburne claims that souls are connected to a body: Julia's soul is connected to her body, and Jack's to his body. A body, however, is not an essential part of the person; it is only contingently a part of the person, and so it contributes nothing to the person's identity. Julia's body—while a part of her—is not Julia. Again, Julia *is* her soul.[38]

Yet this still leaves us wondering how we are to link souls to personal identity. If it's logically possible for a soul to exist apart from the body, our normal way of identifying Julia, or distinguishing her from Jack, is no longer available—these two souls are in principle separable from their respective bodies. Indeed, one who doubts the truth of dualism, will wonder how it is that we "track" or identify a person's psychological states. So what is it that makes one soul *this* individual soul and *that* soul that individual soul?

Swinburne argues that there is a fundamental *thisness* or *haecceity* to each soul. *Haecceity* is a Latin term coined by the medieval philosopher John Duns Scotus (1265–1308). In English, it means *thisness*. For Scotus, haecceity is the source of the unity of the soul.[39] The thisness of a soul is a basic, unanalyzable feature of souls, according to Swinburne. In a sense, because a soul exists, it always exists as *this soul*. To put it roughly, any soul has essentially its special "I'm this one" feature.

Some contemporary views of haecceity or "individual essence" hold that an object's thisness is itself a property. In addition to having properties, such as

---

36 Swinburne 1997, Chap. 8.
37 Swinburne 1997, p. 333.
38 Swinburne 1986, p. 146.
39 Cross 2014.

being the author of *Huckleberry Finn* or having been born in Florida, Missouri, Mark Twain also had the individuating property *being identical with Mark Twain*.[40] Of course, this is a quite special property, and whether this type of property exists is still the subject of debate.

Swinburne recognizes that some critics may think that the haecceity view is "irrational." Two things (souls) can't just be different; they must differ in some respect, or in some characteristic. Indeed our normal way of distinguishing individual things is by means of some property or characteristic. These two glasses are distinct: although both are ruby red, both crystal, both eight inches tall, *something* physical distinguishes them. Similarly we normally distinguish persons' bodies by means of some physical characteristic. In the case of physical objects, then, like glasses or bodies, we can point to physical differences, which make them *distinguishable* from all other physical objects. But what will we point to with an *immaterial* object like a soul? If souls are identified with sets or collections of nonphysical mental characteristics, isn't it possible that there would be two apparently identical souls, having all the same mental characteristics, and thus indistinguishable?

Swinburne's main positive argument can be laid out simply. First, consider a world in which Deirdre's soul is attached to her body and Danny's soul is attached to his. Now, Swinburne asks us, imagine a world in which Deirdre and Danny switch bodies. But these two worlds are obviously different, he suggests: "What could be more obvious?"[41]

It may be obvious that these two worlds are different, but how is that supposed to address the *thisness* of souls? Assuming that the worlds are different, it is not Deirdre's or Danny's bodies that make them different. All that changes is the souls connected to these bodies: *this* soul (Deirdre's soul, say) is now attached to a different body, Danny's. And similarly for Danny's soul. If soul changes are sufficient to make the two worlds different, then it would seem that each soul must have a thisness. One soul must be intrinsically different from the other. For Swinburne, there would be a difference in worlds even if the mental characteristics are the same for each soul. Thus, the difference between these two hypothetical worlds can only be explained, in Swinburne's view, by the thisness of souls.

But there are still questions one might have about the *disembodied* souls. Could such beings come into contact with one another? We might wonder about the "contact mechanism," since disembodied souls will not have our

---

40   Robert M. Adams 1979.
41   Swinburne 1997, p. 341.

normal perceptual apparatus. And *thisness* is similarly a nonphysical, imperceptible characteristic.

Some will dissent of course from the idea that life after death is the life of a disembodied soul; it is the life of a soul in some new (?) body. *Thisness* is a metaphysical fact, it might be further claimed, recognized only by God perhaps. Swinburne does not address the details of life after death, however.

Soul Concerns: Soul Trains and Soul Copies

In a little monograph read by many beginning philosophy students, John Perry imagines a series of conversations over three evenings, occurring between two friends, one whom is about to die.[42] Perry raises two concerns about souls of interest for us here. The first concern is the individuation of souls: there appear to be no clear "identifying characteristics" for a soul. What difference would there be whether a body had just one soul, or series of souls all having the same characteristics—a soul train—moving through?

Swinburne of course has a response to the problem of the soul train. Souls are by nature individuated. This is what it means to say that every soul has an intrinsic thisness. There is in principle then a *metaphysical difference* between souls—that is, uniqueness is one of a soul's metaphysical properties.

The second concern for our purposes is raised by the following hypothetical case. Imagine that you die. Your soul—that is, your self—goes to heaven. Upon your arrival, imagine that God—perhaps because yours is such a remarkable or extremely praise-worthy soul—makes a duplicate of your soul. That is, whatever mental or psychological characteristics possessed by your "original" soul, God manufactures or creates an identical soul. This newly minted soul possesses all the same properties. And so our familiar and fundamental principle of identity reappears: $1 \neq 2$. By being so enamored of you, and making an identical "soul mate," God has effectively killed you off. Again recall that when it comes to identity, competition can be deadly.

Leaving aside whatever other worries a theist might have about this thought experiment, notice that Swinburne's view has a ready, if controversial, response to concern about soul competition. *Not even God can make a soul competitor.* Not even God can make $1 = 2$. The *thisness* of a soul guarantees that it can't be copied in the way imagined.

---

42   Perry 1977.

Key Concepts

- qualitative identity
- numerical identity
- individual identity
- personhood identity
- persistence question
- individuation question
- memory criterion
- fission objection
- body criterion
- hylomorphism

Reading/Discussion Questions

1. What do you think is the strongest objection to Locke's view of personal identity? Do you think the continuity view fares better? Explain.

2. Suppose someone claimed, drawing on the movie *Bedazzled*, that as someone occupies several different bodies in turn, even though some memories are retained, there is still a different person with each new body. Different bodies would yield different sensations, even different emotional reactions—hence, a different person. How might you defend the "same consciousness, same person" view against this sort of claim?

3. First, explain the problem presented by fission or branching cases. Suppose you were the person about to undergo a transplant of a hemisphere; should you be concerned about competitors, that is, duplicates? Explain.

4. Briefly describe Swinburne's view of personal identity. Describe what you see as a major problem with this view. How might Swinburne's view be defended from this objection?

5. Suppose a human person were to receive a bionic part in place of some human body part. Now suppose that someone claims that this bionically modified being is no longer a *human* person, perhaps a bionic person, but not a human person. Given that some discussions now suggest that the implanting of microchips in a person is only a decade or two away, what do you think of this claim? That is, is a bionically enhanced person still a human person? Would a human "Luke Skywalker" cease to be a human person with a bionic hand? How much of a human person's ordinary

human body could be replaced by bionic parts, yet still be a human person? Try to identify the principle behind your answer.

For Further Reading

David Wiggins 1967, perhaps a challenging work for the beginner, identifies a number of important aspects and arguments for both identity generally and personal identity. John Perry 1977, as noted in the text, has served as the introduction for many students to the problems of personal identity; it is both rigorous and readily accessible to anyone. Perry 1975 is an anthology containing some of the more important readings on personal identity. Shoemaker and Swinburne 1984 is an exchange between a materialist, Shoemaker, who nonetheless views himself as a "neo-Lockean," and a dualist, Swinburne. Shoemaker defends the psychological continuity view, based in part on his functionalist view of the mind. Swinburne defends the same soul view; Swinburne's notion of the soul comprises various aspects of our mental life, as noted in the text. This same soul view is also detailed in his 1986, 1994, and 1997; as noted in the text, Swinburne defends a *haecceity* notion of the soul. Amelie Oksenberg Rorty 1976 includes contributions by David Armstrong, Derek Parfit, and David Wiggins, all of whom have significantly contributed to recent discussions of personal identity. Parfit 1986, while about much more, contains an extended and influential discussion of personal identity. Bernard Williams 1973, similarly influential in discussions of personal identity, defends the same body view. Corcoran, ed., 2001b contains a number of essays, authored by philosophers who have played pivotal roles in these discussions, on identity and related matters. A recent, sometimes challenging book surveys historical and contemporary views, including a section on animalism, and standard, well-known objections to the various views, is Harold Noonan 2003. Dwayne Godwin's and Jorge Cham's "Of Two Minds" in the "The Mind in Pictures" section at the back of the March/April 2013 issue of *Scientific American: Mind* is an annotated and illustrated introduction to matters related to split brains.

CHAPTER TEN

FREE WILL

(A Few) Great Moments in the History of Literature on Fate and Free Will

Free will or its lack is not the sole province of theologians and philosophers. Is a life controlled by fate or mechanism, by necessity? Can a person choose—freely—an action that has some significance in one's life? Some of our greatest poets and dramatists have put just these issues before us.

For example, in Homer's *Odyssey* (eighth century BCE), Agamemnon rejoices that Odysseus and Achilles are arguing about who was the best warrior—because he thought this fulfilled Apollo's prophecy that Troy would fall when such a "contest" occurred. If the prophecy was being realized, then *fate* was in control.

In Sophocles' well-known play about Oedipus's attempt to escape his fate (c. 429 BCE), it is suggested that while our "choices" are up to us, their outcome is not. Oedipus's parents, hearing a prophecy that their son will kill his father and marry his mother, have him left outside to die—but he is adopted, grows up with no knowledge of his parentage, and ends up unintentionally doing exactly what was predicted. Indeed, we find throughout Greek literature the suggestion that necessity controls our lives—represented, for example, by the Three Fates of Greek mythology, who spin, measure, and cut the thread of our lives.

Several centuries later, in John Milton's *Paradise Lost* (1667), a different view appears: Milton endorses free will, but he links it to rational behavior. Adam, for example, says to Eve: "God left free the will, for what obeyes / Reason, is free, and Reason he made right" (IX 351–52).

Diane Kelsey McColley 1972 connects this conception of free will to Milton's understanding of the human relationship to the divine, noting that "Man's disobedience ... was not the revelation of his nature, but the violation of it; that is, the voluntary resignation of his free will resulting in the loss of spontaneous love" (p. 107).

The early sixteenth century saw one of the great debates in intellectual history. Erasmus of Rotterdam (1466–1536), the great Renaissance scholar, and Martin Luther (1483–1546), the leader of the Reformation, grew further apart as the debate progressed, even though other scholars tried to effect some reconciliation between them. Many hoped that Erasmus and Luther would find themselves allies in their criticism of the Roman Catholic Church. But it was not to be; they differed too much over the subject of their debate. What lay at the heart of their dispute? The nature and extent of free will.

We won't be following either the theological or philosophical turns in Luther's and Erasmus's contentious dispute. That debate signals, however, the centrality of the conviction that we have free will. The pull of free will can be traced back to the *Meditations* of the Roman emperor Marcus Aurelius (121–180), and it is the focus of St. Augustine's late fourth-century work, *On the Free Choice of the Will*.[1] That we have free will is the default position for many. Indeed, this belief plays a central role not only in how we *understand* our own and others' behavior, but in how we *treat* people. The philosopher, John Searle, once held that we *cannot* give up our conviction that we have free will, even though "Our conception of physical reality simply does not allow for radical freedom."[2]

---

1   Marcus Aurelius 2006; Augustine 1993.
2   Searle 1984, Chap. 6.

One picture of human nature presents us as conscious, rational beings who act on the basis of what we know, believe, desire, or hope. Further, at least some of our actions are of our own choosing. We aren't forced to perform these actions: they aren't simple reflexes. At least some of our actions are the result of *free will*.

No sooner than we complete this description, however, we hear a competing picture, apparently drawn from science. The world, we are told, is a structured, largely predictable world. Everything in it is governed by natural laws, which are revealed to us by scientific investigation. If you take a bowling ball to the top of a church steeple, and drop it, it's going to fall—*it has to fall*. In this picture events don't just happen, but must happen. Given the laws, given past events, this new event *must* happen the way it does. This is a *mechanistic* or *deterministic* picture of the world. If we are part of such a world, then our actions are events no different from dropping the bowling ball.

In the second picture all of our actions are fixed by something beyond us; the first presents at least some of our actions as the result of free will, of our choosing to do them. In a moment, we will be more precise about these notions of free will and determinism. Right now, notice that the conflict between these two seems to have implications for another important notion, that of moral responsibility. It is because we attribute "authorship" or "ownership" of an action to a person that we hold that person morally responsible for the action. This deterministic interpretation of the world seems to say, however, that a person isn't the "author" of an act. Rather that act is authored by—caused by—a very impersonal set of laws and circumstances. So, the outcome of the free will issue has very broad implications. We return to this below.

Before clarifying the notion of free will, we need to set aside one sense of "free." The notions of freedom and liberty appear often in historical, political, and cultural contexts. But in this context, we are not interested in political freedom. And, in our context, the word "libertarian" does not describe a political view. Whether we have free will is a *metaphysical* question, not resolved by consulting experts in political science or political history, or political philosophy, for that matter. The metaphysical question of free will is only about the control of at least some of our actions: are at least some of our actions "up to us," or are all actions "controlled by" a set of laws and prior circumstances?

One more qualification. Libertarians—people who believe that we have free will—do not claim that *all* our actions or behaviors are the result of free will. They willingly admit that some, perhaps many of our actions are indeed determined. Proponents of free will claim only that on some occasions, some agents' actions are free.

(Don't be alarmed by the term "agent." Here the term is used in one of its senses: an "agent" is simply a person or being using a certain power to bring about a certain end. And *agency* is the having this power or this ability to make something happen. A *person's* action and an *agent's* action are for our purposes synonymous.)

Free Will and Determinism

Our intuitive sense of the notion of free will can be characterized more precisely. An agent has free will (or an agent's action is free) if and only if the agent *could have done otherwise*, under the same circumstances. With all the same circumstances at the time the person performed some action, that person could have done something else. Imagine an action that we would normally think of as coming about as a result of free will, say, going to a library and deciding to check out *Dial Emmy for Murder* instead of *Death by Honeymoon*. You check out *Dial Emmy*. This is a free act, we suppose, because it was open to you to do something else. You could have checked out *Honeymoon*. You could have done otherwise ... even if all circumstances had been the same.

This picture fits closely with our commonsense view. We think free will is having different paths or options open to us. We may choose one option, but we *could have done otherwise*; we could have chosen the other option. A somewhat different version of free will has recently been developed. But we will be working with this notion of free will: a free agent is one who, on at least some occasions, *could have done otherwise*.

Why Believe in Free Will?

Sartre and Free Will

One of the most dramatic assertions of human freedom comes from a philosopher who asserted that humankind was a "useless passion."[3]

---

3   Sartre 1956. This quotation is from p. 784; those following are from pp. 710, 567, 707, 566, 640, and 725.

Jean Paul Sartre (1905–80), the French existentialist philosopher, argued for a view of human nature that includes a capacity for almost boundless choice. Indeed, in his view, human beings are responsible for not just some but all of their actions. "I am responsible for everything ... except for my very responsibility," he writes, because choice—and therefore responsibility—is a fact about human *being*, or our being in the world. In other words, Sartre claims, "I am condemned to be free." I cannot escape this freedom, and not because some "higher power" has made it so. Rather my "condemnation" is that nothing can or will relieve me of the responsibility for what I do. Sartre says of any individual human being, "The weight of the whole world is on his shoulders: he is responsible for the world and for himself as a way of being." For Sartre, whether or not we "could have done otherwise" is not the real question. Freedom is not merely "a *property* of my being. It is very exactly the stuff of my being."

How does Sartre arrive at such a conclusion? Sartre's ontology, his inventory of the basic features of the world, recognizes only consciousness and things. As conscious beings, we find ourselves "thrown into" a world in which there is no God, and which has no meaning apart from what we ourselves give to it. Even our own past is significant only because we assign meaning to it.

We are thus always in the process of making, even remaking, ourselves, according to Sartre. And the way we accomplish this is by choosing personal projects. It is only in the choosing and the carrying out of these projects that a person has a character. Unlike the typical approach to free will, in which character can constrain or even preclude freedom, Sartre holds that our freedom makes our character, and we make it from "nothing." This is the corollary of the Sartrean claim that existence precedes essence: "Freedom is existence, and in it existence precedes essence." In other words, at first we are nothing—and who and what we become depends on our choices.

Sartre was a member of the French Resistance during World War II. He had a long and complicated relationship with Simone de Beauvoir. The author of plays, novels, essays, and his most important and most challenging work, *Being and Nothingness*, he was awarded the Nobel Prize for literature in 1964, but declined to accept it.

What reasons do people have for thinking we have free will? There are two principal arguments: one based on the notion of responsibility or accountability and the other based on our experience—how it seems to us—when we undertake some action. Both arguments are controversial; still, they illustrate how deeply connected free will is to other important views.

We hold people *responsible* or *accountable* for many of their actions. Some years ago I gave an informal talk on free will to adult members of the local community; of the about 50 people in attendance, only one person in the audience thought it was likely that we were not in fact responsible for our actions. To the rest, accountability for our actions not only undergirded our understanding of human behavior, but was also a part of the basis for our moral judgments! Bad behavior results in blame; good behavior merits praise.

We move quickly from accountability to free will. We hold people responsible for their behavior because we think *they could have done otherwise*. Deirdre blames Danny for being late because he stayed at the bowling alley an extra twenty minutes. He could have left on time; he didn't have to bowl the few extra frames—*he really could have done otherwise*. Imagine, however, a different scenario. Imagine that Danny is late because he is arrested and hauled off to jail in a case of mistaken identity. Deirdre now cannot hold him accountable for his lateness; she can't blame him. It was not in his control that the police mistook him for someone else. Indeed Danny was held against his will! *He could not have done otherwise.*

This example is easily generalizable. A necessary condition of accountability or responsibility for our actions is that we could have done otherwise. Of course, we are not talking here of reflex behaviors or internally or externally compelled behaviors, or "accidental slips." Leave aside then those behaviors and focus on what we normally consider to be actions that deserve moral praise or blame. We seem committed to the following simple argument. If we are accountable for our actions, then we have free will. Since we believe we are accountable for our actions, the conclusion follows: we have free will. Call this the responsibility argument for free will.

You might be wondering if this argument might be turned around. That is, if there's good reason to think that we do not have free will, then we aren't accountable or responsible for our actions. As we will see below, some hold just this view.

Nonetheless, the idea of accountability for our actions seems inescapable for many. And this inescapability has led to the insistence that we possess free will.

The other argument most commonly made for the existence of free will is the experience argument for free will. The main idea: it sure seems like a lot of our actions depend on our choices; nothing, it seems to us, *makes us* perform those actions. My experiencing *myself* as the source of my actions, rather than some force other than me, is the key to the experience argument. I'm very much awake, in command of my faculties; I'm not ill or taking medication. So, if circumstances are normal, my experience—how it seems to me—is a fairly reliable guide to what is actually happening.

We are now able to see the argument from experience somewhat more explicitly. Assuming circumstances are normal, my experience is a fairly reliable guide of what is actually happening. In such normal circumstances, sometimes I experience my actions as something *I'm in charge of*—actions that I freely perform. But this is just my freely performing this action. Hence, based on my experience of this action and the reliability of my experience, I have free will.

Critics still ask whether or not such experiences are genuinely reliable. They might point to other "experiences" that were thought to be reliable, but weren't. For example, B.F. Skinner, the noted twentieth-century behaviorist psychologist, held that our experience of ourselves as "free" was an illusion founded in our ignorance of the real causes of our behavior.[4] In response, libertarians claim that these experiences aren't like that at all. The experience is, as it were, "transparent." We will pick up on this idea below. For now, it is enough to know that the "reliability" of our experience of free will is controversial.

Together the experience argument and the responsibility argument seem to underlie the conviction that we have free will. Still, some see the attractiveness of a competing picture—the deterministic picture.

Determinism

We have an intuitive idea about determinism: *you can't escape the law*. Of course, the sense of "law" here is physical law, the laws of nature, with which are all very familiar. A historically prominent notion of determinism is that every event has a cause; no event occurs *ex nihilo* (from nothing). Various philosophers, theologians and scientists still make use of this account of determinism. But a different version is becoming more common: determinism is the claim that *every event is the necessary outcome of physical laws and prior circumstances or events.* In other words, events are *necessitated* by a combination of physical law and antecedent conditions. Given certain reasonable assumptions about the notion of cause, one can see that the historical understanding leads to the

---

4   Skinner 1974, Chaps. 8 and 12; see also Crumley 2006.

more contemporary view of determinism.[5] For our purposes, we will work with this more recent view. It's worth taking a look at it in a bit more detail.

Events are familiar enough: Caesar crossing the Rubicon, Washington crossing the Delaware, World War II, Sara dropping Sam off at the train station—all of these are events. But we want to broaden the notion to include some "happenings" you might not normally consider as events. Any object has characteristics or qualities or properties. The rocking chair has the quality or property of being red. Danny has the property of wearing a magenta-colored shirt. The broader sense of event is *any change in the properties of an object.* Change the color of the rocker, have Danny put on a different shirt—those are events. Some events are very complex, made up of other events, World War II, for example. Other events are relatively simple: you pick up your smart phone. The history of the world up to *now* just is all the events that have occurred—from the Big Bang to *The Big Bang Theory.*

Now consider something that you might not have thought of as an "event": *deciding* to go to the library instead of taking a nap. This deciding is sometimes called *volition.* Among a person's many properties are obviously physical properties—height, weight, eye color, chemical makeup, which parts of the brain are activated at a given moment—*and* a person's mental properties. You know these properties: your beliefs and desires, your feelings and emotions, the things you know, your fears, and yes, your "decidings" or volitions. But changing these properties, e.g., changing beliefs, changing your desire ("On second thought, I want the apple pie."), changing your mind: these are one and all events! *Deciding* or *forming an intention* or *volition* is an event.

The implication of seeing mental changes as *events* is not far to seek. If any event is necessitated by a combination of prior events or circumstances and natural law, and deciding is an event, then even deciding or forming an intention is necessitated; it's *determined.* If determinism is true, for any given mental event, *it had to happen.* There's no "could have been otherwise" about it! All of us know what's going to happen if I take any object to the top of the steeple, hold it out over the edge, and let it go. It's going to fall; that *has to happen.* It's necessitated by natural law and prior events. According to determinism, this is no less true of mental events.

In the early nineteenth century, the French mathematician and astronomer Pierre-Simon Laplace (1749–1827) gave a vivid expression of determinism that you may have heard described as "Laplace's demon":

---

5   E.g., Blanshard 1961.

We may regard the present state of the universe as the effect of its past and the cause of its future. An intellect which at a certain moment would know all forces that set nature in motion, and all positions of all items of which nature is composed, if this intellect were also vast enough to submit these data to analysis, it would embrace in a single formula the movements of the greatest bodies of the universe and those of the tiniest atom; for such an intellect nothing would be uncertain and the future just like the past would be present before its eyes.[6]

Laplace's hypothetical "vast intellect" (his "demon") could predict the outcome of any set of circumstances. The knowledge that would be possessed by such an intellect is merely the reflection of the *metaphysical* fact that each and every event is constrained by law; no event escapes the law.

If determinism is right, there are no open futures. Danny's deciding to go see the Radiators down on Decatur Street or his deciding to spend another 20 minutes at Café DuMonde eating beignets while reading his Facebook page is just as determined as whether a piece of litmus paper turns red in the presence of an acid.

IS EITHER OF THESE FREE?

---

6 Laplace 1995, p. 2.

This view of the world certainly seems to leave no room for free will. Determinism implies that there is only one possible future at any moment; natural laws and prior circumstances determine that unique outcome. But if there is only one possible outcome, if the event that happens is necessitated, there is no "being able to do otherwise." And if there is no being able to do otherwise, then—by definition—there is no free will. Determinism precludes free will.

Some determinists also accept an apparent implication, namely, that we are not in charge of our actions, and hence should not be held morally responsible. They are sometimes known as *hard determinists*, a term coined by William James.[7] (It is not always easy, however, to settle whether someone should be classified as a hard determinist.[8])

The thought that determinism and free will are mutually exclusive is presented in a powerful, controversial and much-discussed argument by Peter van Inwagen, known as the *consequence argument*.[9] The conclusion of this argument is the claim that the truth of determinism would rule out free will. The technical framework employed by van Inwagen we must leave aside, but the sense of the argument is reasonably straightforward. The argument assumes the *fixity of the past*—we can't change what's happened; what's done is done. Notice—all the laws of nature and all the events prior to any of our births are part of an unchangeable past. Since we can't change those, and what happens now is *determined* by already set laws and past events, then what we do is similarly fixed. There is no "could have done otherwise." Hence, if determinism is true, there is no free will. Those who accept this argument, both determinists and free will proponents, are known as *incompatibilists*. Incompatibilism holds that determinism and free will can't both be true. The consequence argument is thus an argument for incompatibilism.

In a subsequent section, we see that some have tried to avoid this result; they have tried to argue that determinism and free will are compatible (and hence, that moral responsibility is compatible with determinism).

Que sera, sera!—The song "Que sera, sera," suggests a kind of *fatalist* view: "Whatever will be, will be." Some confuse determinism with fatalism, the view that any event that happens is metaphysically necessary. Determinism says only that if you start with these laws and this set of prior events, a particular

---

7   James 1978.

8   E.g., Marsden 2003, Chap. 26; Blanshard 1961, see n. 4; Paul Edwards 1958.

9   van Inwagen, 1986, Chap. III.

outcome must follow. Fatalism is the much stronger view asserting a metaphysical necessity rather than the physical necessity of determinism. Fatalist views are also sometimes accompanied by the thought that we should simply resign ourselves to the inescapability of what will happen. Recently the philosopher Richard Taylor argued for fatalism, going so far as to suggest that we will lead calmer, more peaceful lives if we accept fatalism as a metaphysical fact. Taylor also appears to reject any real distinction between determinism and fatalism:

> Fatalism is the belief that whatever happens is unavoidable. That is the clearest expression of the doctrine, and it provides the basis of the attitude of calm acceptance that the fatalist is thought, quite correctly, to embody. One who endorses the claim of universal causation, then, and the theory of the causal determination of all human behavior is a kind of fatalist—or at least should be if he is consistent.[10]

In an intriguing presentation of his argument, Taylor asks us to imagine an ordinary man named Osmo, coming across a book in a library entitled *The Life of Osmo*. As Osmo reads *The Life of Osmo*, chapter by chapter, he comes to see that it describes accurately each year of his life. But the book ends three years hence with the death of Osmo in a plane crash! Osmo resolves to avoid the circumstance that brings about the death of "Osmo-in-the-story," yet three years later he nonetheless finds himself boarding the doomed plane. Taylor

---

10   Richard Taylor 1992, p. 55.

argues that, though the rest of us might not be able to read our own biographies in advance, the events of our lives are just as determined as Osmo's.[11]

However, philosophers usually want to distinguish between determinism and fatalism. The latter view is often thought to be that things are "fated" to happen no matter what—that is, regardless of our decisions or any other antecedent events. Determinism, on the other hand, holds that things will happen *given* antecedent decisions or other events. (But these antecedent events are themselves determined.) So a fatalist would say: you'll be killed no matter what you decide. A determinist would say: you'll be killed or not, depending on (among other things) what you decide.

But we must leave fatalist visions of the universe, and focus on determinism, as defined above.

But What If We Believe in Dualism?

Dualism—the idea that minds are different in kind from the physical world—has been thought to be a way to save free will. Free will seems to be in jeopardy because of causal determinism. But this causal determinism seems a characteristic of the *physical* world. Determinism is, after all, tied to *natural law*, the laws that govern physical objects and events. Suppose now, however, that our wills are something *nonphysical*. Following this line of thought, willing or forming intentions would not be subject to the laws of nature. Hence, our wills would not be determined. We can take a moment to spell this out in more detail.

First, a dualism defense of free will holds that choosing or deciding or willing is a nonphysical mental event. In the dualist view, natural or physical law does not apply to mental events. A mind or mental event—such as deciding—doesn't have physical properties, according to the dualist. Natural law, however, applies to physical objects in virtue of their *physical* properties. Gravitational attraction between objects depends on their *masses* and the *distance* between them. Chemical compounds are formed according to certain rules depending on the *charge* of the constituent parts; it's no accident that it takes two hydrogen atoms for every one oxygen atom to yield the molecule water.

But minds don't have physical properties, if we assume dualism. My belief that Jamoca® Almond Fudge ice cream is sold only at Baskin-Robbins doesn't have a charge or a mass, nor is it some distance from my desire to eat something

11   Richard Taylor 1992, Chap. 6.

chocolaty and sweet. Nor does my subsequent intention to go to Baskin-Robbins have a force determined by its mass and acceleration. The mental and the physical are different *kinds* or have different *natures*. So, the mental is the wrong sort of "thing" to be governed by physical law.

Is dualism then the way to save free will? There are problems with this defense of free will. Dualism does not rule out the existence of *mental* laws "necessitating" the forming of certain intentions, given prior beliefs and wants. And the sort of generalizations that we often make about behavior might be an indication that such laws plausibly exist. Note how many of our common-sense observations rely on such generalizations: if Danny wants to see Deirdre, and he believes she will be down in the French Quarter, listening to the Rads tonight, then Danny will decide to go to the French Quarter. Of course, there are a number of complex issues that arise here. Thus, simply appealing to the nonphysical character of the mind won't guarantee that the will is free.

It is sometimes believed that a special creation of humans by a divine being put us outside the causal realm. But an appeal to a divine being as a creator does not really help the dualist here. Creating essentially nonphysical beings does not obviously require giving such beings free will. Any creator the dualist might imagine could have made the mind just as deterministic as the physical world.

What Does Science Say about Free Will?

No Free Will? What about the Criminals?

In the past hundred years, some have suggested that once we recognize that our actions are exclusively caused by biochemical events in the brain, we will need to make compensatory changes in our criminal justice system. Earlier in the last century, B.F. Skinner gave this argument, based on his behaviorism. And now more brain science researchers—those who think free will is an illusion—suggest that we need to see responsibility, even *criminal* responsibility, differently.

In his "The Lucretian Swerve: The Biological Basis of Human Behavior and the Criminal Justice System," Anthony Cashmore, a biologist, claims that as we know more about the chemical basis of our actions, it will become "increasingly untenable to retain a belief in the concept of free will." Cashmore, however, does not think we should unlock the prison gates. We will still need to incarcerate individuals. Our understanding of criminality will need to change, however; we will in fact need to adopt a more utilitarian view of societal punishment—that is, to use it to isolate those likely to offend again, and to discourage future crime.

In her *Mapping the Mind*, an engaging introduction to the brain and its relation to our mental life and our behavior, Rita Carter 2010 intimates a similar point: as we find out more about the brain, our view of culpability, including criminal culpability, will need to change.

Well, that depends on who you ask. Ask Michio Kaku, well-known theoretical physicist, and he'll tell you that modern quantum physics implies that we have free will "in a sense."[12] Or ask Nobel laureate Gerald Edelman, author of numerous books on the brain and consciousness; he claims we have a "degree of free will," but such freedom is not "radical."[13] (He apparently believes that indeterminism produces free will only rarely.) Daniel Wegner, a psychologist at Harvard, thinks free will is but an illusion.[14] On the other hand, Seth Lloyd of MIT suggests that even laptop computers have a kind of free will.[15]

Science proceeds by doing experiments, by testing claims. Is there a way to "test" the existence of free will? In one of the most famous experiments "involving" free will, physiologist Benjamin Libet discovered that subjects reported being conscious of a decision to move a finger only *after* the activation of that part of the brain responsible for sending the movement signal.[16] Many have thought this is genuine scientific evidence *against* free will. The conscious mind—presumably where choosing occurs—seemed not to be in control after all; it seemed to follow what the brain—the physical part—had already done. And if the physical part is in control, that would seem to indicate that it's *determined*, and this counts against free will.

Not everyone accepts the deterministic interpretation of Libet's argument. Alfred Mele argues at length that the brain activity prior to the flexing should not be identified with a "decision."[17] Perhaps surprisingly, Libet does not draw the conclusion that freedom is an illusion: he argues that his experiment showed there was time for the subjects to consciously veto movement of the finger after the signal had already been sent but before the finger moved.

---

12   Kaku 2011.
13   Edelman 1992, p. 170.
14   Wegner 2003.
15   Seth Lloyd 2012.
16   Libet 2004.
17   Mele 2014, especially Chap. 2; also Balaguer 2014, Chap. 7.

And those philosophers who take seriously developments in science are in no greater agreement than the scientists themselves. Robert Kane, a champion of free will, argues that quantum indeterminacy opens the door for free will.[18] On the other hand, Paul Thagard, philosopher and cognitive scientist, claims that recognizing that consciousness or minds are nothing more than brain processes at work leads us to see that free will, at least of the sort promised by dualism, is an illusion.[19]

We have selected out only a few; but we could continue mentioning philosopher and scientist alike, some advocating, some rejecting free will, in light of developments in the sciences.

We might not be able to say definitively "what science says." Still we can sort out matters a bit so that we can see how different thinkers have arrived at their respective claims. Let us begin with determinism and modern physics.

Indeterminism and Free Will

Some have suggested that free will advocates won't find solace in either scientific *in*determinism, the notion that science does not reveal a deterministic world, or the uncertainty and unpredictability of quantum physics. Why not? If determinism is wrong, doesn't that help free will?

Not exactly. We've already seen why determinism seems to preclude free will. But now consider the *randomness* that modern physics seems to bring. According to contemporary science, some events occur randomly: they just happen and there is no rational way to predict their occurrence. Specifying a random sequence or a chance event turns out to be very technical and no easy matter to explain,[20] but suppose this is an example: When you shoot a photon at a barrier with two slits in it, it's (according to some) completely random which slit it will go through. Now shoot photons at the rate of one per minute; given the right arrangement of the slits, it will pass through the right slit half the time. Now put a robot in back of the right slit, with a photon-detector. When it detects a photon, it will push a button. Now, there's a 50% chance the robot will push the button during any one-minute period, but it's completely unpredictable whether it will push the button or not during the next minute.

---

18 Kane 2002b; 1998, Chap. 8.
19 Thagard 2010, Chap. 6.
20 Eagle 2014.

Does that mean that this robot has free will? Obviously not. We wouldn't consider the robot free because of this *unpredictable and random* behavior.

Now imagine that every five minutes or so Sara does something strange. At noon she says "Crustacean!" At 12:05 she walks backwards in a circle. At 12:10 she puts her left index finger into her right ear. At 12:15 she closes her left eye for a full minute. You ask her why she's doing those things, and she replies, "I don't know. I really don't." She goes to a neurologist for very advanced tests, and he discovers (here's where the science fiction comes in) a random signal generator in her brain that fires every five minutes, causing random behavior. Not determined—that means random, right? And this is random, right? But it surely isn't free will.

Genuinely free action isn't random. So believers in free will apparently face a dilemma: a determined action isn't free, but the alternative, a random action, isn't free either. The unpredictable or random character of quantum phenomena on its own simply cannot solve this problem.

Defenders of free will are not without their resources, however. Let us start with the idea of randomness.

The philosopher Robert Kane, and libertarian advocate, has made use of this idea in a quite remarkable way. He suggests that we are at times confronted with differing options, each option supported by good reasons. These differing options correlate with indeterminacy at a subatomic level. Yet there is nothing to determine one option over the other. While the option we choose is "random," it is not arbitrary, since each option is based on good reasons. Our choices in these types of situation form our character. As long as a person "embraces" the character formed by such choices, Kane holds that subsequent choices are free. The original "self-forming actions" are undetermined. But the consequent actions are caused by that "self-formed" character, and consequently free. Kane thus embraces the notion of randomness at two levels (at the quantum brain level and the equally good option level), but claims this leads to free will.[21]

Kane's view perhaps suggests a way to respond to the apparent conflict between the scientific view of the brain, and our feeling of free will. Science recognizes different "levels" of phenomena. We might talk about an atomic level, a biological level, or our "higher" everyday, commonsense level of cabbages, kings, and continents, starfish and stock markets, clothes and clouds—the last having both meteorological and virtual instances. Each of these different levels

---

21   Kane 1998 and 2002b.

has its own properties. A dress may be blue, but protons are not. Electrons are charged, but not a cabbage.

The properties that arise at these "higher levels" are sometimes called *emergent properties*, because they arise from the complex organization of more basic or lower level properties. At the atomic and molecular levels, we find properties that physics and chemistry tell us about. Biochemistry tells us about molecules combining in ever more complex ways, resulting in complex biological properties arising. At the neural level, at the level of brain structure and function, we find still more complex neural properties *emerging from* or coming about because of the way biological structures—neurons—are organized or related. At the most complex level, psychological properties emerge. Because of—some contend—the structure of the brain, its complex organization—consciousness, thought, emotion come about.[22] That is, mental properties emerge.

Building on this, some have suggested that while determinism may be true at the neural or "micro-level," it doesn't follow that determinism is true at the macro-level, the level of conscious thought, of decision and choice. Thus, free will could be an emergent property of a very complicated kind of organism.

Agent Causation: A Different Type of Causation?

Suppose God exists.
Is His Omniscience Incompatible with Our Free Will?

This question has been troublesome for theistic philosophers since St. Augustine. But Nelson Pike's 1965 "Divine Omniscience and Voluntary Action" brought wide and renewed attention to the problem.

God's omniscience implies that he *foreknows* everything. And if he foreknows now that Julia will leave tomorrow to visit the Galapagos to see the blue-footed booby, then Julia *must* leave tomorrow. Otherwise, God would not now have knowledge, and his belief about her departure would be false. But God can't have false beliefs—omniscience precludes that. So, Julia *can't do otherwise* than what God foreknows. So, she isn't free. God knows everything we will choose, and we have no free choice.

Eternalism and *Ockhamism* are two of the main types of response. Eternalism, a view that can be traced back to Boethius and was also

---

22   E.g., Edelman 1992; LeDoux 2002.

championed by Aquinas, holds that God is outside of time. All times at once are present to God; God never looks *back into the past* or looks *forward into the future*. Hence, it would be wrong to say that God *foreknows* (because "past" and "future" do not accurately reflect God's knowledge). Since God does not foreknow, there are no "divine constraints" on human action. Making God *atemporal* presents its own problems, however; how, for example could God intervene in time?

William of Ockham's suggestion, later revised and defended by Marilyn McCord Adams 1967, distinguishes two kinds of fact: *hard* and *soft*. The former do not depend on any reference to some future time. Thus, a hard fact about the past: In 212 BCE a Roman soldier killed Archimedes, the Greek scientist and mathematician of antiquity. A soft fact makes reference to some future, e.g., Archimedes was killed 2288 years before the 300th anniversary in 2076 of the signing of the Declaration of Independence.

The Ockhamist solution claims that God's omniscience extends only to hard facts, not to soft facts. God knows *today* that Julia will leave *tomorrow* for the Galapagos is then a soft fact—and it in no way restricts Julia's ability to do otherwise.

This intriguing issue is still much contested and this brief summary only begins to address the challenges of the topic. See "For Further Reading."

Determinist views, and even some libertarian and compatibilist views, hold that causation is always *event causation*: one event causes another. Only events are causes and only events are caused. Indeed reference to events is integral to the definition of determinism. But another type of causality has been suggested. Roderick Chisholm's 1964 address, "Human Freedom and the Self," continues to be seminal in contemporary discussions of free will. Chisholm argued that we need to see free acts as the result of *agent causation*.

Chisholm remarked on the dilemma for free will that we mentioned above. To accept indeterminism—the idea that our actions had no prior cause *of any sort*—was no help. To do so is to abandon the idea that we are responsible for our actions. Now there had to be a way in which the person, the *agent*, was the cause, but could have done otherwise. And for this he thought we should recognize a different type of causation, that is, agent causation.

Agent causation is a causal power that each of us has, a power distinct from event causation. The self is not just a ripple in a causal stream. The self's choosing is not just another event in the deterministic stream of event causation. As Chisholm noted at one point, agents have a power that some of us might think belongs only to God—we are, each and every one of us, self-moved movers! That is, the power to bring about an intention is unique to agents, and the only source of this power is the agent—not some external cause, or even the *caused* brain events, but the agent. Now Chisholm recognized that *uncaused* acts were not genuinely free. And he held that even human action is caused. But Chisholm claimed that persons—or selves—are the cause of an action, not some sequence of prior events governed by natural or physical law. This self chooses which action to perform, and since the choice is not determined by a prior set of events, the agent *could have done otherwise*. Because the agent is the cause *and* could have done otherwise, the action is free in the requisite sense.

Invoking a different kind of causal power—agent causation—allowed him to avoid "metaphysical indeterminism"—that a free act has no cause whatsoever. It also allowed him to avoid determinism. Tracing back the causes of the agent's actions stops at the agent. When this happens, a person could have done otherwise.[23]

Others have since followed Chisholm in ascribing to agents this different kind of causal ability. Timothy O'Connor explicitly says that fundamental to *agency theory*—agent causation views—is the basic tenet that there are two very different kinds of causal powers. First, event causation is identified as the power one object has to act on another. These powers are of course governed by natural law and exemplified by objects. But there is another kind of causal power, which applies "uniquely to intelligent purposive agents."[24] O'Connor sees these powers as *emergent causal properties*—as manifested in our "reason explanations," that is, appeals to the beliefs and desires of the agent. In his view, the "free choice" of an agent occurs along the following lines. A person has certain desires and beliefs (the "reasons"). The person also "represents"— conceives, or thinks of—various possible courses of action. The agent-causal power then brings about a choice, "an executive intention." Our free will thus lies in our special ability to form certain intentions.[25]

You may well have begun formulating at least one of the questions so often asked by skeptics of this position. This is all very much a mystery, says the critic. We have some idea of what it is for one event to cause another, but what is this mysterious "agent causation"? This has been called the *mystery objection*.[26]

23   Chisholm 1964.
24   O'Connor 1995, p. 177; also O'Connor 2002, especially Chaps. 3 and 4.
25   O'Connor 2001, p. 55.
26   Carroll and Markosian 2010, p. 72.

Defenders of the view have a response: whether you think of event or agent causation, both are mysterious. If libertarians have a hard time explaining agent causation, philosophers (and some scientists) have had an equally hard time explaining the nature of event causation. Indeed Chisholm suggests that we have a *better* understanding of agent causation because we experience it from a first person perspective!

Some related objections:

We apparently have two conflicting, mutually exclusive explanations of our actions. According to the agent causation, Sam—the agent—is the cause of his raising his arm. But a view held by many argues that our actions are brought about by a sequence of neural processes. And this scientific view "trumps" or excludes the agent causation view. Thus, the real causal work is being done by the neural processes, not by any mental process or the agent.[27]

This objection is related to a more general worry that many have. Why should we think that there are two different types of causation in the world? They claim that our best understanding of a cause is an event, located at a particular place and particular time. Thus, agent causation, given such a worry, doesn't offer us any real understanding of the nature of the causes of our actions.

Once again we find a deep fault line in philosophy, one that we leave for now as we turn to still another view.

Science tells us that when Sam raises his arm, this is caused by neural events in his brain. Agent-causation tells us that this is caused by Sam. Are they both right? Can they both be right?

What about an agent is supposed to be the cause of an action? The agent is there long before the action. Why *now*? It looks like something happened to make the agent do it now. But then, why isn't that event the cause? Perhaps this returns us to the central dispute: does the nature of causation require event causation? But we leave the matter here.

Compatibilism

According to many theorists, we have, then, determinism on the one hand—any event had to happen, given prior conditions and the laws of nature—and free will on the other—determinism is false and an agent could have done otherwise in at least some circumstances. In the view of both libertarian and

---

27 See Crumley 2006, Chap. 9 for a survey of the related issues.

determinist, the one position seems to exclude the other. Free will or determinism; take your pick, but you can't have both.

A view known as *compatibilism* picks ... both! Compatibilism is the view that free will and determinism are compatible: determinism is true, yet some of our actions are free. Some see the approach in the work of Aristotle. It is more clearly expressed by David Hume. Another important writer on compatibilism is the theologian and philosopher, Jonathan Edwards (1703–58), who provided a particularly articulate account of the view. While Edwards's principal aims were theological, he also adeptly spells out and defends a philosophical position. Of particular interest to us now is that Edwards defended a view that he thought preserved moral responsibility or accountability. Our choices might be caused, but if there is a sense in which those choices are free, we are morally accountable for our free actions. Both Hume and Edwards agree that liberty—our being able to choose—is necessary for moral responsibility. Hume notes that "... liberty ... is essential for morality...."[28]

According to Edwards, our will is caused, but we possess free will nonetheless, or as he calls it "liberty," because free will is simply "The power, opportunity, or advantage, that any one has, *to do as he pleases. Or in other words, his being free from hindrance or impediment in the way of doing, or conducting in any respect as he wills.*"[29]

Notice that our "being free" consists in the absence of any "hindrance or impediment" in doing as we will, that is, in doing as we want. Still our will is caused, according to Edwards, because it is *determined by* our choice or our motive. The important issue, for compatibilists, is our being able to do as we choose, even if our wants may be determined. It matters that one "*has liberty to act according to his choice, and do what he pleases; and by means of these things, is capable of moral habits and moral acts.*"[30] So, here we have the essence of Edwards's compatibilist view: Our actions are caused, of course, but so long as there are no "hindrances or impediments" to acting as we please, as we want, we are free. Edwards notes that this liberty or agency separates us from "mere machines."

The contemporary compatibilist acknowledges that decisions or intentions to act (and the actions that follow) are indeed caused. For these compatibilists, however, free will isn't the absence of cause; rather it's the absence of

---

28   Hume 1975, Sect. 8, Pt. II.
29   Jonathan Edwards 1835, p. 11; emphasis added.
30   Jonathan Edwards 1835, p. 68; emphasis added.

compulsion. Compulsion happens when our actions aren't the result of our decisions. Our free actions happen when they are—even though our decisions are determined by causes. Compatibilists are sometimes known as *soft determinists*, another term due to William James.[31]

Compatibilists draw our attention to the causal influence of *deliberation* or *rational deliberation* on many of our actions or behaviors. When there is this influence, compatibilists say, we are free, in a sense compatible with determinism, and responsible for our behavior. Understanding the difference between behaviors brought about by deliberation and compelled behaviors is crucial for understanding the compatibilist project.

Our behavior may be compelled by some external physical force, or compelled by some internal "physical force," e.g., some neurological disorder, or because of some psychological disorder. Psychologically compelled or coerced actions may be rare; we perhaps associate them with various disorders, such as obsessive-compulsive disorders, or physical disorders, such as when someone *can't help but* arrange items so they evidence some sort of proportion or symmetry, who *can't help but* knock on a door in a particular fashion. Kleptomania is the compulsion to steal; the kleptomaniac doesn't decide to do it. While these behaviors appear to be in some sense intentional, such behaviors are in fact out of the person's control. Indeed, real patients suffering from a particular disorder will sometimes say that it *felt like* they had to perform some particular behavior. Sara's bizarre behavior imagined above is compelled.

Much more ordinary, however, is external compulsion. Sam sat down because he was pushed into his chair. Sara arrived late because her car got a flat tire. The common element in all compulsion—internal or external—is that it's behavior that is not the result of the agent's decision. In fact, it would have happened even if the agent had decided not to act that way.

Many of our behaviors seem not like that at all—they aren't compelled, and we don't experience them as such. We don't experience those behaviors as coerced. Rather, sometimes we mull things over, as we might say, weighing the pros and cons. After doing so, we come to a conclusion, the outcome of our

---

31 Note that "soft determinism" is not the view that things are mostly determined, or just sort of semi-determined. It's a fully deterministic view. A soft determinist is a determinist who is also a compatibilist. A "hard determinist" is a determinist who is an incompatibilist, and hence denies the existence of free will and moral responsibility. James, by the way, condemned soft determinism, as he found it in Hume, as "a quagmire of evasion under which the real issue of fact has been entirely smothered" (James 1956, p. 149).

deliberation, about large matters or small. We are standing, say, in a Baskin-Robbins, having to choose among 31 flavors, carefully deliberating, and then say, in a loud and clear voice, "Jamoca® Almond Fudge, please." Sometimes it's just a bare decision, without any mulling-over at all, such as when Andy just picks one of his shirts to wear, rather than the other, for no real reason at all. The compatibilist model of "free action" is the model of action brought about by a decision on the part of the agent.

This view of free action is compatible with determinism, according to the compatibilist. There is an identifiable cause—the decision—that brings about the relevant behavior. And as we have noted, the compatibilist may allow that this decision may itself be determined.

Of course critics of compatibilism claim this is too easy. They want to know in what sense a person could have done otherwise. Imagine for a moment that Danny has told Deirdre that he will take her to the airport on Friday. Later he is invited to join as a contestant in a bowling tournament during the time he was to take Deirdre to the airport. He will have to decide; he will have to *choose*. Suppose that he chooses the bowling tournament and texts the news to Deirdre. Is this choosing—on the compatibilist model—a case of free action?

Critics of compatibilism think not. The critics claim that if determinism is true, then Danny isn't choosing at all. Danny's decision is caused by reasons, his desires, his beliefs; and these are one and all determined by relevant natural law and prior events. And the outcome of Danny's deliberations is *necessitated by* all these prior events. The decision to bail on Deirdre and bowl instead was the necessary outcome of Danny's psychological state, his reasons, desires, and beliefs, and these were necessitated by other things. It is simply not true—say critics—that Danny could have done otherwise—if determinism is right. Stretching back far beyond Danny's birth are a chain of events, which lead to but one possibility: Danny's choosing bowling. The German philosopher Arthur Schopenhauer (1788–1860) neatly summarizes the problem: "A man can surely do what he wants to do. But he cannot determine what he wants."

The Schopenhauerian thought captures the problem, according to the critic of compatibilism. If Danny's reasons *necessitate* his visiting bowling alleys instead of visiting the airport, and if other events *necessitate* his having those reasons, there is no room for free will.

Compatibilism responds in the following manner. Again, suppose that an agent, Deirdre, after weighing the various reasons for and against two options (which we will call A and B), does (A)—she goes to a party with Danny—rather than (B), going alone. Deirdre does A because she willed or chose to do A. The compatibilist maintains that *had she chosen to do B, she would have done B*. Deirdre's action is thus free because she did what she willed or chose.

There is a general compatibilist principle here. This is referred to as the *ability analysis of "can."* To say that an agent *could have done otherwise* is to say that the agent would have done otherwise *if the agent had chosen or willed to do otherwise*. Now we can understand why the compatibilist emphasizes an absence of compulsion. If there is no compulsion or coercion or constraint, what an agent does depends only on what is willed or chosen. An action is free because it's voluntary, that is, determined by the agent's will or choice. This makes no mention of whether or not the agent's will or choice is itself determined. According to the compatibilist, it doesn't matter that it is.

Compatibilists who are also determinists (and most of them are) would add that, given the aims and goals of a person, given that person's preferences, the weight attached to particular reasons, this particular decision, and thus this particular act, had to result. As Deirdre thinks about what she wants to accomplish this weekend, and she tries to decide whether to drive to Pensacola for the weekend or attend the Seurat exhibit at the museum, the relative value she attaches to certain activities, given her desires and goals, lead her to choose staying home and attending the exhibit. Character shapes the outcome of deliberation—who Deirdre is, what she values, believes, and desires guides or structures her deliberation. And given that character and those values and beliefs and desires, she had to choose that action. Schopenhauer also held that character determines our deliberation. He quotes the German poet Goethe: "We cannot escape ourselves."

But the compatibilist might also hold that character is sometimes not simply given to us, that perhaps in some way, we can shape our character. Harry G. Frankfurt, points out that we have both *first order desires*—the desire to take a cab to the French Quarter, for instance—and *second order desires*: desires to have (or not have) certain kinds of first order desires. I have a desire, say, for a Godiva truffle. But I may also have the desire to *desire* to eat more vegetables and avoid eating expensive chocolates. The former is a first order desire; the latter is second order, a desire about my desires. Frankfurt claims that we have free will when we act on the desires we want to guide our behavior. And this is the important point, according to Frankfurt: free will is not "escaping" determinism, but rather acting on the desires we want to have. In a sense, then, who we are, what type of character we have, is a function of these second order states.[32] Whether this is sufficient to allay incompatibilist suspicions is a question we will have to leave aside.

We might then think of compatibilism generally like this. The determinism side explains the *what* or the *content* of our deliberation. But the "free will side," the responsibility side, focuses on the fact *that* we deliberate.

Moral Responsibility and Compatibilism

Compatibilists think their position preserves many of our intuitions about moral responsibility. If Andy is texting on his smart phone while driving and just happens to run into the bank robbers' getaway car, thus preventing the robbery, we don't praise Andy for his action. We might be glad the robbery was foiled, but Andy hardly deserves credit. Similarly, if a sudden muscle spasm causes Fred to kick the cat, we do not hold Fred responsible. We may worry about the cat, but Fred is not to blame.

Matters are quite different when a person *decides* to undertake some action. Andy deciding to run his car into the getaway car is an action that we praise, while Fred deciding to kick the cat is an action that merits blame.

Compatibilists think their view explains and supports our understanding of when we should hold a person morally responsible. Moreover, they hold that assigning praise and blame can encourage a person to make the appropriate decision in a future case.

This brief sketch suggests perhaps one reason why so many are drawn to compatibilism.

Key Concepts

- free will
- responsibility argument for free will
- experience argument for free will
- determinism
- incompatibilism
- fatalism
- agent causation
- compatibilism

---

32   Frankfurt 1971.

Reading/Discussion Questions

1. Briefly describe the two main arguments for the existence of free will. Which of these two seems most compelling to you? Explain.

2. In your own words, explain what determinism is. Again in your own words, briefly explain why determinism seems to rule out free will.

3. What is the consequence argument for incompatibilism? Briefly outline the argument. If correct, what view or views does this argument, rule *out*? Briefly explain.

4. Do you think science shows us that free will is an illusion? Explain. If not, do you think science *could* show us that free will is an illusion?

5. Explain how the compatibilist view of "free action" yields a notion of free will that is compatible with determinism. Who do you think is right, incompatibilists or compatibilists? Why?

For Further Reading

Timothy O'Connor 2014 provides an extensive bibliography of both historical and contemporary works on free will and related issues.

Martin Luther's *The Bondage of the Will* is his extensive analysis and critique of Erasmus's view of free will and is accessible to the casual reader; Luther 1957.

The best contemporary introduction to free will is Robert Kane 2006. As noted in the text, his 1998 is a defense of free will, which depends in part on "indeterminacies" found in neural processes. There are of course many book length defenses of free will, including Timothy O'Connor 2002. Laura Ekstrom 2000 is a defense of libertarianism, which does not rely on agent causation. John Martin Fischer is a principal advocate of compatibilism; his 1995 is widely considered one of the most important defenses of that view. Daniel Dennett 1984 is a very accessible—and, like much of Dennett's work, entertaining—defense of compatibilism.

Daniel Wegner 2003 principally draws on research from psychology and cognitive science; Derk Pereboom also argues that our notion of free will is an illusion; his 2014 expands on his earlier work and further argues that our lives can be significant and meaningful, despite the absence of free will.

John Martin Fischer 1989 contains Nelson Pike's 1965 essay and Marilyn McCord Adams 1967, along with Plantinga 1986 and Hoffman and Rosenkrantz 1984, with several other important essays on omniscience and free will. Fischer's "Introduction" is an excellent, longer introduction to the issue. Hasker's 1989 is a book-length treatment of many of these issues; he argues for a unique view of God's knowledge of the future.

CHAPTER ELEVEN

GOD: NATURE AND EXISTENCE

Perhaps it's puzzling to find a chapter on whether or not God exists, and, if so, what God is, in a brief tour of metaphysics. God is not your ordinary "thing," of course. One of the tasks of metaphysics, though, is to tell us what *kinds* of things exist—so the question of the existence of God is a part of what metaphysics considers. And the traditional monotheistic notion of God has played a special role in the history of metaphysics. It is not only theists that had occasion to discuss the nature and existence of God; various philosophers, both theistic and atheistic, have thought that some concept of God has structured our thinking about the nature and make-up of the world. We begin by explaining a few of the attributes usually ascribed to God. Then, we will look at versions of the three main arguments for God's existence: the Design Argument, the Cosmological Argument, and the Ontological Argument. Finally, we look at an argument that claims to show that the existence of God, as he is normally characterized, is logically incompatible with the existence of evil in the world.

Divine Attributes

God is perfect. That is the heart of the traditional monotheistic notion of God, especially of a *personal* God, that is, a divine being that has, to some extent, the same kind of characteristics, in the same way, as ordinary persons do (as opposed to being wholly indescribable, or wholly abstract). We will be exploring five divine attributes in more depth. They are *omnipresence*, *omniscience*, *omnipotence*, *eternality*, and *immutability*.

Omnipresence

Omnipresence is being present everywhere, but this requires clarification. Most philosophers and theologians have not been panentheists. *Panentheism* is the view that God is *in* or *interpenetrates* all that there is, including finite creatures or objects—or, more properly, the view that all is in God. Two influential American panentheists were the essayist Ralph Waldo Emerson (1803–82), and the twentieth-century philosopher of religion Charles Hartshorne.[1]

In *The Divine Attributes*, Joshua Hoffman and Gary Rosenkrantz note that omnipresence can mean literally being at every location. But of course, God is generally understood as a spiritual, not a material or a spatial being. God's omnipresence is not like being located everywhere in the same way that a puppy is located in the living room. So, Hoffman and Rosenkrantz conclude that this ordinary sense of omnipresence is not the sense in which it is a divine attribute.[2] In this they agree with a number of other philosophers and theologians. St. Thomas Aquinas influentially explained omnipresence analogically; that is, he thought of divine omnipresence as describing the extent of God's knowledge and power. God is everywhere in the sense that nothing is *outside* of God's control or his knowledge. An "earth-bound" analogy might serve: laws of nature govern and "control" everything in the physical world; nothing escapes natural law. In that sense, natural law is everywhere present. God is omnipresent then, but in a similar metaphorical, nonphysical sense.[3] Similarly God's knowledge also is *as though* he were present at all places—which leads us to our next attribute.[4]

---

1   See Hartshorne 1967 and 1976; Dombrowski 2013.
2   Hoffman and Rosenkrantz 2002.
3   Swinburne 1977; Hoffman and Rosenkrantz 2002.
4   See Swinburne 1977, p. 104.

Omniscience

God is **omniscient**: God knows everything there is to know. That God's knowledge extends to all truths may seem a truism, but it is more difficult to understand what this actually means, since "knowing all" is no doubt different in kind from ordinary human knowing. Aquinas again interpreted this analogically. Much of human knowledge is based on reasons. Yet God's knowledge is not mediated; rather it is direct and immediate. God doesn't make inferences, draw conclusions based on premises or reasons; much less did he acquire any knowledge by being told by some other being. Nor does God's knowledge depend on some sensory process, as much of human knowledge does. (Though, interestingly, Isaac Newton described space as God's "sensorium"—the sum of perception.) Thus, God's knowledge never requires an intermediary, whether that of some sensory state or some testimony or some inference. All things—all truths—are immediately present to God.

Much, perhaps all, of our knowing depends on or is *through* concepts. God's knowledge, however, is often described as *intuitive* knowledge. His knowledge is not dependent on concepts the way human knowledge is. Thus, the *content* of God's knowledge is perhaps difficult to describe. Yet, as omniscient, as all-knowing, the content of God's knowledge takes in all that there is to know.

Omnipotence

God's unlimited power is of course one of the central divine attributes; God's **omnipotence** is that he can do anything or is all powerful. Yet many theologians and philosophers have recognized a "limitation" on God's power. They suggest that God can't do the logically impossible; to the statement "God can do anything," they add the caveat "so long as that act is logically possible." But why? Wouldn't a genuinely all-powerful being be able to do *anything at all*? Most believers accept that God can defy the laws of nature—that's presumably what miracles are about. So, why not the laws of logic?

When we say "Sam can play the piano," we know what action we are saying he is able to do. Similarly, "God can make a mountain out of pure gold" ascribes a substantive ability that we understand, even though it takes a bit of imagination. Now imagine that someone insists that God can make a triangle with four sides, or an uncle who has no siblings, or a blue thing that's not colored, or a tree that's not a tree. Are we sure that there are things here for God to do?

The logically impossible is the self-contradictory. So if someone asks for a square circle, we want to say *"There's no such thing,"* since a triangle with four sides contradicts its own nature. A triangle, to be a triangle, can't have four sides. Asking me to draw a triangle with four sides is asking me to draw ... nothing. There is nothing that could correspond to this description. Unlike the phrase "gold mountain," which we all understand the meaning of, the phrase "triangle with four sides" names *nothing*. It is thus no limitation on divine power to say that God can't do the logically impossible.

Can God make a rock heavier than he can lift? Of course we should not imagine God as a super Hercules, wrapping his divine arms around a big rock, picking it up and hurling it into Hudson Bay. Still the question seems to involve a bit of a dilemma.

Suppose God makes a big rock, but can't lift it. Then there is something that God can't do—lift the rock. On the other hand, suppose every rock that God can make is a rock he can lift. Again, we stumble across something God apparently can't do—make a rock too heavy for even him to lift. God's power thus seems limited.

Perhaps this is another example of asking whether God can bring about the logically impossible. But some suggest that this example shows that the concept of omnipotence makes no sense; the concept of omnipotence is itself self-contradictory. Hoffman and Rosenkrantz suggest seeing the notion of omnipotence as a comparative notion: God is maximally powerful. No being is nor could be more powerful than God.[5]

Could God do something evil? Could God will a particular bad or evil circumstance to occur? The question immediately draws our attention to another of God's attributes—God's goodness, or *omnibenevolence*—and the issue of how an all-powerful and all-good God could permit the evil that we seem to see in the world. We explore a special version of this question in the last section of the chapter.

Aquinas suggests that God cannot do anything that violates his own nature. Perhaps you are familiar with the part of the lyrics from "I've Gotta Be Me":

> I've gotta be me, I've gotta be me
> What else can I be but what I am

---

5   Hoffman and Rosenkrantz 2002, p. 167; similarly, see Clack and Clack 1988, pp. 66–69; for another view, see Swinburne 1977, pp. 153–58.

While this popular musical number hints at various philosophical questions about identity, it also points to something important about the divine nature. God's "character" is no accident. It's not that God just happens to be an "omni-nifty" guy. Quite the contrary. God's attributes are *necessary*; these attributes are part of what it is *to be* God. To put this another way, these attributes are essential to God's nature. Thus, God essentially wills the good.

Aquinas suggests, then, that is it no limitation on divine power to say that God is limited by his own essence.[6] To be able to will or perform some evil act is to be able to engage in an act that signals some sort of defect. God's inability to do evil is simply a result of possessing no defects. Hence, not "being able to do" evil is no limitation on God's omnipotence.

Brahman and Ātman

For many Westerners, Brahmanism is perhaps the more familiar philosophy of India. This view comes down to us through the Vedas, the Upanisads, and the oft-mentioned *Bhagavad Gītā*. These are the sacred hymns, texts, and scriptures of Hinduism.

While Hinduism is often associated with polytheism—especially Brahman, Vishnu, and Shiva—there is a form of Hinduism that might be seen as monotheistic.

In this view, the one ultimate reality is Brahman. All of creation is ultimately traceable back to Brahman, who is the ultimate creative force. (In some views, Brahman is properly thought of as an ultimate entity, not a person.) Indeed, early Vedic hymns characterize Brahman as *food*, a unique combination of matter and energy. In the monotheistic view, all Hindu gods are ultimately traceable to Brahman.

A particularly important manifestation of Brahman is Ātman, the ultimate consciousness, the (true) Self, or "controller." Each of us experiences our own particular egos, but we make a mistake if we think that this individual empirical ego is ultimately real. In fact, individual egos are but particular manifestations of Ātman. It is Ātman that is real. The *Upanisads* are particularly concerned with the nature of Ātman.

And *moksa*, or liberation from the cycle of suffering, occurs when we attain the knowledge that not only are our egos manifestations of Ātman, but that Ātman and Brahman are in fact one—a unity which is suggested by the metaphor of two birds in one tree in the *Upanisads*. This knowledge can be

---

6   See Swinburne 1977, pp. 158–59.

attained in different ways, including by rigorous yoga practices, but also by study and reflection on the Hindu scriptures.

Eternal

Unlike all humans, God isn't here for a time and then—alas—gone. **Eternality** is one of the essential divine attributes; God wouldn't be God without it. There are, however, two very different interpretations of this attribute. The fundamental difference is whether God is *in* time or *outside of* time. If God is a temporal being, then he extends infinitely back in time and infinitely forward. God has a past, present, and future, and is thus described as *everlasting*. With the latter interpretation, God is atemporal or *timeless*. God is outside of time, and all moments in time are present to him at once.

By way of comparison, think of the number line, extending infinitely back and forward from zero. Let this line represent, not numbers, but moments in time. As a temporal being, God exists through all the moments of the "time line." The atemporal comparison is a bit trickier. God is not "in" the time line, but outside of it. Yet the entire line—every moment in time—is before him. Of course, it is easy to lapse into a description of a timeless God that makes use of temporal terms, e.g., saying that the entire time line is *always* present to him.

There is a significant drawback to the atemporal view. God acts; God creates; God speaks to some individuals; God intervenes through miracles. All these acts are *events*, God doing something. And events seem to be essentially temporal. Put a little differently, if God is to act *in time*, to intervene in temporal affairs, then it would appear that God, too, must be temporal or in time. Aquinas responds to this worry by noting that if God's decisions were made from eternity, there is no need to see God acting in time. The worry about acting *in time* arises because we think of God as "stepping" in at various points in time. But this is not the nature of God's decisions, in Aquinas' view. Still, critics of the timeless view might wonder how a "timeless intention" could nonetheless be manifested in time.

Immutable and Impassable

Does God change? Aquinas argued that since a perfect being is already perfect, there's no room for change.[7] For a supremely perfect being, supreme in

---

7   Aquinas 2008, Pt. I, Q. 9, Art. 1.

power, knowledge, and goodness, remaining perfect requires staying as it is: no changes. Hence, God is often held to be *impassable*; he is held not to be susceptible to "mental changes." But is that right?

Three related concepts are important here. Immutabilty is the idea that there is no changing in any way whatsoever. Often attributed to the influence of Greek philosophy and Plato especially, this view is held by Augustine, Boethius (840–?), and Aquinas, who link immutability to timelessness; change occurs in time, so a God who is outside of time must be unchanging. A weaker notion than this is available, incorruptibility: a being is incorruptible if there can be no changes to that being's character. Finally, there is the notion of impassability, or the idea that a being cannot be a subject of emotions or feelings.

Various reasons suggest that God in fact changes—is not immutable or impassable—yet remains incorruptible. God may change attitude or opinion, or even be the subject at one time of one feeling or emotion and still another emotion at some other time. However, God remains incorruptible since his character—his essential goodness—does not change.

Various theologians and philosophers point to textual evidence in the Old and New Testaments, which seems to indicate God is subject to various feelings: anger, compassion, and sorrow among them. Similarly various passages suggest a God open to persuasion or a change in intent. The most famous perhaps is Abraham "negotiating" with God over the fate of Sodom and Gomorrah, securing successive promises to spare the cities if a handful of good people are found. Similarly, various passages note that God *relents* because of suffering or that he is *concerned* about their distress. And books have been written about Job's "argument" with God over Job's misfortunes, followed by God's apparently defiant, "Who is this that darkeneth counsel by words without knowledge? Gird up now thy loins like a man; for I will demand of thee, and thou answerest me" (Job 38: 3–4).

Some think such passages are not simply metaphors or literary devices. While God remains incorruptible, some claim God can *increase* in value; he does so through the activities of and his interaction with his creatures.[8] Others suggest that God's identifying with our suffering is a necessary component of understanding God's goodness in light of the terrible evil that befalls so many.[9] To some, an impassable being appears "lifeless" or "inhuman" or—worse—"impersonal."

---

8 Hartshorne 1984, pp. 6–10; Viney 1985, pp. 36 ff.
9 Marilyn McCord Adams 1999.

An immutable view of the divine nature is coherent, however. But we leave the matter here. We will look at one additional attribute, *omnibenevolence*, later. But first we turn to three arguments for the existence of God.

Three Arguments

Arguments for the existence of God touch on a number of philosophical and theological issues, such as whether belief in a divine being is rational and what is the extent of what we can know about God. This brief survey leaves aside not only those issues, but also a number of other arguments for God's existence. These three, however, play a significant role in thinking about whether God exists.

The Design Argument

We begin with a version of the Argument from Design (also known as the Teleological Argument), which holds that there is sufficient evidence of purpose or design in even brute and unfeeling nature to lead us to the conclusion that a designer—God—exists. *Telos* is a Greek word meaning "purpose" or "goal." Teleology is linked to design: if something is designed, then it is directed toward an end, some aim that it is designed to serve. Often enough, complexity or coordinated functioning of many components signal design or purpose—a given set of things working together because they were made to achieve some end. Some have found such "signals" of design in nature. As early as the seventeenth century, defenders of the existence of God found this sort of evidence in the complexity of parts of organisms.

At the heart of the Teleological Argument lies the thought that if we observe *design* or *purpose* in nature, then we require a very special explanation of that design. The empirical or *a posteriori* nature of the argument is then evident, since it is observation that leads us to recognize design or purpose in nature. The observation of this apparent purpose serves as the basis for inferring God's existence.

The structure of the argument is fairly simple: observations of nature provide good evidence of design. Some things occur or are found together—say, a pile of rocks and branches at the bottom of a steep slope—because of happenstance or an accidental convergence of factors; parts of the slope gave way after a heavy rainfall. But, in other cases—say, for example, the existence of DNA—there is reason to suspect more than just coincidence. We find parts working together to achieve an apparent goal. Such coordination seems to imply design, which of course implies the existence of a *designer*.

Perhaps the most famous version of this argument is by William Paley (1743–1805). At the beginning of his 1802 book, he encapsulates the spirit of his argument:

> In crossing a heath, suppose I pitched my foot against a stone, and were asked how the stone came to be there, I might possibly answer, that, for anything I knew to the contrary, it had lain there forever: nor would it perhaps be very easy to show the absurdity of this answer. But suppose I had found a *watch* upon the ground, and it should be inquired how the watch happened to be in that place; I should hardly think of the answer I had before given, that for anything I knew, the watch might have always been there. Yet why should not this answer serve for the watch as well as for the stone; why is it not as admissible in the second case as in the first? For this reason and for no other ... when we come to inspect the watch, we perceive—what we could not discover in the stone—that its several parts are framed and put together for a *purpose*.... There must have existed, at some time, and at some place or other, an artificer or artificers, who formed [it] for the purpose which we find it actually to answer; who comprehended its construction, and designed its use.... Every indication of contrivance, every manifestation of design, which existed in the watch, exists in the works of nature; with the difference, on the side of nature, of being greater or more, and that in a degree which exceeds all computation.[10]

Paley continues throughout the book to trace the evidences of design in the natural order. And the evidence of design or purpose in nature is the coordinated functioning we find, just as the coordinated functioning of the parts of the watch evidence design or purpose. In the case of the watch, we reasonably infer a designer ... and *maker*. Similarly, we are reasonably entitled to infer the existence of a designer and *maker* of nature—and by extension, the whole of the universe.

We are then, Paley holds, entitled to infer the existence of a "universe maker," that is, a creator. Of course, such an argument will say nothing about whether such a being possesses all perfections, whether such a being is omnibenevolent or perfectly just, or omniscient or omnipotent. In other words, the argument cannot prove the existence of a supreme being and creator. But as

---

10   Paley 2006, p. 7; second emphasis added.

the last line of the passage above indicates, given that the degree of complexity of design in nature, the creator of that complexity has to be pretty smart and powerful! Thus, the conclusion of the Design Argument is that nature gives us good reason to believe that there is a sufficiently powerful intelligence that made or created the universe. If this proof were compelling, such a conclusion would indeed be remarkable.

One of the more serious objections, heard especially recently, is perhaps the most obvious: Does the existence in nature of complicated coordinated systems warrant the inference to a powerful intelligence? Put another way, is Paley's the only explanation? Couldn't there be some purely non-intelligent explanation of this apparent design? Couldn't all this be explained by a "watchmaker" without purpose ... by a *blind watchmaker*?

> Paley's argument is made with passionate sincerity and is informed by the best biological scholarship of [Paley's] day, but it is wrong, gloriously and utterly wrong. The analogy ... between watch and living organism is false. All appearances to the contrary, the only watchmaker in nature is the blind force of physics, albeit deployed in a very special way.... Natural selection, the blind unconscious, automatic process which Darwin discovered, and which we now know is the explanation for the existence and apparently purposeful form of all life, has not purpose in mind.... It does not plan for the future. It has no vision, no foresight, no sight at all.... If it can be said to play the role of watchmaker in nature, it is the *blind* watchmaker.[11]

The evolutionary biologist Richard Dawkins thus challenges the idea that design requires *intention*. In Dawkins's view, appeal to natural selection provides all the conceptual resources necessary to explain the "apparently purposeful form of all life." It should be noted that Dawkins agrees with Paley about one important matter. Dawkins suggests that prior to 1859 it would have been unreasonable to be an atheist. He thinks that the complexity of life—the complexity of the world—requires *some* explanation, and that Paley drew on the best science available at the time. That story, however, was seriously incomplete, and the fuller story dispels the basis for Paley's inference.

The eighteenth-century philosopher David Hume made several objections to the Teleological Argument. He questioned whether the universe showed features that necessitated a designer: whether it really is orderly and harmonious,

---

11   Dawkins 1986, p. 5.

and whether it is really complex—compared to what? He pointed out that we know by experience that artifacts—watches and buildings and so on—have designers; but we have no such experience of the designing of the universe—obviously a unique, completely different sort of thing. He mentioned that even if there were evidence the universe was intentionally designed, it wouldn't be evidence that there is a single designer, with the attributes conventionally assigned to God.[12]

Criticisms of the Design Argument need not deny the *function* of certain organs or chemicals or proteins. Ribonucleic acid, RNA, for example, serves several roles or functions in living organisms. And thus there is a sense in which, according to some, *purpose* can still be identified in nature. Ernst Mayr, one of the preeminent evolutionary biologists of the twentieth century, explains:

> Where, then, is it legitimate to speak of purpose and purposiveness in nature, and where is it not? To this question we can now give a firm and unambiguous answer. An individual who—to use the language of the computer—has been "programmed" can act purposefully.... [T]hey [organisms] all act purposefully because they have been programmed to do so.[13]

An "internal principle"—the genetic program—sets or fixes the purpose of a wide range of behaviors of individuals in the animal kingdom. Mayr calls this sort of view *teleonomy*. Purpose in nature is the result of law; thus we have "law-governed" purpose. Critics thus claim that teleonomy preempts the need to invoke the Design Argument or a powerful *supra-natural* intelligence as the designer of the natural world. But Mayr claims that science offers an alternative account of what might otherwise appear to be design. This obviates the need for a non-natural explanation of the complexity that so struck Paley, presenting a real obstacle to the Design Argument.

The Fine-Tuning Argument

The Design argument has resurfaced in various ways in the late twentieth century, some of which may be familiar to you. But one version in particular is worth mentioning. This version is called the "fine-tuning" argument. The argument notes that if certain physical constants (such as the ratio of the

---

12   Hume 1980.
13   Mayr 1988, p. 31.

strength of electromagnetism to the strength of gravity) were even slightly different, life would not exist. This, it is argued, cannot be simply the result of happenstance. Hence, there must be a designer. Many also think "fine-tuning" warrants believing in multiple universes; if there were many universes, many inhospitable and a few hospitable to life, we would of course find ourselves in one of the hospitable ones. To some, this notion of multiple universes shows that the fine-tuning we observe does not require a designer; for others, however, the idea plays a role in some of the arguments *for* a designer. In his 2011 *Where the Conflict Really Lies: Science, Religion, & Naturalism*, Alvin Plantinga devotes a chapter to analyzing the argument. He considers several objections to fine-tuning, including those that claim the fine-tuning argument involves a misinterpretation of the probabilities involved. In the end, he thinks that fine-tuning may offer some support for theism, but it is not compelling. A physicist's perspective and book-length treatment is Victor Stenger's 2011 *The Fallacy of Fine-Tuning: Why the Universe Is Not Designed for Us*. Stenger thinks that current physics and cosmology can explain those instances of apparent fine-tuning, without appealing to design.

The Cosmological Argument

Our second argument takes its cue not from a certain subset of natural things, but from all things, and that they all seem to have this feature in common: they come and go.

A NECESSARY BEING?

Qualia ... and God

Robert M. Adams's contributions to metaphysics, philosophy of religion, and philosophical theology are extensive. He is one of the leading proponents of divine command theory and among his many essays, "Primitive Thisness and Primitive Identity" (1979) is still frequently cited in the metaphysics of particulars.

Perhaps you recall the notion of qualia from Chapter 8. Qualia are the *what it is like*, the *how it feels* of various kinds of experience. How something tastes, for example, is a qualitative experience; it's the having of a particular quale.

In an intriguing essay, "Flavors, Colors, and God" (1987a), Adams suggests a surprising response to the difficulty of explaining why some particular neural event should be correlated with some one color rather than another, or some one taste rather than another. The most reasonable explanation for this connection, Adams suggests, is the existence of God: God correlated particular types of neural activity with particular types of qualia.

It is no surprise that many would resist this conclusion. But it perhaps points to the need for a general explanation addressing the relationship between qualia and the brain.

In the science fiction comedy *Back to the Future*, the main character Marty confronts the possibility that he *might not have existed*. The protagonist accidentally travels back in time to 1955, and finds himself caught up in the high school life of his parents. His presence threatens to keep his parents from falling in love, a possibility that threatens his existence. That he exists at all depends on his parents meeting and falling in love. There was nothing necessary about his existence; in fact, during various points in the movie, the character's existence depends on very slender threads—had circumstances been only slightly different here or there, his "future parents" might not have been his parents at all.

Beings that might not have existed—these are *contingent* beings. Beings that must exist, no ifs, ands, or buts about it: *necessary* beings. Of course, like the time-traveling Marty, you and I, the Grand Canyon, the Milky Way, are contingent beings. Is there a necessary being?

The notion of necessity is important in understanding the divine nature and in proofs for the existence of God. In addition to other divine attributes, theists hold that God differs from other beings or objects in this respect: God's existence is *necessary*. Indeed it's part of God's nature to *necessarily exist*. A contingent thing depends for its existence on other things and events; without them, it wouldn't have existed. They thus tend to come and go. A necessary being *must* exist.

The reason for this particular divine attribute, in the theist view, is not far to seek. God's nature is such that he possesses all perfections to an infinite degree. And, in addition to, say, omniscience or omnibenevolence, necessary existence is another perfection. Indeed, how could God only *contingently* exist? Could the divine nature be like that?

The Cosmological Argument trades on the notions of contingent and necessary beings; according to this argument, an adequate explanation of the existence of contingent beings requires the existence of a *necessary being*—God.

Versions of the argument are traced to Plato, to Aristotle, and to medieval philosophers, such as the Persian philosopher Avicenna (980–1037), and the Jewish philosopher Maimonides (1135–1204). Later, Descartes and Leibniz, as well as Samuel Clarke (1675–1729), the English theologian and philosopher, all offered versions of the Cosmological Argument. Here we begin with a version offered by Thomas Aquinas as part of what he called the *Five Ways*.

THE FIVE WAYS

In the thirteenth century St. Thomas Aquinas offered the *Five Ways*, five proofs for the existence of God. There is some disagreement about Aquinas' attitude toward the proofs, and the intended structure of and relationship between the proofs. Some hold, for example, that he was recounting then well-known arguments for the existence of God, ones every theologian should know. Some hold that the first Three Ways are but different presentations of one argument; others consider that the first two make up a single argument, but hold that the Third Way is a distinct argument.[14] All of the proofs, however, are *a posteriori*: they reason from *observed* effects to the nature of the ultimate cause of those effects.

Whatever the final verdict on Aquinas' intent in presenting the proofs, there is wide agreement that the first three are instances (or, an instance) of the Cosmological Argument. Here is one translation of the Third Way:

> Our experience certainly includes things capable of existing but apparently unnecessary [contingent], since they come and go, coming to birth or dying. But if it is unnecessary for a thing to exist, it did not exist once upon a time, and yet everything cannot be like this, for if everything is unnecessary, there was once nothing. But if such were the case, there would now be nothing, because a nonexistent can only be brought into existence by something already existing. So that if ever there was nothing, not a thing could be brought into existence, and there would be nothing now, which contradicts the facts. And so not everything can be an unnecessary kind of being: there must exist some being that necessarily exists. But a thing that necessarily exists may or may not have this necessity from something else. But just as we must begin somewhere in a succession of causes, the case is the same with any succession of things that necessarily exist and receive this necessity from others. Hence we are compelled to suppose something that exists necessarily,

---

14 Davies 1982, p. 39.

having this necessity only from itself; in fact, it itself is the cause why other things exist.[15]

According to Aquinas, it is readily apparent that there are contingent beings. We observe them, and as is the nature of contingent beings, they come and go. They come into existence and then drop out of existence. It's obvious such beings aren't *necessary*, otherwise they would always be there. There must be, then, a necessary being, which brings the contingent beings into existence, otherwise there would have been nothing at some point.

Aquinas infers a necessary being as the ultimate *causal* source of contingent beings. It is through the necessary being's causal power that the contingent universe comes to be. And because this being is necessary, we do not need to look to something outside of it to understand why it exists. A necessary being is its own explanation. The point of the Third Way is to prove that such a necessary being exists.

The crux of Aquinas' argument is a striking assumption: If only contingent beings exist, there would have been a time when nothing existed. Had such a time existed—a time when nothing existed—there would be nothing now. And this is based on the principle, which comes to us from the ancient Greek philosophers, that from nothing, nothing comes; in Latin, *ex nihilo, nihil fit*.

The truth of this assumption, however, is a little less than obvious. Of course, any particular contingent thing will not exist at some time. But how does that fact give us a reason to think that there was time at which no contingent things existed? There might have been an infinite series stretching backwards of contingent beings. Once we recognize this problem, the Third Way seems uncompelling.

Brian Davies, Thomist scholar and philosopher of religion, suggests that Aquinas no doubt was aware of these sorts of obvious failings in the Five Ways; others are not as sure.[16] Perhaps there is a different way to think about the structure of the argument.

ANOTHER VERSION

In 1948, some centuries after Aquinas recorded the Five Ways, a radio debate took place, broadcast by the BBC.[17] No, this wasn't about politics, or public policy, or cultural norms. It was a debate … between two philosophers! Great

---

15   Aquinas 1972, Pt. I, Q. 2, Art. 3, pp. 123–24.
16   Davies 1982 and 1992; Wippel 2006.
17   Transcript in Hick 1964, pp. 167–91.

philosophers to be sure—the great British philosopher Bertrand Russell and the philosopher Frederick Copleston, S.J., the author of a venerable multi-volume history of philosophy. At one point in that debate the issue arose of whether the existence of the universe required an explanation. Russell and Copleston took opposite sides, as they had during much of the debate. Russell held that the existence of the universe is just a brute fact—inexplicable. Once one has observed that the universe exists, there is nothing more to be said. Indeed, nothing more can be said. Copleston, on the other hand, held that the existence of something, even the universe, requires explanation. And Copleston invoked a "revised version" of the Third Way argument, suggesting that some necessarily existent "thing" must be invoked to explain how we have all these contingent beings. So consider the following.

First, contingent beings need not have existed. A contingent being comes about *because of* something else. Generally "local explanations" are enough for us. Where did this egg come from? That chicken. So we point to something else to explain the existence of any contingent being. If this "something else" is itself only contingently existing, the same question can arise. Where did that chicken come from? This is also the story of your ancestors: where did grandma come from? Great grandma. And where did she ... well, you get the idea.

Instead of this "horizontal series"—the linear causal ancestry of any contin-gent being, e.g., grandparents, great grandparents, great-great grandparents ... —consider the "whole" of contingent being. How does a contingently existent being come into existence? Unlike the series including your great-great-great grandma, we are asking how there came to be any contingent beings *at all*.

The Cosmological Argument says: contingent beings came from a nec-essarily existent being. Any other answer—any appeal to more contingent beings—inevitably leaves us with the same question. The only answer—the only *satisfying* explanation—is this necessary being, which is always existing and can't not exist. Here we have the ultimate cause of all contingently exist-ing beings.

Keith Yandell raises the same point about a similar version of the Cosmological Argument, an argument he formulates in considerable detail. Once the question is raised about why there are any contingently existing creatures, citing more contingently existing beings will not suffice, since that is indeed the point of the question. The options, Yandell notes, are three: refuse to answer; claim that this is an inexplicable fact about the nature of the universe; or appeal to something other than a contingently existing being.[18]

---

18   Yandell 1999, p. 196.

Of course the theist is not willing to follow those who, like Russell, want to say that the contingent existence of everything is just a brute fact.

Russell's argument here is that in an endless series of contingent causes and their effects, there is an answer, at every point, in principle, to the question, "Why did X happen?" The answer is, "It was caused by Y." But if we shift the question to "Why did this whole series happen?" Russell claims that this is not a legitimate question. By analogy, he says, the fact that every person has a mother does not imply that there exists one mother for the whole of humanity.

We might spend a moment more on the "endless explanation" option. The theist thinks that tracing the history of contingently existing beings is no explanation at all.[19] Imagine Julia tells Jack that she will explain to him how to solve quadratic equations (e.g., $x^2 + 2x + 1 = 0$). One minor hitch: the explanation *goes on endlessly*. It's easy to see that Jack might think he isn't getting an explanation at all. Similarly, why should anyone be satisfied with being given one contingent being after another, only to be finally told, this goes on forever; that's just the way it is?

So the critic, according to the theist, is left with the option of joining Russell, asserting that the existence of the universe is merely a brute, inexplicable fact. The theist then observes that "Why does this series of contingent beings exist at all?" seems like a legitimate question that deserves a real answer. If it is, it seems reasonable to conclude that a necessary being exists.

BUT IS IT REASONABLE?

Brian Davies addresses precisely this issue: Is this form of the Cosmological Argument reasonable?[20] It might make sense to disagree with Russell about whether or not there is a point to asking how the universe came to be. Davies, however, notes that the Cosmological Argument might be wildly implausible or even irrational, *even if* it makes sense to ask the question of origin.

Davies first examines whether our notion of cause is applicable in this case. Though his argument is considerably more detailed, Davies claims that our natural inclination is to think that it is reasonable to ask about the cause of all contingent being—and he finds that this is indeed the case.

It becomes harder to defend the reasonability of the Cosmological Argument when we ask a further question. Is it reasonable to accept that the cause of contingent existence is itself something *not caused*? Or, in other

---

19   Pike 1977.
20   Davies 1982, pp. 42–47.

words, is it reasonable to accept that the cause of contingent existence is itself a necessary existent, requiring no explanation of what caused it?

The challenge to the defender of the Cosmological Argument can be put in this way. We insist on being told the *cause* of various things. We don't accept an infinite series because we think each new item in the series requires an explanation of its cause. But then we invoke this "new" kind of being, and say it causes *other* things ... but this one doesn't need a cause! Now, how can defenders of the Cosmological Argument do this? How do they keep insisting on being told the cause, and then suddenly assert "Aha! here's 'something' that is itself uncaused!"?

Davies suggests that this uncaused cause not be thought of as a *being* like other beings.[21] The necessary cause is of a different order than contingent beings. The necessary cause isn't a thing. It is instead a source or ground. This idea perhaps fits with the suggestion earlier, an interpretation sometimes given to the first three of the Five Ways. The interconnected causal chains of contingent beings in the universe can be thought of as a linear or "horizontal" series—and the search for an uncaused cause as traversing the series back in a linear fashion until you reach the first item in the series. Instead, Aquinas, and other proponents of the argument, wants us to look at a "vertical" order. That is, we are to look at what is the source of the series *taken as a whole*, and what supports it. That which supports the series as a whole is not part of the series—not a being—and hence, it is reasonable to think of it as a cause which is not itself caused.

One further proviso. Davies takes the Cosmological Argument as reasonable. But, even if we agree, one of Hume's objections to the Teleological Argument seems germane here also: it does not follow that the Cosmological Argument demonstrates the existence of a God, who has the attributes normally of interest in monotheistic traditions. Here are two attributes considered by Davies: perfection and omniscience.[22] Suppose we have something, X, capable of bringing everything into existence. Such causal power will not, however, necessitate omniscience or even awareness. Quite informally, X might have a lot of knowledge by our standards, but be far from omniscient—or X might have no consciousness, and no knowledge at all. The concept of ultimate cause does not entail omniscience or indeed other perfections. Granting the conclusion of the argument still would not suffice to demonstrate the existence of God, at least as Aquinas and others understand "God."

---

21   Davies 1982, pp. 46–47.
22   Davies 1982, pp. 48–49.

So while the Cosmological Argument might be viewed by some as an acceptable or reasonable argument for the existence of a necessary cause, it does not quite get us to the perfect being typically identified as "God." Yet this notion of perfection itself—this notion of a "perfect being"—leads us to one of history's most truly remarkable arguments.

The Ontological Argument

Formulated by Anselm of Canterbury (1033–1109), the Ontological Argument was included in his *Proslogion*. A prior work of Anselm's, *Monologion*, presented a long and difficult argument for God's existence. The Ontological Argument gave Anselm what he wanted—a "master argument," briefer and more readily accessible.[23] The argument drew an immediate and still discussed critical response from the French monk, Gaunilo. It was otherwise largely ignored for a couple of centuries, but in the thirteenth and fourteenth centuries philosophers and theologians began weighing in on the argument. Aquinas rejected it, as did William of Ockham, though it was defended by John Duns Scotus. Later on, Descartes gave a version in the *Meditations*, and Leibniz later undertook to bolster Descartes's version. Kant's criticism is, along with Gaunilo's, one of the two most known criticisms. Two twentieth-century philosophers, Norman Malcolm and Charles Hartshorne, undertook to refocus the argument. There is no consensus about the argument, and it remains one of the more discussed topics in philosophy. The argument's general outline, drawn from Chapter 2 of the *Proslogion*, is very simple. Perhaps this is part of its continuing lure: its apparent simplicity. Alvin Plantinga remarked that although no one has probably ever been led by the argument to believe in God's existence, there remains the suspicion that no one has yet given a full and convincing refutation of the argument.[24]

Why is it called the *Ontological* Argument? The argument proceeds by reflecting on God's nature or *essence*, and claiming to derive God's existence from his nature, or more precisely, from our concept of that nature. This contrasts with both the Design and Cosmological Arguments. Whereas those arguments are *a posteriori*, proceeding from observed effects to the claimed cause, the Ontological Argument is *a priori*.

The outline of the argument is strikingly brief. Chapter 2 of the *Proslogion* is barely a page, and the argument occurs in a long paragraph:

---

23   Thomas Williams 1996a, p. xviii.
24   Plantinga 1967, pp. 26–27.

Now we believe that you [God] are something than which nothing greater can be thought. So can it be that no such nature exists, since "The fool has said in his heart, 'There is no God'" (Psalm 14:1) ... So even the fool must admit that something than which nothing greater can be thought exists at least in his understanding, since he understands this when he hears it.... And surely that than which a greater cannot be thought cannot exist only in the understanding. For if it exists only in the understanding, then that than which a greater cannot be thought is that than which a greater can be thought. But that is clearly impossible. Therefore, there is no doubt that something than which a greater cannot be thought exists both in the understanding and reality.[25]

The concept of God expressed at the outset is what drives the argument. When we think "God," what are we thinking? God is *perfect*. That's the divine nature—he lacks nothing. So to think of God is to think of the greatest being that could ever be conceived.

Is this idea of God perhaps something unique to Anselm, something "subjective"? Anselm takes himself to be expressing the "common concept" shared by all parties to the debate about God's existence, not some idiosyncratic notion. This is what we mean by "God": you can't think of anything greater because there isn't anything greater. If you can think of something greater, you haven't yet understood the concept of God.

Obviously, this concept exists in the mind—or, as Anselm calls it, the "understanding." Thus, the concept of that which nothing greater can be thought is at the very least *mentally real*. It is real because it exists in the mind.

Anselm now wants to draw his readers' attention to a very important point. A concept can be—and often is—about something existing *outside* the mind. The content (what the concept is about) might only exist *qua* mental item, or it might also exist externally, independent of the mind's conception. A whimsical example. You might have overheard someone say that Santa Claus is real because he's "really" in our hearts and minds. And since there's a real thought of that jolly old elf, Santa Claus is real to that extent. Still, famous newspaper editorials aside, Santa Claus doesn't exist *outside* the mind. A more practical example: think now of an American hundred dollar bill, Ben Franklin's likeness and all. That content is of course *mentally real*; as Anselm says, your concept of the hundred dollar bill exists in the understanding. But you'd feel a bit differently about that content if it existed outside the mind, say, tucked into the pages of this book, wouldn't you? Which is "better," the merely *mentally*

---

25   Anselm 1996, pp. 99–100.

real idea of that banknote? Or the referent of that idea existing *external to the understanding*—the money right there in your hand?

Anselm says that if we have a concept of a being greater than which nothing can be thought, that necessarily leads us to the idea that such a being exists not only in the mind, but outside the mind, as well. Compare these two concepts: (a) greater than which nothing can be thought, and existing *only in the mind*, and (b) greater than which nothing can be thought, and existing *outside the mind, as well*.

Which of these two concepts, Anselm asks, is really the concept of a being greater than which nothing can be thought? Anselm thinks that it is obviously (b). Given (b) then, God exists *externally*, not just in our minds, but also objectively, independently of our minds. Our concept of God leads to the conclusion that God exists *outside the mind*, or else we would have contradicted ourselves: we would not yet have the concept of that greater than which nothing could be thought.

By taking the concept of God, which expresses God's nature, and reflecting on that concept carefully, we find that we are committed to a God that indeed exits. The move from concept to conclusion might be put thus:

1. God is that than which nothing greater can be thought.
2. This entity, than which nothing greater can be thought, exists (at least) in the understanding.
3. Either that which nothing greater can be thought exists (a) only in the understanding, or (b) also outside the mind.
4. It is greater to exist outside the mind than to exist only in the mind.
5. So, if God is that than which nothing greater can be thought, then God must be thought as existing outside as well as in the understanding.
6. So, God exists.

GAUNILO: A PERFECT ISLAND

The monk Gaunilo thought he had diagnosed what was wrong with this argument. Given this line of reasoning, *the existence of the perfect anything can be proved!* The perfect apple pie, the perfect golfer, even the perfect island, an island "with an indescribable abundance of all sorts of riches and delights":

Suppose someone tells me all this. The story is easily told and involves no difficulty, and so I understand it. But if this person went on to draw a conclusion, and say, "You cannot any longer doubt that this island, more excellent than all the others on earth, truly exists somewhere in reality. For you do not doubt that this island exists in your understanding, and since it is more excellent to exist not merely in the understanding, but also in reality, this island must also exist in reality."[26]

The island example, says Gaunilo, demonstrates that there is something faulty about Anselm's reasoning. If "existence in reality" could be proved from the existence of the concept of the greatest X that can be conceived, then we would have to be committed to the existence of all sorts of perfect things. But this result is clearly a mistake. So, something is wrong with Anselm's argument.

Put the matter this way: which is better: something that exists or something that doesn't? That doesn't make sense: we aren't comparing two things, which differ only in properties. There's only one thing—the one that exists! This argument, it seems, gets off on the wrong foot from the word go by talking about two kinds of existence. Something that we only imagine doesn't exist, period.

Many agree with Gaunilo: you can't derive existence from a concept or a definition. Once you start with concepts, you're stuck with concepts. You need some further premise or claim to connect the concept (or the mental content) with a really existing object.

26　Thomas Williams 1996b, pp.124–25.

This objection suffers from a misunderstanding, Anselm claims. He notes that there is a difference between the concept of a *contingently* existing thing and a thing than which nothing greater can be thought. No island, perfect or otherwise, is "that which nothing greater can be thought." To put this another way, Gaunilo thinks of the perfect one of a given *type*. But the argument is about the perfect type of thing *period*. There is nothing contradictory about the concept of a perfect island that doesn't exist. There is something contradictory about the concept of that which greater cannot be thought, which still might not exist![27] Gaunilo's mistake is to think that the concept of any isle—"blessed," perfect, or otherwise—is analogous to the concept of an unsurpassable being.

KANT: EXISTENCE ISN'T A PROPERTY

Although Gaunilo's objection is still recounted almost a millennium later, undoubtedly it is Immanuel Kant's objection in his *Critique of Pure Reason* that is now the most widely endorsed objection. Simply, Kant held that existence is not a property, a claim which is sometimes cast as "existence is not a perfection." Kant claimed that nothing was added to the concept of something if we say that it exists. "By whatever and by however many predicates [property] we may think a thing—even if we completely determine it—we do not make the least addition to the thing when we further declare that this thing *is*."[28] If Sam tells Sara about a chair he saw at the department store—blue, a recliner, cotton fabric—he conveys to Sara the properties of the chair. She thus acquires a concept of the chair. Were Sam then to say, "Oh, yeah, and it exists," Kant claims Sara would add nothing to Sara's concept of the chair. Some think Kant's point is reflected in modern symbolic logic, which indeed treats existence differently from other properties. (Modern predicate logic employs an "existential quantifier" *there exists*; its "grammatical position" is different from the "grammatical position" of symbols for properties.)

Aside from modern logic, is there a good reason not to think that existence is not a predicate? Some do claim that existence is not like other properties. And they might offer two kinds of reasons. First, some think that we assume existence when we explain the concept of some object, or "predicate" some characteristic of the object. Deirdre says that Julia is athletic; she's presupposing

27 Anselm 1996, pp. 132–34.
28 Kant 1965, p. 505.

Julia exists. If attributing some property to an object already presupposes the object exists, then why "add in" that it exists? But William Rowe—who describes himself as a "friendly atheist" and has helped shape the current debates in philosophy of religion—thinks that this does not seem terribly convincing. We frequently ascribe properties or "predicates" to nonexistent objects. It seems perfectly legitimate to say that the Mad Hatter is having tea, even though the existence of the Hatter is not assumed.[29]

The second sort of reason stems from the function of our descriptions—we ascribe properties or characteristics to pick out the *type* of thing and the particular *individual*. Saying that the object exists serves neither of these functions. Again, Sam tells Sara the *kind* of thing—a chair—and which *one*. Describing it as existing apparently contributes nothing to this concept.

A defender of the Ontological Argument thinks this is not quite right. There are occasions when existence *adds* something. We learn something new about the concept of a car that drives itself when we are told, "Oh, yeah ... they've made some. It's not just a 'concept car' any longer." Again we can note Rowe's remark that "there is some question ... whether anyone has succeeded in giving a really conclusive argument for the view that existence is not a predicate."[30]

A NEW INTERPRETATION: HARTSHORNE AND MALCOLM

Two twentieth-century philosophers hold that the real version of the Ontological Argument occurs in Chapter 3 of the *Proslogion*. The theologian and philosopher Charles Hartshorne (1897–2000), who gave the first "modal version" of the argument (a proof that uses a system of modal logic), and philosopher Norman Malcolm (1911–90) both held that the core distinction in the argument is between that which can be conceived as contingently existing and that which can *only* be conceived as *necessarily* existing. Anselm's second sentence of Chapter 3 is direct: "For it is possible to think that something exists that cannot be thought not to exist, and such a being is greater than one that can be thought not to exist."[31]

---

29   Rowe 2000, p. 36.

30   Rowe 2000, p. 36.

31   Anselm 1996, p. 100.

Malcolm held that while existence is not a perfection, *necessary existence* is a perfection.[32] He holds that the proof in Chapter 3 argues that God's existence is either impossible or necessary. Since the concept of God is not self-contradictory, God's existence is not impossible. Thus, God's existence is necessary. Hartshorne's modal logic version makes a similar point and is valid.[33]

Here is a slightly different, more informal version of the Chap. 3 argument, drawing on both Malcolm and Hartshorne. It relies crucially on what Hartshorne calls the "True Anselmian Principle," namely that which can only be thought as *necessarily existing* is greater than that which can be thought as *merely contingently existing*.

First, remember that God is that which nothing greater can be thought. Suppose then someone, call him GK, accepts this notion of God but also claims this gives us no good reason to think God exists.

What happens if we or GK suppose God does not exist? What are we imagining? We are apparently imagining a being that might not exist, or that might exist at one time but not another. Hence, this being's existence depends on circumstance or something else.

Once we have arrived here, however, it looks like we have imagined only a contingently existing being. Does this sort of *contingently existing being* sound like a being than which nothing greater can be thought? Anselm, Hartshorne, and Malcolm suspect that even our imagined GK can think of something greater—a being who doesn't exist only contingently, but exists necessarily!

We are now at the heart of Anselm's Chapter 3 argument. When we conceive of a being greater than which nothing can be thought, we have two alternatives. Either we conceive of a being whose existence is contingent, or we conceive of a being whose existence is necessary. And by the "principle" that necessary existence is greater than contingent existence, it appears that we must conclude that God necessarily exists.[34]

Rowe has doubts about granting that a being greater than which nothing can be thought is indeed a possible being. If we grant that, we are in effect granting that God actually exists, or as he remarks, we are ceding a premise "which is virtually equivalent to the conclusion that is to be proved."[35] Perhaps Anselm would not be dismayed by this criticism. Given the nature of the being under discussion, there is indeed a close connection between possibility and

---

32   Malcolm 1960, p. 46.
33   Hartshorne 1962, 1967.
34   Hartshorne 1965, pp. 85–108; Malcolm 1960, pp. 47–50.
35   Rowe 2000, p. 41.

necessary existence. The Ontological Argument leaves us, then, not quite where we started, but with a question still to be resolved.

God and the Existence of Evil: Incompatible?

In 1755, an earthquake in Lisbon, Portugal, killed somewhere between 10,000 and 100,000 people. Four years later, Voltaire famously satirized one type of attempted reconciliation of such evil with an all-good and powerful God in his *Candide*. Candide, the story's protagonist, begins with a naïve and superficially optimistic belief, taught to him by a philosopher, that we live in "the best of all possible worlds." Gradually he becomes disillusioned when he is confronted by the extent of suffering in the real world. We might wonder about the possibility of a supremely good and powerful God given earthquakes and other *natural evils*, and also given *moral evils*—the Holocaust, horrifyingly and brutal abuses and murders of innocent victims, adult, child, and infant.

Theology and philosophy of religion treat this set of issues under the general heading of the "problem of evil." How are we to reconcile such tragedies with the existence of God—more specifically, a supremely powerful and benevolent God? The problem is now thought of as two distinct but related problems: the *logical* problem of evil and the *evidential* problem of evil. Both problems challenge the rationality of theistic belief. These arguments suggest that believing in a God, conceived as an omnipotent, omniscient, all-good being, is incompatible with an incontrovertible fact: evil exists. Either one must reject the existence of evil, it seems, or reject the notion of the existence of God as he is classically conceived.

The Logical Problem of Evil

J.L. Mackie's 1955 "Evil and Omnipotence" was the impetus for much contemporary discussion of the logical problem of evil. Mackie held that two propositions were *logically inconsistent*: that evil exists *and* that God is all-good, all-powerful, and all-knowing. The two propositions can't be true at the same time. Since the existence of evil seems undeniable, then logic would appear to dictate giving up the other proposition, namely, that there is an all-good, omniscient, omnipotent God.[36] It is easy enough to supply the "missing

---

36   Rowe 2000, pp. 92–97; Adams and Adams 1990, pp. 1–3.

steps" and make explicit the incompatibility. So far we have the following two propositions:

(1) God exists, and is omniscient, omnipotent, and all-good.
(2) Evil exists.

An all-good or omnibenevolent being would of course not permit evil, if he had the ability. So, let us add an additional step.

(3) An omnibenevolent being would not permit evil.

Just as an omnibenevolent being would not permit evil, an omnipotent being would have the power to eliminate suffering. And if such a being were omniscient, no instances of evil would go unnoticed. Thus, we have two more steps:

(4) An omnipotent being could prevent the occurrence of evil.
(5) An omniscient being would know of any instances of evil.

To put it somewhat starkly, God would have both "motive and opportunity." God would want to preclude evil—his omnibenevolence at work. And no possible evil could escape God's ability to keep it from ever occurring—his omniscience and omnipotence at work. Thus, we are led to this: if the God of the Ontological Argument exists—*no evil exists*.

Clearly this cannot be right. It seems to be an undeniable truth that there is evil in the world (though a few philosophers and theologians have disputed this). And we cannot have it both ways: the existence of an omni-perfect God is logically inconsistent with the existence of evil. Logical consistency requires us to give up something. Since the fact of the *real existence of evil* seems inescapable, Mackie claims the theist faces the unhappy option of giving up proposition (1), in the argument above.

Alvin Plantinga provided a particular type of *theodicy*, that is, an explanation that reconciles an all-powerful and all-good God with the existence of evil. Plantinga's detailed and rigorous defense centers on free will.[37] He argues that it is logically possible that God could not have created genuinely free creatures while preventing the existence of evil. Human beings possessing genuine free

---

37 Plantinga 1990.

will—making decisions, choosing between options—according to Plantinga, opens up the possibility that evil will also exist.

But could not an omnipotent God create free beings while also preventing evil? God's omnipotence, as we saw in the first section of the chapter, extends only to that which is logically possible. Plantinga argues that a world in which creatures freely choose to do the good must include the existence of bad choices, some of which cause suffering, sometimes great suffering. Free creatures choosing to do good things make a world more valuable than an "evil-less" world in which there is no free will. Further, Plantinga maintains that it may be logically impossible to have a world in which there is both freedom and complete absence of evil. Consider this example: a small child chasing a ball runs into the road and is badly injured; the resulting suffering for the child and his family is enormous. In what sort of world would this sort of thing be prevented by God? Maybe God would prevent small children from playing ball, or briefly take over the control of cars when tragedy is imminent. Either way, we would be controlled by such a God in this sort of case and in countless others, ways that limited our freedom to make our own decisions. Most, including critics of the theistic position, now concede that the "free will theodicy" satisfactorily answers Mackie's logical problem—that is, it shows that it's *logically possible* that a benevolent God and *apparent* evils co-exist—that is, given the possibility that these "evils" are only apparent and are necessary for the greater good.

The Evidential Problem of Evil

Still, many critics of the idea of a perfect God suspect that a more serious version of the problem of evil remains: the *evidential problem of evil*.[38] William Rowe's account of the evidential problem is the center of recent discussion. Rowe does not claim that *any* evil is incompatible with God's existence. Rather he claims that there is *too much* intense suffering. Surely the omni-perfect God could have prevented *at least some*: must the fawn suffer for hours or days after being badly burned in the forest fire? Couldn't such a God have prevented at least a million of the Holocaust deaths?[39] Rowe's version of the argument is elegantly succinct:

---

38   E.g., Rowe 1995.
39   E.g., Taliaferro 1998, Chap. 9.

1. There exist instances of intense suffering which an omnipotent, omniscient being could have prevented without thereby losing some greater good or permitting some evil equally bad or worse.

2. An omniscient, wholly good being would prevent the occurrence of any intense suffering it could, unless it could not do so without thereby losing some greater good or permitting some evil equally bad or worse.

3. [So] There does not exist an omnipotent, omniscient, wholly good being.[40]

The force of this argument is readily apparent. *Some* of the horrible suffering that we read about or see or experience must be unnecessary. Consider the Lisbon earthquake. Had God moved it to a sparsely populated area of the earth, or reduced its force a bit, or eliminated it altogether, a tremendous amount of very serious suffering would have been prevented. Plantinga's point is that it is *logically possible* that all that suffering was necessary for a greater good, and that even a little less suffering wouldn't have done the job. Critics agree that it's logically possible, but wonder whether there's good reason to think that *all suffering* is really necessary for the existence of free will. Suppose we just concentrate on *unnecessary* evils. There appear to be plenty of examples of this. And if there is such unnecessary evil, then an all-powerful, all-good God does not exist. We will touch on three common theistic responses that are worth considering. All these present perspectives for seeing apparent evil as necessary.

God Knows Best

Creatures' relationship to God is like that of child to parent. Children often do not know, indeed, cannot even understand the "why" of their parents' behavior. Yet this doesn't necessarily mean the parents aren't good or that they aren't extremely powerful relative to their children. Similarly, God's creatures might not understand the *reason for* the suffering we witness. Our inability to discern God's purpose or to see justification for the suffering that occurs reflects human limitations. It just might be that the suffering we notice is, after all, necessary, but we don't see how it is. It need not reflect God's lack of power or goodness. We cannot then conclude that God is not both omnibenevolent and omnipotent.[41] But consider this analogy. A small child sometimes cannot

---

40   Rowe 1979; Adams and Adams 1990, pp. 127–28.
41   Wykstra 1984.

understand how his parents could be benevolent when they take him to the dentist or deny him another cookie. But that means that the child, of course, doesn't understand what real benevolence is. If that is like our position with regard to God, then we don't understand what real benevolence is either, and, lacking that concept, our talk is something like nonsense when we attribute "benevolence" to God.

Soul-Making

In his *Evil and the God of Love*, John Hick offered another sort of view on why suffering might actually be good for us: it serves for "soul-making."[42] Also relying on the parent-child metaphor, Hick emphasized our moral development. In Hick's view, suffering is essential to that development and thus essential to the relationship between creature and Creator. Especially important, in this view, is the role that suffering plays in the process of creatures coming to see and accept God's love. So, for example, every bit of the massive amount of suffering caused by the Lisbon earthquake was effective and essential for humanity's moral development. Still some suspect that every bit of the suffering is necessary for our moral development.

God's Participation in Suffering

Marilyn McCord Adams emphasizes a Christian resolution of the evidential problem.[43] She emphasizes the *passability* of God—his emotional nature. God participates in the suffering of created beings by becoming one of them. The incarnation—Jesus, as a person of the Trinity, becoming a human being—is the bond between Creator and creature in which God both experiences the suffering of created beings and honors that suffering, according to Adams. She also claims that her view provides a present justification for intense suffering: a person can find meaning or justification in suffering through seeing God's own experience of that suffering. So this means—again—that suffering is actually a good thing, and God is benevolent in creating or allowing it. This understanding of "benevolence" might seem suspect, however. We perhaps understand parents whose benevolence extends to letting their children "learn from their mistakes" and the suffering of both child and parent that might go

---

42 Hick 1978.
43 Marilyn McCord Adams 1999.

along with such learning. Parent and child perhaps become closer. But do we really think it's reasonable if a mother let her child go through extreme and continued suffering because the mother also suffers and such mutual suffering will draw them closer? Might we not insist instead that more reasonable persons intervene and protect the child from such "bonding"? Whether one finds, or *should* find, satisfactory these or any of the other many responses to the evidential problem of evil need not be settled now. It suffices to note that the evidential problem of evil continues to draw the attention of theist and atheist. In doing so it perhaps draws attention, as critic and proponent alike have noted, to the ultimate nature of the human condition.

Key Concepts

- omnipresence
- omniscient
- omnipotence
- eternality
- immutability
- incorruptibility
- impassability
- Argument from Design
- Cosmological Argument
- Ontological Argument

Reading/Discussion Questions

1. Explain how theists defend the claim that God is omnipotent. Do you think it is a limitation on God's power to not be able to "do" the logically impossible? Do you think it is a limitation if God can't do something evil? Explain.

2. What are the two ways of understanding God's eternality? Which of these two do you think is the better interpretation? Why?

3. Explain the *Proslogion* Chapter 2 version of the Ontological Argument? Do you think Anselm succeeds in responding to Gaunilo? Why or why not?

4. How would you explain the difference between the Hartshorne/Malcolm interpretation of the Ontological Argument and the Chapter 2 version?

Do you think Hartshorne and Malcolm give us a better version of the Ontological Argument? Why or why not?

5. What is the logical problem of evil? The evidential problem?

6. How would you assess Plantinga's response to the logical problem of evil? Which of the three responses to the evidential problem seems most promising? Why?

For Further Reading

Most surveys of the philosophy of religion include sections or chapters on divine attributes. Clack and Clack 1998, Brian Davies 1982, and Charles Taliaferro 1998 are all very helpful. Joshua Hoffman and Gary Rosenkrantz 2002 is a book-length consideration of the relevant issues. Richard Swinburne 1977 is still a classic work, which analyzes various interpretations as well as presenting Swinburne's own view. Chapter 8 explores the question of whether God is free.

Again, standard introductions to the philosophy of religion cover the arguments for the existence of God, e.g., Rowe 2000. David Hume 1980 includes his critique of the Design Argument, as well as his reflections on the problem of evil. Keith Yandell 1999 engages in a very detailed analysis of the Five Ways, especially the Cosmological Argument and the Ontological Argument. Alvin Plantinga 1968 includes several important essays on the Ontological Argument. Charles Hartshorne 1965 is his evaluation of historical views of the Ontological Argument together with a presentation of his own view. Donald Viney 1985 is a helpful account of Hartshorne's work.

Marilyn McCord Adams and Robert M. Adams 1990 is an excellent collection of essays on the problem of evil, which includes Alvin Plantinga 1990. Nelson Pike 1958, although ostensibly a comment on another essay, is also helpful in understanding the traditional problem of evil. Again, philosophy of religion introductions typically explain and analyze the problem of evil; William Rowe 2000 includes a balanced, excellent presentation of the difficulty. Thomas Senor 1995 includes several essays on the rationality of faith, some of which address specific issues related to the problem of evil. Marilyn McCord Adams 1999 offers a unique perspective and approach to the problem of evil. Taliaferro 1998 has a very nice survey of the problem of evil, including extensive quotations from the original sources.

Zimmer 1951, Pt. III, Chap. III is an exploration of Brahmanism, with extensive quotations from the Hindu Scriptures. Michael Molloy 1999, now in its 6th edition, includes an extensive chapter on Hinduism, and is intended for students and lay audiences. It is replete with photographs that Molloy took during his travels through the many historical sites of the world's religions. Carl Olson's 2007 is also a wide-ranging and accessible exposition of Hinduism.

GLOSSARY

a posteriori **knowledge** knowledge that depends on our sense experience (Introduction)

a posteriori **necessary truths** truths known *a posteriori*; that is, knowledge of them depends on experience, yet, they are necessary. Identity statements, it is argued, are examples (Chapter 2)

a priori **knowledge** knowledge that we have independent of sense experience (Introduction)

actual entities the basic units of reality, according to Whitehead. Actual entities are individual, but they are not static elements of reality; rather they are always becoming (Chapter 7)

adverbial theory a direct realist view of perception that holds that sensations are a way of experiencing objects, not mental objects of some sort (Chapter 5)

agent causation a view of causation held by some libertarians. Agent causation differs from event causation and is a causal power that each self has. Actions are thus caused, but caused by the self (Chapter 10)

analytic-synthetic distinction the idea that we can distinguish between analytic statements, which merely reflect the connection between concepts or meanings, and synthetic statements, which reflect what we learn from experience; notably challenged by Quine (Chapter 2)

androcentrism the practice of seeing things exclusively from the male point of view, ignoring the activity and concerns of women (Chapter 4)

Argument from Design an argument for God's existence, which claims that there is sufficient evidence of purpose or design in nature; hence, we must conclude that a designer, God, exists (Chapter 11)

arguments from illusion a family of arguments purporting to show that we are not immediately aware of objects and that their sensible properties are not intrinsic to them (Chapter 5)

behaviorism the view that the best explanation of behavior is to be found in environmental causes (stimuli) and subsequently conditioned behavioral responses (Chapter 8)

Being (Heideggerian view) that which gives the things of our every day world their being; the "presence-ing" of things (Chapter 7)

belief a type of mental state that has a particular content or represents the world as being some way or other; see also *content* and *representational states* (Introduction)

body criterion the view that a person's identity and persistence over time is determined by sameness of body, or sameness of some part of the body, such as the brain (Chapter 9)

bundle theory the view that objects are nothing more than collections, or "co-locations" of qualities (Chapter 7)

categories according to Kant, innate concepts that organize or structure incoming sensory information (Chapter 2)

coherence theory or **coherentism** the view that the justification of beliefs derives from the coherence—that is, the mutual support—of others of the agent's beliefs (Chapter 3)

compatibilism the view that there is a sense of the notion of free will that is compatible with determinism; thus moral responsibility or accountability is also compatible with determinism (Chapter 10)

concepts concepts classify or pick out or designate types of objects and types of properties (Introduction)

conceptualism the view that universals are to be identified as those concepts, located in the mind, standing for many individuals (Chapter 6)

content mental content; the "aboutness" of mental states such as beliefs and desires, which represent the world as being a certain way (Introduction)

Cosmological argument an argument for God's existence that argues that an adequate explanation of the existence of contingent beings must include the existence of a necessarily existing being, specifically God (Chapter 11)

Demon Argument Descartes's argument intended to show that even apparent truths arrived at by reason are possibly mistaken and hence not knowledge (Chapter 1)

determinism the view that every event is the necessary outcome of physical laws and prior circumstances or events; more traditionally the view that every event has a cause (Chapter 10)

direct realism a view of perception that holds that we directly perceive mind-independent, publicly accessible objects (Chapter 5)

Dream Argument Descartes's argument intended to show that our perceptual beliefs may be mistaken (Chapter 1)

dualism the view that the mental is something different in nature from the physical; a complete physical account of the world inevitably leaves something out, the mental. The two main types are substance dualism and property dualism (Chapter 8)

eliminative materialism the view that some significant class of mental phenomena do not exist; in particular, eliminativists typically claim that states like belief and desire—the basic elements of folk psychology—don't exist (Chapter 8)

empiricism the view that our beliefs about the world can be instances of knowledge or justified belief only if those beliefs derive from information gained in sense experience (Introduction)

epistemology the philosophical discipline that attempts to understand and explain the nature and sources of knowledge and justification (Introduction)

eternality a divine attribute; interpreted in two different ways: that God is in time, and extending infinitely backward and forward; or outside of time, that is, timeless (Chapter 11)

evidentialism the view that a belief is justified only if a person's evidence supports the belief and the person has the belief because of that evidence (Chapter 3)

experience argument for free will an argument for the existence of free will that appeals to our experiencing ourselves as choosing or deciding which actions to perform (Chapter 10)

fallibilism theories of justification that hold that further evidence—or the acquisition of further beliefs—can override one's present justification (Chapter 3)

fatalism the view that every event that occurs is metaphysically necessary and would have happened no matter what preceded it; often distinguished from determinism (Chapter 10)

fission objection an objection to theories of personal identity involving imagining a person dividing into two equivalent beings (Chapter 9)

foundationalism the view that at least some of our beliefs do not depend on other beliefs for their justification, but are nonetheless justified (Chapter 3)

free will that a person could have done otherwise, given the same course of events up till that choice; the view that on at least some occasions, a person's future is open (Chapter 10)

functionalism the view that the nature of the mental is seen in its *function*, what leads to or causes it, what it's connected to, and what happens as a result (Chapter 8)

gendered concept the meaning of a concept arises from some social or cultural structure or set of relations, in particular those that reflect relations between sexes, rather than from some "natural" fact or property (Chapter 4)

Gettier cases or **Gettier counterexamples** examples intended to show that a person could have a true belief, good reasons or justification for that belief, but not know (Chapter 2)

Hylomorphism the view, original with Aristotle, that all things, including persons, are a unity of form and matter (Chapter 9)

idealism the view that the world, or the objects in the world, depend on our beliefs. Typically contrasted with realism (Introduction)

immutability the idea that there is no changing in any way whatsoever (Chapter 11)

impassability the idea that a being cannot be a subject of emotions or feelings (Chapter 11)

incompatibilism the view that determinism and free will are incompatible; the consequence argument supports incompatibilism (Chapter 10)

incorruptibility a being is incorruptible if there can be no changes to that being's character (Chapter 11)

indefeasibility view a belief is an instance of knowledge only if it is true *and indefeasibly justified*. A belief is indefeasibly justified only if there are in fact no defeaters, no actually true proposition that would undermine the person's justification (Chapter 2)

individual identity the qualities or personality that constitute the nature of the individual, which may change over time (Chapter 9)

individuation question the question of what makes a person *this* person rather than some other (Chapter 9)

induction (as Hume conceived it) a type of non-deductive reasoning, which attempts to apply generalizations accepted on the basis of past experience, and extend them to new cases (Chapter 1)

infallibility a belief is infallible if it is not possible for that belief to be mistaken. Alternatively, it's not possible for the belief to be false (Chapter 1)

isolation objection the fundamental objection to coherence theories. The claim is that coherence cuts justification off from the world, that they cannot explain why our beliefs are likely to be true (Chapter 3)

linguistic view of the *a priori* we know that certain propositions are true independently of experience because we know the meanings of the words; the necessity and *a priori* character of certain truths are due to the meanings of the words (Chapter 2)

logically possible a proposition is logically possible if it is not self-contradictory (Introduction)

memory criterion a person's identity is determined by conscious memories (Chapter 9)

metaphysics a principal discipline in philosophy that attempts to understand and explain the nature and structure of the most general features of our world (Introduction)

moderate realism moderate realism is the view that our kind concepts refer to universals, but universals exist only in the objects; sometimes called immanent realism (Chapter 6)

monism only one type of thing exists: physical objects with their physical properties, according to physical monists (Introduction)

naïve realism a direct realist view of perception; holds that objects have the properties we sense them to have (Chapter 5)

Naturalism the view holds two central doctrines, one ontological and one epistemological. The ontological doctrine, a doctrine about what exists, holds that everything that exists is natural. The epistemological doctrine tells us that the natural objects and properties are those talked about or referred to in the explanations and theories offered by the natural sciences (Chapter 4)

naturalized epistemology a view that sees epistemology as part of natural science, and its principal aim as discovering, not the "justification link," but the causal link between evidence and theory (Chapter 4)

necessary a proposition is necessary if its truth value cannot be otherwise (Introduction)

necessary and sufficient conditions A is a necessary condition of B if and only if B cannot occur without the occurrence of A; A is a sufficient condition of B if and only if whenever A occurs, B also occurs (Introduction)

no false premise view a belief is an instance of knowledge if and only if it is true, justified, and no false belief is an essential part of its justification (Chapter 2)

nominalism the view that universals do not exist; only particular things or particular occurrences of properties exist (Chapter 6)

numerical identity A and B are numerically identical when A *is* B— that is, when 'A' and 'B' are different names for the same thing. Distinguished from qualitative identity (Chapter 9)

omnipotence a divine attribute, namely that God's power is unlimited. Many hold that this is understood as God's power to do anything that is logically possible (Chapter 11)

omnipresence a divine attribute, namely that God is everywhere. As understood by many theorists God is everywhere because his knowledge and power are everywhere present (Chapter 11)

omniscience a divine attribute, namely that God knows everything there is to know (Chapter 11)

Ontological argument an argument for God's existence, which proceeds by reflecting on God's nature or essence, and claiming to derive God's existence from his nature, or more precisely, our concept of that nature (Chapter 11)

ontology the philosophical study of the different types or kinds of things that exist (Introduction)

Particulars objects or individuals; particulars cannot be instantiated (Chapter 6)

persistence question (personal identity) the question of what makes a person the same person over time (Chapter 9)

personhood identity those characteristics that make something, whether human being, animal, robot, or extra-terrestrial creature a *person* (Chapter 9)

phenomenalism factual phenomenalism holds that there are no mind independent objects and that we are only directly aware of our own sensations; linguistic phenomenalism claims that references to objects are references to collections of sensations (Chapter 5)

physicalism the view that everything is ultimately physical; only physical things and properties exist (Introduction, Chapter 8) –

postmodern epistemology rejects the idea that there are any grand narratives or totalizing views, and in doing so, rejects the assumptions and values of traditional epistemology and sees all knowledge as practical and relative to a particular narrative (Chapter 4)

property dualism the view that there is only one kind of substance—the physical—but distinctly mental properties emerge from particular physical arrangements or structures (Chapter 8)

proposition what is expressed or "meant" by a sentence; different sentences or sentences in different languages might express the same proposition (Introduction)

qualia the qualitative aspects of the mental or the felt quality; sometimes "raw feels" (Chapter 8)

qualitative identity when two or more objects have all the same qualities or properties (Chapter 9)

rationalism the view that at least some of our beliefs are justified and hence instances of knowledge because of the operation of reason; such beliefs do not depend on sense experience for their justification (Introduction)

realism the idea that some area or domain of objects or kinds of thing exist independently of our beliefs (Introduction)

realism (about universals) holds that universals are a special kind of object, which exist separately from the many occurrences or instances (Chapter 6)

regress argument the principal motivation for foundationalism. The argument notes that every belief offered as supporting or justifying some other belief must itself be justified. This seems to set us on an unending process, a *regress*, and the only suitable option for ending the regress is foundationalism (Chapter 3)

reliabilism holds that a belief is justified or an instance of knowledge only if there is a reliable connection between the belief and truth; different versions of reliabilism will vary in the additional conditions required (Chapter 2)

representational states mental states that have contents and represent the world as having certain characteristics or being a certain ways (Introduction)

representative realism a causal theory of perception; sensations are caused by physical objects and somehow represent them (Chapter 5)

resemblance nominalism the view that we classify or group certain objects together because they resemble each other (Chapter 6)

responsibility argument for free will an argument for the existence of free will that asserts that since we are sometimes morally responsible for our actions, and free will is a necessary condition of responsibility, so free will must exist (Chapter 10)

skepticism the view that we do not have knowledge or justified beliefs in some area (Chapter 1)

social constructivism the view that the way the world is represented or known is a social construction, and that what is known—the objects, properties, and relations that make up the external world—are themselves at least in part a social construction (Chapter 4)

strict nominalism the view that it is an unanalyzable basic metaphysical fact that there are only individuals, which we describe using certain predicates but there is no need to explain why we use the same predicate to describe different objects (Chapter 6)

Substance dualism the view that there are two distinct kinds of substances in the world, bodies, or the physical, and minds, or the mental (Chapter 8)

substance view or **substance-attribute view** primary substances are our familiar individuals, and these individuals possess attributes or properties; some properties are essential to the individual, and some are accidental or inessential (Chapter 7)

substratum that which supports or holds together the various properties of an object (Chapter 7)

synthetic *a priori* propositions propositions that are necessarily true, known *a priori,* and carry new information—the predicate tells us more than the subject—hence are not simply asserting connections between concepts (Chapter 2)

Third Man argument an objection to the existence of universals, which holds that the attribute agreement argument for universals leads to an infinite regress of universals (Chapter 6)

token identity theory a view of the mental that holds that every occurrence of a mental state, event, or process is identical with some physical state, event, or process; functionalists usually accept this view (Chapter 8)

traditional view of *a priori* knowledge view that once we acquire the relevant concepts, we can see or grasp by reason alone that a proposition must be true (Chapter 2)

tropes the view that each occurrence of a property is particular and individual; no two property occurrences are of the same type or class (Chapter 6)

type identity theory the view that every type of mental state, event or process is nothing more than some type or pattern of brain activity (Chapter 8)

Uniformity Principle according to Hume, the principle that we tacitly rely on when making an inductive inference: unobserved cases must resemble those we have observed, and that the course of nature continues always uniformly the same (Chapter 1)

universal that which can be instantiated by many objects or particulars at the same time; a universal can be shared by any number of particulars at the same time and can be predicated of or attributed to many things (Chapter 6)

BIBLIOGRAPHY

Abelard, Peter. 1969. "On Universals." In J.F. Wippel and A.B. Wolter, eds. and trans., *Medieval Philosophy: From St. Augustine to Nicholas of Cusa*. New York: Free P. Reprinted in Andrew B. Schoedinger, ed., *The Problem of Universals*, Atlantic Highlands, NJ: Humanities. 1992.

Adams, Marilyn McCord. 1967. "Is the Existence of God a 'Hard Fact'?" *Philosophical Review* 76 (4): pp. 492–503.

——. 1999. *Horrendous Evils and the Goodness of God*. Ithaca, NY: Cornell UP.

Adams, Marilyn McCord, and Robert Merrihew Adams, eds. 1990. *The Problem of Evil*, New York: Oxford UP.

Adams, Robert Merrihew. 1979. "Primitive Thisness and Primitive Identity." *Journal of Philosophy* 76 (1): 5–26.

——. 1987a. "Flavors, Colors, and God," in *The Virtue of Faith and Other Essays in Philosophical Theology*. New York: Oxford UP, pp. 243–62.

——. 1987b. "The Logical Structure of Anselm's Arguments." In *The Virtue of Faith and Other Essays in Philosophical Theology*. New York: Oxford UP, pp. 221–42.

Alcoff, Linda, and Elizabeth Potter, eds. 1993. *Feminist Epistemologies (Thinking Gender)*. New York: Routledge.

Allen, Barry. 2004. *Knowledge and Civilization*. Boulder CO: Westview.

Alston, William. 1989. *Epistemic Justification*. Ithaca NY: Cornell UP.

Anderson, Elizabeth. 2000/2007. "Feminist Epistemology and Philosophy of Science." *The Stanford Encyclopedia of Philosophy*. Edward N. Zalta, ed. <http://plato.stanford.edu/entries/feminism-epistemology/>.

Anselm. 1996. *Monologion and Proslogion*. Thomas Williams, ed. and trans. Indianapolis, IN: Hackett.

Antony, Louise. 1993. "Quine as Feminist: The Radical Import of Naturalized Epistemology." In Louise Antony and Charlotte Witt, eds., *A Mind of One's Own: Feminist Essays on Reason and Objectivity*. Boulder CO: Westview, pp. 110–53.

Antony, Louise. 2002. "Embodiment and Epistemology." In Paul K. Moser, ed., *The Oxford Handbook of Epistemology*. New York: Oxford UP, pp. 463–78.

Aquinas, Thomas. n.d. Commentary on the First Epistle to the Corinthians. Fabian Larcher, trans. <http://www.dhspriory.org/thomas/SS1Cor.htm>.

——. 1953. *Introduction to the Metaphysics of St. Thomas Aquinas*. James F. Anderson, ed. and trans. South Bend, IN: Regenery/Gateway.

——. 1972. *An Aquinas Reader*. Mary Clark, ed. and trans. Garden City, NY: Image Books.

——. 2008. "Whether God Is Altogether Immutable?" *The Summa Theologica of St. Thomas Aquinas*. <http://www.newadvent.org/summa/>.

Aristotle. 1941a. *Categories*. E.M. Edghill, trans. In Richard McKeon, ed., *The Basic Works of Aristotle*. New York: Random House, pp. 7–39.

——. 1941b. *De Anima*. J.A. Smith, trans. In Richard McKeon, ed., *The Basic Works of Aristotle*. New York: Random House, pp. 533–603.

——. 1941c. *De Interpretatione*. E.M. Edghill, trans. In Richard McKeon, ed., *The Basic Works of Aristotle*. New York: Random House, pp. 38–61.

——. 1941d. *Metaphysics*. W.D. Ross, trans. In Richard McKeon, ed., *The Basic Works of Aristotle*. New York: Random House, pp. 681–926.

——. 1941e. *Physics*. W.D. Ross, trans. In Richard McKeon, ed., *The Basic Works of Aristotle*. New York: Random House, pp. 213–394.

Armstrong, D.M. 1973. *Belief, Truth and Knowledge*. Cambridge: Cambridge UP.

——. 1978. *Universals and Scientific Realism.* 2 vols. Cambridge: Cambridge UP.

——. 1988. "Perception and Belief." In Jonathan Dancy, ed., *Perceptual Knowledge.* New York: Oxford UP, pp. 127–44.

——. 1989. *Universals: An Opinionated Introduction.* Boulder CO: Westview.

Ashman, Keith, and Phillip Barringer, eds. 2001. *After the Science Wars: Science and the Study of Science.* New York: Routledge.

Atherton, Margaret. 1993. "Cartesian Reason and Gendered Reason." In Louise Antony and Charlotte Witt, eds. *A Mind of One's Own: Feminist Essays on Reason and Objectivity.* Boulder, CO: Westview P.

Atwell, Jessica, Josh Van Otterloo, Jennifer Zipprich, Kathleen Winter, Kathleen Harriman, Daniel A. Salmon, Neal A. Halsey, and Saad B. Omer. 2010. "Nonmedical Vaccine Exemptions and Pertussis in California." *Pediatrics* 132 (4): 624–30.

Audi, Robert. 1988. *Belief, Justification, and Knowledge.* Belmont CA: Wadsworth.

——. 1993. *The Structure of Justification.* Cambridge: Cambridge UP.

——. 1998. *Epistemology: A Contemporary Introduction to the Theory of Knowledge.* New York: Routledge.

——. 2005. *Epistemology: A Contemporary Introduction to the Theory of Knowledge,* 3rd ed. New York: Routledge.

Augustine. 1949. *The Confessions of Saint Augustine.* Edward B. Pusey, trans. New York: Random House.

——. 1993. *On the Free Choice of the Will.* Thomas Williams, trans. Indianapolis IN: Hackett.

Aurelius, Marcus. 2006. *Meditations.* Martin Hammond, trans. New York: Penguin.

Austin, J.L. 1962. *Sense and Sensibilia.* Oxford: Clarendon P.

Ayer, A.J. 1952. *Language, Truth and Logic,* 2nd ed. New York: Dover.

——. 1956. *The Problem of Knowledge.* New York: Penguin.

Baker, Lynne Rudder. 2000. *Persons and Their Bodies: The Constitution View.* Cambridge: Cambridge UP.

Balaguer, Mark. 2014. *Free Will.* Cambridge, MA: MIT P.

Bambrough, Renford. 1960. "Universals and Family Resemblance." *Proceedings of the Aristotelian Society* 61: 207–22. Reprinted in Andrew Schoedinger, ed. *The Problem of Universals,* 1990, pp. 266–79.

Barnes, Winston F. 1945. "The Myth of Sense Data." *Proceedings of the Aristotelian Society* 45: 89–115.

Baylis, C.A. 1951. "Universals, Communicable Knowledge, and Metaphysics." *Journal of Philosophy* 48 (21): 636–44.

Beauvoir, Simone de. 2011. *The Second Sex*. Constance Borde and Sheila Malovaney-Chevallier, trans. New York: Vintage.

Benardete, Seth. 1997. *The Bow and the Lyre: A Platonic Reading of the Odysssey*. Lanham, MD: Rowman and Littlefield.

Berkeley, George. 1965. *A Treatise Concerning the Principles of Human Knowledge*. Indianapolis, IN: Bobbs-Merrill.

Bernstein, Richard. 1987. "Philosophical Rift: A Tale of Two Approaches." *New York Times*, Dec 29, p. A-1. <http://www.nytimes.com/1987/12/29/us/philosophical-rift-a-tale-of-two-approaches.html>.

Biology and Gender Study Group. 1999. "The Importance of Feminist Critique in Contemporary Cell Biology." In Jennifer McErlean, ed., *Philosophies of Science: From Foundations to Contemporary Issues*. Belmont, CA: Wadsworth, pp. 172–87.

Blackham, H.J. 1952. *Six Existentialist Thinkers*. New York: Harper Torchbooks.

Blanshard, Brand. 1961. "The Case for Determinism." In Sidney Hook, ed., *Freedom and Determinism in the Modern World*. New York UP, pp. 19–30. Reprinted in Neil Campbell, ed., *Freedom, Determinism, and Responsibility: Readings in Metaphysics*. Upper Saddle River, NJ: Prentice-Hall, 2003, pp. 7–15.

Bleier, Ruth. 1986. "Sex Differences Research: Science or Belief." In Ruth Bleier, ed., *Feminist Approaches to Science*. Oxford: Pergamon, pp. 147–64.

Block, Ned. 1978. "Troubles with Functionalism." In Wade Savage, ed. *Perception and Cognition: Issues in the Foundations of Psychology*, vol. 9 of *Minnesota Studies in the Philosophy of Science*. Minneapolis, MN: U of Minnesota P, pp. 261–325.

Bogdan, Radu J. 1976. "Hume and the Problem of Local Induction." In Radu J. Bogdan, ed., *Local Induction*. Dordrecht, Netherlands: Reidel, pp. 216–34.

Boghossian, Paul A. 2005. "What is Social Construction?" In *Theory's Empire: An Anthology of Dissent*, Daphne Patai and Wilfrido Corral, eds. New York: Columbia UP. <http://philosophy.fas.nyu.edu/docs/IO/1153/socialconstruction.pdf>.

——. 2007. *Fear of Knowledge: Against Relativism and Constructivism*. New York: Oxford UP.

Boghossian, Paul A., and Christopher Peacocke, eds. 2000. *New Essays on the A Priori*. New York: Oxford UP.

Boghossian, Paul A., and David Velleman. 1989. "Colour as a Secondary Quality." *Mind* N.S. 98 (389): 81–103.

——. 1991. "Physicalist Theories of Color." *Philosophical Review* 100: 81–103. Reprinted in Alex Byren and David Hilbert, eds. *Readings on Color: Volume 1, The Philosophy of Color*. Cambridge, MA: MIT P, 1997, pp. 105–36.

BonJour, Laurence. 1980. "Externalist Theories of Empirical Knowledge." *Midwest Studies in Philosophy* 5 (1): 53–73.

——. 1985. *The Structure of Empirical Knowledge*. Cambridge, MA: Harvard UP.

——. 1998. *In Defense of Pure Reason: A Rationalist Account of* A Priori *Justification*. Cambridge: Cambridge UP.

——. 2001/2007. "Epistemological Problems of Perception." In Edward N. Zalt, ed., *Stanford Encyclopedia of Philosophy*. http://plato.stanford.edu/entries/perception-episprob/.

Borst, C.V., ed. 1970. *The Mind/Brain Identity Theory*. New York: St. Martin's.

Bouwsma, O.K. 1949. "Descartes' Evil Genius." *The Philosophical Review* 58 (2): 141–51.

Burger, Ronna. 1984. *Phaedo: A Platonic Labyrinth*. New Haven, CT: Yale UP.

Burton, Neel. 2012. "The Vanishing Self." In "Hide and Seek," *Psychology Today*. <http://www.psychologytoday.com/blog/hide-and-seek/201205/the-vanishing-self>.

Byrne, Alex, and David Hilbert, eds. 1997. *Readings on Color: Volume 1, The Philosophy of Color*. Cambridge, MA: MIT P.

Campbell, Keith. 1984. *Body and Mind*. Notre Dame, IN: U of Notre Dame P.

——. 1991. *Abstract Particulars*. Oxford: Blackwell.

Carroll, John, and Ned Markosian. 2010. *An Introduction to Metaphysics*. Cambridge: Cambridge UP.

Carter, Rita. 2010. *Mapping the Mind*. Berkeley CA: U of California P.

Cashmore, Anthony. 2010. "The Lucretian Swerve: The Biological Basis of Human Behavior and the Criminal Justice System." *Proceedings of the National Academy of Sciences of the United States of America* 07 (10): 4499–4504.

Casullo, Albert. 1988. "A Fourth Version of the Bundle Theory." *Philosophical Studies* 54 (1): 125–39.

Chalmers, David. 1996. *The Conscious Mind*. New York: Oxford UP.

Cherniss, Harold. 1936. "The Philosophical Economy of Plato's Theory of Ideas." *The American Journal of Philology* 57 (4): 445–56.

Chisholm, Roderick. 1957. *Perceiving*. Ithaca, NY: Cornell UP.

——. 1964. "Human Freedom and the Self." The Lindley Lecture, U of Kansas, pp. 3–14. Reprinted in Gary Watson, ed., *Free Will*. New York: Oxford UP, 1982, pp. 24–35.

——. 1976. *Person and Object*. LaSalle, IL: Open Court.

——. 1977. *Theory of Knowledge*, 2nd ed. Englewood Cliffs, NJ: Prentice-Hall.

Churchland, Patricia. 1986. *Neurophilosophy: Toward a Unified Science of the Mind/Brain*. Cambridge, MA: MIT P.

Churchland, Paul M. 1981. "Eliminative Materialism and the Propositional Attitudes." *Journal of Philosophy* 78: 67–90.

——. 1988. *Matter and Consciousness*, rev. ed. Cambridge, MA: MIT P.

——. 1996. *The Engine of Reason, The Seat of the Soul: A Philosophical Journey into the Brain*. Cambridge, MA: MIT P.

——. 2013. *Matter and Consciousness*, 3rd ed. Cambridge, MA: MIT P.

Clack, Beverly, and Brian Clack. 1998. *Philosophy of Religion: A Critical Introduction*. Cambridge: Polity P.

Clarke, Thompson. 1972. "The Legacy of Skepticism." *Journal of Philosophy* 69: 754–69.

Clifford, William K. 1999. *The Ethics of Belief and Other Essays*. Amherst, NY: Prometheus.

Code, Lorraine. 1987. *Epistemic Responsibility*. Lebanon, NH: UP of New England.

Cooper, David E. 1999. *Existentialism*, 2nd ed. Oxford: Blackwell.

Copleston, Frederick C., S.J. 1946. *A History of Western Philosophy*, Vol 1. Garden City, NY: Doubleday.

——. 1953. *A History of Western Philosophy*, Vol 3. Garden City, NY: Doubleday.

——. 1966. *A History of Western Philosophy*, Vol 8. Garden City, NY: Doubleday.

——. 1974. *A History of Medieval Philosophy*. New York: Harper & Row.

Corcoran, Kevin. 2001a. "Physical Persons and Post-Mortem Survival Without Temporal Gaps." In Corcoran, ed., *Soul, Body, and Survival: Essays on the Metaphysics of Human Persons*. Ithaca, NY: Cornell UP, pp. 201–17.

——, ed. 2001b. *Soul, Body, and Survival: Essays on the Metaphysics of Human Persons*. Ithaca, NY: Cornell UP.

Cornman, James. 1975. *Perception, Science, and Common Sense*. New Haven, CT: Yale UP.

Cross, Richard. 2014. "Medieval Theories of Haecceity." *The Stanford Encyclopedia of Philosophy* (Summer 2014 Edition), Edward N. Zalta, ed. <http://plato.stanford.edu/archives/sum2014/entries/medieval-haecceity/>.

Crumley, Jack S., II. 1991. "Appearances Can Be Deceiving." *Philosophical Studies* 64: 233–51.

——, ed. 1998. *Readings in Epistemology*. Mountain View, CA: Mayfield.

——. 2006. *A Brief Introduction to the Philosophy of Mind*. Lanham, MD: Rowman & Littlefield.

——. 2009. *An Introduction to Epistemology*, 2nd ed. Peterborough, ON: Broadview P.

Curley, E.M. 1978. *Descartes Against the Skeptics*. Cambridge, MA: Harvard UP.

Damasio, Antonio. 2000. *The Feeling of What Happens: Body and Emotion in the Making of Consciousness*. New York: Mariner Books.

Dancy, Jonathan, ed. 1988. *Perceptual Knowledge*. Oxford: Oxford UP.

Dancy, Jonathan, and Ernst Sosa, eds. 1993. *A Companion to Epistemology*. Cambridge, MA: Blackwell.

Datson, Lorraine J., and Peter Galison. 2010. *Objectivity*. New York: Zone Books.

Davidson, Donald. 1986a. "A Coherence Theory of Truth and Knowledge." In Ernest Lepore, ed., *Truth and Interpretation: Perspectives on the Philosophy of Donald Davidson*. Oxford: Blackwell, pp. 307–19.

——. 1986b. "Empirical Content." In Ernest Lepore, ed., *Truth and Interpretation: Perspectives on the Philosophy of Donald Davidson*. Oxford: Blackwell, pp. 320–32.

Davies, Brian. 1982. *An Introduction to the Philosophy of Religion*. New York: Oxford UP.

——. 1992. *The Thought of Thomas Aquinas*. Oxford: Clarendon.

Dawkins, Richard. 1986. *The Blind Watchmaker: Why the Evidence of Evolution Reveals a Universe Without Design*. New York: Norton.

Dennett, Daniel. 1978. *Brainstorms: Philosophical Essays on Mind and Psychology*. Cambridge, MA: MIT P.

——. 1984. *Elbow Room*. Cambridge, MA: MIT P.

——. 1991. *Consciousness Explained*. Boston: Little, Brown.

——. 1998. "True Believers: The Intentional Strategy and Why It Works." In *The Intentional Stance*. Cambridge, MA: MIT P, pp. 13–42.

Descartes, René. 1968a. *Discourse on the Method of Rightly Conducting the Reason and Seeking for Truth in the Sciences*. In Elizabeth S. Haldane and G.R.T. Ross, trans., *The Philosophical Works of Descartes*, Vol. I. Cambridge: Cambridge UP.

——. 1968b. *Meditations on First Philosophy*. In Elizabeth S. Haldane and G.R.T. Ross, trans., *The Philosophical Works of Descartes*, Vol. I. Cambridge: Cambridge UP.

DeRose, Keith. 2000. "Ought We to Follow Our Evidence?" *Philosophy and Phenomenological Research* 60 (3): 697–706.

DeRose, Keith, and Ted Warfield, eds. 1999. *Skepticism: A Contemporary Reader*. New York: Oxford UP.

Dewey, John. 1920. *Reconstruction in Philosophy*. New York: H. Holt and Company.

——. 1929. *The Quest for Certainty: A Study of the Relation Between Knowledge and Action*. New York: Perigee Books.

——. 1938. *Logic: The Theory of Inquiry*. New York: H. Holt and Company.

——. 1954. *Art as Experience*. New York: Capricorn Books.

Dicker, Georges. 1980. *Perceptual Knowledge*. Dordrecht: Reidel.

Donagan, Alan. 1963. "Universals and Metaphysical Realism." *Monist* 47(2). Reprinted in Michael J. Loux, ed., *Universals and Particulars: Readings in Ontology*. New York: Anchor Doubleday, 1970.

Dombrowski, Dan. 2013. "Charles Hartshorne." The Stanford Encyclopedia of Philosophy (Spring 2013 Edition), Edward N. Zalta, ed. <http://plato.stanford.edu/archives/spr2013/entries/hartshorne/>.

Dreifus, Claudia. 2002. "Taking a Clinical Look at Human Emotions: A Conversation with Joseph LeDoux." *The New York Times*, October 8.

Ducasse, C.J. 1960. "In Defense of Dualism." In Sidney Hook, ed., *Dimensions of Mind*. New York: New York UP, pp. 85–90.

Dummett, Michael. 1978. *Truth and Other Enigmas*. Cambridge, MA: Harvard UP.

Eagle, Antony. 2014. "Chance versus Randomness." *The Stanford Encyclopedia of Philosophy*, Edward N. Zalta, ed. <http://plato.stanford.edu/archives/spr2014/entries/chance-randomness/>.

Eames, S. Morris. 1977. *Pragmatic Naturalism*. Carbondale, IL: Southern Illinois UP.

Edelman, Gerald. 1992. *Brilliant Air, Brilliant Fire: On the Matter of the Mind*. New York: Basic Books.

Edwards, Jonathan. 1835. *Freedom of the Will.* In Edward Hickman, ed., *The Works of Jonathan Edwards.* New York: D. Appleton.

Edwards, Paul. 1958. "Hard and Soft Determinism." In Sidney Hook, ed., *Determinism and Freedom in the Age of Modern Science.* New York: Collier Books, pp. 117–25. Reprinted in Robert Kane, ed., *Free Will,* Oxford: Wiley-Blackwell, 2001, pp. 59–67.

Ekstrom, Laura. 2000. *Free Will: A Philosophical Study.* Boulder, CO: Westview.

Emerson, Ralph Waldo. 1987. *The Essays of Ralph Waldo Emerson (Collected Works of Ralph Waldo Emerson).* Alfred R. Ferguson, Jean Ferguson Carr and Alfred Kazin, eds. Cambridge, MA: Belknap.

Everitt, Nicholas, and Alec Fisher. 1995. *Modern Epistemology: An Introduction.* New York: McGraw-Hill.

Fagan, Melinda B. 2010. "Social Construction Revisited: Epistemology and Scientific Practice." *Philosophy of Science* 77: 92–116.

Feldman, Richard. 1985. "Reliability and Justification." *The Monist* 68 (2): 159–74.

——. 1993. "Evidence." In Jonathan Dancy and Ernest Sosa, eds. *A Companion to Epistemology.* Oxford: Blackwell.

——. 2003. *Epistemology.* Upper Saddle River, NJ: Prentice-Hall.

——. 2012. "Naturalized Epistemology." *The Stanford Encyclopedia of Philosophy* (Summer 2012 Edition), Edward N. Zalta, ed. <http://plato.stanford.edu/archives/sum2012/entries/epistemology-naturalized/>.

Feldman, Richard, and Earl Conee. 1985. "Evidentialism." *Philosophical Studies* 48 (1): 15–34.

——. 2004. *Evidentialism.* New York: Oxford UP.

Fisch, Max H., ed. 1951. *Classic American Philosophers.* New York: Appleton-Century-Crofts.

Fischer, John Martin, ed. 1989. *God, Foreknowledge, and Freedom.* Stanford, CA: Stanford UP.

Fischer, John Martin. 1995. *The Metaphysics of Free Will: An Essay on Control.* Malden, MA: Blackwell.

Fish, William. 2010. *Philosophy of Perception: A Contemporary Introduction.* New York: Routledge.

Flanagan, Owen. 1992. *Consciousness Reconsidered.* Cambridge, MA: MIT P.

Fodor, Jerry A. 1975. *The Language of Thought.* Cambridge, MA: Harvard UP.

——. 1981. "The Mind-Body Problem: A Guide to the Current Debate." *Scientific American* 244: 114–25.

Foley, Richard. 2012. *When Is True Belief Knowledge?* Princeton, NJ: Princeton UP.

Forbes, Graeme. 1986. *The Metaphysics of Modality*. Oxford: Clarendon.

Foster, John. 1985. "Berkeley on the Physical World." In John Foster and Howard Robinson, eds., *Essays on Berkeley: A Tercentennial Celebration*. Oxford: Oxford UP, pp. 83–108.

——. 1991. *The Immaterial Self: A Defence of the Cartesian Dualist Conception of the Mind*. New York: Routledge.

Frankfurt, Harry G. 1971. "Freedom of the Will and the Concept of a Person." *Journal of Philosophy* 68 (1): 5–20.

Fricker, Miranda. 1994. "Knowledge as Construct: Theorizing the Role of Gender in Knowledge." In Kathleen Lennon and Margaret Whitford, eds., *Knowing the Difference: Feminist Perspectives in Epistemology*. New York: Routledge.

Fumerton, Richard. 1985. *Metaphysical and Epistemological Problems of Perception*. Lincoln, NE: U of Nebraska P.

Fung, Yu-lan. 1962. *A History of Chinese Philosophy*. Princeton, NJ: Princeton UP.

Garber, Daniel. 2000. *Descartes Embodied*. Cambridge: Cambridge UP.

Gaunilo. 1996. *On Behalf of the Fool*. In Thomas Williams, ed. and trans., *Monologion and Proslogion*, Indianapolis, IN: Hackett, pp. 121–26.

Genova, A.C. 1983. "The Metaphilosophical Turn in Contemporary Metaphysics." *Southwest Philosophical Studies* IX: 1–22.

Gettier, Edmund. 1963. "Is Justified True Belief Knowledge?" *Analysis* 23: 121–23.

Gilson, Etienne. 1937. *The Unity of Philosophical Experience*. Fort Collins, CO: Ignatius P.

——. 1940. *The Spirit of Medieval Philosophy*. New York: Charles Scribner's Sons.

——. 1960. *Heloise and Abelard*. Ann Arbor, MI: U of Michigan P.

Godwin, Dwayne, and Jorge Cham. 2013. "Split-Brain Patients Reveal Brain's Flexibility." *Scientific American Mind* 24 (1): 5.

Goetz, Stewart, and Charles Taliaferro. 2011. *A Brief History of the Soul*. Oxford: Wiley/Blackwell.

Goldman, Alvin. 1976. "Discrimination and Perceptual Knowledge." *The Journal of Philosophy* 73 (20): 771–91. Reprinted in *Liaisons: Philosophy Meets the Cognitive and Social Sciences*. Cambridge, MA: MIT P, 1992, pp. 85–103.

——. 1979. "What Is Justified Belief?" In George Pappas, ed., *Justification and Knowledge*. Dordrecht, Netherlands: Reidel, pp. 1–23.

——. 1986. *Epistemology and Cognition*. Cambridge, MA: Harvard UP.

Goldsmith, Timothy. 2006. "What Birds See." *Scientific American* 295: 68–75.

Gracia, Jorge J.E. 1992. "The Transcendentals in the Middle Ages: An Introduction." *Topoi* 11 (2): 113–20.

Griswold, Charles, ed. 1988. *Platonic Writings, Platonic Readings*. New York: Routledge.

Guttenplan, Samuel, ed. 1975. *Mind and Language*. Oxford: Oxford UP.

Hacking, Ian. 1973. "Leibniz and Descartes: Proof and Eternal Truths." *Proceedings of the British Academy* 59: 175–88. Reprinted in Ted Honderich, ed., *Philosophy Through Its Past*. Harmondsworth, UK: Pelican Books, 1984, pp. 211–24.

——. 2000. *The Social Construction of What?* Cambridge, MA: Harvard UP.

Hamilton, Edith, and Huntington Cairns, eds. 1961. *Plato: Collected Dialogues*. Princeton, NJ: Princeton UP.

Hardin, C.L. 1986. *Color for Philosophers: Unweaving the Rainbow*. Indianapolis, IN: Hackett.

——. 2003. "A Spectral Reflectance Doth Not a Color Make." *Journal of Philosophy* 100: 191–202.

Harding, Sandra. 1986. *The Science Question in Feminism*. Ithaca, NY: Cornell UP.

——. 1991. *Whose Science? Whose Knowledge? Thinking from Women's Lives*. Ithaca, NY: Cornell UP.

——. 1993. "Rethinking Standpoint Epistemology: What Is 'Strong Objectivity'?" In Linda Alcoff and Elizabeth Potter, eds., *Feminist Epistemologies*. New York: Routledge.

Harman, Gilbert. 1986. *Change in View*. Cambridge, MA: MIT P.

——. 1999. *Reasoning, Meaning and Mind*. Oxford: Oxford UP.

Harris, James F., and Richard H. Severens, eds. 1970. *Analyticity*. Chicago: Quadrangle Books.

Hartshorne, Charles S. 1962. *The Logic of Perfection*. LaSalle, IL: Open Court.

——. 1965. *Anselm's Discovery: A Reexamination of the Ontological Argument for God's Existence*. LaSalle, IL: Open Court.

——. 1967. *A Natural Theology for Our Time*. LaSalle, IL: Open Court.

——. 1976. *Aquinas to Whitehead*. Milwaukee, WI: Marquette UP.

——. 1984. *Omnipotence and Other Theological Mistakes*. Albany, NY: SUNY P.

Hasker, William. 1989. *God, Time and Knowledge*. Ithaca, NY: Cornell UP.

Haslanger, Sally. 1993. "On Being Objective and Being Objectified." In Louise Anthony and Charlotte Witt, eds., *A Mind of One's Own: Feminist Essays on Reason and Objectivity.* Boulder, CO: Westview.

Hegel, G.F.W. 1967. *Phenomenology of Mind.* J.B. Baillie, trans. New York: Harper & Row.

Heidegger, Martin. 1962a. *Being and Time.* John Mcquarrie and Edward Robinson, trans. London: SCM P.

——. 1962b. *Kant and the Problem of Metaphysics.* James Churchill, trans. Bloomington, IN: Indiana UP.

——. 1965. *Existence and Being.* Werner Brock, ed. Chicago: Henry Regnery.

——. 1976. *What Is Called Thinking?* J. Glenn Gray, trans. New York: Harper & Row.

——. 1977. "The Question Concerning Technology." In William Lovitt, trans., *The Question Concerning Technology and Other Essays.* New York: Harper Torchbooks, pp. 3–35.

Heil, John. 1983. *Perception and Cognition.* Berkeley, CA: U of California P.

——. 1998. *Philosophy of Mind.* New York: Routledge.

——. 2004. *Philosophy of Mind: A Guide and Anthology.* New York: Oxford.

Heller, Mark. 1999. "The Proper Role for Contextualism in an Anti-Luck Epistemology." *Philosophical Perspectives* 13: 115–29.

Hetherington, Stephen, ed. 2012. *Epistemology: The Key Thinkers.* London: Bloomsbury Academic.

Hick, John, ed. 1964. *The Existence of God.* New York: Macmillan.

——. 1978. *Evil and the God of Love,* rev. ed. New York: Harper and Row.

Hoffman, Joshua, and Gary Rosenkrantz. 1984. "Hard and Soft Facts." *Philosophical Review* 93: 419–34.

——. 2002. *The Divine Attributes.* Oxford: Blackwell.

Holland, John H., et al. 1986. *Induction.* Cambridge, MA: MIT P.

Hrdy, Sarah Blaffer. 1986. "Empathy, Polyandry and the Myth of the Coy Female." In Ruth Bleier, ed., *Feminist Approaches to Science.* New York: Pergamon.

Hubbard, Ruth. 1983. "Have Only Men Evolved?" In Sandra Harding and Merrill Hintikka, eds., *Discovering Reality: Feminist Perspectives on Epistemology, Metaphysics, Methodology, and Philosophy of Science.* Dordrecht, Netherlands: Reidel, pp. 45–70.

——. 1999. "Science, Facts and Feminism." In Jennifer McEarlean, ed. *Philosophies of Science: From Foundations to Contemporary Issues.* Belmont, CA: Wadsworth.

Huemer, Michael. 2001. *Skepticism and the Veil of Perception*. Lanham, MD: Rowman & Littlefield.

Hume, David. 1975. *An Enquiry Concerning Human Understanding*, 3rd ed., L.A. Selby-Bigge, ed., rev. by P.H. Nidditch. Oxford: Clarendon.

——. 1978. *A Treatise of Human Nature*, 2nd ed. L.A. Selby-Bigge, ed., rev. by P.H. Nidditch. Oxford: Clarendon.

——. 1980. *Dialogues Concerning Natural Religion*. Richard Popkin, ed. Indianapolis, IN: Hackett.

Irvine, Andrew David. 2013. "Alfred North Whitehead." *The Stanford Encyclopedia of Philosophy* (Winter 2013 Edition), Edward N. Zalta, ed. <http://plato.stanford.edu/archives/win2013/entries/whitehead/>.

Irwin, Terence. 1989. *A History of Western Philosophy: 1 Classical Thought*. New York: Oxford UP.

Jackson, Frank. 1982. "Epiphenomenal Qualia." *Philosophical Quarterly* 32: 127–36.

Jacquette, Dale. 1994. *Philosophy of Mind*. Upper Saddle River, NJ: Prentice-Hall.

James, William. 1951a. "The Continuity of Experience." Excerpt reprinted in *Classic American Philosophers*. Max. H. Fisch, ed. New York: Appleton-Century-Crofts, pp. 160–64.

——. 1951b. "Does 'Consciousness' Exist?" In *Classic American Philosophers*. Max. H. Fisch, ed. New York: Appleton-Century-Crofts, pp. 148–60.

——. 1951c. "The Will to Believe." Excerpt reprinted in Max H. Fisch, ed., *Classic American Philosophers*, 1951, New York: Appleton-Century-Crofts, pp. 136–48.

——. 1956. "The Dilemma of Determinism." *In The Will to Believe and Other Essays*. New York: Dover, pp. 145–83.

——. 1975. *Pragmatism: A New Name for some Old Ways of Thinking*. Cambridge, MA: Harvard UP.

——. 1978. "The Dilemma of Determinism." In John J. McDermott, ed., *The Writings of William James: A Comprehensive Edition*. Chicago, IL: U of Chicago P, pp. 146–84.

——. 2004. *The Varieties of Religious Experience*. New York: Barnes and Noble Classics.

Jones, W.T. 1969a. *A History of Western Philosophy: The Classical Mind*, 2nd ed. New York: Harcourt, Brace and World.

——. 1969b. *A History of Western Philosophy: The Medieval Mind*, 2nd ed. New York: Harcourt, Brace and World.

——. 1997. *A History of Western Philosophy: The Twentieth Century to Quine and Derrida*, 3rd ed. New York: Harcourt, Brace and World.

Jones, W.T. and Robert J. Fogelin. 1997. *A History of Western Philosophy: The Twentieth Century to Quine and Derrida*, 3rd ed. Fort Worth, TX: Harcourt Brace.

Kaku, Michio. 2011. "Why Physics Ends the Free Will Debate." <http://bigthink.com/videos/why-physics-ends-the-free-will-debate>.

Kalderon, Eli Mark. 2007. "Color Pluralism." *Philosophical Review* 116 (4): 563–601.

Kane, Robert. 1998. *The Significance of Free Will*. New York: Oxford UP.

——, ed. 2002a. *Free Will*. Oxford: Blackwell.

——. 2002b. "Free Will: New Directions for an Ancient Problem." In Robert Kane, ed., *Free Will*. Oxford: Blackwell, pp. 222–48.

——. 2006. *A Contemporary Introduction to Free Will*. New York: Oxford UP.

Kant, Immanuel. 1965. *Critique of Pure Reason*. Norman Kemp Smith, trans. New York: St. Martin's.

Keller, Evelyn Fox. 1985. *Reflections on Gender and Science*. New Haven, CT: Yale UP.

Kim, Jaegwon. 1988. "What Is 'Naturalized Epistemology'?" In James Tomberlin, ed., *Philosophical Perspectives, 2, Epistemology*. Atascadero, CA: Ridgeview, pp. 381–405.

——. 2007. *Physicalism, or Something Near Enough*. Princeton, NJ: Princeton UP.

——. 2010. *The Philosophy of Mind*, 3rd ed. Boulder, CO: Westview.

Kitcher, Philip. 1993. *The Advancement of Science: Science Without Legend, Objectivity Without Illusions*. New York: Oxford UP.

Kornblith, Hilary, ed. 1985. *Naturalizing Epistemology*. Cambridge, MA: MIT P.

Krauss, Lawrence M. 1995. *The Physics of Star Trek*. New York: Harper.

Kripke, Saul. 1972. "Naming and Necessity." In Donald Davidson and Gilbert Harman, eds. *Semantics of Natural Language*. Dordrecht, Netherlands: Reidel, pp. 253–355.

Kvanvig, Jonathan. 2003. *The Value of Knowledge and the Pursuit of Understanding*. Cambridge: Cambridge UP.

Kvanvig, Jonathan, and Wayne Riggs. 1992. "Can a Coherence Theory Appeal to Appearance States?" *Philosophical Studies* 67 (3): 197–217.

Lahey, Stephen E. 1998. "William Ockham and Trope Nominalism." *Franciscan Studies* 55: 105–20.

Laplace, Pierre-Simon. 1995. *Philosophical Essay on Probabilities.* A.J. Dale, trans. New York: Springer Verlag.

LeDoux, Joseph. 2002. *Synaptic Self: How Our Brains Become Who We Are.* New York: Viking.

Leftow, Brian. 2001. "Souls Dipped in Dust." In Kevin Corcoran, ed., *Soul, Body, and Survival: Essays on the Metaphysics of Human Persons.* Ithaca, NY: Cornell UP, pp. 120–38.

Lehrer, Keith. 1965. "Knowledge, Truth and Evidence." *Analysis* 25: 168–75.

——. 1974. *Knowledge.* New York: Oxford UP.

——. 1990. *Theory of Knowledge.* Boulder, CO: Westview.

——. 1993. "Coherentism." In Jonathan Dancy and Ernest Sosa, eds. *A Companion to Epistemology.* Oxford: Blackwell, pp. 67–70.

——. 1997. *Self-Trust: A Study of Reason, Knowledge and Autonomy.* Oxford: Clarendon.

——. 2003. "Coherence, Circularity and Consistency: Lehrer Replies." In Erik J. Olsson, ed., *The Epistemology of Keith Lehrer,* Dordrecht, Netherlands: Kluwer, pp. 309–56.

Leibniz, G. 1979. *Monadology.* In P.P. Weiner, ed. *Leibniz Selections.* New York: Scribner's, pp. 533–51.

Lepore, Ernest, ed. 1986. *Truth and Interpretation: Perspectives on the Philosophy of Donald Davidson.* Oxford: Blackwell.

Levine, Joseph. 2004. *Purple Haze: The Puzzle of Consciousness.* New York: Oxford UP.

Levitan, William, trans. 2007. *Abelard and Heloise: The Letters and Other Writings.* Indianapolis, IN: Hackett.

Lewis, C.I. 1970. "The Given Element in Empirical Knowledge." In *Collected Papers,* John D. Goheen and John L. Mothershead, Jr., eds. Stanford, CA: Stanford UP, pp. 324–31.

Lewis, David. 1976. "Survival and Identity." In Amelie Oksenberg Rorty, ed., *The Identities of Persons.* Berkeley, CA: U of California P, pp. 17–40.

Libet, Benjamin. 2004. *Mind Time: The Temporal Factor in Consciousness.* Cambridge, MA: Harvard UP.

Lloyd, Genevieve. 1984. *The Man of Reason: 'Male' and 'Female' in Western Philosophy.* Minneapolis, MN: U of Minnesota P.

Lloyd, Seth. 2012. "A Turing Test for Free Will." *Philosophical Transactions of the Royal Society* 370: 3597–3610.

Locke, John. 1975. *An Essay Concerning Human Understanding.* Peter H. Nidditch, ed. Oxford: Clarendon.

Longino, Helen. 1990. *Science as Social Knowledge.* Princeton, NJ: Princeton UP.

Loux, Michael J. 1970. *Universals and Particulars: Readings in Ontology.* Garden City, NY: Anchor Doubleday.

——. 2006. *Metaphysics: A Contemporary Introduction*, 3rd ed. New York: Routledge.

Lovitt, William, and Harriet Brundage Lovitt. 1995. *Modern Technology in the Heideggerian Perspective.* Lewiston, NY: Edwin Mellen.

Lowe, E.J. 1998. *The Possibility of Metaphysics.* Oxford: Oxford UP.

——. 2002. *A Survey of Metaphysics*, New York: Oxford UP.

——. 2005. *Locke.* New York: Routledge.

——. 2006. "Non-Cartesian Substance Dualism and the Problem of Mental Causation." *Erkenntnis* 65: 1–23.

Lowe, Victor. 1962. *Understanding Whitehead.* Baltimore, MD: Johns Hopkins UP.

Luce, A.A. 1941. "Berkeley's Existence in the Mind." *Mind* 50: 258–67.

Luther, Martin. 1957. *The Bondage of the Will.* J.I. Packer and O.R. Johnston, trans. Westwood, NJ: Fleming H. Revell.

Lycan, William. 1987. *Consciousness.* Cambridge, MA: MIT P.

Lycan, William, and Jesse Prinz, eds. 2008. *Mind and Cognition: An Anthology.* 3rd ed. Oxford: Wiley-Blackwell.

Lyons, Daniel. 1998. "Immortality at Last." Forbes. <http://www.forbes.com/global/1998/1130/0118098a.html>.

Lyons, William. 1986. *The Disappearance of Introspection.* Cambridge, MA: MIT P.

Mabbott, J.D. 1931. "The Place of God in Berkeley's Philosophy." *Journal of Philosophical Studies* 6: 18-29.

——. 1968. "The Place of God in Berkeley's Philosophy." Reprinted in C.B. Martin and D.M. Armstrong, *Berkeley: A Collection of Critical Essays.* New York: Anchor, pp. 364–79.

Macdonald, Cynthia. 2005. *Varieties of Things: Foundations of Contemporary Metaphysics.* Oxford: Wiley-Blackwell.

Mackie, J.L. 1955. "Evil and Omnipotence." *Mind* 64: 200-12.

——. 1976. *Problems from Locke.* Oxford: Clarendon P.

Maclachlan, D.L.C. 1989. *The Philosophy of Perception.* Englewood Cliffs, NJ: Prentice-Hall.

Maffie, James. 1990. "Recent Work on Naturalized Epistemology." *American Philosophical Quarterly* 27: 281–93.

Malcolm, Norman. 1960. "Anselm's Ontological Arguments," *Philosophical Review* 69 (1): 41–62.

Marenbon, John. 1997. *The Philosophy of Peter Abelard*. Cambridge: Cambridge UP.

Markosian, Ned. 1999. "A Compatibilist Theory of Agent Causation." *Pacific Philosophical Quarterly* 80 (3): 257–77.

Marsden, George. 2003. *Jonathan Edwards: A Life*. New Haven, CT: Yale UP.

Martinich, A.D., and Avrum Stroll. 2007. *Much Ado About Nonexistence: Fiction and Reference*. Lanham, MD: Rowman and Littlefield.

Marx, Werner. 1984. *The Philosophy of F.W.J. Schelling*. Thomas Nenon, trans. Bloomington, IN: Indiana UP.

Maund, Barry. 2011. *Colors: Their Nature and Representation*. Cambridge: Cambridge UP.

Mayr, Ernst. 1988. *Toward a New Philosophy of Biology: Observations of an Evolutionist*. Cambridge, MA: Harvard UP.

McCarthy, Michael. 2013. "Vaccine Refusal May Have Contributed to California's 2010 Pertussis Outbreak, Study Finds." *BMJ*; 347:f6109.

McColley, Diane Kelsey. 1972. "Free Will and Obedience in the Separation Scene of *Paradise Lost*." *SEL Studies in English Literature, 1500–1900* 12 (1): 103–20.

McKeon, Richard.1941. *The Basic Works of Aristotle*. New York: Random House.

Meinwald, Constance C. 1992. "Good-Bye to the Third Man." In Richard Kraut, ed., *The Cambridge Companion to Plato*. Cambridge: Cambridge UP, pp. 365–96.

Mele, Alfred R. 2014. *Free: Why Science Hasn't Disproved Free Will*. New York: Oxford UP.

Merleau-Ponty, Maurice. 1962. *The Phenomenology of Perception*. New York: Routledge.

Merricks, Trenton. 2001. "How to Live Forever Without Saving Your Soul: Physicalism and Immortality." In Kevin Corcoran, ed., *Soul, Body, and Survival: Essays on the Metaphysics of Human Persons*. Ithaca, NY: Cornell UP, pp. 183–200.

Mesle, C. Robert. 2008. *Process-Relational Philosophy: An Introduction to Alfred North Whitehead*. West Conshohocken, PA: Templeton Foundation P.

Meyers, Robert. 1988. *The Likelihood of Knowledge*. Dordrecht, Netherlands: Kluwer.

Mittag, Daniel. 2013. "Evidentialism." The Internet Encyclopedia of
Philosophy. <http://www.iep.utm.edu/>.

Molloy, Michael. 1999. *Experiencing the World's Religions*. Mountain View,
CA: Mayfield.

Moore, G.E. 1957. "Proof of an External World." In *Philosophical Papers*.
London: George Allen and Unwin, pp. 127–50.

——. 1966. "A Defence of Common Sense." In Morris Weitz, ed., *20th Century
Philosophy: The Analytic Tradition*. New York: Free P, pp. 99–123.

Moser, Paul K., ed. 1987. *A Priori Knowledge*. New York: Oxford UP.

Moyer, Melinda Wenner. 2013. "Brain Implant Could Enhance
Our Senses." <http://www.scientificamerican.com/article/
brain-implant-could-enhance-our-senses/>.

Nagel, Thomas. 1974. "What Is It Like to Be a Bat?" *Philosophical Review* 83
(4): 435–50. Reprinted in *Mortal Questions*. Cambridge: Cambridge UP,
1979, pp. 165–80; and in Jack Crumley, ed., *Problems in Mind: Readings
in Contemporary Philosophy of Mind*. Mountain View, CA: Mayfield,
1999; and <http://organizations.utep.edu/portals/1475/nagel_bat.pdf>.

——. 1989. *The View from Nowhere*. New York: Oxford UP.

Nammour, Jamil. 1973. "Resemblances and Universals." *Mind* 82 (328):
516–24. Reprinted in Andrew Schoedinger, ed., *The Problem of Universals*.
Atlantic Highlands, NJ: Humanities P, 1992, pp. 346–53.

Nelson, Jack, and Lynn Hankinson Nelson. 1994. "No Rush to Judgment." *The
Monist* 77 (4): 486–508.

Newberg, Andrew, Eugene D'Aquili, and Vince Rause. 2001. *Why God Won't
Go Away: Brain Science & the Biology of Belief*. New York: Ballantine
Books.

Noonan, Harold. 2003. *Personal Identity*, 2nd ed. New York: Routledge.

Ockham, William. 1969. *Predestination, God's Foreknowledge, and Future
Contingents*. Marilyn McCord Adams and Norman Kretzmann, trans.
New York: Appleton-Century-Crofts.

——. 1974. *Ockham's Theory of Terms: Part I of the Summa Logicae*. Michael J.
Loux, trans. Notre Dame, IN: U of Notre Dame P.

O'Connor, Timothy. 1995. "Agent Causation." In Timothy O'Connor, ed.,
Agents, Causes, and Events: Essays on Indeterminism and Free Will, New
York: Oxford UP, pp. 173–200.

——. 2001. "Causality, Mind and Free Will." In Kevin Corcoran, ed., *Soul, Body,
and Survival: Essays on the Metaphysics of Human Persons*. Ithaca, NY:
Cornell UP, pp. 44–58.

——. 2002. *Persons and Causes: The Metaphysics of Free Will*. New York: Oxford UP.

——. 2014. "Free Will." The Stanford Encyclopedia of Philosophy (Fall 2014 Edition), Edward N. Zalta, ed. <http://plato.stanford.edu/archives/fall2014/entries/freewill/>.

Olson, Carl. 2007. *The Many Colors of Hinduism: A Thematic-Historical Introduction*. New Brunswick, NJ: Rutgers UP.

Olson, Eric T. 1999. *The Human Animal: Personal Identity without Psychology*. New York: Oxford UP.

Paley, William. 2006. *Natural Theology*. New York: Oxford UP.

Parfit, Derek. 1986. *Reasons and Persons*. New York: Oxford UP.

Paul, G.A. 1951. "Is There a Problem about Sense Data?" *Aristotelian Society Supplementary Volume*, pp. 61–77.

Penner, Terry. 2006. "The Forms in the *Republic*." In Gerasimos Santas, *The Blackwell Guide to Plato's Republic*. Oxford: Blackwell, pp. 234–62.

Pereboom, Derk. 2014. *Free Will, Agency and Meaning in Life*. New York: Oxford UP.

Perry, John, ed. 1975. *Personal Identity*. Berkeley, CA: U of California P.

——. 1976. "The Importance of Being Identical." In Amelie Oksenberg Rory, ed., *The Identities of Persons*. Berkeley, CA: U of California P, pp. 67–90.

——. 1977. *A Dialogue on Personal Identity on Immortality*. Indianapolis, IN: Hackett.

Philipse, Herman. 1998. *Heidegger's Philosophy of Being*. Princeton, NJ: Princeton UP.

Pike, Nelson. 1958. "God and Evil: A Reconsideration." *Ethics* 68 (2): 116–24.

Pike, Nelson. 1965. "Divine Omniscience and Voluntary Action." *Philosophical Review* 74 (1): 27–46.

——. 1977. "If There Is No Necessary Being, Nothing Exists." *Noûs* 11: 417–20.

Place, Ullin T. 1956. "Is Consciousness a Brain Process?" *British Journal of Psychology* 47: 44–50.

Plantinga, Alvin. 1967. *God and Other Minds: A Study of the Rational Justification of Belief in God*. Ithaca, NY: Cornell UP.

——, ed. 1968. *The Ontological Argument*. London: Macmillan.

——. 1986. "On Ockham's Way Out." *Faith and Philosophy* 3: 235–69.

——. 1990. "God, Evil and the Metaphysics of Freedom." In Marilyn McCord Adams and Robert Merrihew Adams, eds., *The Problem of Evil*. New York: Oxford UP, pp. 83–109.

——. 2011. *Where the Conflict Really Lies: Science, Religion, & Naturalism*. New York: Oxford UP.

Plato. 1951. *Parmenides*. In Francis M. Cornford, *Plato and Parmenides: Parmenides' Way of Truth and Plato's Parmenides*. Atlantic Highlands, NJ: Humanities P.

——. 1961a. *Laches*. Benjamin Jowett, trans. In Edith Hamilton and Huntington Cairns, eds., *Plato: The Collected Dialogues*. Princeton, NJ: Princeton UP, pp. 123–44.

——. 1961b. *Meno*. W.K.C. Guthrie, trans. In Edith Hamilton and Huntington Cairns, eds., *Plato: The Collected Dialogues*. Princeton, NJ: Princeton UP, pp. 353–84.

——. 1961c. *Phaedo*. Hugo Tredennick, trans. In Edith Hamilton and Huntington Cairns, eds., *Plato: The Collected Dialogues*. Princeton, NJ: Princeton UP, pp. 40–98.

——. 1961d. *Theaetetus*. F.M. Cornford, trans. In Edith Hamilton and Huntington Cairns, eds., *Plato: The Collected Dialogues*. Princeton, NJ: Princeton UP, pp. 845–919.

——. 1974. *Republic*. G.M.A. Grube, trans. Indianapolis, IN: Hackett.

Popkin, Richard H. 1979. *The History of Skepticism from Erasmus to Spinoza*. Berkeley: U of California P.

Price, H.H. 1932. *Perception*. London: Methuen.

Pritchard, Duncan. 2004. "Epistemic Luck." *Journal of Philosophical Research* 29: 193–222.

——. 2009. *Knowledge*. London: Palgrave Macmillan.

Pritchard, Duncan, and John Turri. 2014. "The Value of Knowledge." The Stanford Encyclopedia of Philosophy (Spring 2014 Edition), Edward N. Zalta, ed. <http://plato.stanford.edu/archives/spr2014/entries/knowledge-value/>.

Quine, W.V.O. 1951. "Two Dogmas of Empiricism." *The Philosophical Review* 60 (1): 20–43. Reprinted in W.V. O. Quine, *From a Logical Point of View*, 2nd ed. New York: Harper, 1961, pp. 20–46.

——. 1961. *From a Logical Point of View*, 2nd ed. New York: Harper.

——. 1969. *Ontological Relativity and Other Essays*. New York: Columbia UP.

——. 1975. "The Nature of Natural Knowledge." In Samuel Guttenplan, ed., *Mind and Language*. New York: Oxford UP.

——. 1981. "Things and Their Place in Theories." In W.V.O. Quine, *Theories and Things*. Cambridge, MA: Harvard UP.

Quine, W.V.O., and J.S. Ullian. 1978. *The Web of Belief*, 2nd ed. New York: Random House.

Raloff, Janet. 1997. "Does Yo-Yo Dieting Pose Cancer Threat?" *Science News*, March 15, 1997. The Free Library. Science Service, Inc. <http://www.thefreelibrary.com/Does+yo-yo+dieting+pose+cancer+threat%3f-a019249832>.

Redding, Paul. 2009. *Continental Idealism: Leibniz to Nietzsche*. New York: Routledge.

Reid, Thomas. 1975. "Of Mr. Locke's Account of Our Personal Identity." In John Perry, ed., *Personal Identity*. Berkeley, CA: U of California P, pp. 113–19.

Roberts, John Russell. 2007. *A Metaphysics for the Mob: The Philosophy of George Berkeley*. New York: Oxford UP.

Robinson, Howard, 1994. *Perception*. London: Routledge.

Rorty, Amelie Oksenberg, ed. 1976. *The Identities of Persons*. Berkeley, CA: U of California P.

Rorty, Richard. 1972. "The World Well Lost." *Journal of Philosophy* 64: 649–65.

——. 1976. *Philosophy and the Mirror of Nature*. Princeton, NJ: Princeton UP.

——. 1982. *Consequences of Pragmatism*. Minneapolis: U of Minnesota P.

Rosen, Stanley. 2008. *Plato's Republic: A Study*. New Haven, CT: Yale UP.

Rosenthal, David M., ed. 1971. *Materialism and the Mind-Body Problem*. Upper Saddle River, NJ: Prentice Hall.

Rosenthal, David M., ed. 1991. *The Nature of Mind*. New York: Oxford UP.

Ross, Andrew, ed. 1996. *Science Wars*. Durham, NC: Duke UP.

Ross, David. 1971. *Aristotle*. London: Methuen.

Rouse, Joseph. 2004. "Barad's Feminist Naturalism." *Hypatia* 19: 142–61.

Rowe, William. 1979. "The Problem of Evil and Some Varieties of Theism." *American Philosophical Quarterly* 16 (4): 335–41. Reprinted in Marilyn McCord Adams and Robert Merrihew Adams, eds. *The Problem of Evil*. New York: Oxford UP, 1990, pp. 126–37.

——. 1995. "William Alston on the Problem of Evil." In Thomas Senor, ed., *The Rationality of Belief and the Plurality of Faith*. Ithaca, NY: Cornell UP, pp. 71–93.

——. 2000. *Philosophy of Religion: An Introduction*, 3rd ed. Belmont, CA: Wadsworth.

Russell, Bertrand. 1959. *The Problems of Philosophy*. New York: Oxford UP.

Sainsbury, R.M. 2010. *Fiction and Fictionalism*. New York: Routledge.

Sartre, Jean Paul. 1956. *Being and Nothingness.* Hazel E. Barnes, trans. New York: Washington Square P.

Sarup, Madan. 1993. *Post-Structuralism and Postmodernism,* 2nd ed. Athens, GA: U of Georgia P.

Schelling, F.W.J. 1809/1936. *Schelling: Of Human Freedom.* James Gutmann, trans. LaSalle, IL: Open Court.

Schmitt, Frederick F. 1992. *Knowledge and Belief.* New York: Routledge.

——. 1995. *Truth: A Primer.* Boulder, CO: Westview.

Schoedinger, Andrew B., ed. 1992. *The Problem of Universals.* Atlantic Highlands, NJ: Humanities P.

Schutte, Ofelia. 1998. "Latin America." In Alison M. Jaggar and Iris Marion Young, eds. *A Companion to Feminist Philosophy.* Oxford: Blackwell, pp. 87–95.

Schwarz, Robert. 1986. "I'm Going to Make You a Star." *Midwest Studies in Philosophy* 11: 427–39.

Scruton, Roger. 2002. *A Short History of Modern Philosophy.* New York: Routledge.

Searle, John. 1984. *Brains, Minds, and Science.* Cambridge, MA: Harvard UP.

——. 2001. "Free Will as a Problem in Neurobiology." *Philosophy* 76 (298): 491–514.

——. 2005. *Mind: A Brief Introduction.* New York: Oxford UP.

——. 2008. *Freedom and Neurobiology: Reflections on Free Will, Language, and Political Power.* New York: Columbia UP.

Senor, Thomas, ed. 1995. *The Rationality of Belief and the Plurality of Faith.* Ithaca, NY: Cornell UP.

Sherburne, Donald. 1971. *A Key to Understanding Process and Reality.* Bloomington, IN: Indiana UP.

Sherman, Daniel. 2013. *Soul, World, and Idea: An Interpretation of Plato's Republic and Phaedo.* Lanham, MD: Lexington.

Shields, Christopher. 2012. *Ancient Philosophy: A Contemporary Introduction,* 2nd ed. New York: Routledge.

Shoemaker, Sydney. 1963. *Self Knowledge and Self Identity.* Ithaca, NY: Cornell UP.

——. 1982. "The Inverted Spectrum." *Journal of Philosophy* 79 (7): 357–81.

——. 2008. "Persons, Animals, and Identity." *Synthese* 162 (3): 313–24.

Shoemaker, Sydney, and Richard Swinburne. 1984. *Personal Identity.* Oxford: Blackwell.

Shope, Robert K. 1983. *The Analysis of Knowing.* Princeton, NJ: Princeton UP.

Sider, Theodore. 2006. "Bare Particulars." *Philosophical Perspectives* 20 (1): 387–97.

Skinner, B.F. 1974. *About Behaviorism*. New York: Alfred A. Knopf.

——. 1990. "Can Psychology Be a Science of the Mind?" *American Psychologist* 45: 1206–10.

Smart, J.J.C. 1959. "Sensations and Brain Processes." *Philosophical Review* 68 (2): 141–56.

——. 2004. "The Identity Theory of Mind." The Stanford Encyclopedia of Philosophy (Fall 2004 Edition), Edward N. Zalta, ed. <http://plato.stanford.edu/archives/fall2004/entries/mind-identity/>.

Smith, A.D. 2002. *The Problem of Perception*. Cambridge, MA: Harvard UP.

Snyder, Michael. 2012. "They Really Do Want to Implant Microchips into Your Brain." Website: "End of the American Dream." <http://endoftheamericandream.com/archives/they-really-do-want-to-implant-microchips-into-your-brain>.

Solomon, Robert C. 1988. *Continental Philosophy Since 1750: The Rise and Fall of the Self*. New York: Oxford UP.

Sosa, Ernest. 1980. "The Raft and the Pyramid: Coherence versus Foundations in the Theory of Knowledge." *Midwest Studies in Philosophy* 5 (1): 3–25.

——. 2007. *A Virtue Epistemology: Apt Belief and Reflective Knowledge*. New York: Oxford UP.

——. 2011. *Knowing Full Well*. Princeton, NJ: Princeton UP.

Spector, Dina. 2013. "Is There a Humane Way to Kill a Lobster?" Business Insider <http://www.businessinsider.com/scientist-lobsters-can-feel-pain-2013-1>.

Stenger, Victor. 2011. *The Fallacy of Fine-Tuning: Why the Universe Is Not Designed for Us*. Amherst, NY: Prometheus Books.

Sterelny, Kim. 1990. *The Representational Theory of Mind*. Oxford: Blackwell.

Steup, Mathias. 1996. *An Introduction to Contemporary Epistemology*. Upper Saddle River, NJ: Prentice-Hall.

——, ed. 2001. *Knowledge, Truth, and Duty: Essays on Epistemic Justification, Responsibility, and Virtue*. New York: Oxford UP.

Steup, Matthias, and Ernest Sosa. 2005. *Contemporary Debates in Epistemology*. Oxford: Blackwell.

Strauss, Leo. 1964 *The City and Man*. Chicago: Rand McNally.

Strawson, P.F. 1952. *Introduction to Logical Theory*. London: Methuen.

——. 1983. *Skepticism and Naturalism: Some Varieties*. New York: Columbia UP.

Strawson, P.F., and Paul Grice. 1956. "In Defence of a Dogma." *Philosophical Review* 65: 141–58.

Stroud, Barry. 1975. *Hume: Arguments of the Philosophers*. New York: Routledge.

Stump, Eleonore, 2003. *Aquinas*. New York: Routledge.

Suzuki, D.T. 1963. *Outlines of Mahayana Buddhism*. New York: Schocken.

Swain, Marshall. 1974. "Epistemic Defeasibility." *American Philosophical Quarterly* 11 (1): 15–25. Reprinted in George Pappas and Marshall Swain, eds., *Essays on Knowledge and Justification*. Ithaca, NY: Cornell UP, pp. 160–83.

Swartz, Robert. 1965. *Perceiving, Sensing and Knowing*. Berkeley: U of California P.

Swinburne, Richard. 1977. *The Coherence of Theism*. Oxford: Clarendon.

——. 1986. *The Evolution of the Soul*. Oxford: Clarendon.

——. 1994. *The Christian God*. New York: Oxford UP.

——. 1997. *The Evolution of the Soul*, rev. ed. New York: Oxford UP.

——. 1998. "Soul, Nature and Immortality of the." In E. Craig, ed., *Routledge Encyclopedia of Philosophy*. New York: Routledge. <http://www.rep.routledge.com/article/K096>.

Taliaferro, Charles. 1998. *Contemporary Philosophy of Religion*. Oxford: Wiley-Blackwell.

Tanesini, Alessandra. 1999. *An Introduction to Feminist Epistemologies*. Oxford: Blackwell.

Taylor, A.E. 1949. *Aristotle on His Predecessors: Being the First Book of His Metaphysics*. LaSalle, IL: Open Court.

——. 1955. *Aristotle*. New York: Dover.

Taylor, Richard. 1992. *Metaphysics*, 4th ed. Upper Saddle River, NJ: Prentice-Hall.

Thagard, Paul. 2000. *Coherence in Thought and Action*. Cambridge, MA: MIT P.

——. 2010. *The Brain and the Meaning of Life*. Princeton, NJ: Princeton UP.

Thijssen, Hans. 2013. Winter Edition. "Condemnation of 1277." The Stanford Encyclopedia of Philosophy. Edward N. Zalta, ed. <http://plato.stanford.edu/archives/win2013/entries/condemnation/>.

Thomasson, Amie L. 1999. *Fiction and Metaphysics*. Cambridge: Cambridge UP.

Tipton, I.C., ed. 1977. *Locke on Human Understanding*. Oxford: Oxford UP.

Tollefsen, Deborah. 1999. "Princess Elisabeth and the Problem of Mind-Body Interaction." *Hypatia* 14 (3): 59–77. <http://muse.jhu.edu/journals/hypatia/v014/14.3tollefsen.html>.

Tong, Rosmarie. 2013. *Feminist Thought: A More Comprehensive Introduction.* Boulder, CO: Westview.

Tye, Michael. 1984. "The Adverbial Theory of Perception." *Philosophical Review* 93: 195–226.

——. 1992. "Visual Qualia and Visual Content." In Tim Crane, ed. *The Contents of Experience.* Cambridge: Cambridge UP, pp. 158–77.

Tyson, Peter. 2010. "The Future of Brain Transplants." <http://www.pbs.org/wgbh/nova/body/brain-transplants.html>.

Van Cleve, James. 1985. "Three Versions of the Bundle Theory." *Philosophical Studies* 47 (1): 95–107.

van Inwagen, Peter. 1986. *An Essay on Free Will.* New York: Oxford UP.

——. 1990. *Material Beings.* Ithaca, NY: Cornell UP.

——. 2008. *Metaphysics.* Boulder, CO: Westview.

Veatch, Henry B. 1974. *Aristotle: A Contemporary Introduction.* Bloomington, IN: Indiana UP.

Viney, Donald. 1985. *Charles Hartshorne and the Existence of God.* Albany, NY: SUNY P.

Vision, Gerald. 2004. *Veritas: The Correspondence Theory and Its Critics.* Cambridge, MA: MIT P.

Vlastos, Gregory. 1954. "The Third Man Argument in the Parmenides." *Philosophical Review* 63: 319–49.

Wagoner, Robert E. 1997. *The Meanings of Love.* Westport, CT: Praeger.

Watson, John. 1930. *Behaviorism*, rev. ed. Chicago: U of Chicago P.

Wegner, Daniel. 2003. *The Illusion of Conscious Will.* Cambridge, MA: MIT P.

Weiss, Paul. 1958. *Modes of Being.* Carbondale, IL: Southern Illinois UP.

Welton, William A., ed. 2002. *Plato's Forms.* Lanham, MD: Lexington Books.

White, Nicholas P. 1976. *Plato on Knowledge and Reality.* Indianapolis, IN: Hackett.

Whitehead, Alfred North. 1925. *Science and the Modern World.* London: Macmillan.

——. 1929. *Process and Reality.* London: Macmillan.

Wiggins, David. 1967. *Identity and Spatio-Temporal Continuity.* Oxford: Blackwell.

——. 1980. *Sameness and Substance.* Cambridge, MA: Harvard UP.

Williams, Bernard. 1973. "Personal Identity and Individuation." In *Problems of the Self.* Cambridge: Cambridge UP, pp. 1–18.

Williams, Donald C. 1953. "The Elements of Being, I." *Review of Metaphysics* 7 (1): 3–18.

Williams, Thomas. 1996a. "Introduction." In Thomas Williams, ed. and trans., *Monologion and Proslogion*. Indianapolis, IN: Hackett, pp. xi–xx.

——, ed. and trans. 1996b. *Monologion and Proslogion*. Indianapolis IN: Hackett.

Wilson, Margaret Dauler. 1978. *Descartes: Arguments of the Philosophers*. New York: Routledge.

Wippel, John. 2006. *"The Five Ways."* In Brian Davies, Leonard Boyle, and John Wippel, eds. *Aquinas's Summa Theologiae*. Lanham, MD: Rowman and Littlefield, pp. 45–110.

——. 2007. *Metaphysical Themes in Thomas Aquinas II*. Washington, DC: Catholic U of America P.

Wisnewski, J. Jeremy. 2011. *Heidegger: An Introduction*. Lanham, MD: Rowman and Littlefield.

Wittgensteing, Ludwig. 1922. *Tractatus Logico-Philosophicus*. Frank P. Ramsey and C.K. Ogden, trans. London: Routledge and *Kegan Paul*.

——. 1968. *Philosophical Investigations*, 3rd ed. G.E.M. Anscombe, trans. London: Macmillan.

Wolterstorff, Nicholas. 1970. "Qualities." In Michael J. Loux, ed., *Universals and Particulars: Readings in Ontology*. Garden City, NY: Anchor Doubleday, pp. 87–105.

Wykstra, Stephen. 1984. "The Humean Obstacle to Evidential Arguments from Suffering: On Avoiding the Evils of 'Appearance.'" *International Journal of Religion* 16: 73–93. Reprinted in Marilyn McCord Adams and Robert Merrihew Adams, eds., *The Problem of Evil*. New York: Oxford UP, 1990, pp. 138–60.

Yandell, Keith E. 1999. *Philosophy of Religion: A Contemporary Introduction*. New York: Routledge.

Zagzebski, Linda. 1994. "The Inescapability of Gettier Problems." *Philosophical Quarterly* 44 (174): 65–73.

Zimmer, Heinrich. 1951. *Philosophies of India*. Joseph Campbell, ed. Princeton, NJ: Princeton UP.

Zimmerman, Michael E. 1986. *Eclipse of the Self: The Development of Heidegger's Concept of Authenticity*. Athens, OH: Ohio UP.

——. 1990. *Heidegger's Confrontation with Modernity: Technology, Politics, and Art*. Bloomington, IN: Indiana UP.

——. 1997. *Contesting Earth's Future: Radical Ecology and Postmodernity*. Berkeley, CA: U of California P.

INDEX

being *qua* being, xx
belief, xxiii–xxiv, 15–17, 46, 128, 207, 218, 229, 232–33
    acquiring, 138–40
    background beliefs, 24–25, 65
    basic (*See* basic beliefs)
    belief-formation, 23, 56, 97
    can be either true or false, 44
    content of, xxiii
    Demon Argument and, 10
    fallible, 91
    false, 44, 54, 84
    justified when it is good for the believer, 86
    legitimacy of inductively based beliefs, 26
    memory beliefs, 223
    pragmatic grounds for holding beliefs, 85
    as representation, xxiii, 3, 76
    "self-evident" or "self-presenting," 70
    true (*See* true belief)
    "web of belief" metaphor, 78
    why of a belief, 63
belief and environment, connection between, 55
belief-desire psychology, 228
belief resulting from reliable belief forming processes, 56
belief without evidence, 85–86
benevolence, 322
Berkeley, George, 116–17, 122, 131–34, 178, 184, 187, 189
"The Beverly Hillbillies," 17
Bhagavad Gītā, 297
bias in research design, 100
Bible, 12
Big (film), 238
biological properties, 253
biology, 93
blind watchmaker objection to Design Argument, 302
blindsight, 118
body criterion for individuation numerical identity, 256
body criterion for personal identity, 245
body theorists, 250

From the Publisher

A name never says it all, but the word "Broadview" expresses a good deal of the philosophy behind our company. We are open to a broad range of academic approaches and political viewpoints. We pay attention to the broad impact book publishing and book printing has in the wider world; we began using recycled stock more than a decade ago, and for some years now we have used 100% recycled paper for most titles. Our publishing program is internationally oriented and broad-ranging. Our individual titles often appeal to a broad readership too; many are of interest as much to general readers as to academics and students.

Founded in 1985, Broadview remains a fully independent company owned by its shareholders—not an imprint or subsidiary of a larger multinational.

For the most accurate information on our books (including information on pricing, editions, and formats) please visit our website at www.broadviewpress. com. Our print books and ebooks are also available for sale on our site.

On the Broadview website we also offer several goods that are not books— among them the Broadview coffee mug, the Broadview beer stein (inscribed with a line from Geoffrey Chaucer's *Canterbury Tales*), the Broadview fridge magnets (your choice of philosophical or literary), and a range of T-shirts (made from combinations of hemp, bamboo, and/or high-quality pima cotton, with no child labor, sweatshop labor, or environmental degradation involved in their manufacture).

All these goods are available through the "merchandise" section of the Broadview website. When you buy Broadview goods you can support other goods too.

broadview press
www.broadviewpress.com